Decolonizing the Diet

Decolonizing the Diet

Nutrition, Immunity and the Warning from Early America

Gideon A. Mailer and Nicola E. Hale

ANTHEM PRESS

Anthem Press
An imprint of Wimbledon Publishing Company
www.anthempress.com

This edition first published in UK and USA 2019
by ANTHEM PRESS
75–76 Blackfriars Road, London SE1 8HA, UK
or PO Box 9779, London SW19 7ZG, UK
and
244 Madison Ave #116, New York, NY 10016, USA

First published in the UK and USA by Anthem Press 2018

British Library Cataloguing-in-Publication Data
A catalogue record for this book is available from the British Library.

ISBN-13: 978-1-78527-158-8 (Pbk)
ISBN-10: 1-78527-158-X (Pbk)

This title is also available as an e-book.

[…] our fathers had plenty of deer and skins, our plains were full of deer, as also our woods, and of turkies, and our coves full of fish and fowl. But these English having gotten our land, they with scythe cut down the grass, and with axes fell the trees; their cows and horses eat the grass, and their hogs spoil our clam banks, and we shall all be starved […]

—Miantonomo, 1642

Any person […] who neglects the present opportunity of hunting out good lands […] will never regain it.

—George Washington, 1767

The circumstance of my Nation is changed, the game is gone, our former wilderness is now settled by thousands of white people, and our settlements are circumscrib'd and surrounded, and it bec[o]mes necessary that my Nation should change the Custom, and leave our forefather's ways.

—David Folsom (Choctaw), 1824

If the misery of the poor be caused not by the laws of nature, but by our institutions, great is our sin.

—Charles Darwin, *The Voyage of the Beagle*

There is no death, only a change of worlds.

—Duwamish Native American Proverb

CONTENTS

ACKNOWLEDGMENTS

This book was inspired by a collaboration that began several years ago. We began to draw together materials from history, anthropology, evolutionary biology, genetics and nutritional biochemistry, for a unique interdisciplinary course at the University of Minnesota, Duluth, on nutrition, evolutionary medicine, and early American and Native American history. We soon realized that no existing text synthesizes the science of immunity and autoimmunity in light of historical case studies of nutritional change.

We noticed the ways in which the history of the agricultural transition 10,000 years ago—and its health dynamics—could inform the history of the Euro-American assault on Native American subsistence and nutrition after 1492. In writing and researching the book over the last few years, we also became increasingly aware of its place within broader public health debates.

We are grateful to the anonymous peer reviewers in both stages of the review process. This book required a great deal of cross-disciplinary expertise from the reviewers, as well as specific knowledge in their various fields (whether in biological science, history or Native American studies). Thus, we are extremely grateful for their time and their recommendations. Without their comments and critiques, this book would not be what it is today.

Nicola is grateful to all those who have helped her skills in research and synthesis at the University of Cambridge over the years, particularly during her time at the Glover lab under Dr. Nikola Dzhindzhev and as a research assistant at the Laura Itzhaki lab investigating protein structures and protein-protein interactions. She is also grateful for the mentorship she received during her year working at the Kevin Hardwick lab at the University of Edinburgh, Wellcome Trust Centre for Cell Biology, in 2012. She is grateful to the anonymous reviewers at the *Journal of Evolution and Health*, who refined her thinking on the genetic adaptations relating to nutrition and disease resistance.

Gideon is grateful to the Department of History and the dean of the College of Liberal Arts, at the University of Minnesota, Duluth, Dr. Susan Maher, for their support in this project, and the Academic Affairs Committee for its help and comments during the development of the course that gave birth to this book. He is also grateful to David Woodward for his advice and recommendations in discussions on the ethnohistory and archaeology of early America. He is grateful to the Ancestral Health Symposium for providing a framework to present some of the ideas in this book, over the last few years.

Finally, we are both grateful to the editorial and production team at Anthem Press, for believing in this project, and for taking so much time to make sure that it was finally born. We are also grateful to Heather Dubnick for her editorial and indexing expertise.

Duluth, Minnesota, February 2018

Introduction

NUTRITION AND IMMUNITY IN NATIVE AMERICA: A BIOLOGICAL AND HISTORICAL CONTROVERSY

This book argues that resistance to disease is often contingent on historical context; particularly in relation to the protection or destruction of the long-evolved nutritional and metabolic building blocks that underlie human immunity. It joins other recent scholarship in modifying the common claim that Native American communities were decimated after European contact because their immunity was somehow distinct from populations in the Old World. A dominant thesis has drawn from, and sometimes oversimplified, work by Crosby and others to suggest that Native Americans in a virgin land were unable to cope with the pathogens inadvertently introduced by Europeans after the arrival of Christopher Columbus.[1] These diseases, as Trigger and Swagerty have summarized, were introduced by germs, spores and parasites from European and African sources, and included smallpox, measles, influenza, bubonic plague, diphtheria, typhus, cholera, scarlet fever, trachoma, whooping cough, chicken pox and tropical malaria.[2] We argue that contingent human interventions in subsistence frameworks contributed greatly to the marked decline in Native American health and fertility, and the increase in mortality, in the centuries after the arrival of Columbus in the western hemisphere—as distinct from the notion of an amorphous "biological exchange" involving a mismatch between European and Native American immunity.[3]

Comparing the European and Middle Eastern transition from Paleolithic hunting and gathering around 10,000 years ago with Native American subsistence strategies before and after 1492, and synthesizing the large and diverse literature on the historical contact between Europeans and Native Americans, we offer a new way of understanding the link between biology, ecology, and history. After examining the history and bioarchaeology of ancient Europe, the ancient Near East, ancient Native America and Europe during the medieval Black Death, we set out to understand the subsequent collision between indigenous peoples and Europeans in North America from 1492 to the present day. Combining and synthesizing the latest work in the science of nutrition, immunity and evolutionary genetics with the vast scholarship on the history of indigenous North America, *Decolonizing the Diet* highlights a fundamental model of human demographic destruction: populations have been able to recover from mass epidemics within a century, or slightly more than a century, whatever their genetic heritage. A key determinant of their failure to recover from epidemics can be found when their ability to hunt, gather and farm nutritionally dense plants and animals is diminished by war, colonization and cultural destruction.

Scholarship of global infectious disease has shown that societies have often been able to recover demographically from near collapse following massive outbreaks, usually in around 150 years. Disturbances such as epidemics have tended to result in only short-term demographic decline, with populations returning to pre-disease levels of growth, decline or stability. Describing the response to the European Black Death, for example, McNeill points out that medieval European populations only required around five generations, or just over a century, to recover their numbers after renewed exposure to the plague.[4] As Gottfied has demonstrated, fourteenth- and fifteenth-century Europeans suffered multiple epidemics including the Black Death, typhus, influenza, and measles; yet their populations were able to recover demographically after around a century.[5] Herring has even shown that early twentieth-century Native American populations outside reservations were able to recover numbers following influenza, smallpox, and measles epidemics, largely thanks to their different settlement patterns and their nutritional diversity.[6]

Taking such general studies as a starting point, the chapters that follow caution against assuming certain communities are more prone to syndromes and infectious diseases, whether due to genetic differences or a comparative lack of exposure to specific pathogens. They refocus our understanding on the ways in which human interventions—particularly in food production, nutritional accessibility and subsistence ecology—have exacerbated demographic decline in the face of disease, whether in terms of reduced immunity before infection, reduced ability to fight pathogenic invasion or compromised health among subsequent generations of survivors in affected populations. They provide case studies in Native American history to illustrate such a phenomenon. They show how contemporary scientific studies can inform an analysis of the role of nutrition in enhancing or reducing the potential for recovery after mass epidemics in Native America.

As Jones and Kelton have pointed out in pioneering work, the notion of differing immunity to pathogens among geographically distinct populations rests on several problematic assumptions from the perspective of biological science and epidemiology. Contingent rather than innate contextual factors are more accurately related to the relative immunological health of communities—including their nutritional status. There is no doubt that Native American communities and Europeans retained partial differences in the nature of their inherited immunities during the period of contact.[7] But suggesting that Native Americans were predisposed to *near-total* demographic collapse solely due to their relative lack of immunity overlooks the disruption of their deeply rooted nutritional frameworks as a cofactor in such a phenomenon. The notion of a biological exchange of infectious disease incorporates an overly deterministic account of health outcomes, eschewing the unsettling role of human interventions against ancestral food ways—either in exacerbating Native American susceptibility to infectious disease or metabolic syndromes, or even as a primary factor in their increasing mortality and declining fertility after European contact. Interventions that altered the nutrient-density or metabolic profile necessary for optimal immune function often took place at just the point when disease epidemics became more likely due to new movements of people and increased population density in sedentary settlements.[8]

In the centuries after European contact, many (though not all) Native American communities were forced to move away from diets that incorporated important starch and plant sources such as wild rice, tubers, chenopods, beans, seeds, maize, squash, berries and leafy vegetables, and which were often high in animal proteins, animal fats and fat-soluble vitamins. Notwithstanding regional variations, the precontact Native American diet was relatively nutrient dense, incorporating varied macronutrients and micronutrients through hunting and gathering practices and indigenous forms of horticulture and agriculture that were subsequently disrupted.[9] Thanks to the deleterious and often deliberate effects of colonization, deeply rooted food systems were ruptured. From as early as the sixteenth century, new postcontact circumstances forced many Native Americans to adopt diets that favored imported European grain cultivars, to maintain greater calorific reliance on relatively nutrient-poor New World maize species and to reduce their consumption of traditionally hunted animals and fish, and cultivated or gathered plant sources.[10]

According to Snow, had "European expansion been less rapid, and had lethal epidemics not swept the landscape clear of Indian resistance as effectively as they did, the dynamics of historic cultural adaption" on the Great Plains and at the previous sites of European contact might have been different.[11] But it is worth asking a slightly different set of questions: Did the inability to reproduce horticultural and hunter-gathering methods actively *contribute* to Native American demographic decline following epidemics, rather than simply demonstrating another unfortunate result of the Biological Exchange?

Did the change in Native American diets following European contact directly impact the attendant increase in mortality rates—as distinct from epidemics elsewhere in the world where demography could restabilize after around a century?

To consider these possibilities, we turn to the literature on medical anthropology, bioarchaeology and modern experimental data on the link between health, immunity and the consumption of important vitamins, minerals, fatty acids and other nutrients. Disrupted access to macronutrients and micronutrients—whether derived from hunted and gathered animals and plants, from indigenous agricultural practices, or from a combination of both—should be defined as a highly influential cofactor alongside predetermined genetic loci or the exchange of diseases across the Atlantic.

We join several scholars in highlighting the delay that often occurred between first European contact, in so-called protohistoric eras, and first mass epidemics. To be sure, once disruptive colonial frameworks were in place, allowing new diseases to spread more efficiently, even the most nutritionally optimal food strategies would have been unlikely to prevent the initial mortality rates that followed the proliferation of diseases such as smallpox. Though we do not discount the role of optimal nutrition in allowing some individuals to survive diseases associated with initial mass epidemics, it is a stretch to claim that broader demographic numbers would have been affected by nutrition in the short term. Even the strongest immune system, for example, would have found it extremely difficult to fight off smallpox. Rather, we suggest that the degradation of available food sources and the decline in nutrient diversity compromised immunity and fertility among affected communities in the medium to long term, requiring a wider definition of the epidemiological effects of disease on the demographic stability of colonized communities. A sudden mismatch between evolved nutritional needs and available food made secondary infections such as pneumonia more likely, or allowed other infections to increase mortality and reduce fertility among survivors of earlier epidemics. Here we should recall those other global instances where communities were able to recover their population numbers after a century, notwithstanding initially disastrous responses to new diseases. They remind us of the need to focus on the contingency of health, immunity and fertility in the decades *after* epidemics, and how it has likely determined the eventual survival of groups in the long term, as distinct from short-term individual losses.

Initial survivors may have been lucky to avoid contact with infected vectors, or lucky enough to possess genetic mutations that reduced the likelihood of their mortality after infection. In either case, nutritional degradation may have prevented these individuals from rebuilding their communities in demographic terms, as distinct from those whose societal mechanisms and nutritional strategies remained in place. Individuals in some Native American contexts became more likely to leave their populations in search of food or better land for subsistence, thus rupturing demography even further and lowering the number of reproductive-age individuals who might rebuild the demography of communities affected by epidemics. Thus, the role of contingency in allowing particular communities to rebuild *after* infection should be defined as a primary factor for consideration when assessing the final nadir in Native American population numbers in the nineteenth century.[12]

Using gendered insights from Merchant, we suggest that reproduction and fertility must be understood in relation to communal recovery from disease, rather than focusing on immediately infected bodies as a primary point of analysis. The ability to recover from epidemics, after all, required nutritional health to aid reproductive success as well as maternal, neonatal and infant health. If colonial disruption reduced nutritional diversity, then biological reproduction likely became less viable, further preventing communities from demographic recovery during and following disease epidemics.[13] Malnutrition may have increased infant mortality for generations after epidemics, either among weaning infants or because breast milk was less available, thus decreasing the immunological protection provided by maternal lactation and increasing infant infections at a time when populations were already under stress.

Decolonizing the Diet thus provides the first extended analysis of the biological link between nutrition and immunity, and nutrition and fertility, to understand Native American demographic losses over an extended period. Whether we examine the literature of contact in Florida during the sixteenth century; in the American Southeast, the American Southwest and the Atlantic Northeast during the seventeenth century; or in Alaska and California during the early nineteenth century, we see how contingencies of context allowed immunity to be strengthened or weakened as different indigenous communities struggled to maintain their subsistence strategies at a time when the effects of colonization were prone to shatter them irrevocably. Societal contingencies impacted the interaction between Native American subsistence strategies and biological immunity above and beyond the inherited genetic determinants of specific populations.

Highlighting the contingency of human actions and reactions, indeed, also allows us to examine those Native American communities that initially prospered demographically after contact, such as the Comanche peoples in the Great Plains. Notwithstanding their living in supposedly virgin soils, population numbers increased in the century after European contact. They could achieve greater access to nutrient-dense foods, such as bison, thanks to their adoption of European technologies and horse power.[14]

Conceptual and Moral Minefields between the Humanities and Science

Educational theorists have recently begun to call for more immersion of trainee scientists and medical practitioners in the humanities, particularly through the study of history as part of their educational program. In a widely circulated analysis that first appeared in an August 2014 *Inside Higher Education* supplement, Elizabeth H. Simmons suggests that "to fully prepare for careers in science, it is essential that students grasp how the impetus for scientific work arises from the world in which the scientist lives, often responds to problems the scientist has personally encountered, and ultimately impacts that society and those problems in its turn." Every nascent scientist, according to Simmons, "should read, think, and write about how science and society have impacted one another across cultural and temporal context" because "ethical concepts absorbed" in such study will help them "hew more closely to the scientific ideal of seeking the truth."[15]

Since C. P. Snow's famous 1959 Rede Lecture lamented the gap between the "Two Cultures" of the sciences and humanities, academic initiatives such as Stanford University's Science, Society, and Technology program have been founded to assert the wider societal impact of the natural sciences.[16] Yet far fewer programs and courses have been designed to show how scientific endeavors might benefit from the study of the humanities, particularly history. The newest version of the Medical School Admissions Test (MCAT 2015) now encompasses questions on the psychological, social and biological determinants of behavior to ensure that admitted medical students are "prepared to study the sociocultural and behavioral aspects of health." But as Simmons notes, while "pre-medical and engineering students are being required to learn about issues linking science and culture, most students in science fields are still not pushed to learn about the human context of their major disciplines."[17]

As well as reaching as wide an audience and possible, therefore, we hope this book offers a new way for students and scholars to approach the conceptual and pedagogical relationships between the humanities and the sciences in general, and between historical narrative and biological science more specifically. It endeavors to present new material and ideas in ways that might complement and supplement the teaching and research in recently formed institutes and scholarly networks such as the Evolutionary Studies Institute at SUNY New Paltz, the Center for Evolution & Medicine at Arizona State University,

UCLA's Evolutionary Medicine Program, McGill University's Centre for Indigenous Peoples' Nutrition and Environment, and the Decolonizing Diet Project at Northern Michigan University. As a historian and a research scientist, with very different methodological and educational backgrounds, we seek to show how the study of early American history can inform public policy and health-care paradigms, while also impacting the agenda of cutting-edge research in the biological, nutritional and ecological sciences. We hope to show the ways in which published scientific data and research can inform historical case studies of the encounter between colonial Americans, Native Americans and Europeans from the fifteenth century to the twentieth century—and vice versa. Historical narrative can illuminate the reading of scientific papers and research, which can in turn inform the writing of history. This book joins other recent attempts to bridge the scholarly gap between the disciplines of evolutionary biology and historical narrative—disciplines that have remained surprisingly separate.[18]

To be sure, many of the syllogistic assertions that drive our interdisciplinary synthesis are unavoidably speculative, such as: scientific studies confirm that vitamin D is important to immunity; indigenous foods often provided dietary sources of vitamin D; and the restriction of those foods by European disruption likely compromised Native American immunity irrespective of their genetic predisposition to suffer from infections. There are occasions when we are able to cross-reference such assertions with available skeletal data from sites of first European contact, such as those uncovered by bioarchaeologists who examine sixteenth- and seventeenth-century Florida. In those instances, we are able to highlight material evidence that confirms micronutrient deficiencies, such as iron and vitamin B-12, alongside heightened risk for infection.[19] But our assessment of many other case studies is necessarily speculative. In these instances, we care to highlight those speculations that are stronger or weaker, based on the nature of historical evidence or the quality of the methodological foundations for the scientific studies that we use to interpret historical evidence. We are careful to distinguish between scholarly consensus on the association between any contingent nutritional factor and optimal immunity, and more speculative or less consensual claims, which might derive from cutting-edge but hitherto underexamined associations, including those that rely on animal rather than human studies or problematic epidemiology, or that consider nutritional science in light of evolutionary paradigms that are intellectually convincing but tricky to verify quantitatively.

Aside from the necessary complexity of its interdisciplinary focus, this has also been a difficult book to think through, research and write, because it intervenes in debates that are filled with potential minefields: scientific and historical, conceptual but also moral. It examines the nature and extent of

European culpability for what some scholars have referred to as a "holocaust" within Native American demography.[20] It also moves into (and hopefully beyond) the heated dispute that has been apparent among scholars of Native American history and anthropology since—and even before—the publication of Shepard Krech's *The Ecological Indian: Myth and History* in 1999. What has been described as "anti-modern romanticism" has used the example of precontact Native American ecology—including its various subsistence strategies—to distinguish American environmentalism since the 1960s from the tendency toward unsustainability and environmental degradation in capitalistic growth. In his 1983 *American Indian Ecology*, for example, Hughes described the "[Native American] secret of how to live in harmony with Mother Earth […] without destroying, without polluting, without using up the living resources of the natural world."[21] As Krech, Lewis, Nadasky and others have suggested, such a depiction of Native Americans as timelessly ecological before European contact removed agency from indigenous peoples in their ability to change and determine their environments. By denying their human agency and suggesting they were natural land stewards who could do no wrong in ecological terms, the trope of the "Ecological Indian" placed Native Americans in a "static rather than reciprocal culture-nature relationship" that denied them "their history, their biological human nature, and their humanity" while ignoring the work of more nuanced ecologists who "no longer think of ecosystems in terms of climax or stable equilibrium (with humans as intrusive agents) but rather in terms of intrinsic disequilibrium and long-term dynamic flux, with humans as one of those natural forces."[22]

In highlighting the distinction between colonial agricultural strategies and precontact Native American agriculture, horticulture, and hunting and gathering, we are thus aware of the danger in exoticizing precontact Native Americans as the ultimate ecologists, as perfectly at one with the land and as infallible proponents of environmental sustainability. We are careful to avoid any crude interpretative framework that might suggest precontact Native American communities avoided any form of managed agriculture, crop monoculture or organized land husbandry.[23] Recent historical research, after all, has often employed the metaphor of "gardening" to question the notion that precontact Native Americans relied solely on hunting and gathering methods for sustenance. Other studies emphasize the complex forms of agricultural intensification that were enacted in many communities for several thousand years.[24]

It is also important to avoid overlooking the distinct variations between indigenous food cultures both during and after the period of European contact: veering between the cultivation of maize, tubers and starchy seeds alongside hunted animals in the American Southwest to a relatively (but not entirely) homogeneous reliance on fat and protein gathered from hunted meats and fish in subarctic North America, as well as many gradations in between, such as the cultivation of wild rice alongside more traditional hunting and gathering patterns in the Great Lakes region. Yet this book seeks some degree of generalization in discussing the differences between indigenous food systems and those that were introduced after European contact, and in discussing how we can view those distinctions in light of the modern scientific literature on metabolic and nutritional health.

Proponents of the so-called Paleolithic diet template endeavor as far as possible to match foods that appeared among many human communities thousands of years before the transition to agriculture around 10,000 years ago, a transition that may have introduced macronutrient ratios and micronutrients that were maladapted to the evolved nutritional needs of humans before that transition. Problematically, however, a number of those proponents have tended to describe Native American subsistence strategies relatively crudely, to offer a distinction between their purported role as ideal hunter-gatherers (with an emphasis on meat consumption) and Anglo-European populations whose earlier transition to agriculture apparently cursed them with grain-oriented diseases of civilization. We take care to avoid similar stereotypes and tropes. Yet in questioning crude definitions of precontact Native Americans as noble hunter-gatherers or natural (read unthinking) ecologists—including those that are sometimes used by advocates of Paleolithic nutritional principles—we avoid going to the other extreme by de-emphasizing indigenous Native American knowledge and practice of sustainable ecology, or by minimizing the relative environmental and dietary importance of hunting and gathering systems in many different parts of North America immediately prior to, and even after, European contact. While indigenous agricultural activities were present throughout the American continent, hunter-gathering practices were also continued to a far greater extent than in post-Paleolithic Europe and the Middle East—potentially heralding important ecological and nutritional differences between the Old World and indigenous North America over the following centuries. Those differences should inform our understanding of the role of nutrition in health, particularly by comparing the precontact and postcontact history of Native Americans.

The attempt to avoid the trope of the naturally environmental Native American has been problematic in encouraging some to eschew aspects of indigenous subsistence strategies that were indeed unique, that did allow ecological environments to remain fecund and stable, and which do in fact provide models of sustainable nutritional systems that preserved biodiversity. If Native Americans were not the ultimate ecologists, it has been pointed out (often with an element of mischief), then colonial and postcolonial land deprivation must be mitigated, or even justified, as necessary and realistic in societal and environmental terms.[25] So long as the historical and biological record allows, conversely, we support the qualitative distinction between precontact Native American nutritional strategies and those that were imposed on relatively delicate ecological systems after 1492.

Synthesizing the fields of nutrition, immunity and evolutionary genetics with a new history of indigenous North America also requires our entry into separately thorny controversies in the scientific disciplines. Oddly, given its relationship with fundamental functions of the human body, rigorous scholarship linking nutrition to immunity has only begun to appear in the last few decades. The topic remains an inchoate field, with a number of questions still to be answered. It is difficult to determine experimentally the extent to which specific nutrient deficiencies affect immunity, due to the complexity of human diets and the vast number of dietary and other influences on the immune system. To understand the link between nutrition and immunity, then, it is necessary to examine the cellular and biochemical mechanisms that make nutrition so vital—both in metabolic terms, relating to energy production, and in functional terms, relating to micronutrients and minerals.

We try as hard as possible to avoid ahistoricism in our discussion of optimal macronutrient ratios in and out of Native America. We define macronutrients as the class of chemical compounds that are consumed in the greatest quantity by humans, measured in terms of mass or volume, and which are usually required as a source of energy—either through the conversion into glucose, fatty acids or ketones, depending on the relative use of carbohydrate, protein or fat as the primary macronutrient source. They are most likely to appear in discussions of metabolic health, relating to the means by which humans fuel movement and other essential processes.

We define micronutrients as those nutrients that are found in animal and plant products (including starch sources), which are vital for immunity and general well-being, and which are often provided partially or even entirely exogenously. They include vitamins, minerals, essential fatty acids and essential amino acids. Generally, we define minerals as those chemical elements that organisms require for their survival, other than the carbon, hydrogen, nitrogen, oxygen and sulfur present in common organic molecules. They can include trace elements such as iron, iodine, manganese, selenium and zinc. We define essential amino acids as those that cannot be synthesized within the body, and are therefore required from dietary sources. They include phenylalanine, methionine, leucine and histidine. Though essential fatty acids might be classed as a macronutrient along with other fats, we treat them as micronutrients, distinct from our discussion of the use of fat, protein and carbohydrates for the production of energy in the body.

As is shown by contemporary debates over the ideal human diet, and its distinction from potentially problematic recommendations in politically mandated nutritional guidelines, both the public and the scholarly understanding of optimal macronutrient ratios and the centrality of micronutrients remains opaque, riddled with ambiguity, overstatement and understatement. Medical students in most developed nations receive only a few hours of nutritional instruction in four years of academic study that is ostensibly centered on the human body.[26] Over the last decade, therefore, scholars and activists have begun to question the relatively jarring lack of rigor and scientific literacy underlying national food guidelines, which are often followed by government-accredited nutritionists and health practitioners. They have focused in particular on those recommendations that until very recently called for a reduction in cholesterol and saturated fat; for increased consumption of nutrient-poor and insulinogenic grain products and low-fat foods; which advocate the potentially problematic consumption of industrial seed and vegetable oils and other polyunsaturated fats; and which avoid focusing on the consequences of a high sugar intake combined with a high ratio of omega-6 fatty acids in comparison to omega-3 fatty acids.[27]

Some now suggest a correlation between the implementation of the Food Pyramid's emphasis on a low-fat and high-carbohydrate diet and the subsequent development of heightened obesity, heart disease, diabetes, inflammatory conditions and even certain mood and neurological disorders in the United States, Britain and other developed nations. The so-called "French Paradox"—according to which the French eat a higher-fat diet yet enjoy lower instances of cardiovascular disease—has recently been described as not much of a paradox at all. The French Mediterranean Diet, some now suggest, simply recommends less processed and more nutrient-dense foods, including animal and marine fats, which might protect individuals from negative health outcomes, rather than cause those outcomes as once claimed.[28]

This book considers the recent critiques outlined above. It incorporates burgeoning scientific scholarship on the importance of more nutrient-dense foods as viewed from an evolutionary perspective—including those relatively high in fat as well as other macronutrients and micronutrients. If those foods—and their relatively fixed proportion in relation to other nutrient sources—have been central to the development of human health and immunity over millennia, any deviation from their proportional dietary constituency may have deleterious consequences.[29] In our reading of the assault on Native American subsistence strategies after European contact, therefore, we take note of these conceptual developments in evolutionary medicine and nutrition, and apply them to our assessment of the interaction between changing nutritional context and demographic decline in Native America after 1492.

We also take note of the methodological problems that underlie many of the studies that have been marshaled in support of public nutritional recommendations during the last half-century—particularly in their unfortunate tendency to muddle the distinction between association and causation. Using epidemiological assessments based on surveys and subjective human actors, they have made nutritional claims that may well be confounded by several factors and cofactors that are not accounted for when discussing the health of certain populations, and the perceived association between health and particular food groups. Such claims are also often supported by studies that have often been carried out on rats, or other nonhuman organisms, or that make nutritional assessments that are belied by the actual micronutrients or macronutrients used in the examination, which do not in fact conform to or reflect the actual diets or food systems that those studies purport to support or repudiate (though animal studies can still be useful).[30]

Failing to distinguish association from causation, then, bedevils too much modern nutritional science. These problems make it even trickier to find solid nutritional studies that allow us to move beyond hypothesis when discussing the similarly vexing link between nutrition and immunity to infectious disease. Therefore, when examining the role of key micronutrients and macronutrients in human health, fertility and immunity, and their potential contribution to the survival or loss of Native American communities before and after contact, we always endeavor to support historical assertions with scientific evidence that is grounded in sound experimental procedure and interpretation, rather than using problematic studies whose own methodological failings might then compromise our subsequent historical inferences.

Yet we are also aware of the dangers in veering from one nutritional paradigm to another. Sensible critiques of government food recommendations have sometimes inspired other actors to make claims that are unsubstantiated, either due to lack of available data, a misreading of data or even special pleading. In a field of nutritional science that remains in its infancy, there ought to be room for acknowledged uncertainty, ambiguity, tentativeness and qualification about difficult cellular and biochemical processes that are still not entirely understood. Just as some scientists and public policy actors may have been overly confident in recommending the reduction of cholesterol and saturated fat, it is important to assure that their opponents are not simply food gurus whose own arguments from authority may mask tendentious readings of the scholarly literature or even willful misreading of data to support controversial arguments that increase the public profile of their proponents.

Those who claim that animal products are vital to human health and development may have an important point to make. But in the same manner as those who advocate a solely plant-based diet, proponents of high animal fat and very low carbohydrate diets risk overplaying their hand in discussions of optimal human health, whether in terms of human longevity or with respect to quality of life. Saturated fat, for example, may be problematic if consumed in proportions that do not reflect human evolutionary principles, just as the increased consumption of insulinogenic and fructose-dense carbohydrate sources is likely problematic for optimal human well-being. Although high blood insulin levels are increasingly connected to metabolic and inflammatory syndromes, such a paradigm need not suggest that reducing *any* stimulation of insulin in the blood will provide positive health outcomes. The stimulation of some insulin from dietary carbohydrate, rather than merely through the process of gluconeogenesis of protein molecules, may have a role in human health and well-being, notwithstanding the evolutionary importance and centrality of fat and protein in the human diet.[31]

If we adopt an evolutionary biological model to understand optimal human health, indeed, it is pertinent to note that wild animals—including those which likely roamed during the Paleolithic era—incorporated proportionally less saturated fat into their tissue and more omega-3 fat sources. Wild animals were leaner than present-day animals (many of which are grain-fed, thus increasing the saturated fat content even further). As Larsen has argued, the "reason for the low prevalence of cardiovascular disease in traditional hunter-gatherers is likely due to the fact that the animal tissues they consumed contained the same amount of fat as consumed by humans living in developed settings today, but the fat eaten by traditional hunter-gatherers was high in monounsaturated and polyunsaturated fatty acids [...] Herein, then, lies another key point: if meat consumption is to be significant in living populations in the developed and developing world, the lipid characteristics should more closely approximate the lipid characteristics of meats (e.g., ruminants) consumed by traditional hunter-gatherers and our prehistoric forebears."[32]

Thus, the debate on the optimal metabolic state for cardiovascular and other forms of health (including immunity) is far from over, even if the loudest advocates of high-carbohydrate and low-fat diets or low-carbohydrate and high-fat diets might think differently. And so, we are careful to avoid allowing their competing claims to govern our examination of macronutrient use in Native America, which was likely more varied than merely centered on maize (a metabolic state likely focused on the consumption of carbohydrate) or solely on animal fats (a metabolic state focused on the consumption of fatty acids that then allow the creation of ketone bodies as a metabolic fuel alternative to glucose). Varying according to region and season, precontact Native American communities most often combined macronutrients in proportions that we take care to specify according to time and place.[33]

To be sure, we note the problems associated with diets whose reliance on carbohydrate likely prevented the consumption of more necessary macronutrients such as fat and protein, separate from their role in providing metabolic energy. Those macronutrients also contained vital micronutrients. Animal meat, for example, contains fat-soluble vitamins as well as minerals. Their decreased consumption in relation to carbohydrates would likely have entailed negative health consequences. Moreover, high carbohydrate consumption over the course of a day, combined with increased sedentary behavior, is also problematic in creating a metabolic state of decreased insulin sensitivity and increased negative health outcomes, including compromised immunity.[34] Greater reliance on carbohydrates—particularly through maize—caused these associated problems before and after European contact, just as high blood sugar levels and poor-nutrient density has contributed to problematic metabolic syndromes in the contemporary era. That said, we avoid any stark dichotomies between carbohydrate and fat as metabolic fuels when such a reading does not reflect the historical record.

In a seminal article on the food economy of Native Americans in seventeenth-century New England, Bennet suggests that maize dominated the indigenous diet before and after contact. Yet Bennet's model, which focused on the calorific content of macronutrients rather than the density and diversity of micronutrients, is problematic in privileging energy expenditure over all other nutritional measures. When calories (mainly in the form of starch) are high following the introduction of energy-dense grains, we now are more aware, the availability of vitamins, minerals and essential fatty acids may be proportionally diminished, affecting the functioning of cells and enzymes in the human body. We certainly note the gendered nature of many Native American subsistence strategies before contact, which allowed women an increasingly dominant role in producing agricultural products such as beans, squash and maize. Carbohydrates did likely increase as a proportion of the Native American diet in the centuries before contact, providing more energy to those who sought to reach reproductive age without suffering from scarcity of calories. But we avoid the pitfall in Bennett's influential estimation that animal products only constituted around 10 percent of the Native American diet in regions such as New England. Though they may have only constituted 10 percent of calories consumed, their contribution of nutrients—rather than readily available energy to burn—was likely far higher as a proportion within the overall diet.

Bennet's emphasis prefigures the modern nutritional debate on macronutrient ratios, which has led vital micronutrients and macrominerals to be pushed aside in conceptual discussions of health and immunity. By taking into account the importance of micronutrients in plants and animals, as well as fat and protein, this book questions the scholarly tendency to focus on maize consumption at the expense of other plants and animals consumed by Native Americans. The European perception of maize consumption in New England and elsewhere often represented a Native American reaction to threats to their more diverse subsistence frameworks, which centered on a hybrid between agriculture and hunting and gathering. Before contact, indeed, increasing consumption of maize was not necessarily at the expense of other nutritional sources. Rather, it may have provided a readily available source of energy that enabled longer and further-reaching hunting practices, allowing other more nutrient-dense food sources to be located and consumed. Calorie-dense macronutrients like maize could facilitate the consumption of nutrient-dense foods such as fish, animals and other plant sources, with attendant physical activities in cultivating the maize or in hunting and gathering, thereby preventing adiposity or other inflammatory markers that are associated with high resting blood sugar.[35]

The tensions and ambiguities outlined above are not erased in the chapters that follow, as we attempt to apply the latest work in nutritional science to our reading of Native American history before and after European contact. We show how the interaction between nutrition and immunity resulted from a delicate balance between wild animal products and cultivated and wild plant sources, and between diets that were often (but not always) relatively high in animal and marine fats, but which also tended to incorporate starch from plant sources. This balance encouraged a relatively sustainable and biodiverse ecological environment in precontact North America. It also allowed a combination of nutritional sources that, from the perspective of modern science, would have encouraged relatively strong human immunological health and fertility. Where biodiversity was reduced in precontact Native America, indeed, the bioarchaeological record suggests that health and immunity also suffered—most notably during the move toward indigenous cultivation and consumption of maize at the expense of other plant and animal sources. Yet even here, we will see, the historical context allowed other nutritional strategies to mitigate these consequences, unlike during the postcontact era, when nutrient-poor food sources often increased as a proportion of the Native American diet.

Chapter 1

THE EVOLUTION OF NUTRITION AND IMMUNITY: FROM THE PALEOLITHIC ERA TO THE MEDIEVAL EUROPEAN BLACK DEATH

To understand the biological effects of nutritional disruption on Native American immunity and fertility after 1492, it is necessary to consider what we know, and what we do not yet know, about three vital stages in human nutritional history. The earliest two stages affected the nature of human evolution. The first began more than 2.5 million years ago, when nutrient-dense foods from land mammals allowed an increasingly small human gut to complement an expanding brain.[1] The second, according to a newer and more controversial hypothesis, took place between 200,000 and 90,000 years ago, when coastal marine migrations from Africa provided greater access to the omega-3 fatty acid docosahexaenoic acid (DHA). Those migrations contributed to what some scholars now describe as a second stage in the evolving growth of the human brain, due to the greater reliance on DHA as an exogenous nutrient.[2] These evolutionary interactions, and their nutritional basis, coincided with a hunter-gatherer lifestyle and preceded the intensified farming of "Neolithic" foods such as wheat and corn, which began around 10,500 years ago throughout the world. We consider the rupturing of hunter-gatherer food systems as a third major stage in human nutritional history, beginning with the rise of Neolithic agriculture in Europe and Asia, and slightly later with the rise of maize intensification in parts of North America.

Assessing what we define as the third stage in human nutritional history allows us to consider how immunity, and thus demography, might be compromised by rupturing the food requirements that developed during the two earlier evolutionary stages. Scholarship on declining health markers and increasing disease in Europe and Asia during the Neolithic era, and slightly later during the rise of maize intensification in North America, offers an important model and conceptual framework to explain similarities and differences in post-contact North America, when populations were also faced with sudden changes to subsistence strategies and threats to their immunological health. There is still much that we do not know regarding the evolution of the human immune system, including the extent to which it continued to evolve and adapt during the rise of the Homo genus around two million years ago; or even the nature of the role of an immune system during the evolutionary divergence between vertebrates and invertebrates before that period. Nonetheless, we are comfortable with the suggestion that selective pressures may well have contributed to ongoing refinement of the inflammatory and immunological response during the Paleolithic era, coinciding with the development of a small gut in relation to a large brain, including in relation to the micronutrient and metabolic requirements for optimal immune function.[3]

The brain utilizes micronutrients as well as energy. The former is required for the proper function of enzymes and other features that underlie chemical and hormonal signaling between the brain and the rest of the body. The relatively recent enlargement of the brain thus risked constraining the function of other parts of the body that preceded its evolutionary growth, including the cellular processes that allow the immune system to function against pathogens, or perceived pathogens. The consumption of nutrient-dense foods during the Paleolithic era thus allowed a smaller digestive system in relation to the enlarged brain, while also continuing to supply the immune system with all that it continued to require; or even with micronutrients and metabolic sources that allowed it to continue to evolve advantageously. If those micronutrient-dense foods were suddenly replaced with nutrient-poor foods, the consequences for optimal health, including immune function, would be deleterious. We ought to examine those consequences at relevant historical junctures. The problematic health consequences of the Neolithic transition to agriculture 10,000 years ago, for example, may have compromised immune function at just the point when the changing societal context made diseases more likely to proliferate. Examining that phenomenon provides a paradigm to understand the problematic curtailment of nutrient-dense foods in Native American history, particularly if we can inform our assessment of both historical phenomena and their mutual relevance with new insights from the fast-developing scientific literature on the association between nutrition and immunity.

The scientific literature on the link between nutrition and immunity has developed significantly since anthropologists and archaeologists first identified declining health in transitional Neolithic populations. It has evolved even further since historians such as Jones and Kelton began to highlight ruptured food access as one of several contingent factors in the decline of post-contact

Native American populations.[4] A vast number of human immune cells reside in the human gut. The immune response to pathogens that enter the body via the gut begins with these immune cells.[5] Yet we have only very recently begun to realize the full extent of the inflammatory response that follows the gut's encounter with foods that are maladapted to its evolved structural and hormonal mechanisms: a release of inflammatory proteins that upregulate the human immune response, often chronically.[6] It is likely that in such a chronically inflamed state, the efficacy of the acute immune response to pathogens is reduced.[7] In this chapter we examine whether such a state was likely during the third stage of human nutritional history, which corresponded with the rise of Neolithic grains in Europe and the Middle East, and which also witnessed the proliferation of new diseases.

We take care to avoid overstating the importance of the concept of chronic inflammation, given that its scientific literature is still in its infancy, leading some in the sphere of functional medicine toward possible exaggeration or misunderstanding. Doing so will require examination of the optimal operation of the immune response to invading pathogens both in relation to and separate from the process of inflammation. We consider the connection between inflammatory health markers, declining working immunity to disease and the introduction of new subsistence patterns in the Neolithic Old World. Scholarship on these connections—including that which has examined Neolithic skeletal evidence—offers important models and conceptual frameworks to explain similarities and differences in post-contact North America, when populations were also faced with sudden changes to subsistence strategies and threats to their immunological health.

By synthesizing the latest historical, archaeological and anthropological assessments of Neolithic health outcomes with the most recent biological literature on nutrition, inflammation, autoimmunity and immunity, we will be able to form a related hypothesis, which will frame the chapters that follow: whether during the intensification of maize agriculture in precontact indigenous North America from around 4,500 years ago, or following the disruptive arrival of Europeans and European agriculture among Native Americans, autoimmunity and chronic inflammation, and a compromised immune system, could have been strongly affected by dietary changes that deviated from the repertoire of foods that Native Americans, like all human populations, had evolved to consume during the Paleolithic era (from around 2.4 million years ago to around 10,000 years ago). This phenomenon represented a centrally important contingent factor in Native American demographic decline, which was distinct from any supposed genetic differences in the working immunity of Native Americans as compared to Old World populations.

Expanding the Expensive Tissue Hypothesis: Evolutionary Nutritional Interactions between the Small Gut and the Large Brain

It is now well accepted among evolutionary biologists that the increased consumption of animal meat by early hominids played a profound role in the evolution of modern humans. It was fundamental in allowing the development of the exceptionally large brain of Homo sapiens.[8] A new generation of scholars has identified the importance of marine animals during a later period of brain evolution, separate from that which was enabled by access to land mammals. It is worth identifying and synthesizing the latest scholarship on these interactions, to understand why nutrition is central to the enhancement or diminishment of working immunity in human populations, including those in indigenous North America who suffered an assault on long-evolved nutritional frameworks at just the point when diseases began to proliferate. The nutrient sources that allowed the development of a small human gut in relation to a large human brain likely included other benefits, particularly in relation to the growth and optimal function of the human immune system.

The exact point in our evolutionary history at which we started eating meat is uncertain, but meat eating likely originated before the appearance of "a human-like primate some 6–8 million years ago," before the Paleolithic period that extended from the earliest known use of stone tools by early hominids, around 2.4 million years ago, to the end of the Pleistocene around 11,500 years ago.[9] Several lines of evidence, including changes in morphology through the evolution of early hominids to modern humans, and archaeological evidence of tools used in hunting and meat consumption, suggest that meat eating increased from the earliest hominids to modern humans. By 500,000 years ago, moving from the Upper Paleolithic toward the Middle Paleolithic, there is clear evidence of meat consumption by modern humans.[10]

With these evolutionary and archaeological discussions in mind, scholars have drawn an association between meat consumption and the inverse relationship between the size of the human gut and the human brain. Animals with large (and even multiple) guts, such as ruminants, spend much energy converting nutrient-poor foods, such as grass, into nutrient-dense end products (their own tissue). With an increasingly small gut, conversely, evolving humans required nutrient density exogenously, from other animal meats. There is a linear correlation between body weight and basal metabolism in terrestrial mammals, suggesting that the supply of metabolic fuel to the brain is a limiting factor for brain growth, and that an increase in brain volume must be compensated for by a decrease in the size of other organs.[11] In The

Expensive Tissue Hypothesis, therefore, Aiello and Wheeler propose that gut tissue was sacrificed as brain tissue expanded in human evolution.[12] As brain growth occurred alongside the increased consumption of animal products, the digestive organs were able to decrease in size without compromising nutrient supply: the nutrient density of meat enabled a smaller digestive system to provide all the nutrients required for a metabolically demanding larger brain.[13]

As Hardy et al. have recently suggested, it is not necessary to rule out the consumption of plant carbohydrates in any discussion of the important role of animal meat in the evolution of the brain. Both, in their view, were "necessary and complementary dietary components in hominin evolution." Discussing work by Conklin-Brittain et al. and Wrangham, they do not discount the hypothesis that "concentrated starch from plant foods was essential to meet the substantially increased metabolic demands of an enlarged brain [...] [and] to support successful reproduction and increased aerobic capacity." Immune cells require glucose, either from gluconeogenesis (the production of glucose from non-carbohydrate sources within the body) or from ingested carbohydrates, suggesting that starch consumption may have been important even as animal meats contributed to the enlargement of the brain and the shrinking of the gut. Animal products, as we shall see, supply many of the nutrients that are necessary for the multicellular processes that enable optimal immune function. But the metabolic energy used for sound immune function may have relied in part on exogenous starch consumption throughout the history of modern human beings.[14]

More recent human evolutionary studies have suggested an association between marine animal consumption and enhanced brain function, revising our focus solely on land animals. The Expensive Tissue Hypothesis ought to be understood alongside, and even synthesized with, an expanding separate literature on the role of DHA, in human evolution. Though the levels of DHA from terrestrial sources might have been sufficient for smaller-brained early humans, several recent assessments suggest that exploitation of seafood resources from coastal and estuarine environments later in human evolution was vital in allowing a continued increase in brain size, coinciding with changes in human behavior that likely required greater processing capacity.[15]

The brain began to increase in size long before the evolution of modern humans.[16] Between the evolution of Homo erectus and modern humans, brain size almost doubled. Yet as recently as in the last 200,000 years, the increase in size may have been "exponential."[17] The negative logarithmic relationship between body size and brain size to which most other mammalian species conform, does not apply to modern humans.[18] Given that DHA is thought to be one of the nutrients whose abundance acts as a limiting factor for brain size, some scholars have posited that increased consumption of DHA was central in allowing the possible continued expansion of the brain in more recent human evolutionary history.[19]

Although early humans may not have been able to exploit marine resources intensively, they may have consumed marine foods sporadically, similarly to the periodic consumption of marine foods by primates such as monkeys and chacma baboons, thereby consuming more DHA than could be found in terrestrial sources alone.[20] Intense exploitation of coastal resources would have required regional societal knowledge of the association between lunar dates and tidal cycles. The seasonal variability of marine foods would have necessitated movement toward and away from the coast at different times of year. The high level of cognition required for the exploitation of marine resources may in part explain why marine foods did not form a substantial part of the human diet earlier in human history.[21]

Alpha-linolenic acid (ALA), the precursor for all omega-3 fatty acids, cannot be manufactured by mammals, and so must be obtained from dietary sources.[22] Plants contain ALA, which can be converted into the omega-3 fatty acids eicosa-pentaenoic acid (EPA) and DHA. However, this conversion is thought to be inefficient and unreliable.[23] Consequently, several researchers now suggest that DHA is "conditionally essential"—challenging previous assumptions that "ALA is the essential omega-3 nutrient."[24] Thus the brain size of other mammalian species may have been limited by their lesser supply of DHA, which is not manufactured by the "primary source of the terrestrial food chain" and can only be produced in small quantities in mammals, making it a scarce resource for terrestrial mammals in their historical development.[25] A significant part of human evolution, conversely, occurred with at least some access to coastal regions with abundant availability of marine foods, which would have supplied their nutrients.[26]

We can also point to the potential importance of other trace elements (particularly iodine and selenium) that are found at much higher levels in marine foods than terrestrial foods, and which are crucial for brain function. Their scarcity may also have acted as limiting factors in brain size before the widespread consumption of marine foods.[27] Thus the more recent dramatic expansion of the brain from 200,000 to 90,000 years ago may have required a higher consumption of DHA, and therefore more intense and organized exploitation of marine resources, through a process defined by scholars as "coastal adaptation."[28] In this framework, we can identify "a potential early coastal route of modern humans out of Africa via the Red Sea coast."[29] This second evolutionary stage may have increased brain size further, and possibly also reduced the size of the gut, thanks in part to newly abundant dietary DHA from marine animals.

Such a hypothesis, to be sure, does not reflect a consensus among scholars of the nutritional framework for human brain evolution, not least due to the vexing nature of identifying marine fossil evidence versus that from land mammals. But although the hypothesis remains relatively controversial, the overlooked evolutionary importance of DHA for immunity and health more generally, as described by Crawford, Cunnane and other proponents of the hypothesis, is much less contentious.[30] DHA has been defined as anti-inflammatory both within and without the gut, and has been linked to enhanced immunological function, in addition to its role in cognitive reasoning and brain development.[31]

Immunity, Inflammation and the Evolution of Nutritional Needs

The majority of human immune cells reside in the gut, below the epithelial layer in the lamina propria of the gastrointestinal tract.[32] That which the gut evolved to incorporate for most of human history—land animal products, including protein, fat and myriad micronutrients; marine animal products, containing DHA and vitamin D; and preagricultural plants such as non-starchy vegetables—likely influenced its cellular structure and function, and its evolving relationship with the rest of the human body, including the immune system. Selective pressures that coincided with the evolution of the small gut in relation to a large brain led to the upregulation or downregulation of inflammatory responses that evolved to require specific nutrients. Preventing access to those nutritional sources, or replacing them with foods to which the human gut has had less time to adapt, may cause autoimmune responses that dysregulate the acute immune response, by causing chronic overreaction to inflammatory food molecules. Doing so might also prevent consumption of certain micronutrients and macronutrients that various parts of the immune system require for optimal function. These or similar nutritional disruptions ought to be defined as a vital contingent factor in the ability of communities to maintain health and immunity, not least in contexts where the sudden proliferation of infectious diseases requires immunity to function as optimally as possible.

It is logical to suggest that any mismatch between evolved nutritional needs and substances that enter the gut might portend negative consequences in relation to the interaction between working immunity and the inflammatory response. An understanding of the biological consequences of such a mismatch ought to frame archaeological and bioanthropological work from human sites that shows a relationship between declining meat consumption, increasing grain consumption, nutrient deficiencies, compromised immunity and even inflammation.[33] But before we examine historical case studies that confirm such an association, we need to understand the biological interaction between nutrition, inflammation and immunity in a little more detail. Such an understanding will underscore why nutrition cannot merely be defined as one of several nebulous factors that prevent populations from surviving or recovering from epidemics. Rather, it is central to the sound function of human immunity, fertility and broader health, all of which have evolved to become contingent on specific micronutrient and macronutrient requirements.

The surface of the human body—the skin on the external surface, and mucous membranes lining the internal cavities—acts as a physical barrier to pathogens, which must be breached for infection to occur. Invasion of pathogens through these barriers is inhibited by acidic secretions such as sweat, mucous and stomach acid, which contain antimicrobial compounds. Pathogen invasion is inhibited by cilia, microscopic protrusions from cells that resemble small hairs, which line internal cavities such as the respiratory tract and move mucus and debris, including pathogens, out of the body. When one of these barriers is breached, an immune response ensues.[34]

Two major types of immunity, innate immunity and adaptive immunity, work contiguously to identify and eradicate an invading pathogen. The innate response developed earlier in evolution and involves a nonspecific response to pathogens. The lack of immune memory and adaptability in the innate immune system means that the response of the innate immune system to a specific pathogen will not depend on previous exposure to the pathogen. The adaptive, or acquired, immune response involves a more flexible response to pathogens. It is also sometimes referred to as antibody-mediated, or humoral, immunity. The adaptive response can stimulate an immune response to a newly encountered pathogen that evades the innate immune system as well as orchestrate a more rapid response to a previously encountered pathogen.[35]

The innate response depends on immune cells known as phagocytes and natural killer cells. Phagocytes kill pathogens in the process of phagocytosis, whereby pathogens are effectively consumed by immune cells. Phagocytes include cells such as neutrophils, monocytes and macrophages. Natural killer cells destroy host cells infected with pathogens and release inflammatory and toxic molecules that further activate the immune response. After recognizing a pathogen, innate immune cells subsequently display pathogen-derived molecules, known as antibodies, on their surface. These cells are thus referred to as "antigen-presenting cells."[36] Cell-surface proteins known as major histocompatibility complex (MHC) proteins are required for this process. Different MHC molecules recognize and display different classes of pathogen-derived molecules. Variations in MHC proteins between individuals are thus linked with differences in immunity.[37] Importantly, the identification of pathogens by the innate immune system depends on pattern recognition receptors (PRRs) detecting characteristic molecular signatures of pathogens, such as lipopolysaccharides in the cell walls of bacteria. This pattern-recognition system is primitive, and the molecules recognized by PRRs are encoded genetically, such that a newly encountered pathogen may not be recognized by this system.[38]

The adaptive immune response involves the secretion of a range of cytokines, which are signaling molecules that allow communication between immune cells as well as other proteins, such as clotting factors and antibacterial proteins. Two main types of immune cells, B and T lymphocytes, are involved in the response. B and T lymphocytes constantly circulate around the body, and during an infection are attracted to the point of infection by cytokines.[39] The adaptive response depends on antibodies, also known as immunoglobulins. These are Y-shaped molecules with variable regions that bind to a specific antigen derived from a pathogen. B lymphocytes, as well innate immune cells such as macrophages, process antigens and display antigen fragments on their surface in combination with the MHC. When a T lymphocyte encounters these antigen-MHC complexes (via the binding of a T-cell receptor to the antigen), it becomes activated against the pathogen. In doing so, it enlarges and secretes cytokines and toxins. T cells are divided into subclasses that recognize different MHC molecules and respond in slightly different ways to pathogens.[40] The differentiation (conversion) of T cells into specific subclasses is an important aspect of immune function. Perturbations in differentiation can result in a less effective response to invading pathogens.[41] Following an encounter with an antigen, memory B cells and T cells are created, which allows the immune system to generate a superior secondary immune response on a subsequent encounter with the same pathogen.[42]

That pattern recognition receptors in the innate immune system are encoded genetically makes them fixed within an individual. The number of genes encoding such receptors is thought to be only in the hundreds, and new receptors can only be generated through mutations in individuals, which must then be inherited and subjected to natural selection over many generations.[43] This creates a weakness: a pathogen may be able to escape this pattern recognition system and therefore evade detection by the innate immune system. In contrast, the antibodies and T-cell receptors of the adaptive immune system are highly variable, thereby allowing recognition of molecules from newly encountered pathogens. Antibodies and T-cell receptors are generated through the process of genetic recombination during the formation of new immune cells within each individual (recombination involves the rearrangement, or shuffling, of genes from different segments).[44] Around 400 genes encode these variable regions. The diversity is generated by the recombination of these genes.[45] Each immune cell therefore contains a unique arrangement of genes so that the antigens produced by each cell are specific to that cell. It is estimated that immune cells can create around 10^{30} different variable regions, including those on B cells and T cells, thereby creating the capacity for the identification of an almost infinite variety of pathogens.[46]

These processes underlying the human immune system are contingent on the health of the human body, irrespective of any invasion of pathogens. Other factors might arouse an immune response, prior to infection, thereby perturbing the immune system and potentially compromising the ability of the acute immune system to respond to pathogens. Chronic inflammation in the gut, and eventually elsewhere in the body, is one such factor. A chronic inflammatory response is distinct from the acute inflammatory response associated with infection and injury. An acute inflammatory response involves the movement of immune cells to the site of injury or infection, and the production of inflammatory mediators such as cytokines, eicosanoids and prostaglandins primarily by mast cells and macrophages residing in the injured or infected tissue. Such a response is intended to upregulate working immunity to eliminate pathogens and allow repair of damaged tissues. Following elimination of the pathogen and damaged tissue, this inflammatory response is resolved.[47] In the state of chronic inflammation, however, the inflammatory reaction is not resolved. Inflammatory cells remain in inflamed tissues, producing inflammatory molecules such as reactive oxygen species (ROS) and cytokines, resulting in the chronic sustained activity of immune cells.[48] In autoimmune conditions, the immune system loses the ability to distinguish pathogen-derived antigens from host proteins. Thus, the immune response of T lymphocytes becomes directed at the body's own tissue, potentially leading to damage to the tissue of the host.[49]

There is an increasing body of evidence that immune function is altered by chronic inflammation and autoimmunity, supporting our hypothesis that immunity to pathogens is decreased by the overactivation of the immune system in conditions of chronic inflammation and autoimmunity. One reason that inflammation and autoimmunity may decrease the immune response to invading pathogens may relate to the consumption of resources—particularly glucose—in the reaction. This process risks limiting the resources available to the immune system to respond to pathogens.[50]

Diabetes and excess adiposity, both hallmarks of the metabolic syndrome associated with chronic inflammation, have been shown to be associated with decreased immunity to pathogens. While the nature of this association is not currently well understood, the observation that patients suffering from diabetes and obesity have lower immunity, and animal and in vitro experiments illustrating potential mechanisms for this effect, provide support for this hypothesis.[51] One potential mechanism involves the effects of immunomodulatory adipokines and inflammatory cytokines secreted by adipocytes.[52] For example, the hormone leptin, secreted by adipocytes, has been shown to have complex and wide-ranging effects on immune cell function, including the production of proinflammatory cytokines by immune cells, the activation and activity of phagocytes, and the generation of reactive oxygen species in specific types of neutrophils.[53] The hormone adiponectin, also secreted by adipokines, has been shown to affect the function of several different classes of human immune cells in vitro, including inducing or decreasing the production of various anti-inflammatory cytokines in abnormal ways.[54] Since the levels of leptin, adiponectin and inflammatory cytokines such as IL-6 are altered in obese individuals, it is highly plausible that the increased secretion of these substances in the state of obesity will affect immune cell function.[55] As Myles suggests, the production of these immune-stimulating compounds creates signals that "act as false alarms [...] that [can] cause the entire system to dial down its responsiveness"—analogous to the down-regulation of the endogenous steroid response in steroid users.[56]

Another potential mechanism by which acute immune function may be altered due to a chronic inflammatory response in obese individuals involves the alteration in immune function by increasing levels of circulating glucose and fatty acids, due to deranged metabolic profiles. Markers of poor metabolic energy use can be defined according to problematic macronutrient ratios, usually where carbohydrates vastly outweigh protein and fat. They are strongly associated with inflammation, often, but not always, in conjunction with obesity.[57] Glucose is known to be important as a substrate for immune cells, and some recent experiments have shown that exposure of immune cells in vitro to high glucose concentrations can alter their activity.[58] Fatty acids are also used as a substrate for immune cell metabolism. In vitro experiments have shown that exposure of immune cells to different levels of fatty acids can affect their function.[59] Saturated fatty acids have been found to activate Toll-like receptors, which are central to signaling between immune cells.[60] While there is little research into the effects of the changing levels of glucose and fatty acids on immune function, it is clear that glucose and fatty acids affect the process. It is highly plausible that the increased levels of these substrates in the state of chronic inflammation may adversely affect the immune response to pathogens.

Hyperglycemia increases the formation of advanced glycation end products (AGES), which form when glucose reacts with proteins, thereby detrimentally affecting their function.[61] AGES have been shown to affect immune responses, including the migration of phagocytes, and to affect cell signaling in ways that promote inflammation.[62] Hyperglycemia can activate the polyol pathway, which metabolizes glucose during conditions of excess consumption. This has been shown to compromise innate immunity by affecting the function of neutrophil immune cells. Neutrophils have consequently been shown to be less effective at killing bacteria in diabetics.[63]

The accumulation of oxidative damage within a cell, caused by oxidation of cellular constituents, often known as oxidative stress (OS), is common
among those with chronically raised blood sugar. OS describes an "imbalance
of pro-oxidants and antioxidants" within the cell during the metabolism of
macronutrients for energy, with an accumulation of oxidizing molecules that
can damage cellular components.[64] OS plays an important role in cell signaling,
particularly in immune cells.[65] It stimulates the inflammatory response by activating cell signaling pathways, as shown in studies of diabetic, prediabetic and
even in nondiabetic control populations.[66] Thus continued OS is thought to
play a profound role in the chronic inflammatory response and in compromising working immunity. Oxidizing molecules ROS are produced as part of
the immune response by cells such as macrophages and neutrophils, and aid
in destruction of the pathogen.[67] Since these highly oxidizing molecules can
result in damage to host cells, mechanisms have evolved to prevent their accumulation: enzymes such as glutathione peroxidase, and antioxidant molecules
are involved in the neutralization of ROS, thereby maintaining homeostasis
of cellular oxidation status.[68] When these mechanisms are insufficient to maintain homeostasis, oxidizing molecules can damage cellular components.[69] As a
result, OS may contribute to chronic inflammation by disrupting immune cell
signaling, also potentially limiting the function of the acute immune response
to pathogens when needed.[70]

Chronic inflammation is now thought to increase insulin resistance, even
among those not diagnosed with type 2 diabetes.[71] An evolutionary perspective helps us explain this phenomenon: activation of the highly metabolically demanding immune system could potentially threaten the brain's glucose
supply. Therefore, immune activation results in a level of insulin resistance
in other parts of the body: a mechanism that has likely evolved to ensure an
adequate supply of glucose for the brain.[72] The insulin resistance of these
tissues causes fat to replace glucose as the primary metabolic fuel in these
tissues.[73] The increase in insulin resistance during chronic inflammation
results in a positive feedback loop, increasing inflammation further.[74] Due to
chronic hyperglycemia and inflammation, diabetics have been shown to be
particularly susceptible to periodontal pathogens, urinary tract infections and
soft tissue infections, and to infections by gram-negative bacteria.[75] Diabetics
also suffer from impaired healing of fractures, likely to be a result of altered
regulation of the immune system.[76]

Though many of the studies referenced so far have focused on the effects
of raised blood glucose among those who have developed type 2 diabetes
(which is strongly associated with chronic inflammation), scholars have begun
to extrapolate beyond diabetic subjects to define the immune dysregulation
caused by chronically raised glucose in very high carbohydrate diets more

generally. Immune cells require some glucose to function. But excess glucose from exogenous carbohydrates, we are beginning to learn, can cause an inflammatory state even before the diagnosis of diabetes. This inflammatory state, in turn, may compromise immune function. Such an extrapolation is in its infancy in the scholarly literature. Thanks in part to the deeper scholarly literature on diabetes, nonetheless, a new consensus is developing on the problematic immunological effects of chronically raised blood glucose among those who are not formally considered as diabetic. They derive from the interaction between several factors, including the disruption of signaling among gut bacteria, the reduction of immune cell regeneration due to the prevention of autophagy by the chronic presence of insulin in the blood, declining insulin sensitivity due to raised blood glucose and increased inflammatory adiposity due to the conversion of glucose to triglycerides, which disrupts immune signaling pathways. We hypothesize that the above effects may result in the diversion of immune cells that the acute immune system requires, due to low-level inflammation caused by chronically raised insulin.[77]

Aside from the inflammatory and immunological effects of chronically raised blood glucose, we ought to note another possible problematic effect of diets that depart from those experienced by humans for the most part of their history: a sudden mismatch in the ratio between omega-3 fatty acids and omega-6 fatty acids, which may increase the occurrence of inflammatory cytokines and compromise immunity to pathogens.

The omega-6 fatty acid linoleic acid (LA) is found in most plants, including in grains, and is metabolized to the biologically active arachidonic acid (AA).[78] Omega-6 fatty acids are generally required for activation of the inflammatory response. When the omega-6 fatty acid arachidonic acid becomes oxidized under enzymatic activity, it forms eicosanoids, which are signaling molecules that are necessary to mount an inflammatory response.[79] In the first phase of the inflammatory reaction, these proinflammatory mediators are generated from arachidonic acid by specific enzymes.[80] This process results in immune responses such as the activation of neutrophil immune cells, vasodilation and extravasation of fluid (the movement of immune cells from the capillaries to the tissues around them).[81]

Omega-3 fatty acids, conversely, inhibit the inflammatory reaction via several mechanisms. The omega-3 fatty acids ALA, EPA and DHA are the precursors for anti-inflammatory molecules called resolvins, which are required for the resolution of the inflammatory reaction as well as the production of anti-inflammatory molecules.[82] Omega-3 fatty acids are incorporated into cell membranes, where they have a number of physiological effects that in turn affect immune cell signaling and behavior.[83] They have been shown to alter gene expression of molecules involved in the production of other proinflammatory molecules, thereby lowering the production of these molecules.[84] They are able to inhibit the production of proinflammatory eicosanoids produced from omega-6 fatty acids by competing with them as a substrate for the enzymes involved in the production of proinflammatory eicosanoids.[85] They are even able to change the composition of signaling molecules in the cell membrane. Incorporation of omega-3 fatty acids into the cell membrane has thus been shown to result in a shift to the presence of less biologically active molecules in the cell membrane, which in turn affects immune cell signaling and behavior.[86] Incorporation of EPA and DHA into the membranes of lymphocytes is thought to affect the proliferation of T cells and their activation by antigen-presenting cells, essential to the working of the immune system in response to pathogens.[87]

If omega-6 fatty acids are not balanced in equal ratio with omega-3 fatty acids, the interaction between inflammatory and anti-inflammatory response risks being thrown off-kilter. Such a phenomenon has been noted in discussions of metabolic derangement in the contemporary Western diet.[88] The effects of omega-3 and omega-6 fatty acids on immune function, then, are directly influenced by the consumption of these fatty acids in equal ratio.[89] The new scientific literature on the interaction between omega-3 and omega-6 fatty acids thus further supports our working hypothesis regarding the link between curtailed nutrition and compromised immunity. Any historical move away from omega-3-rich wild animals and marine products toward omega-6 dominant grains might herald problematic health outcomes, including increasing inflammation and declining immune function.

Our working hypothesis regarding the link between chronic inflammation and compromised immunity will be important as we go on to examine declining health markers among individuals in communities that began to consume inflammatory food sources, or who were subjected to new macronutrient ratios that encouraged inflammation and obesity, particularly due to chronically raised blood glucose or a sudden increase in oxidized omega-6 fatty acids relative to omega-3 fatty acids.

Evolutionary Health and the Rise of Neolithic Agriculture: A Useful Category of Historical Analysis

Understanding the mechanisms involved in the processes of immunity and inflammation allows us to explore how diet may affect the immune response during periods of societal upheaval or distress, when invading pathogens became more problematic. Let us begin with the health consequences of the move toward agricultural intensification in the Middle East and Europe, around 10,500 years ago.[90] The diet of hunter-gatherers in the region during the Paleolithic era is thought to have consisted of some combination of meat, fish and plant foods such as nuts, berries, wild fruits, nonstarchy plants and starchy roots, tubers and rhizomes.[91] The transition to agriculture, defined by a shift from hunting and gathering to the cultivation of plants for dietary purposes, and the domestication of animals, resulted in the increased consumption of grains, including in relation to animal products.[92] The transition to agriculture also corresponded to changes in living conditions, from a nomadic to a sedentary lifestyle, and an increase in the size and density of populations.[93]

Agriculture originated in at least eight different areas around the world around 10,500 years ago: including the Near East (the earliest known center of domestication), South China and North China, New Guinea and sub-Saharan Africa.[94] Maize intensification occurred in North America several thousand years later (though as we shall see, important facets of horticulture preceded those later developments).[95] The multiple origins of domestication around the same time have led scholars to propose that global climate change at the end of the Pleistocene, and the consequent effects on the availability of plant and animal species for consumption by hunter-gatherer populations around the world, may have driven the impetus for agricultural transition. Unpredictability of food acquisition may have been a strong motivator for the exploration of alternative methods of attaining food.[96]

It was once thought that the physical demands of hunting and gathering during the Paleolithic era were grueling and drove individuals to an early grave.[97] Such a view was driven by the assumption that the growth of the population following the Neolithic revolution was the result of food surplus that allowed increased health, fertility and life expectancy.[98] Research since the 1960s has challenged the distinction between Paleolithic and Neolithic health and nutrition, supporting a now generally well-accepted consensus that certain facets of biological health declined after the adoption of agriculture. The rise in population that followed agricultural intensification can be attributed to energy-dense storable food allowing more individuals to reach reproduction age, combined with early weaning and decreased birth spacing. Yet skeletal and other evidence confirms a significant rise in disease effects, compromised bone density and even decreased immunity to infection.[99] Comparison of skeletal and dental remains before and after the use of agriculture at archaeological sites in Europe and the Middle East provide insight on the interaction between sedentary subsistence frameworks, decreasing nutritional diversity and increased infectious disease.[100] Skeletal indicators of health, such as a reduction in tooth size, jaw size, cortical bone thickness and an increase in nutritional deficiencies such as iron deficiency followed the move to agriculture in regions around the world.[101]

To be sure, regional variations in the availability of noncultivated foods, population density and local culture determined whether and how the agricultural transition impacted communal health.[102] Therefore, it is important to consider multiple factors that may have impacted health, rather than assuming the introduction of grains was unanimously harmful. In some regions, analysis of skeletal remains suggests that health increased following the adoption of agriculture.[103] The use of domesticated animals alongside grains was an important contingent factor in maintaining nutritional diversity, from the Near East to Europe.[104] It is also important to note distinctions in the kind of grains used in different regions. Barley and wheat were cultivated in the Near East; millet, sorghum, yams and dates in Africa; millet and rice in northern China; and rice, sugarcane, taro and yams in Southeast Asia. Each staple varied in its capacity to affect health. For example, rice and European domesticated plants have been suggested to be more cariogenic than maize.[105] Some grains, such as rice, are particularly deficient in protein, which can inhibit vitamin A activity and absorption.[106]

Dental caries are useful markers to distinguish between communities that did or did not adopt intensified agriculture in the Old World during the Neolithic era.[107] Metabolism of dietary carbohydrates by oral bacteria produces acids that cause demineralization of the enamel and other tissues.[108] A high prevalence of dental caries in a population does not necessarily indicate an increase in grain consumption. Some hunter-gatherer groups also suffer a high frequency of dental caries. For example, preagricultural remains from the Mesolithic period in Sicily and Portugal show a high prevalence of caries. These caries likely resulted from the consumption of high-carbohydrate plants as well as honey and sweet fruits.[109] Nonetheless, an increase in caries following the adoption of agriculture has been documented by numerous researchers in various settings worldwide.[110] Larsen has suggested that increased carbohydrate consumption due to grain intensification acted as the primary causal factor in many of the most well-studied Neolithic communities.[111] In the majority of postagricultural societies, women have been found to suffer increased dental caries compared to men.[112] Such a phenomenon, according to the best available hypothesis, derived from a higher carbohydrate and lower protein diet among females, possibly as a means to provide readily available energy while pregnant and breastfeeding.[113]

Periodontal disease, deriving from inflammation of tissues around the teeth, which potentially results in the loss of teeth, has also been linked to the move toward Neolithic grains in the Middle East, Europe and beyond.[114] In skeletal remains, careful examination is required to distinguish exposure of the tooth root as a result of periodontal disease from exposure as a result of mechanical wear and tear due to the consumption of hard foods or other activities.[115]

Such assessments have revealed that in the Nile Valley, for example, tooth loss increased from the Mesolithic period (c. 15,000 years ago) to agricultural societies in the Meroitic era (350 BC–AD 350) and after.[116] This trend is echoed at several other locations around the world during the adoption or intensification of agriculture.[117]

The isotopic analysis of bones has been particularly informative in pinpointing the transition to agriculture in specific communities, and in linking this to nutrient and mineral deficiencies, and evidence of a rise in infection by diseases. Isotopes are forms of a chemical element that differ in the number of neutrons. Stable isotopes in skeletal remains do not decay over time, and so can provide valuable information regarding the types of foods consumed during an individual's lifetime. Isotopic analysis of carbon and nitrogen has been used by anthropologists in the determination of ancient diets. Isotopic signatures from skeletal tissue, which remodels throughout life, is representative of diet for around a decade before death.[118] Isotopic signatures from tooth enamel, which does not remodel after formation, is representative of diet over a lifetime.[119] Different food sources have different proportions of carbon and nitrogen isotopes, allowing us to discern differences in food consumption patterns in bioarchaeological evidence, including among different plant types, different animal types and between plants and animals. We are then able to cross-reference other health markers according to those differences. Various global populations exhibit greater prevalence of skeletal indicators of growth disruption and enamel defects such as hypoplasias, and even greater prevalence of disease and infection indicators, alongside evidence of newly introduced grain products. These associations are markedly different in comparison to other populations where those products were not yet introduced, and which did not display the same negative health markers.[120]

With these general indications in mind, and their association with intensified grain agriculture, other more specific inferences have been gained from isotopic and other analyses of skeletal evidence. Many global regions, for example, show a decline in adult stature during the agricultural transition, or during agricultural intensification.[121] Several studies demonstrate cortical bone thinning in currently living populations experiencing nutritional deficiency.[122] In particular, a lack of protein or overall energy intake in children has been associated with the thinning of cortical bone.[123] Bone mass has been found to decrease during the transition to agriculture, particularly in later life, notwithstanding a degree of regional variation due to differences in physical activity.[124]

Aspects of craniofacial, jaw and tooth morphology have also changed since the transition to agriculture, including decreases in tooth size and increased prevalence of malocclusal abnormalities. The mechanisms behind such changes are a matter of debate, but are likely to be a result of several interacting factors, including the degradation of nutrients and decreasing mastication requirements, associated with the consumption of grain-dominated food sources.[125] Several scholars emphasize the potential role of nutrition in affecting the growth of the teeth.[126] The association of smaller teeth with a shorter life span allows the hypothesis that small teeth may be symptomatic of poor overall health.[127] The association between low birth weight, poor maternal health status and small tooth size suggests that compromised nutrition in utero has affected the growth of teeth in historical populations.[128] There may also be a genetic component to the decrease in tooth size, due to smaller teeth being less likely to develop caries, thereby providing a selective advantage.[129] Increasing consumption of cariogenic grains following the Neolithic revolution may have resulted in genetic changes in tooth size, particularly among the earliest agricultural European and Middle Eastern populations, where such changes could occur over the longest period. Craniofacial growth and tooth growth in transitional Neolithic populations may also be controlled by epigenetic mechanisms—an adaptive response to poor nutrition, which might indicate other associated health problems.[130]

Aside from occlusal abnormalities, bone lesions provide an important source to define and understand the impact of nutritional change on the health of ancient populations. Unlike other archaeological measures, they are useful in providing possible ways to detect the prevalence of infectious diseases in populations, and to assess whether that prevalence was correlated with compromised immunity and diminished nutritional status. To be sure, it remains difficult to know whether such a suggested correlation was causally related to changed living conditions in sedentary agricultural communities, which increased the spread of pathogens, or to dietary changes, which decreased immunity to those invading pathogens (some combination of the two seems likely). Nonetheless, it is possible to draw some inferences for several diseases and conditions.

Porotic hyperostosis and cribra orbitalia, for example, are descriptive terms for lesions found on the parietal and orbital bones of the cranium.[131] These lesions are found commonly in archaeological remains and are thought to be most commonly associated with "iron deficiency anemia caused by consumption of iron-poor foods, parasitism, infantile diarrhoea, and other chronic stressors that influence iron metabolism."[132] Iron deficiency has been suggested to cause the condition by triggering the "expansion of the blood-forming tissues in order to increase production of red blood cells."[133] These lesions are found in skeletal remains at increasing frequency in agricultural societies, as distinct from earlier Paleolithic skeletons, likely as a result of increasing prevalence of iron deficiency, particularly during childhood.[134]

Some scholars have challenged the hypothesis that iron deficiency is the chief cause of porotic hyperostosis and cribra orbitalia in archaeological populations.[135] They argue that deficiency in iron would not allow the increase in red blood cell production that occurs in the condition. Nonetheless, even this hypothesis supports our broader contention that micronutrient deficiencies are linked to the condition and its evidence in skeletal remains. Rather than looking to iron deficiency, the evidence may be more consistent with a model in which the overproduction of red blood cells is a result of haemolytic and megaloblastic anemias, which can be caused by a deficiency in vitamin B12, folate or vitamin C.[136] The latter are required for the regulation of red blood cell production as well as immunity, and their reduction would have followed the diminishment of plants and animals rich in those nutrients, in favor of wheat and other grains.[137] Breastfeeding infants are particularly vulnerable to vitamin B12 deficiency, which can lead to compromised tissue and bones in adulthood.[138]

Harris lines, which are defined as "dense traverse lines visible in longitudinal sections or radiographs of longbones," have been used as skeletal indicators of short-term stresses, including nutritional degradation and (potentially associated) increasing propensity for infection in Neolithic communities in Europe and the Middle East.[139] They tend to occur as a result of a historical period of arrested growth followed by growth recovery over the period of approximately one week.[140] They are likely to be indicative of acute, episodic stress, and have been associated with "measles, scarlet fever, infantile paralysis, pneumonia, starvation, vitamin A, C, and D deficiencies, protein-energy malnutrition, kwashiorkor, and mechanical restriction."[141] Other stress indicators should be used in conjunction with Harris lines to suggest episodic stress, allowing nutritional degradation to be inferred when there is supporting evidence from other skeletal indicators.[142]

Global analyses of bone mass, stature and specific skeletal lesions thus all indicate stresses such as nutritional deficiencies and infections, and dental analyses indicate defects such as hypoplasias and malocclusion. They suggest nutritional stress at different points in the lifetime of the individual. Comparisons of such indicators of health in archaeological remains before and after the agricultural transition provide insight into how the health of individuals was affected in specific regions—including as defined by increasing evidence of susceptibility to diseases. As Armelagos has pointed out, the "incidence of infectious disease and the influence of disease-related mortality on population growth is consistently found to be less in the Paleolithic than formerly assumed, but to have risen markedly in sedentary Neolithic groups."[143] Larsen corroborates such an assessment, noting the increased pattern of infectious diseases in populations following adoption of agriculture.[144] Tuberculosis

'r infections increased in Western Europe during the Mesolithic to
... transition.[145]

More recent epidemiological and laboratory studies provide a further framework to understand skeletal evidence from Neolithic populations, supporting the notion that decreased consumption of meat and nutrient-dense plants in favor of grains heralded profound consequences in health and immunity.[146] We now know that diets without animal products may suffer deficiencies of nutrients such as vitamin B12 and iron, for example, leading individuals to suffer health conditions, including compromised immunity.[147] Extrapolating evidence from modern studies that demonstrate such a correlation, it is fair to hypothesize that deficiencies in micronutrients and minerals among individuals in Neolithic populations decreased their immunity to disease, at least to some extent, while increasing the onset of infectious diseases that were likely to exacerbate nutrient deficiencies even further.[148]

If we can determine that agricultural intensification resulted in failure to satisfy evolved nutritional needs, therefore, a resulting hypothesis can be developed: immunity might have been compromised within a chronic inflammatory state, caused by deficient nutrient or metabolic status following the introduction of Neolithic foods. A suboptimal diet, as we have noted, has been linked to chronic inflammation, oxidative stress and even compromised immunity in contemporary populations.

To understand the possibility of similar outcomes in historical populations, when changing subsistence strategies coincided with the greater prevalence of diseases, we can examine how those changes may have affected or enacted the inflammatory or anti-inflammatory role of certain components in foods, particularly protein molecules, antioxidants, glucose and polyunsaturated fatty acids. If less nutrient-dense foods, especially those lower in essential fatty acids and proteins, and higher in glucose, replace those that were prominent throughout most of human history, we would expect to see problematic effects in immunological and inflammatory markers. Defining the general biological mechanisms underlying such a hypothesis provides us with an updated language and conceptual framework to approach seminal archaeological and bioanthropological assessments of compromised health during the Neolithic agricultural transition. Such a definitive framework, moreover, provides insights to understand maize intensification in North America. It also allows us to comprehend the nutritional degradation heralded by the arrival of Europeans among Native American communities.

As well as being low in micronutrients compared to the foods they replaced, the grains that proliferated during and after the Neolithic era have other properties that may have affected immune function of individuals after their introduction. Nutritional allergy, defined as an "adverse response to food proteins," is linked to inflammatory responses with autoimmune aspects.[149] Allergic reactions involve a decrease in oral tolerance, which involves antigen-presenting cells such as intestinal epithelial cells and dendritic cells, as well as T cells.[150] Given our discussions in the previous section, it is clear why allergic responses to food may be associated with a chronic inflammatory response.[151] Grains, indeed, contain large proteins, such as glutenins, gliadians and the lectin wheat germ agglutin (WGA) in wheat, which may induce an immune response in and beyond the gut—not merely among those individuals who suffer from celiac disease (CD), an inflammatory response in the small intestine.[152] Two main mechanisms are likely to be involved in the allergic immune response caused by gliadins and WGA: increased intestinal permeability and the binding of gluten fragments and WGA to immune cell receptors, which then triggers an immune response.[153] It is worth pointing out that the consumption of other cereal grains such as oats and even maize has been shown to have potentially negative effects on health, due to the presence of similar proteins that can also cause immune responses.[154]

To cause an immune response, gliadin and WGA must cross the intestinal barrier. This barrier is designed to allow the uptake of nutrients from the intestine but to prevent the movement of pathogens and toxins. The barrier consists of the epithelial cells lining the intestine, which can take up and destroy pathogens and toxins. Protein complexes known as "junctional complexes" bridge the gaps between intestinal epithelial cells and regulate the movement of substances across the intestinal barrier. Yet as several recent studies have demonstrated, gliadin increases intestinal permeability in some populations by binding to specific receptors on intestinal epithelial cells and triggering the release of a protein called zonulin, which increases intestinal permeability.[155] Zonulin is thought to increase intestinal permeability in affected individuals by causing rearrangements in actin filaments (structural proteins) in intestinal cells, which can displace proteins from the junctional complexes, thus compromising the function of these complexes.[156] High zonulin levels and increased intestinal permeability are found in a vast array of autoimmune and inflammatory diseases, suggesting that the increase in intestinal permeability is a central factor in the immune response triggered by gliadin.[157] In vitro experiments suggest that WGA also increases intestinal permeability.[158] The increase in intestinal permeability caused by proteins such as WGA and gliadin can exacerbate the immune responses triggered both by WGA and gliadin and by other dietary substances and pathogens: more of these substances will be able to cross the intestinal barrier and cause an immune response.[159] The inflammatory response to these agents increases intestinal permeability further, thereby creating a positive feedback loop between inflammation and movement of particles across cells lining the gut wall.[160]

Some gliadin fragments, moreover, activate an innate immune response involving inflammation, whereas others activate T cells.[161] Even in individuals who do not suffer from celiac disease, gliadin has been shown to cause an immune response involving the production of various inflammatory cytokines, the signaling proteins central to the immune response following inflammation. Such an association suggests that gliadin has negative effects on immune function, to some degree, in a broader cross section of the human population than once assumed.[162] WGA, moreover, has been demonstrated to have several effects on immune function in humans and animals, including the upregulation of the activity of immune cells such as neutrophils, increased release of several cytokines and increased activity by T cells and natural killer cells.[163]

The high glucose content of grains introduced during the Neolithic transition also likely contributed to aberrations in immune function, such as autoimmunity and chronic inflammation, separate from the problematic inflammatory responses caused by plant protein molecules such as WGA.[164] Such aberrations, we suggest, decreased immunity to invading pathogens by altering the behavior of immune cells and limiting the metabolic substrates available for immune activity. Our hypothesis is supported by evidence of decreased immune function in conditions involving chronic inflammation due to raised blood glucose and declining insulin sensitivity. It is further supported, of course, by the skeletal evidence in Neolithic populations, surveyed above.[165] We can expand our assessment of the link between compromised immunity and raised blood glucose beyond the literature on diabetes, as discussed in the previous section, to suggest the problematic effects among (seemingly) nondiabetic individuals in historical populations. Such an extrapolation illuminates bioarchaeological evidence from Neolithic populations that experienced a sudden turn toward glucose-inducing foods, and which display evidence of greater propensity for infectious disease than among Paleolithic populations. As we shall see, the proximity of living conditions in Neolithic societal contexts certainly increased the likelihood that infectious diseases would proliferate. But we suggest that contiguous dietary changes—including those that raised blood sugar chronically—also heightened the risk of infection due to compromised immunity. Even if the latter occurred subtly, irregularly or among a subset of populations, it would have been enough to alter the broader bioarchaeological record.

Indeed, we need not solely focus on the problematic occurrence of proinflammatory nutritional sources, such as proteins in grains, or the higher blood sugar levels associated with grain intensification, in elucidating the link between evolutionary mismatched nutritional frameworks and potentially compromised immunity in the Neolithic context. Returning to our discussion of omega-3 fatty acids, derived from marine and some wild land animals, it is worth highlighting their anti-inflammatory role, their attendant contribution to immune function and the potentially problematic effects of their curtailment in favor of other nutritional sources, such as Neolithic grains, whose oils are much higher in omega-6 fatty acids. The effect of omega-6 and omega-3 fatty acids in inflammation and metabolic health, as we saw in the previous section, is now well supported in scientific literature.

To be sure, a propensity for infection in Neolithic communities need not only be related to the association between suboptimal nutrition and compromised immunological health. In a period of "epidemiological transition," changing living conditions transformed the way pathogens and humans interacted, exposing populations to a new repertoire of diseases and greatly increasing the impact of several others—whether or not communities within those populations were already compromised in their working immunity.[166] Hunter-gatherer societies tended to maintain much smaller populations than early agricultural communities, with less population density. As Armelagos has summarized, they "were involved in a highly stable equilibrium system with respect to their population size and realized rate of growth."[167] Their potential for infectious diseases was limited by the inability of pathogens to spread easily between disparate settlements and by the diverse nutritional profile provided by hunting and gathering. Sedentary agricultural lifestyles, conversely, allowed Neolithic populations to increase, thanks to energy-dense storable grains and declining birth spacing due to early weaning on grains. Increased population density around grain stores, as well as increasing trade movements between those sedentary populations, allowed pathogens to spread between hosts more easily, becoming more endemic.[168]

The proximity of domesticated animals to sedentary agricultural settlements also allowed some zoonotic diseases to transfer from animals to humans.[169] Domestication of animals in the Neolithic era exposed individuals in denser populations to a new array of pathogens. Prior to the Mesolithic, the dog was likely the only domesticated animal. In the Middle East, domestication of cattle, sheep and goats occurred around 8,000–9,000 years ago, followed by pigs, chickens and other animals.[170] Domesticated animals such as pigs, sheep and fowl would have carried bacteria such as *Salmonella* and parasitic worms such as *Ascaris*. Domesticated animals may also have increased the spread of trypanosomes.[171] The milk, skin, hair and dust of domesticated animals may have transmitted anthrax, Q fever, brucellosis and tuberculosis.[172] The clearing of land for agriculture, and the new proximity of human populations to human and animal waste, provided favorable conditions for many parasitic worms and protozoal parasites.[173] The cultivation of land increased the spread of other infectious disease such as scrub typhus.[174]

In Neolithic Europe and the Middle East, zoonotic diseases combined problematically with greater sedentary population density. Proximity to animals increased the spread of parasitic and pathogenic disease. In previous hunter-gatherer populations, frequent migrations limited the contact of individuals with human waste. In more sedentary populations, concentrated around grain production and domesticated animals, human and animal waste became more likely to contaminate drinking water. In Neolithic and post-Neolithic European and Middle Eastern societies, conversely, a greater proportion of individuals came into close contact with concentrated animal pens. Populations therefore became more liable to infection from diseases that followed animal byproducts.

Yet it is more accurate to suggest that the increase in infections during the Neolithic transition was the result of a combination of "increasing sedentism, larger population aggregates, and the [...] synergism between infection and malnutrition." The changing societal context of agricultural communities interacted with the nutritional deficiency that appeared in such communities, providing dual social and biological reasons for the spread of new diseases. The changes in diet following the Neolithic transition are likely to have had some influence on immune function, at least temporarily, at a time when humans were exposed to more pathogens because of their changing lifestyle. Immunity was potentially compromised at just the point when diseases were more likely to impact populations that lived closer together, and in greater proximity to domesticated animals that might transmit diseases zoonotically (from animal to human).[175] Neolithic peoples, according to Ulijaszek, experienced "greater physiological stress due to under nutrition and infectious disease."[176] Declining nutritional diversity may also have reduced the ability of individuals in Neolithic contexts to fight off those pathogens—particularly if their immune systems were already compromised by an autoimmune response triggered by suboptimal foods entering the gut. Dietary changes such as the curtailment of micronutrients and increased glucose and omega-6 fatty acid consumption compromised immunity, making individuals, and entire populations, potentially more susceptible to increasingly prevalent pathogens.

Thus, we propose a link between evolutionarily mismatched nutritional frameworks and potentially compromised immunity during the Neolithic era. We speculate more specifically about the role of chronically raised blood glucose, declining access to micronutrient dense and anti-inflammatory foods, and increased consumption of nutrient-poor and proinflammatory foods. Having placed the literatures on blood glucose derangement, problematic grain proteins, and DHA in conversation with the scholarly consensus on problematic Neolithic health outcomes, we are provided with an interpretative framework to approach other historical contexts that encompassed a growing mismatch between evolved nutritional needs and new subsistence models, and which also demonstrated seemingly greater susceptibility to disease among their constituent populations—not least in native North America. Before we do so, however, it is worth considering the ways in which Neolithic populations were able to mitigate the health problems detailed so far, not least to underscore the distinction from the later European–Native American encounter, when adaptation and mitigation were far less likely.

Mitigating Nutritional Degradation through Genetic or Societal Adaptations: A Neolithic Model Denied to Native Americans after European Contact

In Europe and the Middle East, Neolithic population numbers stabilized and then increased following the introduction of grains and domesticated animals, notwithstanding other declining health markers that accompanied demographic growth. Energy-dense and storable forms of food allowed individuals in expanding populations to reach reproductive age without a shortage in calories (as opposed to micronutrients).[177] The avoidance of starvation up to reproductive age allowed population expansion at the expense of the metabolic and immunological health of individuals within those same expanding communities. These processes were gradual enough to allow adaptation and survival, in the absence of external disruptions such as colonization.

Diminished overall health, as indicated by anthropological and bioarchaeological evidence, deriving from the nutrient-poor status of grains in comparison to previously hunted and gathered foods, was offset by increased reproductive capacity. Agricultural intensification allowed early weaning onto semi-solid grain products, leading to less spacing between births.[178] Yet early weaning onto a higher-carbohydrate, low-protein diet in post-Neolithic societies is thought to have left the very young particularly vulnerable to nutritionally induced immunological degradation.[179] Nonetheless, the "reproductive core" of Neolithic society was protected by an acquired immune response. In combination with decreased birth spacing in agricultural societies, population numbers could recover following epidemics, despite a high mortality among those infants who were born in such an environment.[180] This was part of the Neolithic paradox: though the death rate from disease likely trended slightly higher in agricultural societies than in Paleolithic communities that preceded them, increased associated mortality was offset by increased birth rates.[181] In Europe, for example, women birthed an average of four children during the Mesolithic and six during the Neolithic.[182]

The paleopathological and archaeological assessments that underlie our synthesis above are supported by contemporary research, which notes a strong association between declining breastfeeding and compromised immunity.[183] Though their associations tend to be drawn from epidemiological rather than laboratory-tested methodologies, other studies in vitro and in animals have begun to show the profound effect of breastfeeding on the production of immune cells and immune system function.[184] Similarly, biochemical studies support the hypothesis that breastfeeding increases immunity to pathogens. Breast milk contains a number of substances, including various immune cells, antibodies, hormones, cytokines and growth factors, that appear to increase infant immunity.[185] Early colostrum contains high levels of immune cells (including macrophages, neutrophils, T cells, natural killer cells and B cells), which then decrease to lower levels in mature milk.[186] These immune cells most likely survive passage through the infant's digestive system and arrive in the lymph nodes, where they can influence the immune response.[187] The lower incidence of autoimmune diseases in breastfed infants compared with non-breastfed infants, following the cessation of breastfeeding, further suggests that breastfeeding helps the development of the infant's own immune system and reduces the chronic inflammatory state.[188]

It can be hypothesized, then, that Neolithic weaning diets, which were high in carbohydrate and low in protein, would have compromised infant immunity, even if only to a small extent, further contributing to infant mortality. Protein deficiency reduces immune function, among other nutritional deficiencies. Yet as we have seen, population could still expand, despite an increasing rate of infant mortality, thanks in no small part to early weaning and less birth separation.[189]

Given the population growth described above, notwithstanding declining Neolithic health markers, it is worth considering the possible adaptive role of genetic mutations as well as acquired immunity, both of which may have enabled subsequent generations to tolerate new subsistence strategies and the societal contexts that they required. Both genetic and acquired forms of immunity may have helped develop heritable immunological benefits to withstand those infectious diseases that became more abundant in agricultural communities. It is especially important to consider these potential developments because they have often been drafted into explanations of the purported inherited immunological differences between Old World and New World communities, particularly as defined by proponents of the virgin soil thesis, who seek to explain the demographic collapse of post-contact Native American populations.

The acquisition of disease resistance among Neolithic peoples may have been provided to individuals through childhood exposure to pathogens. European populations that would eventually send settlers to the New World may have acquired immunity to pathogens through childhood exposure in sedentary agricultural contexts, which made those pathogens more apparent.[190] Such immunity acquired within the lifetime of an individual would have depended on the adaptive immune response, which allows a more rapid and efficient response to a previously encountered pathogen.[191] Viral infections such as chickenpox, smallpox and measles are usually less severe in children and less likely to cause mortality.[192] Hence, in regions in which these viruses were not endemic, mortality may have been greatly increased by the lack of acquired immunity among native populations.[193] Thus it has been suggested that Europeans evolved greater immunity to diseases in the centuries after the Neolithic transition through childhood exposure.

Moving from the potential role of acquired immunity to a discussion of more specific genetic adaptations, it is worth noting that several genetic differences have been discovered in the immune systems of Native American and European populations, offering some support for the hypothesis that populations gained increased resistance through selection of the most resistant individuals through the Neolithic agricultural transition in Europe, the Middle East and parts of Asia. For example, genetic differences in macrophage immune cell behavior have been proposed to explain the susceptibility of Native Americans to tuberculosis.[194] Studies have noted a distinctly limited genetic diversity of major histocompatability (MHC) protein molecules in Native Americans compared to Europeans. Such limited diversity, it has been suggested, may have increased the susceptibility of the population to diseases, given that parasites would have been more virulent in hosts of similar MHC genotypes.[195]

Whether these examples of limited genetic diversity played a significant role in disease susceptibility is currently unknown. The literature on the genetic propensity of populations to withstand diseases better than others is by no means settled. Opponents of the adaptive immunity hypothesis have argued that the time for significant disease resistance to have evolved distinctly in Europeans after the Neolithic transition is too short. Measles and smallpox are thought to have arrived in Europe around the second or third centuries AD, giving only around 12 centuries for immunity to evolve. Although evolution can work within such a timescale, a strong selection pressure is required. It is difficult to know whether the selection pressures from the European diseases were great enough to allow such rapid evolution in the European population. Some of the genetic differences in the immune systems of Europeans and Native Americans could therefore instead be a result of neutral genetic variation rather than natural selection, making it tricky to explain the difference in immunity between the populations in a biologically deterministic way.[196]

Moreover, when considering whether Europeans may have benefited from disease resistance provided by specific genetic adaptations within their distinct agricultural context, it is necessary to discuss the extent to which human populations can ever truly adapt genetically to changing environmental conditions over the timescale that is associated with the transition from hunting and gathering to intensified agriculture (a period of several hundred years, and less than a millennium). Such a suggestion can inform our discussion of the negative health impacts of a changing diet. Until recently, a scholarly consensus accepted the human evolutionary stasis argument (HESA), which suggests that "human biology was fundamentally shaped by an ancient African Plio-Pleistocene experience" and that genetic adaptation ceased before the Neolithic revolution.[197] The HESA notes that the post-Neolithic period of human history represents less than 0.5 percent of human evolutionary history from the earliest Homo species around two million years ago.[198] Although the environment changed in significant ways following agricultural intensification around 10,500 years ago, the HESA maintains that the selection pressures from these environmental changes would not have been great enough to allow natural selection to occur, given the short time period involved.

The HESA consensus, however, has been challenged by geneticists who have cited genetic evidence for post-Neolithic selection. It is now accepted among geneticists that the changing environment since the Late Paleolithic era—including changing climate, diet and disease patterns—created at least a few selective pressures that were strong enough to drive human evolution through genetic adaptation in some specific ways—including to offset some of the negative health consequences of the move to grain agriculture and domesticated animal husbandry.[199] The change in skin pigmentation in populations moving away from the equator provides a well-known example of a genetic change that has occurred in recent human history. It has been suggested that the effects of low vitamin D levels, including rickets, increased infection and that compromised reproductive fitness may have provided a strong selection pressure for lighter skin pigmentation to absorb more UVB light from the sun at higher latitudes.[200] In some populations, moreover, light skin may have evolved in part as a response to diminishing dietary levels of vitamin D after the adoption of agriculture, making greater production from sunlight more necessary.[201]

The increase in the copy number of salivary amylase (AMY1), conferring greater ability to digest starch, has been suggested to be another evolutionary response to increased consumption of carbohydrate since the Neolithic transition, or earlier in human history.[202] Contemporary populations consuming diets high in starch since the earliest part of the Neolithic transition tend to have more copies of AMY1 than those that descend from communities that have consumed lower concentrations of starch in the era since the Neolithic transition.[203] Genome-wide analysis of variation between populations consuming larger proportions of starch and sugar and those that have remained closer to a pre-Neolithic diet (up to the present era) has also found changes in the folate biosynthesis pathway. The changes correlate with some high-starch diets, which are often deficient in folate.[204]

Genetic evidence for the presence of lactase, required for the digestion of lactose in milk, offers another example that can be distinguished among populations, depending on their encounter with domesticated animals in post-Neolithic contexts.[205] The evolution of lactose intolerance and the continued selection for higher copies of AMY1 illustrate the potential for population-wide genetic change to occur in a relatively short timescale, requiring us to question the extent to which populations have become adapted to the Neolithic diet, or how any population might adapt to dietary change. Other adaptations among post-Paleolithic communities might be related to the relative triggering of an immune reaction in the presence of certain wheat protein fragments, such as gliadin. The incidence of autoimmune conditions such as celiac disease follows a gradient from high levels in northern Europe to low levels in the Mideast.[206] It has therefore been suggested that natural selection conferred less susceptibility to celiac disease and other autoimmune disorders among regions with the most concentrated and earliest experience of agriculture.[207]

However, due to the small amount of time since the Neolithic revolution, the variants above only show slight changes in prevalence between different populations, illustrating the insufficient time that has passed since the adoption of agriculture for genetic changes to affect the whole population.[208] Other research in human genetics has begun to examine genetic data from multiple populations to search for signatures of recent genetic change, including those related to diet. While these analyses have revealed evidence of changes in genes relating to the immune response, they reveal very few other changes in diet-related genes. A small number of genes related to diet show small signatures of positive selection, but these affect only a tiny proportion of the population, illustrating the insufficient time that natural selection has had time to select for these variants.[209] It therefore appears that the evolution of lactose tolerance is a unique example in which population-wide genetic change occurred with extreme rapidity as a result of an usually strong selection pressure.[210] Even the narrative regarding the AMY1 gene, moreover, may need revision. Recent research, including genome analysis of an 8,000-year-old Mesolithic hunter-gatherer, suggests that the duplication of AMY1 may have occurred long before the Neolithic revolution.[211] This analysis suggested that selection since the Neolithic revolution may have maintained a greater copy number of AMY1 in populations consuming more starch. In populations consuming less starch, genetic drift may have resulted in the loss of AMY1.[212]

Indeed, the observation that some genetic variants associated with autoimmune disorders appear to have actually increased in the population since the Neolithic revolution has led to the suggestion that the increased exposure of Neolithic populations to pathogens resulted in the positive selection of genetic variants that resulted in a more vigorous immune response. While these variants may have been beneficial in improving the immune response to pathogens, the trade-off may have been an increase in the immune response to nonpathogenic molecules, including those from grains.[213]

Diet may have influenced the selection of lesser-known genes distinguishing southern Europe and the Middle East from northern Europe in the post-Neolithic era. Variants associated with inflammatory bowel disease, for example, may have increased in frequency due to "hitchhiking" alongside a genetic variant, known as 503F, which is common among southern European and Middle Eastern populations, and which allows increased transport of an antioxidant known as ergothioneine (ET) into cells.[214] Hitchhiking refers to the common inheritance of regions of DNA that are close together on a chromosome, due to a decreased chance of recombination separating these genes.[215] While the genetic variants associated with bowel disease are harmful, the neighboring genetic region encompassing 503F may be beneficial: the genetic variant 503F may be an adaptation to low dietary levels of ET among early Neolithic farmers, which would have resulted in positive selection for a variant that allowed increased cellular uptake of ET.[216] Due to its role in protecting against UV-induced oxidative stress, ET may have been particularly important if the farmers had already developed a lighter skin color.[217]

The genetic adaptations outlined above likely accompanied other genetic adaptations, which occurred due to the changing societal frameworks heralded by agriculture. Over several generations, natural selection can select for individuals that are more resistant to diseases, thereby allowing populations to adapt to new living conditions involving increased pathogen exposure. Several genetic variants are likely to have been selected for in communities that turned away from hunter-gatherer subsistence systems, increased their population density and lived in greater proximity to animals. These contexts amplified the potential for disease epidemics. But they also allowed inherited immunity to develop among later generations that descended from those which survived infection or which enjoyed certain mutations that provided an evolutionary advantage in the circumstances that led to the flourishing of diseases. Agricultural intensification in Europe, the Middle East and part of Africa was thus gradual enough to allow the manifestation of a degree of inherited immunity.[218] Individuals who survived epidemics became genetically less susceptible so that secondary epidemics in the same populations or regions resulted in fewer deaths, including among offspring of those survivors.[219]

Recently, geneticists have identified specific genes that provide increased disease resistance, which are likely to have been selected by natural selection. Potential mechanisms involved in the evolution of disease resistance have been proposed, most of which relate to genetic components of the innate immune system that are thought to be subject to natural selection. These include variations in genes encoding the MHC proteins (for example, the affinity of different MHC molecules for antigens); genes causing variations in the behavior of immune cells such as the cytotoxic and cell signaling molecules secreted; and genes affecting the responses of cells to such signals. All might have been subject to natural selection in the last 10,000 years, given a strong enough selection pressure.[220]

In the explanation of mechanisms allowing the evolution of disease resistance, two types of natural selection have been commonly invoked: heterozygote advantage and frequency dependent selection. Heterozygote advantage describes a scenario in which individuals with genotype Aa are fitter than individuals with genotype AA or aa. Natural selection therefore favors the maintenance of both alleles A and a in the population.[221] Heterozygote advantage has been proposed to explain the selection of variants of immune cell proteins that provide immune system advantages in certain circumstances.[222] Frequency-dependent selection occurs when the fitness of an allele decreases as it becomes more common. Such a process may have caused the selection of genes involved in disease resistance, particularly in cases in which the pathogen quickly evolves to the host. Hosts with less common genotypes may have greater immunity to a pathogen adapted to a more common genotype.[223] Frequency-dependent selection has been suggested to have resulted in selection for less common MHC variants in response to measles, which has been shown to be more virulent when passed between two hosts with similar MHC molecules.[224] Though there is contention over whether disease resistance has provided a driving force for evolution in human populations, therefore, the current consensus is that there are at least some instances in which such selection has occurred for genes providing increased resistance to infectious disease in the post-Neolithic era.

Epigenetic changes may also have affected human physiology in Europe, the Middle East and Asia since the Neolithic revolution due to changing diet and stress levels, potentially allowing a degree of adaptation to changing lifestyle and nutrition.[225] Epigenetics refers to the chemical modifications to the genome that result in changes in gene expression, and therefore changes in the phenotype of the organism. Unlike genetic evolution, the rate of generation of new mutations is not a limiting factor.[226] Such changes can occur in individuals because of a specific environmental influence and can be passed down generations through prenatal exposure, on a shorter timescale of one or a few generations.[227]

Prenatal exposure has been shown to be a particularly crucial time for epigenetic changes to occur. Maternal stress in animals has been shown to cause profound, long-term changes in the physiology of the offspring. Starvation during the gestational period is thought to cause epigenetic changes in the offspring, such as in the insulin-like growth factor (IGF2) gene, involved in the regulation of growth and development. In one interpretation of this effect, offspring are primed to form fat, for energy storage, to a greater extent than their parents. Starvation in the womb effectively signals that the offspring will be born into an environment of scarcity, where energy storage in the form of fat is more necessary.[228] Experiments in mice also suggest that poor nutrition, specifically a lack of micronutrients required for epigenetic modifications to occur, can alter gene expression in ways that are detrimental to health.[229]

There is currently little research into the effects of changing diet and lifestyle on epigenetic modifications in humans. We can speculate that some genes involved in metabolism, such as IGF2, may have undergone epigenetic changes in response to changing environmental conditions since the transition to agriculture, and that a deficiency of specific micronutrients might have caused harmful epigenetic changes. It is possible that changes in genes involved in immunity, fertility and other aspects of human physiology may have also been affected by the move to agriculture. Future research in the field of epigenetics may shed light on these effects.

Yet the notion that individuals in Neolithic and post-Neolithic populations eventually developed inherited immunity to diseases still requires several caveats. First, diseases that had animal reservoirs may have repeatedly infected humans during the Paleolithic, thus supplying a selective pressure for disease resistance to evolve among hunter-gatherers, such that the evolution of disease resistance is not an entirely post-Neolithic phenomenon.[230] Secondly, host defense involves overlapping functions that might have been trickier for natural selection to select during the Neolithic era than one assumed. The adaptive immune response may provide sufficient variability in the immunity of all humans to override any genetic variation in disease resistance between individuals.[231]

Thirdly, genetic adaptation or epigenetic changes in response to new food sources, or in response to new societal contexts that enhanced disease proliferation, need not suggest those foods optimal contribution to nutrition and immunity. They may still have triggered an autoimmune response, as suggested by contemporary nutritional studies that highlight inflammatory markers among those who consume Neolithic foods, even if they do not present symptoms for conditions such as celiac disease. The Neolithic agricultural transition may have provided the context and impetus for genetic adaptations to its otherwise problematic health consequences. Genetic changes may have mitigated against the loss of nutritional density, in some specific instances, or against the consolidation of food sources that had initially been more difficult to digest in the gut. Nonetheless, those new food sources would never reach the levels of nutrient density—or even the anti-inflammatory capacity—of nutritional frameworks from the pre-Neolithic era.

The Medieval European Model of Nutrition and Contingency

Consider, finally, the pandemic of plagues that took place in medieval Europe. Before the medieval era, population decline following plagues in the Middle East and Europe from AD 541 to AD 750 cannot easily be linked to monocausal biological explanations. The disease was likely carried to Mediterranean ports from the Indian subcontinent, where black rats fed from grain on ships before becoming vectors in Europe. Yet in this instance, societal determinants of the proliferation of disease, rather than the biological immutability of disease resistance, must be considered when understanding possible demographic outcomes after the initial period of infection.[232]

A new generation of scholarship on the medieval Black Death (AD 1347 to AD 1353) has similarly shown that contingent factors allowed a minority of survivors to reproduce in gradually improving circumstances, thereby providing eventual demographic growth more broadly. Originating in East Asia, likely present-day China, as Mongol armies returned from war in the Himalayan foothills, *Yersinia Pestis* was an anaerobic bacterial organism that is thought to have used rats and rat fleas as a vector before then infecting human populations (moving from the Asian continent, to Crimea, to Sicily, and then elsewhere into Western and northern Europe). Unlike among

Native American communities during the extended period of European contact, populations in these cases could improve their living circumstances during and after epidemics, allowing survivors to rebuild societally and demographically. Thus, the demographic shock of the medieval European Black Death was followed by a recovery of all population numbers in just over a century. Central to that recovery was the ability of individuals within affected populations to maximize their working immunity, irrespective of the novelty of incoming pathogens, or to avoid those pathogens altogether, thanks to adaptive movements in living circumstances or to greater sanitation.[233]

Populations that were most negatively affected by the Black Death tended to have suffered nutritional degradation for several generations before infection. Intensification of energy-rich but nutrient-poor grain products in towns in Italy, Flanders and England allowed populations to increase. More individuals could gain energy to carry them to reproductive age, even if the health of those within such communities became potentially less optimal. As more people were born, even more grains were required, leading populations into marginal lands that were less able to store nutrients and transfer them to plants and animals before human consumption. Famine became more apparent as grain stores could not always be guaranteed. And among those who could incorporate calories into their diet, nutrient density declined. It would be a great scholarly stretch to suggest that nutritionally compromised communities would have differed from others in their initial mortality rates following the arrival of *Y. pestis*. Rather, as we shall soon note in the Native American example, prior or contiguous nutritional degradation may have compromised immunity and made secondary infections such as pneumonia more likely, or allowed other infections to increase mortality and reduce fertility among survivors of first epidemics. Initial survivors may have been lucky to avoid contact with infected vectors, or perhaps even lucky enough to enjoy genetic mutations that reduced the likelihood of their mortality after infection. In either case, nutritional degradation may have prevented these individuals from rebuilding their communities in demographic terms, as distinct from other communities in Europe where societal mechanisms and nutritional strategies were more optimal, allowing surviving generations to regroup and reproduce.

In cases such as the Black Death, malnutrition may also have increased infant mortality, either among weaning infants or because breast milk was less available. The immunologically protective qualities of breast milk were reduced, increasing infant infections at a time when populations were already under stress. Individuals in specific European contexts, moreover, became more likely to leave their populations in search of food or better land for subsistence, rupturing demography even further and lowering the number of reproductive-age individuals who might rebuild communities affected by plague epidemics. Conversely, communities whose societal mechanisms remained in place during and immediately after the Black Death enabled survivors to rebuild demographic strength.[234] Thus, the role of contingency in allowing communities to reconstruct their demography after infection is a primary factor that requires consideration. We do not have to make the more difficult case that nutrition or other contextual factors could somehow have prevented initial population losses in the face of deadly new diseases.[235]

Ironically, where mortality rates in many towns and regions exceeded 60 percent of the total population, those who remained alive could move their subsistence farming from marginal lands to those that yielded greater volumes of more nutrient-dense plants and animals. As Miskimin has shown, the ability to use richer soils to feed surviving populations enabled individuals to cultivate nutritional sources without having to rely on more nutrient-poor "staples"—as had been the case when higher populations required readily available sources of energy. Slightly higher disposable income also allowed these populations to buy foods from other regions, increasing their nutrient density. More varied vegetables and crops, and a greater variety of meat and fish all appeared in the diet. Thus, these communities could take advantage of available land, without the external societal or civic constraints (unlike the example of Native America after European contact, as we shall see).[236]

These factors distinguished demographically successful communities from those that were less successful in the century after the Black Death. They also allowed communities to stabilize, psychologically and politically, without having to preoccupy themselves with secondary infections, continued declining immunity and deterrents to fertility. Within such a context, moreover, civic authorities were provided breathing space and time to examine the nature of epidemics, allowing them to diagnose their general manifestation as contagion and to construct special adaptive mechanisms to avoid such an epidemic and to prevent its vectors.[237]

That postagricultural communities could recover from mass epidemics is important to note as we go on to consider why Native American communities were unable to recover from infectious diseases after European contact. The arrival of new pathogens in communities has tended to result in only short-term population decline, with populations returning to pre-epidemic demographic trends (whether they were positive, neutral or negative) if certain contextual and contingent factors are in place, including a return to nutritional density, or at least an avoidance of malnutrition.

Whatever our understanding of their exact contribution to immunological development in the Old World, therefore, the various adaptations detailed in this chapter are vital to consider because they allow us to envision a Neolithic and post-Neolithic societal framework that can be contrasted with the subsequent inability of Native American populations to withstand nutritional changes at a time of increasing infectious disease. The earlier contexts of agricultural intensification, and even the period after the medieval European Black Death, differed from the perfect storm of sudden nutritional change and pathogenic invasion in Native America after 1492. They were gradual enough to allow adaptation to changes and mitigation of negative consequences, permitting population numbers to increase. External context—contingent circumstances—required adaptation to problematic nutritional developments. Other contingent contextual circumstances allowed adaptation and mitigation following the rise of Neolithic agriculture, including greater sanitation, improved access to nutrient dense foods to supplement grains and new measures to prevent the spread of diseases. When new diseases proliferated, moreover, nutrition proved to be a key factor and determinant in the eventual demographic recovery of communities. As we shall see, post-contact Native American populations were often prevented from enacting similar contingent adaptations—above and beyond any notion that they suffered from distinct immunological differences. Colonial disruption prevented population growth and recovery to mitigate the nutrient-poor status of intensified agricultural products and the occurrence of diseases in the centuries after the arrival of Europeans in North America.

Chapter 2

MORE THAN MAIZE: NATIVE AMERICAN SUBSISTENCE STRATEGIES FROM THE BERING MIGRATION TO THE EVE OF CONTACT

This chapter synthesizes the vast but hitherto scattered literature on the complex and regionally specific nature of Native American subsistence before European contact. It moves beyond a narrower focus on maize domestication and cultivation, which has often appeared in general works on Native American nutritional heritage, or those studies, conversely, that focus entirely on the hunting of animals at the expense of other contributing subsistence strategies. While taking critiques of the trope of the "ecological Indian" into account, we are wary of veering in an opposite analytical direction by de-emphasizing the positive and unique aspects of Native American subsistence strategies before contact, both in their theory and in their practice, and in their impact on ecology, health and demography.[1]

Several health outcomes were compromised by the rise of maize domestication and cultivation in Native America, as shown by evidence of increasing diseases. Yet, as in the earlier transition to Neolithic agriculture from the Middle East to Europe, these effects were often mitigated by higher birth rates as well as other adaptive measures over time, such as through new forms of sanitation, nutrient supplementation and even, potentially, in the evolving genetic status of individuals within communities. Thus, having noted the possibly deleterious consequences for health and immunity during the rise of maize, as well as its positive demographic consequences, it will be important to consider how, exactly, those consequences were mitigated over time. Population growth was not overly compromised by the translation of diseases into pandemics, or through the occurrence of chronic diseases linked to suboptimal metabolic fueling (generally, though not always, associated with excessively high blood glucose over an extended period, leading to inflammation within the body).[2]

Modifying traditionally held assumptions about the nature of precontact Native American subsistence thus raises questions about the optimal

interaction between nutrition and immunity, and its association with ecological models that developed among the indigenous peoples of North
America for thousands of years before the arrival of Europeans. The "three
sisters" of Native American nutrition—beans, squash and maize—were often
very important. But their supplementation with other plants and animals—
which tended to be more nutrient dense than energy dense in comparison—is
often overlooked. Conversely, the seasonality of hunted meats and fish, and
their supplementation by foods other than maize—from acorns, to insects, to
seaweed—has tended to be eschewed by historians, particularly generalists.[3]

While it is important to examine the regional diversity of Native America
before contact, it is possible to isolate certain general trends: the relationship between horticulture, agriculture, and hunting and gathering was rarely
antagonistic or dichotomous; subsistence was often seasonal; nutrient-dense
foods were often prized, particularly among those of reproductive age;
animals were rarely domesticated and thus their byproducts were rarely close
to living settlements; an often gendered division of labor allowed women to
cultivate plants (often starch sources), while men hunted animals away from
those semisedentary zones; and those settlements were often surrounded by
nonpopulated zones, limiting the spread of disease from one region to another.

Indigenous subsistence strategies underlay the protection of immunity
both on the cellular level, through the supply of necessary macronutrients
and micronutrients, and on the societal level, through the construction of
living and working conditions that prevented diseases reaching a pandemic
level. Problematic health markers that accompanied the population increase
during maize intensification were not sufficient to curtail the demographic stability of communities, whether through pandemics or other potential effects.
Sufficiently low living density in many settlements, coupled with uninhabited
zones surrounding them, prevented the transfer of pathogens in many cases.
Though semiautonomous, settlements in regions such as the Ohio Valley
and the Lower Illinois River Region could trade, if necessary, to gain seasonal nutritional diversity, without requiring constant year-round movements
between regions. Overhunting did not seem to follow population increase.
Rather, animal products tended to supply nutritional density alongside an
increasing proportion of energy needs provided by maize. These adaptations
to agriculture were ruptured during the period of European contact, without
either the time or the societal context that might have allowed further adaptation to such attendant disruption.[4]

This chapter, then, considers the specific nutritional profile of precontact
North America, in all its regional variation and complexity. It reduces the
dichotomy between hunting and gathering, and horticulture, showing why
any disruption to their symbiosis would entail serious consequences during the

later period of European contact, when the nutritional frameworks underlying human immunity were ruptured.

The Earliest Indigenous North American Subsistence Strategies

As our discussion of the Expensive Tissue Hypothesis has shown, the evolution of the small human gut in relation to the enlarging human brain required nutritional sources that progressively decreased in mass and volume but were increasingly nutrient dense: land animals and, perhaps, marine animals. The systems of hunting and fishing that indigenous peoples developed in North America from around 13,500 years ago support the implications of this hypothesis, demonstrating the continued role of animal products in providing necessary micronutrients and relative metabolic health, long after the development of the large human brain.

As the first indigenous people spread into North America, their nutritional needs were met by a combination of nutrient-dense hunted land mammals, marine foods and gathered plants. Immigration onto the so-called Bering Land Bridge, the area between present-day Far Eastern Siberia and Alaska, now covered by the Bering and Chukchi Seas, likely took place more than 13,000 years ago, and potentially more than 22,000 years ago. The movements responded to the area having become gradually available due to lowered sea levels, which followed the ice fixation of global freshwater supplies. As proponents of the Beringian Standstill Hypothesis have argued, it seems likely that the region was populated for far longer than once assumed, before the eventual migration of its population into mainland North America around 13,500 years ago, as the land became covered with water. Before that point, a "shrub tundra refugium" provided the setting for hunted land mammals, and woody plants to facilitate the burning of bones for fuel. Those animals are thought to have included the woolly mammoth, the woolly rhino, Pleistocene horses, camels and bison—all of which could be found on the steppe-tundra of the interior of Alaska and the Yukon and inland northeastern Siberia. The former areas, and the Bering Bridge more specifically, may also have incorporated elk, bighorn sheep and many other small mammals.[5]

In addition to those whose ancestors followed game and other animals along the shrubby tundra of the Bering Land Bridge, it is hypothesized that others moved along a "Kelp Highway" from coastal Japan to Baja California at the end of the Pleistocene, taking advantage of nutrient-rich marine life as they made their way from west to east in small boats from island to island in the far northern Pacific.[6] This hypothesis supports what we know about the human nutritional need for omega-3 fatty acids, particular DHA, as discussed in the previous chapter. As the brain grew larger in the evolution of modern humans from earlier hominids, the gut grew smaller, requiring nutrient-dense foods, including marine animals containing DHA. Much later in human history—at the point when people moved across the Bering Land Bridge, for example—DHA still remained a vital nutrient, given its centrality to the earlier evolution of the gut and brain. It is not surprising, therefore, that it may have contributed to health, immunity and fertility among those who moved to North America along marine-rich island routes.

In fact, we see no need to discount either the Beringian Land Bridge Hypothesis or the Kelp Highway Hypothesis, particularly if we consider the important nutritional role of DHA in both contexts. As studies of Paleolithic hunting and gathering have suggested, herbivorous wild land mammals contained significantly higher proportions of omega-3 fatty acids than farmed animals today, which contain far more saturated fat and omega-6 fatty acids due to their grain-based diets. Thus, whether they relied on land mammals in the Beringian region, or on marine sources of sustenance on the Kelp Highway from Siberia to North America, omega-3 fatty acids would have been important to the sustained health of those migrating populations.[7]

Archaeological evidence for animal consumption through the hunting of large mammals in mainland North America following the Beringian period has been found in Alaska, California, the Great Plains and elsewhere (from the Late Pleistocene and Early Holocene, c. 14,000 BP to 8,000 BP.[8] Archaeological and paleoarchaeological studies have suggested that more than 12,000 years ago, "megafauna" such as mammoths and mastodons were hunted by ancestral Native Americans in the Southeast.[9] From around 9,000 years ago, excavations and ethnographic analyses suggest that generalized foraging—hunting animals as and when needed—became less apparent as North American climate change allowed a more focused pattern of seasonal hunting for prime-age animals such as wapiti and female bison.[10] Particularly during the winter, the earliest Native American communities relied on hunting and gathering fatty cuts of meat for optimal nutritional health. Frison's classic work on the prehistoric practices of the High Plains, Great Plains and Rocky Mountain regions, for example, suggests that nutritious organs and fats from buffalo meat were especially consumed.[11]

Through the mid-to-late Holocene, from around 6,000 years ago, smaller game, shellfish, birds and some plants also became popular among indigenous communities in North America, as scholars have shown in their discussion of mobile populations in California. They rarely stored nutritional resources and did not necessarily favor large game hunting, as is sometimes suggested in discussions of Holocene-era indigenous subsistence strategies.[12] Indeed, the consumption of smaller animals—particularly salmon—complemented the hunting of larger animals, rather than offering an alternative food source. Trends in salmon and cervid use for the south-central Northwest Coast and northern Columbia Plateau from the Holocene to the ancient era in precontact history, suggest that slight population increases were sustainable with respect to food resources. The deliberate burning of dense forests seems to have allowed a habitat for cervids to thrive, thus supplementing the diet of populations that relied on increasing volumes of salmon for health and fertility, without having to depress either their human populations or those of the salmon.[13]

As the climate warmed from around 8,000 years ago, and certainly by around 4,000 years ago, high-status resources were increasingly supplemented with cultivated plants as well as wild animals. It is tricky to assess the exact use of plant resources in these early historical circumstances—whether from gathering or from cultivation—due to the quick degradation of moist organic matter that might otherwise have provided archaeological evidence.[14] But it is thought that a gradual move toward supplementing nutrition from animals with gathered plant materials occurred from the Pacific Northwest to the Atlantic Southeast. In coastal California, archaeologists have claimed to find evidence of stored grass seeds even before these dates, along with evidence for the hunting and processing of animals and fish.[15] The floodplains of Mississippi, Ohio, Missouri and Illinois all provide evidence of wetland cultivation. In the Upper Midwest and Great Lakes regions, mounding, weeding, tillage and wild-rice cultivation are all shown by archaeological and historical evidence from the period. In the Northern Plains, gardens were found near houses, including seedbeds. In California, indigenous populations manipulated the harvest of wild plants, making the endeavor horticultural in practice. In the Great Basin, among other activities, inhabitants manipulated canals to irrigate wild grasses in regions such as the Owens Valley. In the Pacific Northwest, plants were protected and cultivated, to make "stretching" the term agriculturalist appropriate.[16]

These phenomena resulted in the fulfillment of multiple nutritional needs as well as a relatively sustainable form of subsistence, long before the domestication of maize, beans and squash from around 4,000 years ago. After the period of large mammal hunting ended in North America, and as European and Middle Eastern communities transitioned to Neolithic agricultural practices, Native Americans developed a hybrid between agriculture, horticulture, and hunting and gathering. It provided seasonally inflected nutritional diversity and required living circumstances that prevented the translation of diseases into epidemics, most often through uninhabited "buffer zones" that allowed hunting and gathering yet prevented human chains of settlement translating diseases from one setting to another.[17] This hybrid, indeed, helped mitigate some of the more problematic consequences of maize intensification during the same period. Before we examine the nutritional frameworks that were associated with its interlocking ecological system, therefore, let us assess the ambiguous role of maize intensification in early Native American health and immunity.

The Positive and Negative Consequences of Maize Intensification in Native America

Recent techniques have enabled more accurate dating of fossilized plant remains, improving our knowledge of the time of domestication of specific species. For example, early remains of maize cobs in Oaxaca, Mexico, were recently dated at around 6,250 years old.[18] Many Native American communities in North America adopted agricultural practices as early as 4,000 years ago.[19] The earliest evidence for domesticated maize in the Southwest, originally introduced from Mesoamerica, dates to around 4,000 years ago in present-day southern Arizona. The Tucson Basin and uplands of northern New Mexico show evidence of irrigation canals for maize cultivation around 2,400 years ago.[20] Domesticated maize cultivation appeared in the Southwest, the Southeast and the Midwest regions to a greater extent around 2,000 years ago, and was intensified around 1,200 years ago.[21] Deriving from the same Mesoamerica species that were cultivated from 4000 BC, maize became more widely consumed in the Southeast by AD 900.[22] The species cultivated in the region was larger and more drought resistant than earlier versions that had been introduced in the Southeast as early as AD 200. By AD 1250, beans became more widely introduced, also from original Mesoamerican domesticates.[23]

Maize began to be introduced into the eastern Mississippi region and the Southeast thanks to migration and trade routes leading to and from Mesoamerica around 100 BC. During this early period, it was smaller and less densely glycemic than later cultivated varieties. It was often used sparingly, or even ceremonially, rather than dominating the region's nutritional profile. By around AD 1000, however, maize began to be used more widely in the regions. Chiefdoms such as Cahokia, near present-day St. Louis between the Mississippi and Missouri Rivers, included central communities and satellite communities that numbered up to 40,000 people by around AD 1500. Other Mississippi chiefdoms include Etowah in present-day Georgia, Moundville in present-day Alabama, and the large community in Natchez, Mississippi. Examining settlements across the South Atlantic and Gulf Coastal plains, scholars have suggested that the shift toward maize cultivation as a vital source of calories heralded the development of "socially ranked societies" and "fortified civic ceremonial centers" placed near maize storage centers. Maize came to be central to the activities of Iroquois confederations stretching from the east coast to the Ohio River valley, as well as in the Mississippian chiefdoms that grew along the riverways of the Southeast and the Midwest.[24]

It is important to attend to differences in periodization, regional context and cultural distinctions in assessing and comparing agricultural intensification in North America with the European and Middle Eastern examples discussed in the previous chapter. But there are indeed similarities in the consequences of grain domestication and in the reduction of hunting and gathering in both cases. Both allowed expanding populations to avoid starvation and reach reproductive age, without necessarily providing the density of micronutrients that had once been available during their preagricultural eras. It is thus possible—and fruitful—to draw conceptual similarities between the biological and ecological consequences of Native American maize intensification and the European transition to agriculture several centuries earlier.

Scholarship on disease and nutrition in South America provides a framework to assess the possible link between North American maize intensification and a greater propensity for diseases. Discussions of diseases and seasonal nutritional inadequacies begin to dominate the "calendrics" of ancient communities, such as those found in the Andean region, following maize intensification. They also appeared in sources and narratives provided by early Spanish settlers in their encounter with indigenous peoples. Sixteenth-century Peruvians viewed "maize sickness" as an important impetus for ritual attacks carried out by Inca leaders. According to Buikstra's close reading of these events, it is possible "to link the maize sickness of 'sara onvuy' to a nutritional disease such as pellagra [...] [given that] the poor quality of maize protein, deficient in lysine and tryptophan, has been implicated in health problems wherever maize-dependence is intense."[25] Verano's summary of paleopathological evidence for the health challenges faced by prehistoric Andean populations suggests that as they moved away from hunter-gatherer lifestyles toward more sedentary agriculture, with "increasing population size and density came inevitable problems of sanitation, parasitism, and increase in infectious diseases. Agricultural intensification and social stratification led to a less varied diet for many, exacerbating the effects of infectious disease and parasitism." This density made populations even more vulnerable to European diseases at contact.[26]

Scholars have noted similar associations for other indigenous peoples in the Americas, including in North America. The cost-to-yield ratio of precontact maize cultivation may have become more attractive because of an increased demographic pressure on both wild and domesticated resources. Increased mortality due to food scarcity from hunted and gathered sources might have been diminished by the calories provided by maize.[27] Yet as communities came to rely on maize during agricultural intensification (particularly in the

Southeast), their demographic growth sometimes led to the overhunting of animals to supplement energy-dense but nutrient-poor maize, requiring an even greater reliance on the grain as those animals became less abundant. As Kelton has pointed out, "such actions to promote group survival came at the expense of individual health."[28] Archaeological and paleoanthropological studies of bones and other markers of nutritional stress and disease underline the distinction between famine prevention and optimal nutritional health. Maize, as Larsen summarizes, "is deficient in amino acids lysine, isoleucine, and tryptophan. Moreover, iron absorption is low in maize consumers."[29] From around 950 years ago, as Gremillion has suggested, maize was "both readily stored and a significant source of food energy, but also relatively poor in most of the minerals, vitamins, and macronutrients required to maintain adequate health." Furthermore, the "amino acid profile of maize [made] it a poor source of protein, and in conjunction with the depletion of wild game that inevitably accompanies population aggregation and persistent settlement, dietary reliance on this productive staple carried significant health risks. Exacerbating these risks is the fact that maize contains phytates, which actually inhibit the absorption of iron."[30]

Given the link between nutrition and immunity, therefore, it is unsurprising that analysis of skeletal remains suggests that tuberculosis and other infectious diseases increased to a greater extent in regions of North America that had partially transitioned to maize agriculture than those that had not.[31] That which prevented famine was not necessarily nutritionally optimal as a dominant calorie source, particularly from the perspective of immunological health.[32] Modern research highlights a link between iron deficiency and greater susceptibility to infection.[33] Evidence is provided by indicators of porotic hyperostosis, a skeletal gauge that has been extensively studied in archaeological populations of Native Americans in the Southwest and elsewhere. It can be measured through lesions on parietal and orbital bones of the cranium. Bones that are the most active in producing red blood cells are thought to be affected by anemia.[34] The general distribution of the lesion corresponds with the increasing reliance on agricultural products such as maize, which are low in bioavailable iron, and which can be detected through chemical and isotopic signatures in human remains.[35] From the Great Lakes region to the southern plains, and from eastern coastal to Pacific populations, the regular consumption of bison, deer and fish likely prevented protein and iron deficiencies such as porotic hyperostosis, which later accompanied the reliance on maize for a greater proportion of the daily calorie output.[36]

Other micronutrient deficiencies likely also affected health and immunity among maize-intensifying populations. Archaeological evidence of skeletal remains from Ancestral Puebloans in the American Southwest at least suggests a coincidence between newly evident nutritional deficiencies, aside from those which were demonstrated through instances of porotic hyperostosis, and the shift toward maize cultivation. It has highlighted evidence that suggests a concomitant increase in scurvy, dental cariesporotic hyperostosis and *cribra orbitalia*. In North America, periosteal reactions are a commonly found bone abnormality, correlated by paleopathologists with the experience of infection.[37] Moreover, children under six in nascent maize-producing societies seem to have suffered growth retardation compared to hunter-gathering communities from nearby excavations.[38] Thus, a correlation developed between increasing social stratification in maize-intensified societies and a decline in several health markers, including bone density, potentially reduced immunity, anemia and pellagra.[39]

Consider archaeological evidence from late prehistoric Dickson Mounds populations in west-central Illinois, which shows that agricultural intensification (AD 950 to AD 1350) led to a decline in skeletal weight and height as well as other problematic health outcomes introduced above. Periosteal reactions show a nearly fourfold increase in skeletal remains from the Dickson Mounds during the transition from foraging to intense agriculture. These lesions correlate with occurrence of porotic hyperostosis, suggesting that poor nutrition may have compromised immunity to some extent.[40] Studies of child stature in the lower Illinois Valley demonstrate a correlation of depressed growth rates in children with other skeletal indicators suggesting nutritional deficiencies, such as cribra orbitalia and defects in tooth enamel, further implying that the smaller stature is a result of nutritional deficiency.[41] Palaeopathological studies have found a decrease in life expectancy in all age classes in the Dickson Mounds population, moving from around AD 950 through mixed hunting-gathering and agricultural occupations to the Middle Mississippian intensified agricultural occupation (AD 1200 to AD 1300). Over the course of 100 years, life expectancy decreased and infant mortality increased even while overall fertility increased in terms of numbers of children born. Evidence of decreased life expectancy, notwithstanding overall population growth, correlates with increases in other indicators of stress such as enamel hypoplasias, infectious lesions and porotic hyperostosis.[42]

Similar phenomena are evident in other historical populations. A low bone mass in maize agriculturalists in Southern Ontario in comparison to currently living populations has been attributed to an overreliance on maize in the former which may have again resulted in protein deficiency.[43] Among populations that retained a high intake of marine foods, such as those on the southeastern Atlantic Coast, skeletal lesions indicative of iron deficiency are less prevalent, suggesting that marine foods were able to protect against iron deficiency and other problematic health markers.[44] Scholars have noted a decrease in life expectancy for all age groups with increased reliance on maize in the Ohio River Valley, moving from around 3,000 years ago to as early as 500 years ago.[45] Individuals living at Toqua on the present-day Little Tennessee River saw their life expectancy decrease by 50 percent as maize production in concentrated settlements increased, in contrast to their experience 950 years earlier.[46] Conversely, decreasing maize consumption in several North American sites (likely a response to climate change) is correlated with fewer bone lesions, and fewer other signs of the association between nutritional stress and infectious disease.[47]

Carbon isotopic analysis of late prehistoric Mississippian communities around Cahokia, in present-day southern Illinois, are particularly useful to identify the distinction between maize intensification and more diverse nutritional frameworks. Maize consumption was greater in regions outside of Cahokia than more centrally, suggesting that higher-status individuals were able to supplement their diet with more nutrient-dense foods.[48] According to Milner, therefore, porotic hypertosis was less evident in central Cahokia because it was a place of exchange, where communities were able to access other more nutrient-dense plants and animals, in contrast to lower-status outer settlements, which were more reliant on maize.[49] Isotopic markers for maize are highly variable in the late prehistoric central Mississippi River Valley around Cahokia, which is likely to reflect differences in maize consumption as a result of cultural variations or variability in access to other resources. Here, too, scholars have noted an inverse relationship between the relative intensity of maize consumption and bone health measures.[50] Scholars have noted that among twelfth-century Mississippian communities, the prevalence of porotic hyperostosis increased as maize agriculture intensified. A nearly fourfold increase in parietal lesions (caused by nonspecific infections) in Mississippian burials through the transition is said to have resulted in large part from iron deficiency following an overreliance on maize in the diet.[51]

Paleopathological evidence from the Southwest suggests a link between declining immunity and deficiencies in vitamin B12. Assessing the health of Ancestral Pueblo communities that began to cultivate maize at the expense of meat consumption between AD 500 and AD 1000, scholars have suggested that B12 deficiency rather than iron deficiency was the major cause of porotic hyperostosis and cribra orbitalia in this population.[52] Vitamin B12 scarcity, thought to compromise immunity in infants, may have contributed to their community's decreased immunity more generally.[53] A hierarchical structure of society, centered on the storage and distribution of maize, may also have contributed to vitamin B12 deficiency in lower-status Puebloans.[54] It has even been hypothesized that the depletion of wild game and an overreliance on maize was perceived as problematic by Ancient Puebloans, who became keen turkey farmers during this period in order to alter their nutritional intake. Doing so would have likely beneficially increased their consumption of vitamin B12, iron, tryptophan and protein.[55] Their health decline can also be informed by modern scientific studies that have linked protein energy malnutrition to a significant impairment in immunity.[56]

Greater consumption of maize in regions such as Cahokia and the Dickson Mounds also corresponds to a dramatic increase in prevalence of dental caries, leading a number of scholars to suggest that the grain is more cariogenic than other grains.[57] We can note a distinction between the dental pathology of sedentary grain-producing populations in the Southwest, such as Gran Quivira, and California populations that retained hunter-gatherer lifestyles to a greater extent.[58] Moreover, enamel hypoplasia, defined as a "deficiency in enamel thickness," visible as "lines bands, or pits of decreased enamel thickness," is a potential indicator of metabolic stress from infection and malnutrition.[59] We can find a correlation between age of death and number of hypoplasias in an individual, suggesting that the number of hypoplasias correlates with general health.[60] Assessments of the mean age-of-death of individuals with and without hypoplasias from the Dickson Mounds have found an increase in life expectancy of individuals without hypoplasias of around six years.[61] Hypoplasias are nonspecific lesions, and so the cause in specific cases must be inferred with contextual evidence.[62] The transition to agriculture, and agricultural intensification, often corresponds to increases in hypoplasias and other enamel defects. This trend is particularly evident in the Eastern Woodlands region of North America among maize-intensifying communities.[63]

Notwithstanding the growing birthrate that accompanied the intensification of maize in Native America, particularly in the region east of the Mississippi, it is erroneous to suggest that fertility and life expectancy improved in other general ways, including maternal and infant mortality. Early weaning and readily available energy stores allowed less birth spacing and thus a higher number of births.[64] Maize, according to Kelton, "when processed into gruel provided an alternative food source for infants, permitting mothers to wean their children at an earlier age than hunter gatherers" so that "shortened periods of breastfeeding allowed women to conceive sooner after giving birth and produce more children over the course of their lives."[65] Yet that which allowed greater fertility—sedentary lifestyles and early weaning thanks to greater reliance on insulinogenic maize—may have masked declining health and immunity. Women became more likely to die after birth, due to complications of bleeding, porotic hypertosis and anemia (including reduced immunity to infections). It has been hypothesized that women became more likely to die after childbirth, due to loss of blood, if already in an iron-compromised state.[66] Developing insights from Cook, Buikstra has summarized a number of findings from archaeological sites and skeletal examinations in west-central Illinois, focused in particular on evidence for the transition to maize during the Late Woodland period, which was associated with "increased number of deaths during the weaning period, lower rates of stature attainment per dental age, decreased adult stature, and relatively thin long bone cortices," all of which "paint a relatively somber picture of juvenile health status during the terminal Late Woodland period when maize agriculture began."[67] Similar findings can be detected in the Dickson Mounds in Illinois between around AD 950 and AD 300.[68]

In addition to evidence of micronutrient deficiencies, compromised immunity and dental caries, other problematic effects of maize intensification can be detected in Native American populations. Waterborne diseases such as dysentery, for example, appeared near agricultural communities in the pre-Columbian Southeast, particularly among sedentary horticultural villages aside oxbow lakes, which allowed human waste and disused plant matter to accumulate.[69] At the Larson site, around 26 percent of skeletal remains of hunter-gatherers demonstrated damage to connective tissue covering bones, a key sign of bacterial infection. Eighty-four percent of a genetically related horticultural population, however, showed the same signs.[70] At the horticultural Toqua community site, 77 percent of skeletal remains of infants under one year old demonstrated similar reactions, likely from a combination of "pneumonia, septicemia, staphylococcal infection or gastroenteritis"—all of which increased infant mortality rates during the transition to agriculture even while the overall demographic numbers of the community increased.[71] Only "after indigenous peoples made the switch to maize-intensive horticulture and established permanent settlements in flood plain environments," according to Kelton, "did the proper ecological conditions emerge" for diseases such as typhoid and dysentery "to spread frequently from person to person."[72]

These phenomena allow us to begin to question the virgin soil paradigm, given the likely existence of diseases in precontact North America. Contingent disruptions caused by colonization, as we shall see, heralded demographic destruction, rather than supposed immunological distinctions among groups who had not experienced diseases in the way of Old World communities.[73] A rich scholarly debate has developed regarding the possibility of tuberculosis as a pre-Columbian disease in North America.[74] It is well known that the sexually transmitted disease syphilis is likely to have originated on the western side of the Atlantic, and that it became more prevalent in Europe as well as North America in a new postcolonial context that allowed it to flourish in ways that had been restricted in the Americas.[75] Hepatitis B likely came along the Bering Strait to the Americas, possibly then allowing the hepatitis germ, a "delta agent" that can be deadly if combined with the B virus, and which may have originated from the Old World rather than being transmitted across the Bering Strait.[76] Communities such as the Iroquois sometimes lived in relatively dense settlements before contact and "experienced both endemic and epidemic episodes of numerous diseases prior to the introduction of whatever new pathogens Europeans may have brought."[77] Greater density of population in maize-producing communities, such as those in the lower Mississippi Valley from around AD 700, demonstrated the potential for social effects of agriculture to produce the context for disease epidemics, though not pandemics.[78] As we shall see, adaptation and mitigation in response to the problematic effects of maize intensification likely prevented the latter.

Adapting to Agricultural Intensification through Continued Hunting and Gathering

A Little Ice Age from AD 1350 to around AD 1550 decreased agriculture output among many indigenous communities in North America, particularly Mississippi chiefdoms and Eastern Woodlands communities, which refocused on hunting animals and gathering plants, reducing maize and bean cultivation.[79] These changes in the immediate precontact era suggest the capacity for adaptation in Native American subsistence strategies. But even before this era, in regions such as the lower and central Mississippi Valley, it is tricky to find evidence of full maize intensification. From AD 300 through AD 800 (and likely later) maize was often supplemented by continuing hunting and gathering practices by men and women, as well as alternative systems of horticulture. These systems mitigated the problematic nutritional deficiencies in maize, while allowing the benefits of its production as a storable energy source.[80] This hybrid model of subsistence is often overlooked by those who only focus on hunting among Native Americans (as supposedly distinct from Old World populations during the same era), or by those who, conversely, solely emphasize the domesticated "three sisters" of beans, squash and maize.

Adaptations had taken place long before the Little Ice Age, allowing communities to retain hunting and gathering systems as well as alternative forms of horticulture and agriculture, distinct from maize cultivation. The adaptations mitigated against the effects of maize intensification and prevented them from threatening demography and health more seriously. They prevented disease epidemics from becoming pandemics, thanks to their encouragement of buffer zones between settlements. Those zones encompassed wild hunting spaces while preventing the spread of diseases between humans, or from animals to humans. Let us, then, examine the nutritional profile of indigenous plant and starch sources that remained important in many regions of North America even after the shift toward maize, before then turning to the hunting and gathering strategies that remained geographically separate from agricultural and horticultural settlements. Both phenomena provided frameworks to supply nutrient-dense foods that strengthened immunity. They also decreased the context for broader epidemics.

Southeast North America

In the Southeast, as we have seen, intensified cultivation of maize began between around AD 100 and as late as AD 750 in the easternmost coastal zones.[81] Nutritional deficiencies and a greater propensity for metabolic and infectious diseases have been linked to this trajectory, even while the intensification of energy-dense and storable grains allowed populations to increase. The community and satellite communities of Cahokia, near present-day St. Louis between the Mississippi and Missouri Rivers, thus numbered up to 40,000 people by around AD 1500.[82] Yet members of its population continued to consume native plants that had been gardened, gathered or cultivated for more than 3,000 years.[83] Before the introduction of maize, plants had become more prevalent in the Southeast after a relatively marked climate shift at around 3000 BC, when often female-centered agricultural communities developed ways to cultivate nutritious resources such as gourds, squash, sunflowers, chenopodium and marsh elders.[84] The domestication of indigenous eastern North American seed plants can thus be categorized into four species: *Cucurbita pepo, Helianthus annuus, Iva annua and Chenopodium berlandieri*. Their cultivation alongside other "crops" such as berries and tubers required engaging in tree management, expanding floodplains, collecting seed plants, starting fires and establishing "orchards."[85] Their continued consumption represented one of several "countermeasures" to mitigate maize's nutrient deficiencies. Those countermeasures required careful land management and interventions, which became more difficult to carry through after European colonization.[86]

The assumed centrality of maize in the Southeast partially reflects colonial European misperceptions following the disruption of indigenous subsistence strategies, when storable grain was required to a greater extent than earlier, and as European markets for the resource grew. These misperceptions have influenced subsequent historical accounts. As Fritz has pointed out in a broader discussion of Eastern North America, until the last few decades of the twentieth century, "textbooks and articles minimized the economic importance of any kind of food production in eastern North America that did not include maize." Rather, the "subsistence systems of the early gardeners and farmers [before the introduction of maize] remained diversified in terms of the crops they planted as well as the wild resources they continued to harvest."[87] The claim that maize catalyzed the growth of the civilization of Cahokia, allowing mounds to be built in increasingly sedentary and dense settlements, "frequently fail[s] to point out that the cropping system of the time was diversified, with maygrass and chenopod seeds outnumbering maize fragments in many features."[88] Stable carbon isotopic analysis of late-prehistoric Cahokia settlements, moreover, has demonstrated that their inhabitants, irrespective of social status, did not always eat high volumes of maize with consistency.[89] Even after AD 1200 when maize began to achieve ascendancy over other seed crops in the Mississippi Valley Cahokia population, other plants supplemented the crop.[90]

The diversified crops of the precontact Southeast also included tree nuts, such as acorns, hickory nuts and walnuts, as well as lesser volumes of chestnuts, butternuts and hazelnuts, which were consumed seasonally and through storage. Hickory nuts and acorns are relatively nutrient dense, and contributed to metabolic health as a macronutrient containing both fat and protein. Acorn was the dominant plant staple in the Southeast until the introduction of maize, particularly as populations grew, and continued to be consumed even later in indigenous history.[91] Nuts and acorns were often ground up into powders that resembled grain or maize flour, but which were in fact higher in fat and lower in carbohydrate, when we consider their fundamental macronutrient profile.[92]

Beans began to be cultivated in the Southeast by around AD 900, though they assumed slightly less importance than in the Southwest.[93] Evidence from southern Florida and elsewhere in the Southeast shows that fresh greens such as amaranth, poke and cabbage palmettos were also consumed before and after maize and beans began to be cultivated.[94] In these and other cases, female-centered farming techniques were often adopted. Matrilineal kinship, where women farmed collectively and passed their land through the maternal line, was central to what has come to be described as the Mississippi horticultural tradition in the Southeast.[95] From around AD 900 in the riverine "horticultural villages" on the Great Plains, along the Missouri and its tributary rivers flowing into the lower Mississippi, beans, squash, melon, corn and sunflowers were cultivated by Caddoan-speaking Native American communities.[96] In Tidewater Virginia and the wider Southeast, rivers and floodplains offered areas for gardening and horticulture, often within the matrilineal tradition, without swidden practices. In at least one region, near Ocmulgee, Georgia, archaeological evidence suggests the existence of ridged fields to aid cultivation and watering in some way. In the Ohio-Mississippi Valley, as shown by evidence in Kentucky caves, indigenous people cultivated, gathered and even domesticated several woody and herbaceous plants, including squash.[97] In one of the earliest European observations of Native American subsistence and ecology in the Jamestown area of coastal Virginia, during the early seventeenth century, English settler John Smith described evidence of landscaping, gardening and horticulture before the arrival of the English and other Europeans.[98]

Archaeological and paleopathological studies have revealed that in addition to the nuts, berries, fruits, roots, plants and tubers described above, land animal products remained central to subsistence long after the introduction of maize, thus mitigating its nutrient-poor status.[99] If we consider the nutrient density of land and river animals, as distinct from their overall volume and mass in comparison to maize, then it is likely that they offered much in the way of sustenance for many Southeastern communities, both before and after agricultural intensification. Archaeological evidence demonstrates the consumption of nutrient-rich clams and shellfish, as well as smaller mammals, through the Archaic period, from 10,000 years ago to 3,000 years ago.[100] The Archaic period allowed consolidation of marine and river resources, including shellfish, all of which remained important up to and including AD 1500.[101] Between the Woodland Period (beginning around 1000 BC) and the Mississippian Period (around AD 1000 to AD 1500), deer became a vital source of animal meat throughout the Southeast, hunted by stalking as well as by communal drives in the fall and winter months. Raccoons, squirrels, opossums, rabbits, turtles and other mammals supplemented the deer consumption. Even bears were hunted and eaten, with their fat used as oil, nutritional supplement and exchange commodity.[102] Excavations demonstrate the consumption of migrating waterfowl alongside fish in predictable seasonal zones.[103] As English settler John Smith noted in his early account of Virginia, Native Americans seemed to "have plenty of fruits as well planted as naturall, as corne greene and ripe, fish, fowle, and wilde beastes exceeding fat."[104] Smith's writings also confirm that Virginia Algonquians hunted deer in fall and winter, inland and away from sedentary agricultural settlements. As Fritz has summarized in a discussion of Smith and other testimony, the "richness component of Mississippian diets was at least as great as it had been during the preceding period in most regions"—even while maize become more dominant after AD 1200.[105]

Fish and marine animals remained particularly important during the Woodland Period up to the period of contact, demonstrating the indigenous adaptation of so-called fall zones where fish spawned at particular times. Fish and shellfish were gathered all year round and eaten smoked during winter.[106] The developing Powhatan chiefdom benefited from its position near freshwater spawning grounds for anadromous fish, which moved from their saltwater homes at specific points in their lifecycle, and thus allowed populations to predict when and where they would appear en masse. Powhatan societal structures thus evolved to consolidate fertile riverine soils, leading to demographic increase but also placing eventual population pressure on those same lands.[107] Population growth depleted resources such as deer, as well as the soil, more than concentrated aquatic nutrition sources such as anadromous fish. Powhatan chiefdoms developed at the "fall line" between eastern marine and aquatic resources, including spawning grounds, and the ongoing demographic pressure provided by migrating people to those same regions. As agriculture supplemented animal resources, existing populations increased, while also becoming warier of external arrivals in the region. Thus, they developed defensive strategies to protect natural and agricultural resources, whether spawning rivers and lakes, or maize stores. Those who could be charged with overseeing the protection of environmental resources would also become stratified from lower members of the same societies.[108] Such activities are underscored by John Smith's observation of the seasonal adaptations of indigenous peoples: "In March and Aprill they live much upon their fishing, weares; and feed on fish, Turkies and squirrels. In May and Iune they plant their fieldes; and live most of Acornes, walnuts, and fish. But to mend their diet, some disperse themselves in small companies, and live upon fish, beasts, crabs, oysters, land Torteyses, strawberries, mulberries, and such like. In June, Julie, and August, they feed upon the rootes of Tocknough, berries, fish, and greene wheat." Smith's account confirms archaeological and ethnographic evidence that communities became more densely populated when certain animal products or plants were temporarily abundant, such as around spawning fish or seasonal plant harvest, before then dispersing into smaller groups to hunt and gather.[109]

Smith's account can be read as evidence that foods that were richer in fat and protein were consumed during the season for planting maize and other crops. Roots and tubers such as Tuckahoe also supplemented these foods. By mid-to-late summer, squash, pumpkins, beans, gourds and other domesticated plants were harvested and eaten.[110] As Smith highlighted, the point where the greatest volume of maize was harvested also coincided with the fattening of animals, making them more nutrient dense and calorific to consume. "From September until the midst of November," according to Smith, "are the chiefe Feasts and sacrifice. Then have they [Virginia Algonquians] plenty of fruits as well planted as natural, as corne, greene and ripe, fish, fowle, and wilde beastes exceeding fat."[111] Thus, we are offered an account of indigenous practices just before they were suddenly altered by the expansion of European settlement in the region. Consumption of maize, it appears, was supplemented by more nutrient-dense seasonal foods. Any disruption to that supplementation, we suggest, would have reduced nutrient density at just the point when it became even more important to support the immune system, due to the proliferation of infectious and metabolic diseases.

Other useful evidence of the supplementation of maize with nutrient-dense foods can be found in John Lawson's 1709 description of the

"Hunting-Quarters" of Native American communities in present day South Carolina. The English settler noted their separation from maize-producing agricultural settlements and highlighted the diverse animal products they supplied. Lawson's analysis was ethnographic in nature, as it sought to highlight the subsistence strategies that Native Americans had employed before the arrival of his party, which he claimed were the first Europeans to encounter the region. Though we should not discount the possibility that indigenous peoples had altered their behavior in response to earlier European settlers, we can use this account to underscore the supplementation of energy-dense maize with nutrient-dense animal products: "All small Game, as Turkeys, Ducks, and small Vermine, they commonly kill with Bow and Arrow, thinking it not worth throwing Powder and Shot after them. Of Turkeys they have abundance; especially, in Oak-Land, as most of it is, that lies any distance backwards. I have been often in their Hunting-Quarters, where a roasted or barbakued Turkey, eaten with Bears Fat, is held a good Dish; and indeed, I approve of it very well; for the Bears Grease is the sweetest and least offensive to the Stomach (as I said before) of any Fat of Animals I ever tasted." In addition to maize, Lawson noted, "[t]hey plant a great many sorts of Pulse, Part of which they eat green in the Summer, keeping great Quantities for their Winter-Store, which they carry along with them into the Hunting-Quarters, and eat them. The small red Pease is very common with them, and they eat a great deal of that and other sorts boil'd with their Meat, or eaten with Bears Fat."[112] Here Lawson noted the centrality of animal fat to the diet, whether in association with other cuts of meat or to prepare plants and starch sources. Fat, as we should note, is one the most nutrient-dense portions of meat. Lawson's description reflected that of John Smith in Virginia, several decades earlier. Smith noted the growth and cultivation of a seed-bearing plant crop named "mattoume" that was used by Native Americans in "a dainty bread buttered with dear suet." A root crop, known as Tockawhoughe, was also cultivated and eaten with fat and other animal products.[113] These observations provide further evidence of deeply rooted interactions between formal agriculture and hunting and gathering, their products eventually finding themselves on the same serving dish. These were interactions, moreover, that would soon become disrupted as colonization moved into the region.

Lawson's account also corroborates what we know about the prevention of zoonotic or crowd diseases by the separation of hunting zones from horticultural and agricultural settlements before the era of European disruption. The interaction between hunting, horticulture and agriculture impacted the structure of Southeastern village life by preventing diseases from entering sedentary zones in the first place. It would be easy to conclude that the concentration of people around mounds and chiefdoms in areas such as Cahokia—some of the most densely packed polities north of Mexico—would have predisposed them to rapid decline when new pathogens were introduced into these settlements, either before or after European contact. Yet in fact, the combination of horticulture and seasonal hunting between around AD 600 and AD 1400 allowed nutritional diversity (contributing to robust immunity to existing diseases in the region). It also required living circumstances that prevented new diseases from spreading zoonotically or from populations in other regions. Dispersed settlement patterns, in smaller chiefdoms, tended to be preferred when there was no threat of any warfare that made nucleation of towns more appropriate.[114] Chiefdoms were often surrounded by "buffer zones" that were noted by all explorers—unoccupied regions or "deserts" that protected richer natural resources for hunting and gathering, while preventing the spread of diseases between populations, and from animals.[115] Fields, orchards, meadows and agricultural fields were often surrounded by hunting zones (sometimes burned) "in forested areas away from settlements, probably less than 3 mi wide."[116] In areas of the Southeast between AD 700 and AD 1400, the buffer zones that developed between chiefdoms and subchiefdoms concentrated animals as a resource to be hunted but also to regain numbers in periodically uninhabited spaces—evidence of conscious land selection and resource management.[117]

Sources from the early period of contact between Native Americans and Spanish explorers—sometimes described as the "protohistoric" period in the Southeast—offer further evidence of the role of buffer zones. Provided we account for potential biases, inaccuracies or contemporary misreading in these colonial observations, they can be useful for understanding subsistence strategies that required the interaction between sedentary agriculture and hunting and gathering, in ways that also prevented the spread of pathogens. An account from the de Soto expeditions in present-day South Carolina, for example, between around 1539 and 1543, provides evidence of indigenous orchard cultivation, which supplied fruits and nutrient-dense and fat-rich nuts. The orchards were near to riverine agriculture, which was then surrounded by less inhabited hunting zones.[118]

Notwithstanding their deliberate refusal to inhabit areas around semiautonomous agricultural settlements, Southeastern communities still engaged in land management of their space, including by burning. Recent work on indigenous biodiversity has shown that the burning of land in and around buffer zones was a deliberate attempt to increase the fertility of soil for plants as well as to provide fodder for animals that could then more easily be hunted. Contrary to Krep and other historians, who have used burning to unsettle the notion of Native Americans as "ecological" actors, recent scholarship has indeed shown the contribution to sustainability and biodiversity of burning rituals. They concentrated minerals in the soil, which in turn aided the nutritional health of those animals that ate plants from the same zones. Those animals, in turn, may have become more nutritionally dense when consumed by humans.[119]

Increased evidence for social stratification around mound sites in Cahokia during the Mississippi Period, as we have seen, has often been linked to the consolidation of maize as a nutritional resource. Those who controlled its storage and protection, according to such an analysis, gained positions of power and authority. Yet it is important to note that hierarchical cultural developments near ceremonial mound centers also turned on the consumption of animal products. In Cahokia, archaeological evidence suggests that seasonal ceremonial feasts were attended by guests from surrounding hamlets, who competed for social status. All attendees consumed deer and other meat. These findings corroborate ethnographic assessments of war and ceremonial feasts based on eighteenth- and nineteenth-century narratives.[120] Other populations in the Southeast show similar evidence of meat-driven status and also the trade in meat across chiefdom boundaries. There were many communities in the region, to be sure, that showed little evidence of status-driven differentiation in meat consumption or external trade and supply of the resource. All community members ate meat alongside plants and maize. The ceremonial nature of intra-regional feasts and the nonregular nature of trade in animal products also suggest that each chiefdom, and even each hamlet, maintained a degree of autonomy and isolation, supported by the existence of uninhabited buffer zones and hunting spheres around their settlements. Where necessary, however, trade or ceremonial events could provide nutritional resources above and beyond those used on a daily basis.[121]

Southwest North America

Most archaeological evidence suggests that the people who formed the Clovis complex (c. 1300 BC–9000 BC) and Folsom complex (c. 9000 BC–7500 BC) in the Southwest hunted large mammals for sustenance.[122] In addition to evidence for stone implements designed to grind plant and seed matter during the Archaic Period (c. 7500 BC–2000 BC), ground-stone tools designed to pulverize meat and bones have been identified, alongside remains of birds, smaller animals and reptiles, in several archaeological sites.[123] Following the Late Archaic period (3000 BC–1000 BC), however, the descendant populations of hunter-gatherers in the Southwest are often said to have become increasingly sedentary and maize-centered. The earliest evidence for domesticated maize in the region, originally introduced from Mesoamerica, dates to around 4,000 years ago in southern Arizona.[124] The Tucson Basin and uplands of northern New Mexico show evidence of irrigation canals for maize cultivation around 2,400 years ago.[125] We are only able to date its use and domestication to around 4,000 years ago in present-day southern Arizona. Elsewhere in the Southwest, we have evidence for greater introduction and domestication of squash around 3,000 years ago. Beans appear to have been domesticated in the region around 2,600 years ago.[126]

Studies of the Basketmaker people (c. 2100 BC–AD 750) and other allied communities do indeed reveal more sedentary agricultural techniques, including riverine irrigation, diversion of predictable storm water sources onto fields and the use of nutrients to enhance soil yields.[127] Between around AD 200 and AD 550 , subsistence strategies in the Southwest synthesized farming and foraging among small village communities. By AD 1000, domesticated plants such as maize, beans and squash were preferred to a far greater extent than during the Early Pithouse period, leading communities to live in terraced spaces near to fields.[128]

With these developments in mind, historical narratives have tended to define the notion of precontact "civilization" in the Southwest according to an association between high population density and sedentary agriculture. Yet as in the Southeast, we should be wary of reading later European perceptions into our account of earlier subsistence. Disruption to the symbiosis between agriculture, horticulture and hunting and gathering forced many Southwestern communities into focusing solely on maize cultivation in increasingly sedentary zones, which encouraged the spread of disease more than ever before. Before that point, however, a good degree of biodiversity in nutritional supplies was provided by the intersection between agriculture, horticulture and hunting outside sedentary zones, as well as by the movement of populations from one semiautonomous settlement to another as an adaptation to ecological or sociopolitical factors. These nutritional frameworks supplemented maize consumption with more nutrient-dense plants and animals. Rather than domesticating animals or relying solely on cultivated crops in sedentary settlements, populations engaged in migratory movements in search of game and seasonal hunting grounds, and wild plant sources as well as farm lands. Understanding the importance of movement rather than stasis in the indigenous Southwest, encompassing present-day Arizona and New Mexico, parts of Colorado and Utah, and parts of Northwest Mexico and Southwest Texas, highlights the relative ecological and nutritional diversity of the region, so important for the health and immunity of its populations in the centuries before contact.[129]

The Hohokam, Basketmaker and Mogollon cultures all left evidence of faunal bones from hunted animals in their settlements, notwithstanding the purported move toward sedentary agriculture.[130] Among the same populations, we can find pottery evidence that wild plants were gathered both before and after the transition to agriculture. From 8,500 years ago until the precontact era, as Adams and Fish have summarized, those plants included "chenopods, grasses, amaranths, globemallow, bugseed, purslane, beeweed, sunflower, wild buckwheat, stickleaf, tansy mustard, winged pigweed and ricegrass." Upland areas of the Southwest yielded perennial plants such as "agave, yucca, stool, beargrass, acorns, piñon nuts, juniper berries, and manzanita and sumac berries." Lowland areas provided grass grains, pods of "mesquites, walnuts, wild grapes, cattails" and various edible cactus and cactus flower sources. Some of the above appeared on both sides of the region's Mogollon Rim, while others tended to appear either in the southern or the northern side of the Rim.[131]

Plants consumed in the Southwest for at least the last 3,000 years were adapted to riverine habitats and gardens, demonstrating their potential synergy with fishing resources. The seasonality of wild plants required periodic population movements to harvest their nutritious supplies, just as similar movements responded to seasonal migrations of animals and fish. In the northern Rio Grande, households and even villages exchanged plants and animals to respond to climatic or seasonal weather differences, demonstrating continued movements and nutritional exchange during the precontact era.[132] The Southern Plains, according to Doolittle's assessment of ethnobotanical and archaeological evidence, became "a corridor for plants, and perhaps by extension, agricultural information being transferred between east and west." Thanks to the many protohistorical sources from early Spanish movements into the Southwest, moreover, including the de Soto expeditions in the 1530s and 1540s, we can find rich evidence of highly sophisticated farm irrigation techniques that were not always diverted toward maize production.[133]

As Pueblo communities such as Acoma, Hopi and Zuni moved toward intensifying maize, bean and squash crops, to be sure, they constructed new advanced population centers. Yet these examples of advanced civilization continued to incorporate seasonal hunting and gathering activities into their nutritional frameworks. They could also encompass wholesale movement of populations from one region to another, depending on political or ecological developments. To ignore these phenomena would be to define a static and sedentary population, without much agency in response to climatic or demographic necessities. The Pueblo, then, were not solely sedentary farmers who lived in timeless communities built around the cultivation of a few crops.[134]

Indeed, energy from stored maize likely fueled the movements of those such as the Apache bands, who carried the grain with them as they hunted increasingly further afield during the centuries before the arrival of the Spanish in the region. For the Western Apache, crop surpluses rarely occurred and annual agricultural consumption never usually moved beyond 25 percent of total calorific intake. Thus, we can hypothesize that maize was used for energy rather than for nutrients, allowing them greater physical movement to hunt and gather nutrient-dense animals and plants, thereby accounting for the remaining part of their calorific intake. Maize—from sedentary agriculture—could fuel movements out of settled zones, encouraging seasonal behaviors that were anything but immobile.[135] A retreat to greater sedentism, as we shall see, followed colonial disruption. It impacted the health of communities that were faced with new diseases which required immunity to be as strong as possible, yet that found themselves cut off from mobile nutritional networks which had once provided relatively nutrient-dense foods to supplement energy-dense maize, thereby providing a more optimal nutritional contribution to working immunity.[136]

The Northeast Atlantic, New England and Iroquois Country

Bennet has estimated that an increasing proportion of plant products—particularly maize, beans and squash—were incorporated into the southern New England Native American diet in the several centuries before European contact.[137] This analysis has enjoyed a wide scholarly impact, given its focus on a region that would fall under the gaze of modern historians. It uses an estimation of calories to define dietary composition among indigenous people in New England before European contact. Yet even when calorie intake is high, we have suggested, nutrient density—the availability of vitamins and minerals that are necessary for the functioning of cells and enzymes in the human body—can be low. According to Bennet, the gendered division of labor between hunting and agriculture in New England demonstrates that women became responsible for 90 percent of the precontact Native American diet. But if we define dietary intake beyond calorific consumption, which merely relates to a unit of energy, we are required to include nutrient profiles that fall beyond those metabolic values. Though animal consumption likely decreased as agriculture increased, its *nutritional* role in the diet was not likely to have been at under 10 percent, if we aggregate higher nutrient density alongside energy density. Agriculture, as elsewhere, allowed population size to increase in the centuries before contact, even if health measures for those who lived were not necessarily qualitatively superior.

Indeed, the precontact archaeological record for the cultivation and consumption of maize in many more northern parts of New England has been described as "minimal" in comparison to other regions in North America, beginning as late as AD 1100. Ethnohistoric examinations using early-contact sources between New England, Maritime and European communities, as well as earlier archaeological evidence, have demonstrated that Native American "settlement and subsistence patterns, both prehistorically and at contact, were based on a generalized, broad-spectrum hunting, fishing, and gathering economy [...] [including] both coastal and terrestrial resources, associated with a seasonally mobile settlement pattern [...] [providing] a varied diet that met or exceeded minimum adequate nutritional needs in terms of proteins, carbohydrates, vitamins, and fats."[138] The relatively late introduction of maize, coupled with the continuation of other seasonal nutrient-dense resources, thus minimized the problems of health and immunity that scholars have noted in other regions of greater agricultural intensification, such as the Dickson Mounds in Illinois. According to Carlson et al., the "prehistoric Native Americans of southern New England should not have been suffering the type or degree of nutritional deficiencies and infectious disease seen in maize horti-cultural communities elsewhere in precontact North America." The "types of nutritional deficiencies associated with maize as a staple would not have been a health problem" for New England and the Maritimes before European con-tact, with a "low incidence of infectious disease associated with crowding" due to the seasonal nature of settlement, which also likely meant that "nutritional stress episodes would be acute and seasonal, rather than chronic."[139]

Despite "the impact of agriculture on population size and settlement patterns," as Salisbury has pointed out, "the annual subsistence cycle in the south was still timed to coincide with the appearance of favored wild food sources."[140] As in other regional examples, energy-dense but nutrient-poor foods were often supplemented with more nutrient-rich products, and hunting and gathering remained synergistic rather than dichotomous with horticulture and agriculture. In as early as 1524, for example, Giovanni da Verrazano noted that indigenous people in Narragansett Bay "move [their] houses from one place to another according to the richness of the site and the season." English writers during the seventeenth century noted similar seasonal movements.[141] As the Massachusetts Bay settler William Wood described in the early 1630s, hunters in the region kept dwellings "where they know the deer usually doth frequent," and many were "experienced in the knowledge of all baits, and diverse seasons; being not ignorant likewise of the removal of fishes, knowing when to fish in rivers, and when at rocks, when in bays, and when at seas." Bird movements, as well as the occurrence of wild plants and tubers, were also monitored closely by many indigenous peoples throughout New England before (and even after) European contact.[142] Writing in 1616 among Algonquian hunters in the Maritimes and Northern New England, Pierre Biard recorded a seasonal cycle of fall and winter hunting, spring stream fishing, summer ocean fishing and a group of peoples who in his view did "not till the soil at all." Wood also noted similar seasonal hunting and gathering, without also discounting agriculture in delicate and seasonal balance.[143]

In a number of communities in the Atlantic Northeast from the eleventh century to the fifteenth century "Late Woodland" period, particularly in the southern region, a gendered division of labor in food production developed to match that which appeared elsewhere. Women began to cultivate the "three sisters" of maize, beans, and squash, to complement the hunting, gathering and fishing that men continued to engage in outside female-dominated horticultural settlements.[144] But while maize may have increased by volume and mass in relation to hunted animal products consumed, they supplemented rather than replaced animal food. Northeastern women became more equal players in a delicately balanced food system that included many other plants, alongside animal products. Native American farmers in the Eastern Woodlands, for example, domesticated sunflower and sumpweed over 4,800 years ago.[145]

Some plants, indeed, should neither be labeled as wild or domesticated. Rather, they were tended in ways that allowed them to survive and thrive in habitats that were altered by Native American populations. They included the Jerusalem artichoke, maypops, giant Ragweed and a variety of greens.[146] In addition to maize, beans and squash, therefore, Late Woodland women grew pumpkins, cucumbers and Jerusalem artichokes in single fields with regularly apportioned mounds in which maize and bean seedlings grew. Their roots and stems intertwined, protecting them from weeds and wind as well as increasing nitrogen in the soil. Beans contained the amino acid lycine, which increased the nutritional bioavailability of the little protein in maize, the zein.[147] The gendered division of labor prevented epidemics of zoonotic diseases by separating animals into buffer zones, where they could be hunted, rather than domesticating them in the same space as crop agriculture. Child rearing—and thus overall fertility—was also enhanced as children could remain close to their mothers within sedentary horticultural settlements, particularly when those settlements grew folate-rich plants such as beans and squash, which as we shall see, are so vital to maternal nutrition and immunity.[148] As in the Southeast, moreover, plant products could provide portable and storable energy sources—"a form of trail mix"—to enable longer hunts for nutrient-dense animals, or expeditions to gather more nutrient-dense plants and tubers.[149]

When trying to understand land use and subsistence in precontact New England, and in Iroquois lands between the Eastern Great Lakes and the northern Atlantic coast, scholars have more recently employed the metaphor of gardening to describe the way that wild zones were managed and even cultivated, including slashing and burning as well as tilling soil for non-maize crops and plants. Those plants included small grain-like grasses and chenopods.[150] In what came to be known as Massachusetts, nut-bearing trees and plants were managed and improved through fire from at least 8,000 years ago.[151] River valleys in southern New England incorporated fire management to clear growth for wild and cultivated plants as well as to increase nutrient density in the soil. In what came to be known as upstate New York and French Canada, ethnographic and historical sources show "slashing-and-burning" in permanently cultivated, rather than rotated, fields. In the Delaware Valley, as Doolittle suggests, swidden practices involving field rotation were likely introduced by Europeans rather than reflecting indigenous practices.[152] Burning portions of forest and brush for subsistence, in contrast, encouraged more new fauna to develop, and even increased available food for grazing deer, who entered the zones in increasing number. The fires also rarely affected nut and acorn-producing trees, maintaining their role in subsistence while clearing areas below them for new plants to be gathered.[153] In 1656, the Dutch settler Adriaen Van der Donck noted that Native Americans in New Netherlands maintained "a yearly custom of burning the woods, plains and meadows in the fall of the year, when the leaves have fallen, and when the grass and vegetable substances are dry [...] Those places which are then passed over are fired in the spring in April. This is done [...] to render hunting easier, to thin out and clear the woods of all dead substances and grass, which grow better in the ensuing spring [...] to circumscribe and enclose the game [...] and because game is more easily tracked over burned parts of the woods."[154]

From around AD 800, then, the Atlantic Northeast rarely reproduced the cultural complexes built around maize, corn and beans, which are often used to describe Southeastern communities such as Cahokia (but which, as we have seen, were in fact more diverse in their nutritional formation). The spread of the crops was restricted to southern New England. Yet even here, agriculture supplemented rather than replaced hunting, fishing and gathering. As Salisbury has summarized, while "domesticated plants increased in economic and dietary importance from about A.D. 1000, Mississippian influence in southern New England, on the margin of the agricultural zone, was strong enough only to modify, rather than transform, the patterns established during and after the Late Archaic." Moreover, like "their fellow Algonquian speakers just to the north of the zone, the natives here approached the European contact era in autonomous village bands that were optimally "fitted" to the food-producing capacities of their local environments." These models were similar, in fact, to those that scholars have used to modify our understanding of Mississippi chiefdoms, which we now know were more autonomous than once assumed. Buffer zones, and uninhabited hunting spaces, often surrounded settlements that reproduced each other in structure without requiring too much interaction that might encourage the spread of pathogens between mound centers. We can therefore identify far more continuity between the Late Archaic period and the era directly preceding European contact—in contrast to the period that followed, when subsistence strategies were often discontinued without further time to adapt to such change.[155]

From the Great Plains to the Great Basin

Between 13000 BC and 9000 BC, the Clovis people in what is now present-day Oklahoma relied on animal meat from large mammals such as mammoths. Archaeological evidence even suggests that bison were herded into ravines to increase the efficiency of their slaughter by Folsom projectiles.[156] From 12,000 to 8,000 years ago, Great Plains communities of Paleoindians were highly mobile, ordered into bands that hunted large mammals such as bison. They achieved a niche in the region after climatic changes reorganized the environment into one dominated by grasslands.[157] Elsewhere on the Great Plains, and further west in the Great Basin between the Colorado River basin in the south, the Rocky Mountains in the east and the Sierra Nevada mountains in the west, similar animal-hunting patterns appeared. Paiute, Panamint and Western Shoshone communities in the Great Basin, and their ancestors, hunted large and small game, including bighorn sheep, pronghorn, deer, rabbits and porcupines.[158] We even have evidence for fishing expeditions among Great Basin communities along rivers, marshes and lakes from as early as 10,000 years ago. Freshwater clams and other mollusks provided nutritional resources in lakeshore regions such as the Utah Valley and Carson Lake for thousands of years.[159] Nineteenth-century exploratory accounts detail encounters between Euro-Americans and indigenous peoples in the Great Basin. Groups such as the Northern Paiute and Utes were reported to maintain long-standing nutritional systems with insect protein as an important resource, including cicadas, grasshoppers and crickets.[160]

In the Great Basin, as elsewhere in precontact North America, most native mammal species were unlikely to become domesticated because of their innate behavioral features. As Smith has summarized, they included white-tailed and mule deer, elk, moose, pronghorn, bison, bear and bighorn sheep. Thus, zoonotic diseases were far less prevalent, even as the region began to incorporate aspects of horticulture and agriculture through the domestication and cultivation of certain plants, or the gardening of wild plant resources.[161]

Further east from the Great Basin, in the Great Plains, subsistence systems from at least 8,000 years ago were dominated by bison-grazing grasslands, from present-day central Nebraska to northern Texas, and between western Nebraska and northwest Texas, encompassing present-day Kansas and Oklahoma. Yet we should move beyond the postcontact era vision of bison dependency in the region, emphasizing instead the important nutritional interactions between plants and animals. After contact, to be sure, European markets and technologies stoked rivalries that made the region central to the mass slaughter of bison, eventually leading to overhunting and overconsumption, including by communities that had not inhabited the region until relatively recently. But before that point, the picture is more nuanced than once assumed, showing greater use of plant sources than popular narratives suggest.[162] Deer, small animals, fish and waterfowl remains have been located by archaeologists of the Archaic Period (8,000 years ago to 2,000 years ago) and the Woodland Period in the Great Plains (2,500 to 1,100 years ago) alongside archaeobotanical evidence of sunflower, goosefoot and native squash consumption that supplemented animal products. Along migrating streams, groups made use of seasonally available resources such as mussels, small mammals and plants that were adapted to periodic bogginess in these zones.[163] The Woodland Period is most often defined according to evidence of emerging ceramic use, generally linked to the consumption and storage of cultivated plants in more sedentary settings, where hunting took place on the outskirts of horticultural fields and gardened patches. Weedy annuals, likely semicultivated during the earlier Archaic period, appeared in greater volumes in settlements. Small amounts of maize appeared during this period, but much less than is traditionally assumed in general studies of North American dietary change during this era.[164]

The Plains Village period (around 1,000 to 350 years ago) witnessed the construction of diverse villages and communities, and the influx of new groups into the region. Particularly in the western plains, maize became more prevalent after around AD 1000.[165] Yet as Bozell et al. have summarized, large animals continued to be hunted outside those settlements, including bison, pronghorn and deer, as well as smaller animals including rabbits, skunk, beaver, raccoon and wild turkey.[166] In the eastern prairies and central plains, moreover, groups supplemented hunted animals with "a multicropping strategy," rather than one entirely focused on maize, including "seed-bearing annuals harvested in the spring (little barley) and fall (chenopod, sunflower, marsh elder), combined with the cultivation of the tropical cultigens maize, squash, and beans."[167] As Ostler has suggested, Hidatsas, Mandans and Arikaras "lived in permanent villages where they combined farming with hunting and gathering."[168] Plants supplanted animal products, which likely made their fat-soluble nutrients more bioavailable. Large mammal bone, "crushed into small fragments has been interpreted as a by-product of manufacturing bone grease and extraction of bone marrow as nutritional supplements." On the southern Plains, evidence for "marrow processing" and "grease rendering" can be found during the Plains Village period, "likely indicating production of pemmican, a storable mound of animal fat mixed with plant fibers or berries."[169]

In the Great Basin, similarly, hunting and fishing was supplemented by gathered plant resources, more than among the region's sedentary southern and eastern neighbors. Of most importance for plant consumption was the Piñon Complex, developed more than 8,000 years ago in the Great Basin, and increasingly common from around 2,000 years ago. The Complex centered on the collection and preparation of piñon nuts from August to November. They would be tapped out of their cones and stored for their starch, fat and protein. Most commonly, they were roasted and ground up into a flour that was mixed with water and eaten as a form of gruel—or even frozen in winter.[170] Wild seeds were collected and processed for consumption, including Indian ricegrass, goosefoot, saltbush, sunflower and blazingstar.[171] An Acorn Complex also developed, though not as widespread as in California. Western Shoshone communities used mesquite pods throughout the Mojave Desert.[172] Yucca remains appear in archaeological settlements in the southern Great Basin.[173] The Oregon Northern Paiute, Northern Shoshone and Bannock collected root vegetables such as camas, balsamroot and swamp onion many centuries before European contact.[174] The earth ovens used to break down those roots provide us with the most accurate evidence for relatively nutrient-dense root vegetable consumption during the precontact era, dating back to at least 4,500 years ago.[175]

Gardening activities in the Great Basin also predate European contact, according to archaeological assessments. Wild leafy greens were managed and replanted (though not domesticated). Southwestern crops also found their way into some Great Basin communities.[176] Plants were sometimes exchanged for the cultivated crops supplied by southern Pueblo neighbors, allowing the interaction between foraging and farming subsistence in the centuries before contact.[177]

Between around AD 1400 and AD 1450, a shift to intensification of maize and bison consumption took place in the Great Plains, and to a lesser extent in the Great Basin. As in other regional case studies, energy from storable maize could be deployed to hunt wild animals, rather than replacing the latter as a nutritional resource. Such a phenomenon, to be sure, strained sustainable systems even before European contact. It likely also required more trade with other regions for plants and animals that had hitherto been incorporated into more diverse nutritional contexts. These new interactions, as we shall see, only increased after the arrival of Europeans and their horses. Communities came to be shattered by overhunting, new diseases that were transported in dense trade networks and the effects of the trade in enslaved Native Americans.[178]

Ancient and Precontact California

Precontact California indigenous communities, such as the Chumash and their ancestors, supplemented hunted small animals and marine resources

with plants. Roots and tubers, for example, provided supplementary carbohydrate sources in inner California from around 5,500 years ago.[179] Ecological
sustainability was culturally contextualized from at least 4,000 years ago,
allowing a shift from high-ranking larger animals to the consumption of
smaller game and the processing of acorns. Precontact California Native
Americans have thus been defined as proto-agriculturalists and hunter-
harvesters; that is, people who used fire and other methods to manage their
surrounding subsistence sources.[180] Deliberate fire burning in California
promoted the growth of game foraging plants as well as those that could be
gathered by humans.[181]

Climatic changes allowed acorn growth and storage, providing a resource
for sedentary populations that were less inclined to move around in search
of small animals and game. Intensive acorn use began around 2,500 years
ago, remaining supplemented by smaller seed plants and roots.[182] Yet
smaller game and birds continued to be retrieved by individual hunters
without any intervention or organization by the wider community, until
European contact.[183] Chumash, Gabrieleno, Tolowa, and Yurok peoples
continued to hunt sea mammals long after the intensification of acorn
production along the middle and northern California coast.[184] Seaweed
provided important sources of salt and iodine to coastal communities up
until the contact era.[185] Several indigenous groups made use of anadromous fishing resources in the streams and rivers of northern California,
particularly in order to obtain DHA-rich fish oil resources, so central to
health and immunity.[186] Anthropological and ethnographic examinations
of California fishing practices have highlighted the special preference for
preserving salmon oils for use outside fishing seasons, at least several hundred years before European contact, so that the "rich oil was tried out and
dripped almost in a trickling stream into the steatite dishes kept for the pur-
pose of catching and preserving this oil."[187] Even grasshoppers were used
as protein resources, particularly after fires.[188]

At its peak, California's Acorn Complex could yield up to half of the macronutrient energy requirements for populations such as the Pomo, Nomlaki
and Nisenan peoples—including protein, fat and carbohydrate.[189] Leached
acorns were used as a staple throughout precontact California, having had
concentrations of tannic acid removed through pulverizing, soaking and
chemically binding to iron sources. In the coastal ranges and the foothills
of the Sierra Nevada mountains, buckeye was leached in a similar way to
reduce some of its associated toxins.[190] Gender customs were modified over
time, to reward the time-consuming and costly harvesting of acorns and other
nuts, allowing intensification to become worthwhile. Women, therefore, spent
more time processing and grinding.[191] Pine nuts were also harvested from

the prehistoric era onward, transformed into fatty nut butters. When the nut butter was combined with the nutrients in plants that were consumed in the same meal, those nutrients likely became more bioavailable, given their fat-soluble status.[192]

California's acorn economy could produce partially stratified and sedentary communities, depending on the local context, analogous with societal structures that developed following the introduction of maize in other regions. Some individuals gained representative power and authority by guaranteeing the storage, protection and exchange of the resource for the wider community. Storage-based economies, with acorns at their core, nonetheless allowed "logistically based" hunting to emerge. Acorns provided a storable and transportable energy source for organized hunts, favoring higher-status game, away from sedentary zones.[193] Several centuries before European contact, hamlets from the mid-California coast stretching to the Sacramento River tended to comprise around 1,000 people. Chumash and Tongva communities exchanged foods, including animals and acorns, while others competed and even fought for resources. By the late eighteenth century, approximately 300,000 Native Americans lived in California, having stabilized their demographic growth and adapted to changing climate with a mix between the production of acorns, other nuts, and hunting and fishing. Population growth under the Acorn Complex was low enough to prevent those concentrated settlement patterns that might allow the proliferation of diseases.[194]

As in other regions, therefore, we can see that sedentary forms of plant cultivation, and the sedentary processing of wild gathered plant products (including acorns) was not antagonistic to the continuation of seasonal or even year-round hunting and fishing. Storable macronutrients provided by ground acorns provided the energy for hunts outside developing sedentary settlements. Animals were prevented from entering those settlements in ways that encouraged zoonotic diseases. Elk, deer and bighorn sheep were variously hunted in prairie, oak, woodland and highland zones in the centuries before contact.[195] In the California foothills, acorns and grasses provided fodder for animals, which were hunted in the fall and winter seasons before communities moved into higher ranges during the summer.[196] It is often claimed that large game populations recovered after the decimation of Native American populations following European contact in the early nineteenth century. Yet by at least 1,300 year ago, resource use among indigenous people in what is now California had focused on small rather than large game. More distant resource areas were also favored, to allow buffer zones between settlements, and potentially due to intergroup conflicts, allowing animals to proliferate.[197]

The Pacific Northwest before Contact

Within the Pacific Northwest, generally defined as those cultures north of the Columbia River, stratified status was often found among those who were positioned to define access to ecological resources within a hunting-fishing-gathering context. Around 200,000 Native Americans lived in the Pacific Northwest by the mid-eighteenth century, enjoying a diet rich in salmon, other marine products, and without grains. Ethnographic assessments show that villages tended to be semisedentary, without crops or domesticated animals.[198] Plateau communities between the Fraser River Basin and the Great Basin in the Pacific Northwest interior numbered more than 50,000 by the mid-eighteenth century. Men often caught salmon, which was a prime nutritional source, while women often gathered wild plant foods. Women also processed and prepared fish and game.[199]

During the centuries before the Lewis and Clark expedition into the Pacific Northwest, no plants were domesticated in coastal and interior regions. But indigenous peoples managed, gardened and controlled yields of plants and animals, engaged in tilling and applied careful controls on harvesting through communal land mechanisms and seasonal constraints, which were manifested in ceremonial and cultural norms.[200] As in California, fire burning techniques enhanced yields of nutritional sources from roots, tubers and berries.[201]

Archaeological and ethnographic analysis of historic Pacific Northwest communities demonstrates the use of green leafy plants, fruits, roots, bulbs, rhizomes, corms and tubers, providing sources of fat, carbohydrate and fiber for many centuries before contact.[202] Though there was no marked gendered division between sedentary horticulture and more mobile hunting, gender divisions could be found in the distinction between gathering and preparing animal and plant products.[203] Ethnographic analysis of Wapato and Plateau Pacific Northwest peoples has suggested that trade practices still evident in the eighteenth century were deeply rooted in precontact subsistence strategies, which allowed far more nutritional diversity than once assumed. During summer, individuals brought smelt and candlefish to trade exchanges where they encountered other groups offering venison, corms and roots, dried salmon and berries as well as buffalo meat obtained from long networks stretching south to the Great Plains.[204]

We can also gain much understanding from oral histories, archival collections, archaeological records, interviews and participant observation of contemporary practices, using methods and materials from ethnographers such as Daly, which have noted the historical preference for fish fats among Delgamuukw indigenous peoples in British Columbia, going back several centuries in communal memory. According to Daly, fat "rendered from salmon heads was prepared in summer, hung in bladder pouches in the rodent-resistant family meat caches, and saved for winter use." Oils were "prepared from fatty fish and meat such as oolichan, salmon and beaver. Special processes were involved in preparing the heads—drying or boiling them for oil—as well as the eyes, bellies and eggs." Moreover the "arrival of the oolichan [...] was traditionally announced with the cry, 'Hlaa aat'ixshi halimootxw!' or, 'Our Saviour has just arrived!'" Ooligan grease was thus a prized gift in feasts and between neighbors.[205]

Surveying modern communities of Native Americans, Weston A. Price's 1939 *Nutrition and Physical Degeneration* noted a similar preference for animal and fish fats, and organ meats, and suggested its provenance in ancestral food patterns that dated back centuries and even millennia. The indigenous communities Price encountered were seen to prize the fattiest parts of meat and fish, including organ meats, rather than muscle cuts. According to one summary, Price linked a diet high in fats from mammals and fish to "an almost complete absence of tooth decay and dental deformities among native Americans who lived as their ancestors did [...] [including among] the nomadic tribes living in the far northern territories of British Columbia and the Yukon, as well as the wary inhabitants of the Florida Everglades, who were finally coaxed into allowing him to take photographs [...] Skeletal remains of the Indians of Vancouver that Price studied were similar, showing a virtual absence of tooth decay, arthritis and any other kind of bone deformity."[206] As in other regions, these traditions were rooted in much more ancient practices, including those from several thousand years ago, when larger megafauna were consumed. The traditions would become disrupted by the arrival of European settlers and colonizers, to the detriment of their health and immunity, albeit more than a century later than more southerly indigenous communities.

Precontact Alaska and Arctic North America

Indigenous communities in what is present-day Alaska are often described as outliers in discussions of precontact subsistence strategies in North America. Given their regional context, it is often suggested that their diet was dominated by land and marine mammals rather than plants, which could not thrive in the environment. It is sometimes even claimed that Alaskan communities would, until very recently, have lived in a state of permanent ketosis, gaining metabolic energy solely from the conversion of fatty acids rather than glucose provided by carbohydrates, given their purported reliance on fatty animals above all other macronutrient sources.[207] Yet even in this region, recent studies have shown, plants and horticulture were employed in strategies that were more biodiverse than once assumed.

In southwestern Alaska and the Aleutian Islands, to be sure, archaeo-logical sites show remains for sedentism centered on subsistence on seals, sea lions, migratory water birds and codfish. Salmon was also vital, particularly if the communities were oriented toward the Pacific rather than the Bering Sea. Hunting of larger sea mammals, such as whales, was also increasingly common among many Aleut communities from around AD 1000 until the period of European contact.[208] In the Western Arctic regions of Alaska, near the Bering and Chukchi seas, from 2500 BC to 1600 BC, stone and bone materials were adapted and used to hunt and harvest marine animals, from fish to walrus.[209]

More sedentary cultural intensification developed from around 500 BC as indigenous communities in southwestern Alaska came to rely on predictable—and even managed—spawning salmon zones.[210] The Thule period of "proto-Eskimo" culture is usually defined as taking place from around AD 1000. Studies of the Seward Peninsula during this period have revealed fish, mussels, mollusks, duck, geese, hares, squirrel, fox, wolf, dog, bears, caribou, whales, seals and walrus. It has been suggested that planned hunting of whales, caribou and birds was marked seasonally, with more "opportunistic foraging" for other animal products to supplement those activities. Though Caribou came to be the most highly prized nutritional source by AD 1500, other animals continued to provide regularly diverse subsistence strategies.[211] Archaeological evidence from the last 8,000 years demonstrates that ancestral Athapaskans in the far Northwest followed seasonal movements of caribou and used smaller animals and fish as supplementary resources.[212]

Yet traditional conceptions of arctic and subarctic subsistence as completely dominated by land animals and fish may need slight modification. While there are far fewer named plant categories dating back to precontact eras, there are still around 200 named species and a substantial ethnobotanical literature for populations such as the Chugach Eskimo of Prince William Sound, Alaska; the Tanaina people of coastal Alaska; and even the Arctic Red River and Peel River bands in the Northwest Territories.[213]

In 1999, indeed, the body of a young man was found at a high elevation in a melting glacier in the southern part of the Saint Elias Mountains in British Columbia. Estimated to be between 550 and 600 years old, the man was found with preserved mountain sweet-cicely (a member of the celery family), hemlock and chenopod pollen in stomach samples. Crab and salmon were also traced to his body, demonstrating that he had lived in or traveled from coastal Alaska. Other archaeological, paleobotanical, ethnobotanical and ethnographic studies have shown that arctic and subarctic peoples used—and in some cases relied on—around 140 plant species.[214]

Around 25 species of tuberous root vegetables, corms, bulbs and rhizomes were also gathered and consumed throughout the Alaskan and Arctic region in the centuries before major European contact, demonstrating a slightly higher carbohydrate intake for Arctic peoples than usually assumed by those who suggest they must have remained in a permanently ketotic state, relying on ketones for energy, gained from a high fat intake, rather than glucose gained from carbohydrates. Scholars have identified around 50 species of fruits and berries, seasonally harvested by indigenous inhabitants of the arctic and sub-arctic. The inner bark of trees was even used by some peoples, as were partially digested lichens from animal stomachs.[215] Seaweed was harvested for trade and consumption, allowing a historically important source of iodine among coastal settlements.[216]

We can also trace evidence of precontact plant use from accounts given by the earliest explorers in the region, who survived by combining animal meats—often high in fat—with plants. The special preparation of those plants was taught by indigenous people they encountered.[217] The historical role of pemmican, made from animal fats and plants, demonstrates a similar nutritional interaction. In the centuries before contact, generally defined as the late eighteenth century, Arctic Chipewyan communities made pemmican from dried caribou meat, caribou rendered fat and several berries and herbs.[218]

Seventeenth- and eighteenth-century European observations of indigenous communities in the northernmost parts of continental North America show how the fattiest animal parts, and organs, were preferred above other nutrient sources. Hunting and gathering patterns in those regions were less altered by colonization, and so provide a more accurate picture of their ancestral nutritional profile within their regional context. Their populations relied on fats from fish and land animals as a greater proportion of their diet due to their climate and ecology.[219] Consider, for example, the case of Samuel Hearne, an explorer writing in 1768, who described the preparation of caribou among indigenous populations around the Hudson Bay area in Canada. The populations he encountered had maintained a hunter-gathering lifestyle in contrast to their southern neighbors suffering from European interventions:

Of all the dishes cooked by the Indians, a *beeatee*, as it is called in their language, is certainly the most delicious that can be prepared from a deer only, without any other ingredient. It is a kind of haggis, made with the blood, a good quantity of fat shred small, some of the tenderest of the flesh, together with the heart and lungs cut, or more commonly torn into small shivers; all of which is put into the stomach and toasted by being suspended before the fire on a string. (italics in original)

As Hearne noted elsewhere, community members tended to select only the fattiest parts of the animal, or nutrient-dense organ meats, throwing the rest away: "On the twenty-second of July we met several strangers, whom we joined in pursuit of the caribou, which were at this time so plentiful that we got everyday a sufficient number for our support, and indeed too frequently killed several merely for the tongues, marrow and fat."[220]

Notwithstanding Hearn's claim that the area had been uncontacted by other Europeans, it is possible that indigenous people in the area had become aware of disruptions to subsistence systems elsewhere in North America, and that their concentration on intensified animal hunting reflected a response to potential European disruption, rather than reflecting their precontact strategies altogether.[221] Nonetheless, the practices outlined by Hearne do seem to be corroborated by other anthropological and ethnographic histories of the region, as already outlined, at least to a large degree.

In this chapter, then, we have noted the positive and negative consequences of agricultural intensification in Native America, and the nutritional and societal adaptations that responded to those consequences, in regionally specific ways. The purported difference between Native American hunter-gatherers and European pastoralists becomes problematic if it is used to de-emphasize the role of indigenous agriculture and formal plant cultivation (horticulture) before European contact. Focusing entirely on the centrality of maize horticulture, to be sure, misses the important nutritional role of many other plants and starch sources that were gathered, gardened and cultivated in the centuries before contact. Doing so also overlooks the important nutritional and metabolic contribution from animal products during an era when agriculture and hunting and gathering were not dichotomous, as is sometimes suggested in discussions of the human transition to agriculture.

Hunting and gathering supplemented agriculture and horticulture to a greater extent than in Neolithic and post-Neolithic Europe and the Middle East, even after the introduction and intensification of maize, both in the nutritional basis of Native American diets and in the ways that indigenous societies, settlements and chiefdoms were structured within their wider ecological environments. A broad range of relatively nutritious plants, above and beyond domesticated maize, was often available to supplement animal products—even as far north as Alaska. To avoid emphasizing one subsistence strategy over the other, it is most accurate to highlight the hybrid between the two: a relationship between horticultural and hunting practices that provided energy-dense plants where necessary, and a gradual rather than unsustainable population increase; without abandoning more nutrient-dense plants that were gathered, or animals that could be hunted and fished; and creating living circumstances where disease pandemics were less likely, even while diseases certainly existed.[222]

In some postcontact contexts, as we shall see, a reversion to hunting animals at the expense of plant horticulture represented a Native American response to suddenly degraded agricultural lands, or the need to supply new European markets for animal furs. In other postcontact regions, conversely, the abandonment of hunting practices in favor of year-round maize consumption tended to reflect the loss of hunting lands to colonizers and the settlement of shattered communities in sedentary zones. Both these examples erroneously influenced European perceptions, and have often provided an imbalanced account in historical narratives that describe precontact subsistence as either dominated by hunting and gathering or by the cultivation of bean, squash and maize plants. A hybrid between hunting-gathering and agriculture or horticulture enabled Native Americans to avoid the problematic consequences of maize intensification, as initially experienced in communities such as Cahokia during the precontact era. It also avoided the problematic consequences of overhunting, as eventually experienced by some postcontact communities.

Having uncovered myriad micronutrient-dense hybrid subsistence frameworks in this chapter, we are well positioned to consider the deleterious immunological consequences of their subsequent curtailment. European disruption of indigenous nutritional frameworks was too sudden to allow the societal adaptations that Neolithic Europeans eventually adopted to mitigate against the nutrient-poor status of grains, or the adaptive hybrid between hunted animals and cultivated plants that preceded and then continued alongside the intensification of maize in many precontact Native American communities.

Chapter 3

MICRONUTRIENTS AND IMMUNITY IN NATIVE AMERICA, 1492–1750

Populations in Europe, Native America and elsewhere mitigated or adapted to the negative consequences of agricultural intensification over time, allowing demographic growth despite initially suboptimal health effects. This chapter shows how declining access to micronutrients after extended European contact made Native American communities less likely to recover from infectious epidemics in the medium to long term, and may also have threatened working immunity before infection—as distinct from epidemics elsewhere in the world, where demography restabilized after around a century, thanks in part to contingent nutritional improvements.

There is a risk in using the conceptual distinction between Paleolithic hunter-gatherers and Neolithic agriculturalists to understand changing Native American health outcomes after European contact. The link between negative Native American responses to European domesticated farming and the problematic health patterns associated with Neolithic agriculture must not be emphasized too specifically; not least because the latter occurred between 8,000 and 10,000 years prior to the Native American encounter with colonial-European agriculture. Such a link also risks constructing an overly reductive formula focused on Native Americans as engaged in perfectly sustainable land management (overlooking, for instance, the role of land burning, overhunting and the potential negative consequences of the indigenous move toward maize long before colonization).

But although the move toward agriculture in Native America took place in a separate region and era from that in Europe, the methodological approach to understanding health outcomes in both contexts is broadly similar. Europeans eventually developed an increased level of immunity to some of the diseases that proliferated in sedentary agricultural contexts. They also improved sanitation and supplemented nutrient-poor grains with nutrient-dense foods, including domesticated animals. Native American subsistence strategies prevented the problematic health effects of agricultural intensification from becoming chronic or pan-regional. The continued synergy between hunting and gathering, horticulture and agriculture provided nutrient mixtures that we can now identify as vital for optimal immune function. It also relied on buffer zones around sedentary plant cultivation regions. Seasonal hunting rather than permanent human settlement was encouraged in those zones, preventing movements of humans and animals from spreading diseases pan-regionally, zoonotically or otherwise.

Understanding these complex interactions allows us to view the subsequent era of disruption in new ways. We define the notion of contact in regionally and temporally specific ways, noting that instances of colonial disruption and demographic decline took place in a different era in Alaska and California than it did in the Southwest or the Northern Atlantic coast, and that nutritional degradation lasted for decades and centuries, preventing demographic recovery in the long term—rather than requiring our focus on immediate population decline as a sole marker of biological exchange. Whether we examine the literature of contact in Florida after the protohistoric era in the American Southeast, the American Southwest and the Atlantic Northeast during the seventeenth century; in Alaska during the eighteenth and nineteenth centuries; or in California during the early-nineteenth century, we can see how contingent nutritional factors allowed immunity to be strengthened or weakened as different indigenous communities struggled to maintain their subsistence strategies.

If we can detect a decline in health and immunity among precontact Native American communities that moved away from their ancestral nutritional traditions, as we noted in the previous chapter, it seems reasonable to apply a similar hypothesis to the postcontact era, when those traditions were uprooted to a far greater extent—whether in relation to hunted animal proteins and fats or in relation to indigenous plant sources. It is often suggested that precontact "baseline malnutrition" left Native Americans vulnerable to disease after the arrival of Europeans. Yet our synthesis has found evidence of diverse nutritional strategies that were less reliant on nutrient-poor staples, such as maize, than once assumed. Though population numbers in many communities were static immediately before contact, or even slightly decreasing, these phenomena tended to reflect a self-sustaining demographic balance. Many regions, as we have seen, had developed subsistence templates that incorporated nutrient-dense foods, even if they offered less readily available energy for expanding populations.[1]

It bears repeating that even the most nutritionally dense subsistence strategies could not have prevented much of the initial mortality that followed the proliferation of the deadliest new diseases, such as smallpox. Though we do not eschew the potential role of peak nutrition in allowing *some* community members to strengthen their immunity and to survive debilitating infectious diseases from their first occurrence, we avoid the more radical notion that nutrition could have prevented most losses in the short term, during the first periodic epidemics. Rather, we consider how the deprivation of nutrient diversity compromised immunity among affected communities in the medium to long term, over a century or more, suggesting a modified periodization for the epidemiological effects of disease on the population of colonized communities.

If even a small percentage of affected populations were directly compromised by ruptured micronutrient access, that would likely have affected demographic stability in the medium to long term. Using the latest scientific studies to frame our new historical synthesis, we show in the greatest possible detail how nutrition might have compromised immunity and fertility among those who faced secondary infections, or infections by other less deadly diseases, at a time when their communities could not afford any further losses, either to survivors of previous epidemics or to new generations. As scholars have begun to note, after all, a small percentage population decline per year over a century of colonial disruption is enough to reach demographic collapse.[2] Thus we define the curtailment of subsistence strategies as a fundamental marker to explain a fall in population that should be measured in decades and even centuries, rather than merely measuring the relative occurrence of major disease epidemics in the short term.

We are careful to signpost those nutritional disruptions that were severe and sudden enough to directly compromise immunity, based on our synthesis of historical evidence and the secondary literature on contact history, and our earlier synthesis of precontact nutritional strategies. We are particularly concerned to highlight the sudden diminishment of food sources that had been central to indigenous nutritional complexes, which provided certain micronutrients that other foods did not, and then to define the immunological importance of those corresponding micronutrients, isolated from other nutrients, using modern peer-reviewed scientific data. Doing so allows us to distinguish between direct and indirect immunological importance, synthesizing and integrating scientific and historical literatures to differentiate between strongly supported speculation and broader conjecture. If either the scientific or historical literatures are less direct for any particular case study or immunological paradigm, we flag our discussion as one that provides useful speculation, rather than one that engages in stronger speculation which is corroborated by several mutually reinforcing interpretative frameworks.

Beyond Virgin Soils: Nutrition as a Primary Contingent Factor in Demographic Loss

Whether we choose to follow the highest or the lowest scholarly estimates, figures for the decline of Native American populations in the several generations after the sixteenth century are stark. Based on work carried out in the 1930s, Kroeber's assessment of the precontact indigenous North American population suggested a number around 900,000, which was relatively unaffected by disease thereafter. Dobyns, using new scholarly methods in Native American demography, significantly modified Kroeber's analysis and suggested a population of around 18 million before European contact, eventually decimated by 95 percent in just a few decades.[3] New diseases, introduced by germs, spores and parasites from European and African sources, are most often linked to such a drastic population decline. They included smallpox, measles, influenza, bubonic plague, diphtheria, typhus, cholera, scarlet fever, trachoma, whooping cough, chicken pox and tropical malaria.[4] More recently, a partial consensus on demographic figures has been achieved. While noting that precontact North America was not disease free, and that warfare, violence and ethnocultural competition could curtail exponential population growth, scholars have suggested that disease decimated populations that had stood at around 2,360,000 before contact, but which declined between 1500 and 2000, in direct contrast to European, African and Asian populations on the same continent.[5] According to the most widely used recent estimate by Ubelaker for all-cause mortality among North Americans from the contact era to the present, the proportion stands at around 80 percent.[6]

Notwithstanding continued debates over exact population estimates, since the 1970s the conceptual model of a "virgin soil" epidemic has remained popular in our understanding of Native American demographic decline after European contact. Among historians and anthropologists, the term "virgin soil" has been traditionally used to define those populations "lacking previous exposure to a particular pathogen, such as variola major (smallpox)," while among epidemiologists the term has more narrowly referred to populations "in which an organism has not been present for many years, if ever."[7] Dobyns examined Native Americans as a "virgin population of susceptible individuals lacking immunities." Cockburn similarly suggested that the steep demographic decline of Native Americans after European contact represented "the typical reaction of a 'herd' to a pathogen not previously exposed."[8] Crosby's seminal definition in 1976 defined "virgin soil epidemics" as "those in which the populations at risk have had no previous contact with the diseases that strike them and are therefore immunologically almost defenseless." These and other assessments, as Jones has noted, continue to suggest some sort of "racial susceptibility" among Natives Americans during the period of contact—a lack of inherited resistance to specific pathogens that predisposed them to demographic destruction simply by virtue of contact.[9]

We certainly do not discount the broad insights provided by scholars of the "biological exchange," such as Crosby and Cronon, who have highlighted the unsettling consequences when plants, pathogens and animals invaded various ecological settings in North America in the centuries after 1492. Crosby's seminal discussions of European "ecological imperialism" following the "Columbian exchange" moved beyond the trope of the "ecological Indian" by suggesting that Native Americans had indeed altered their ecological environment through farming, hunting and subsistence strategies—including strategies that led to the domestication of plants that would eventually appear for the first time on the eastern side of the Atlantic; and strategies that (perhaps) led to the overhunting of large mammals during the Pleistocene era, around 13,000 years ago. Early overhunting, and subsequent farming and hunting practices, according to Crosby, created ecological niches—such as the consumption of deer, buffalo and maize—that would be filtered by Europeans into their own broader market economies.[10]

Yet a conceptual problem can be detected in such an influential analytical framework. Focusing on the necessary construction of niches, within ecologically determined contexts, risks reducing the role of human agency in the environment, so that, as Fisher has suggested, "while Indians were certainly portrayed as environmental actors [in Crosby's narrative, as distinct from antimodern romanticism], they, like the weedy European invaders, came across as just one more organism struggling to exploit ecological niches." Similar critiques have been used to question Diamond's influential and popular work on the fate of peoples in their environment, including Native Americans before and after European contact.[11] The discussion of niches risks paving a path of environmental determinism, reducing the role—and culpability—of European colonization in facilitating the demographic decline that followed the spread of new pathogens in North America. Diseases are described in abstract and inevitable terms, separate from the contingent human choices and actions that prevented any recovery from them in time. As environments—rather than humans—are said to have determined niches, then new biological frameworks (such as diseases) are often described in similarly deterministic ways.

In response to the problem of determinism, therefore, scholars have begun to reexamine many of the case studies that once supported the "virgin soil" thesis, including those that have extrapolated analytical models from the Caribbean and South America to North America. In doing so, they have highlighted the role of contextual contingency rather than biological immutability. They have questioned the received narrative of causation by altering our understanding of periodization.

During the conquest of Peru, for example, resistance to the Spanish lasted many decades, ebbing and flowing, while demographic decline was associated more closely with contextual constraints on population recovery and fertility than with immediate "virgin soil" epidemics. The protracted rather than immediate population decline of indigenous peoples in the Inca Empire has made scholars rethink causal accounts, as well as periodization, in understanding indigenous demography elsewhere in postcontact areas of the New World.[12] In Peru and Central America, as Newson has shown, the percentage of people in communities who died from diseases during the same period of contact varied greatly according to living conditions and regional context.[13] A more nuanced assessment of Taino and Arawak demography in Hispaniola and the surrounding Caribbean islands after the arrival of Columbus in 1492 tells a similar story. Disease epidemics became more likely to spread among populations that suffered political, social and cultural disruption—a sudden descent into physical labor that accompanied new policies enacted by Nicolás de Ovando y Cáceres more than a decade after Christopher Columbus's first arrival.[14]

Conditional historical circumstances, as distinct from immediate and inherent biological differences, may also explain similar delays in the decline of populations in mainland North America during the so-called Protohistoric period of European contact. Spanish expeditions in the Southeast included those of Juan Ponce de León (1513), Lucas Vázquez de Ayllón (1526), Pánfilo de Narváez (1528), Hernando de Soto (1539–43), Tristán de Luna y Arellano (1559–61) and Juan Pardo (1566–68). They also led to the first permanent settlement of St. Augustine, Florida, in 1565, and to the construction of a network of missions from Georgia to western Florida. It is erroneous to suggest that these expeditions ignited disease epidemics, which somehow cleared the way for subsequent generations of colonizers, including the English.[15] It is more likely that a combination of common bacterial infections, food poisoning and pathogens spread by unsanitary conditions contributed to the death of Cofitachequi peoples following the move of De Ayllón's settlers from Hispaniola to present-day South Carolina in 1526—conditions that reflected the contingent nature of settlement rather than discrete and immutable biological conditions, as suggested by proponents of the "virgin soil" thesis.[16] Diseases such as dysentery, associated with poor sanitation, proliferated as the Spanish began living among pigs and other animals near to settlements. Their effects were slow to develop, and eventually spread among indigenous villages that had previously separated horticulture from animal hunting outside their sphere. Spanish settlers defecated in and around waters where indigenous people had gathered oysters and other marine organisms for subsistence— food sources that are known to retain dysentery-related pathogens despite their nutrient density.[17]

Although Spanish expeditions in the Southwest began in the 1540s, disease epidemics can only be detected from the late 1630s. A century of contact, therefore, preceded what were once described as "virgin soil" epidemics.[18]

Evidence for the abandonment of communities more likely related to nonepidemiological causes, including the growth of the slave trade to Spanish settlements.[19] We can find a similar story in the Northeast Atlantic region following Dutch, French and English attempts to open colonial settlements in the region between 1616 and 1619, before concentrated European settlement. The disease epidemic that destroyed Native American communities near the islands off Massachusetts Bay in 1616, it is often claimed, made Massasoit and Wampanoag people less confident in their ability to withstand or even repel larger numbers of English settlers, who began arriving in the region from the late 1620s.[20] Yet even where seventeenth-century North American epidemics resulted in high Native American mortality rates, such as those between 1616 and 1619, they tended to be localized and serial, determined by contingencies of circumstance rather than interregionally pandemic.[21]

Demographic difficulties suffered by the earliest European settlers in Virginia provide further evidence that contingent circumstances, rather than innate immunity, were likely key to the health and survival of communities, including Native Americans. Regional distinctions in the rate of death or survival among white English settlers demonstrate that the proliferation of population-destroying diseases resulted from poor sanitation, problematic living circumstances, malnutrition, and the inability or refusal to adapt to new environmental contexts. They also reflected demographic imbalances that were caused by human decisions, such as those to prevent female labor migration—all distinct from biologically determined factors within organisms. As Morgan has shown, more than 50 percent of the population of white settlers in Virginia died in a place where context mattered, beyond inherited immunities or Old World heritage. The debilitating effects of malaria among white, predominantly male, Virginia settlers during the early decades of the seventeenth century show how malnutrition combined with poor living conditions within an environment that required adaptation rather than the series of errors that ensued. It came to be hosted in malnourished and physically overworked individuals who lived in saltwater-freshwater boundary zones. In those zones, people and animals defecated near the same mosquito-infested water from which they bathed and drank. Malaria, like yellow fever, bubonic plague and typhus, were all zoonotic diseases, requiring animals, insects and ticks, and thus all contingent on the relative behavior of individuals and their living contexts.[22]

In his well-known early twentieth-century assessment of Native American susceptibility to tuberculosis, Hrdlirka rejected the theory of "greater racial susceptibility" in favor of "other conditions" that might have predisposed postcontact communities to higher rates of infection and suboptimal immunity—contingent factors that may have included nutritional degradation.[23] In a more recent assessment, by an immunologist, several Native American tribes were shown to mount "normal immune responses to measles, and against vaccines for measles, mumps, rubella, polio, yellow fever, pneumonia and bacterial meningitis."[24]

Thus, we stress the role of contingency, rather than immutable biology, in the historical functioning of human immunity in general, and Native American immunity more specifically. The most commonly used scholarly estimate for eighteenth-century Native American demography suggests a decline from 1.4 million in 1700 to 1.0 million in 1800. Such a drop coincided with the increase of the African and European population in North America from 250,000 to 5.3 million because of higher birthrates and migration.[25] But the two populations only met in number in around 1750, before the rapid rise in European migration during the second half of the eighteenth century. The increasingly disruptive context of colonialism provided the framework for the slow and steady decline of indigenous communities, which were unable to adapt to or recover from diseases in the medium to long term.[26]

As Jones has summarized, epidemics that killed so many in such a short time "would be dramatic and unprecedented, something that would require remarkable explanations. But substantial losses over the course of a century [or even more] would not require a special mechanism. A population that loses just 2–3 percent annually will, by the end of a century, have experienced a 90 percent decline."[27] "Disrupted subsistence" strategies accompanied the "simultaneous introduction of new pathogens" in ways that likely "increased mortality because of the synergistic effects of widespread illness." Demographic decline did not require innately differing genetics among virgin soil communities, because any "factor that causes mental or physical stress— displacement, warfare, drought, destruction of crops, soil depletion, overwork, slavery, malnutrition, social and economic chaos—can increase susceptibility to disease"—beyond biologically determined distinctions in the ability to fight off pathogens.[28] As Kelton has argued in his work on the Southeast, "the non epidemiological aspects of colonialism had to transform the lives of Natives before they became vulnerable to regionwide outbreaks [...] the disease com- ponent of the Columbian Exchange was a mediated process in which the larger aspects of colonialism heightened Native vulnerability to infection and mortality. In other words, epidemics and massive death tolls among indi- genous peoples occurred not simply due to their virginity to European—and African—introduced germs. Colonialism created conditions in which many new diseases could spread and in which those diseases produced extremely high fatality rates."[29]

In his work on virgin soil epidemics, Crosby was more willing to take contingent factors into account than subsequent readings of his work have suggested. Crosby describes the eventual point when the "fire goes out and the cold creeps in; the sick, whom a bit of food and a cup of water might save, die of hunger and the dehydration of fever; the seed remains above the ground as the best season for planting passes, or there is no one well enough to harvest the crop before the frost." Such a description highlights the potential for adaptation to new disease contexts—through nutrition, farming or better living conditions—that was thwarted by colonial disruption in the medium to long term.[30]

Several other scholars include subsistence and nutrition, often in general reference, as a contingent factor, countering the biological determinism of the "virgin soil" paradigm. According to Larsen, the emphasis on disease in the biological exchange thesis "has overshadowed a host of other important consequences of contact such as population relocation, forced labor, dietary change, and other areas."[31] Meister similarly notes that "later population decline resulting from disease was made possible because Indians had been driven from their land and robbed of their other resources [including hunted animals and cultivated crops]."[32] According to Anderson, "before long, the expansion of livestock-based agriculture ceased being a model for Indian improvement and instead served almost exclusively as a pretext for conquest, a very different expression of the cultural impact of distinct farming practices" among Europeans and Native Americans in eastern North America from the 1600s.[33] As Kunitz has pointed out in a discussion of the paleoepidemiology of southwestern Native American communities following European colonization, "one does not need to invoke large-scale dramatic epidemics; prosaic entities like malnutrition [...] are more than sufficient to do the job [in demographic collapse]."[34]

Though it remains difficult to address the direct triggers for final mortality, Thornton has assessed much evidence on the history of Plains Native Americans in the two centuries after contact, for example, and concluded that their "mortality and fertility" were severely impacted "when the great herds of buffalo were destroyed" by European agricultural patterns, Native American overhunting in response to curtailed nutritional sources and open warfare. Other scholars concur that an association can be drawn between worsening health; the declining ability to hunt, gather and cultivate; and a new reliance on European agricultural production as animals on the Great Plains came to be overhunted.[35]

We can build on the scholarly insights above, and our earlier synthesis of precontact subsistence history, to begin to think about the role of nutrition more specifically in postcontact population instability. Native American demography was negatively affected by a relatively sudden mismatch between long-evolved food consumption frameworks and newer European agricultural methods. As an important contingent factor, disrupted subsistence exacerbated the spread of diseases that Native American communities were already struggling to fight due to their impaired immunity. Health and demographic outcomes associated with the function of biological immunity are contingent on historical context, not least in relation to the protection or destruction of long-evolved nutritional building blocks that underlie human immunity in the first place.

New Ways to Approach the Link between Nutrition and Immunity

Let us examine how nutritional differences between susceptible and less susceptible populations ought to be considered in discussing the history of Native American immunological health. We should begin by synthesizing the literature on the link between nutrition and immunity more generally—a link that has been exposed, startlingly, only recently. The association between nutrition and immunity would seem to be obvious—even axiomatic—given that most human immune cells reside in the gut; that the immune system requires many nutrients from a diverse diet to function optimally; and that suboptimal nutrition risks affecting a chronically inflammatory state in and beyond the gut, to the detriment of working immunity.[36] Yet these links have rarely been drawn together in the scientific literature, let alone in historical and anthropological studies of population health. Before the last half-century, as Scrimshaw and Shetty have shown, "the relationship between nutrition and infection was unrecognized except for limited reference to tuberculosis," so that with "only minor exceptions, the textbooks on nutrition made no reference to infection, and those on infectious disease were similarly lacking mention of nutrition."[37]

Research on the interaction between nutrition and immunity was pioneered by Scrimshaw, who noted in 1959 that "many of the important infections of human populations are rendered more serious in their consequences by the presence of malnutrition."[38] Only in the last two or three decades, in fact, has "cell-mediated immunity, its complex control by cytokines and the contribution of immunoglobulins to resistance to infections" begun to enter discussions of nutritional health, allowing us to consider how various aspects of immune function are affected by even mild malnutrition.[39] Deficiencies in overall energy intake and in several micronutrients are associated with poorer disease outcomes and with increased mortality.[40] We now know that infectious disease can often exacerbate original deficiencies, leading to a vicious cycle of malnutrition and infection.[41] According to Chandra, scholars ought to consider how "nutritional deficiency is commonly associated with impaired immune responses, particularly cell-mediated immunity, phagocyte function, cytokine production, secretory antibody response, antibody affinity and the complement system."[42] Protein energy malnutrition and micronutrient deficiencies also seem to have far-reaching effects on immunity.[43]

Notwithstanding our growing understanding of the link between nutrition and immunity, the literature on the specific mortality outcomes of malnourished or undernourished communities that encounter infectious diseases remains ambiguous, and even inconclusive, possibly because scholars who have attended to the potential link between infectious disease and nutrition have most often focused on the historical occurrence of smallpox—a disease so deadly that variations in nutritional status fail to distinguish between affected populations. Smallpox, as Riley has summarized, "was the leading cause of death in eighteenth century Europe, accounting for between five and ten percent of all deaths [...] [and] was more devastating still in the New World. In Europe, smallpox slowed population growth. In the Americas, it was the chief factor in the depopulation of the American Indians."[44] According to Riley, then, the hypothesis that malnutrition would have affected the immunity of the Native Americans to smallpox is confounded by the deadly nature of the disease, irrespective of population dynamics.[45] Research on the twentieth-century history of smallpox in India has considered the hypothesis that nutritional status may have affected host resistance, but has not found conclusive evidence.[46]

Moreover, it is not clear whether malnourishment has been defined according to the diminishment of calories in general (metabolic energy) or micronutrients more specifically (nutritional density).[47] Some researchers have suggested that postcontact Native Americans suffered from protein energy malnutrition, which affected their immunity against smallpox.[48] Yet more research is needed to test this hypothesis.[49] Other contingent factors ought to be brought into these assessments, including those that are associated with disrupted subsistence, but that can be distinguished from the internal biology of immunity in individuals. Population movements that spread smallpox more widely, for example, may have followed routes of individuals searching for nutritional diversity after colonial disruption.[50]

It is less problematic to link nutrition and immunity to general demographic stress following primary epidemics than to suggest that such a link might have predisposed communities to suffer from initial outbreaks (although we do not discount such a possibility). Rather than solely focusing on the role of immunity in preventing disease outbreaks such as smallpox, it is just as important to assess how and why communities were likely to suffer from what ought to have been less deadly pathogens, or how they were prevented from recovering their population numbers over subsequent decades and even centuries—whether in the wake of deadly epidemics, less unforgiving diseases or even weaker secondary infections. Understanding the link between nutrition and immunity provides a key framework to understand these different factors and their broader periodization, beyond initial contact.

Let us therefore turn to the immunological importance of micronutrients in plants and animals, to consider how disruption to their consumption following European colonization became so problematic for Native American demography, beginning with Florida and the Southeast, before moving to other regions.

Nutritional Degradation and Compromised Immunity in Postcontact Florida: Understanding the Effects of Iron, Protein and B-12 Deficiencies

The sixteenth-century entry of Spanish explorers and early missions into Florida and the Southeast is often described as the "Protohistoric" era of the European-Native American encounter—a period of inchoate European settlement, before the disruption that later followed. Protohistoric European settlement patterns, to be sure, disrupted Native American living circumstances, including nutritional strategies, making individuals more susceptible to bacterial diseases that were already present in their environment, but which had been less likely to flourish.[51] Yet Protohistoric European interventions were too geographically isolated to herald the shattering of indigenous life—including indigenous subsistence strategies—which remained largely intact. During the sixteenth century, at least, the scale of disruption was too small. As shown in archaeological work carried out near present-day St. Augustine, mammals, birds and marine animals continued to be consumed, and significant demographic decline was not witnessed.[52] Rather, those conditional circumstances that impacted health and immunity offer a portent of that which would become far more prevalent during the subsequent historical era of European colonization in the Southeast, the Southwest and elsewhere.[53]

Consider the distinction between sixteenth-century Spanish exploration in Florida and the consolidation of European agriculture in Spanish missions a century later. The region provides some of the richest bioarchaeological assessments of disease, which we can synthesize with new historical insights about the contexts that prevented the consumption of immunologically important sources of protein, iron and vitamin B-12 from the Protohistoric period to the historic mission era. Such a synthesis provides a convincing framework to explain the contingent link between nutrition and immunity in other similar historical case studies that might lack confirming bioarchaeological evidence.

Jesuit and Franciscan Spanish missionaries were first founded in the coastal Carolinas, in what is now present-day Georgia, and in the Florida peninsula.

The founding of St. Augustine as the first permanent Spanish settlement in La Florida in 1565 allowed the establishment and coordination of missions in four regional centers: Guale, along coastal Georgia; Timucua, east of the Aucilla River in Florida; Apalachee, between the Aucilla and Ochlockonne Rivers; and Apalachicola, on the river of the same name.[54] Yet massive Native American depopulation was not evident for more than two generations after their construction. Localized diseases were associated with the pollution of marine waters, where shellfish and other foods were harvested. But they never amounted to "virgin soil" epidemics as defined in the scholarly literature for other regions and contexts.[55]

Only by the seventeenth century, as settlements such as St. Augustine became more frequently visited by ships from ports such as Havana and Seville, and as their inhabitants fanned out across indigenous buffer zones to encounter people such as the Apalachees, the Guales and the Timucuas, often through Catholic missionary activities, did communities become devastated by disease. The smallpox epidemic in northeast Florida in the 1650s was the worst culprit.[56] Most European accounts from the Protohistoric era in southern Florida noted the deserted nature of buffer zones such as those between the Ochlockonee and Apalachee Rivers. The transfer of diseases into major epidemics was therefore relatively limited before extended European contact, suggesting that changed contexts after colonization made the spread of diseases—including smallpox—so extensive and so difficult for eventual demographic recovery to occur. The ability to isolate settlements from epidemics was eventually lost as semi-independent chiefdoms were shattered by war, slavery and new markets. They were consolidated in ways that prevented the implementation of appropriate disease responses—including by reducing access to indigenous nutritional frameworks.[57]

Following the Protohistoric era, as examinations of dental evidence and the stable isotope ratios of carbon and nitrogen in skeletal material have shown, "native populations in La Florida quite likely experienced dramatic changes in diet, changes that were probably not for the better and may have contributed to the decline of these populations."[58] These changes help explain the gradual weakening of immunological health, which preceded the arrival of pandemics, but which also prevented communities from recovering numbers during the following century.[59] The Native American diet in regions around Florida missions became less diverse and nutritious, as individuals relied more on the primary staple of maize rather than wild game or fish, whose hunting and fishing was restricted by new European enclosures and settlements.[60] In addition to their religious duties, the latter added the coordination of Native American labor conscription for maize cultivation—at the expense of other forms of plant horticulture, hunting and gathering.[61]

More specifically, declining access to hunted animal products likely increased protein and iron deficiency in populations that sought to recover from initial epidemics. Those epidemics need not have precluded communities from eventual demographic recovery, if external circumstances had allowed gradual adaptations. Bioarchaeological investigations suggest that rates of iron deficiency and anemia appeared among missionized Native American communities in Florida and other parts of the Southeast to a far greater extent than among those that did not live among Spanish missions.[62] Recent work on the importance of iron and protein for working immunity allows us to flesh out the notion that secondary infections and lesser diseases heightened mortality among survivors of communal epidemics, as well as their offspring, contributing to the eventual demographic nadir of affected communities.[63]

A high incidence of anemia may indicate an attempt to fight off infectious disease, at a point when a variety of nutrients were required to facilitate that process. It is unlikely that a concentration on maize consumption, as experienced among those Native Americans who lived in mission communities, would have provided those nutrients.[64] Evidence of iron deficiency through skeletal analysis can be linked to infection by disease in two related ways. Decreased iron in the blood may signal a defense against pathogens, demonstrating the occurrence of new diseases in the community (decreasing iron being a biochemical response to the increased activity of immune cells). In studies on contemporary populations, moreover, low iron values have been linked to chronic inflammation, the biological state in which the immune response is continually stimulated, potentially degrading the acute immune response required to fight off invading pathogens.[65]

Protein energy malnutrition is associated with a markedly decreased immune response. While the effects are usually caused by an inadequate overall energy intake, including a lack of protein, the state can also derive from a diet of sufficient calorie intake (usually from carbohydrate) but insufficient protein. Since proteins are required for the formation of enzymes that affect all aspects of cell function, including DNA synthesis and the manufacture of structural cellular components, protein deficiency has far-reaching effects on immunity.[66] In children with protein energy malnutrition, the lymphoid organs undergo several changes, indicative of changes in the immune system: the spleen, thymus, gut-associated lymphoid tissue, tonsils and adenoids all appear smaller and have an associated reduction in lymph cells, and the number of circulating lymphocytes is also often reduced.[67] All of these changes likely lead to prolonged infections and poorer outcomes.[68] A number of mice studies have demonstrated an association between protein malnutrition and diminished immunity. Though the immune system of mice is not identical to the immune system of human beings, these processes should at least remind us of the distinct possibility that a sudden turn to low-protein diets among many Native American communities—particularly those that moved toward maize consumption above all other nutritional sources—likely compromised the immunological health of individuals as they sought to recover population numbers in areas such as the Guale mission region.[69]

Studies of the effects of iron deficiency are complicated by the fact that it does not usually occur in isolation. Iron, after all, is often present alongside protein in animal products—including those whose availability was threatened by European contact. Animal meat, such as deer, contains haem iron in myo-globin and haemoglobin, which is absorbed efficiently in the gut.[70] Non-haem iron, which can be found in salts, metalloproteins and contaminants in plant sources, is less readily absorbed. Polyphenols in vegetables and grains, and phytates in grains, moreover, can actually inhibit iron absorption.[71] Additional complications in determining the effect of iron status on immunity arise from the iron-depleting nature of some infections, making it hard to disentangle cause from effect.[72]

Nonetheless, it is worth considering the potential link between iron and immunity. Among communities prevented from hunting animals, such as those around Florida missions during the seventeenth century, declining con-sumption of haem iron may have compromised their immunity. It is a catalyst in several different processes in the body, including those related to the growth of new immune cells.[73] Iron deficiency results in compromised immunity through a variety of mechanisms, separate from those related to protein and other deficiencies. It is associated with decreased cell-mediated immunity, par-ticularly in pregnant woman and children.[74] In one study, fewer circulating T cells, which are necessary for the immune response, was correlated with chil-dren suffering from iron deficiency. The number of cells were increased with subsequent iron repletion.[75] Iron deficiency has been shown to affect antibody production in rats, an effect that may also occur in humans, given the relative similarity of the immune systems of different mammalian species.[76] Several other effects have been noted in studies of iron deficiency, including changes in the behavior of macrophages, natural killer cells and impaired interleukin-2 production by T lymphocytes. Interleukin-2 is a protein that is central to the inflammatory response, which in turn upregulates the immune response. White blood cells, which are vital for immunity, also tend to be reduced in association with decreased iron serum levels.[77]

In diets that tended toward greater intensification of maize, or experienced other forms of nutritional degradation, an increase in gastrointestinal infections and diarrheal disease followed the move toward greater popula-tion density, sedentism and refuse accumulation. Those infections may also have been exacerbated by disruptions to the balance of different species of symbiotic and parasitic bacteria residing in the gut, caused by nutritional deficiencies or food allergens in grains and other newly introduced food products. These infections, in turn, may have depleted micronutrients due to immune activity, without then being replenished. The immune response following infection, after all, is known to decrease plasma levels of vitamin B12, vitamin D, iron, DHA and other micronutrients, compromising immunity even further in a negative loop.[78]

The metabolic state during infection, furthermore, becomes perturbed by increased production of the stress hormone cortisol, as well as insulin, upregulating the conversion of protein to glucose (gluconeogenesis) and protein catabolism to provide extra amino acids and glucose for energy.[79] This process may lead to protein energy malnutrition even when access to protein is sufficient. In infections that are not immediately associated with the gut or digestive tracts, moreover, gastrointestinal function is still known to become affected, potentially leading to poor absorption of macronutrients, micronutrients, water and electrolytes. Among Native American communities facing the contiguous threats of new diseases, the concentration of familiar diseases and nutritional degradation, infections exacerbated nutritional deficiencies by decreasing nutrient absorption even further, making secondary infections more likely. Vitamin B-12 deficiency, after all, is thought to have contributed to cribra orbitalia in skeletal samples from Amelia Island, Florida, and St. Catherine's Island, Georgia. Increased occurrence of gastrointestinal infections and diarrheal disease due to increased population density, sedentism and refuse accumulation, as well as an increase in maize consumption over animal consumption, likely caused such a phenomenon.[80]

The immune response of Native Americans in Spanish Florida missions may also have become perturbed by chronically raised blood sugar following sudden intensification of insulinogenic maize consumption. Declining access to anti-inflammatory nutrients such as DHA (a form of omega-3 fatty acid) may have exacerbated such a situation. DHA, recent studies have suggested, is strongly linked to the development of optimal insulin sensitivity (the efficiency at which glucose is necessarily removed from the blood following the consumption of carbohydrates).[81] Isotopic analysis demonstrates a decline in anti-inflammatory DHA fatty acids from marine food sources in Florida missions such as Guale by the seventeenth century.[82]

European domesticated animals certainly became available as a supplementary food source around Spanish missions. But their potential to provide micronutrients for immunological health seems to have been negatively offset by their encouragement of zoonotic diseases, due to their proximity to rivers, lakes and dwellings.[83] In missions that surrounded maize cultivation fields and maize storage facilities, animal pens also appeared nearby, most often to supply European tables.[84] Archaeological examinations of the seventeenth-century San Martin de Ayaocuto mission site among the Timucua in north-central Florida has revealed refuse pits near the mission church and convento in the native village as well as agricultural materials. Evidence of pig consumption alongside wild animal products demonstrates that animal husbandry came closer to sedentary settlements during the latter part of the Protohistoric period, increasing the attendant risk of disease. On the Georgia coast, mission sites demonstrate declining venison consumption in favor of European-introduced domesticated animals, likely residing relatively close to European and indigenous dwellings.[85] Even in the Protohistoric period, livestock associated with the de Soto expedition in the region (1539–43)—particularly pigs—were periodically attacked, with the suggestion that they were somehow linked to degraded living circumstances. Though Spanish horses were later readily adopted by Native Americans elsewhere in North America, even those animals were met with suspicion during the second half of the sixteenth century and through the historic era in Florida.[86]

In the latter part of the Protohistoric period, and during the early historical era, unsustainable population loss in Florida thus became contingent in part on the gradual disruption of subsistence strategies and nutritional diversity, at just the moment when mission settlements became more concentrated and movements between them became more frequent. Colonial disruption increased the proliferation of diseases. Those who suffered from those diseases required the best nutritional frameworks for a strong immune response—a requirement that was not often met. The creation of deleterious colonial contexts after the Protohistoric period provided the circumstances for disease to flourish in the medium term rather than in the short term, diminishing the notional effects of biological immediacy associated with narratives centering on lightning-speed pathogenic invasions.

Nutritional Degradation and Immunity in the Postcontact Southeast: Framing Deficiencies in Zinc, Magnesium and Multiple Vitamins

Smallpox was a deadly epidemic, with higher than 40 percent mortality rates in some Southeastern communities by the early eighteenth century. Scholars once emphasized the interconnected nature of precontact chiefdoms in the region and suggested that they provided ideal circumstances for the spread of the disease, given its relatively long incubation period in subjects and its ability to remain biologically active on inanimate objects. Yet as we have seen, precontact Southeastern chiefdoms were far more self-sufficient and self-enclosed than once thought. Populations relied on animals from rivers and lakes, and gathered or cultivated plants from specified sedentary zones. They hunted land animals outside their own jurisdiction, but generally remained separate and dispersed from the hunting grounds used by other chiefdoms. The distribution and trade of surplus foods and other goods tended to take place on ceremonial rather than regular occasions. Tributes within chiefdoms do not seem to have been obligatory. The trade in exotic materials, such as seashells from the Gulf of Mexico, gave status to chiefs precisely because the trade that brought them to communities was not regular.[87]

Yet the semiautonomy and deliberate ecological isolation of Southeastern chiefdoms waned as the region from the Mississippi Valley to the Atlantic became one of many "shatter zones" in postcontact North America. From the 1640s, English commerce from Virginia into the Atlantic world began to incorporate Native Americans in the Southeast. They consumed, or were pressured into consuming, munitions, clothing, animals and alcohol from around 1650.[88] The practice of English settlers in Virginia and the Carolinas buying Native American enslaved people likely began formally in 1659, when Native slavers armed with English guns raided communities along the Savannah River, including in the Spanish mission system.[89] Several chiefdoms in the region formed what have been described as "paramount" unions, where smaller settlements confederated to facilitate trade or defensive activities. Disruptions allowed new indigenous leaders to assume authority as they sought to steady the chaos. They were not always successful, resulting in new disorder and new concentrations of defensive settlements.[90]

By the 1660s, the legal status of Native American enslaved people was situated between that of white indentured servants and imported enslaved Africans. But as was so often the case, legal definitions tended to give way to the effects of brute power or economic exigency, making the lives of enslaved Native Americans less contingent on constitutional definitions of liberty and more affected by the economic desires of particular settlers.[91] Exchange networks expanded from around 1686, when English settlements in South Carolina—themselves an offshoot of Caribbean settlement and trade in the Barbados islands—began to trade with interior Mississippi communities, allowing diseases to be transmitted across hitherto separate boundaries.[92] By the early eighteenth century, more than one-quarter of enslaved people in the Southeast were Native American.[93] As diverse people trying to survive upheaval, they formed the large confederacies we know today, notably the Cherokee and Creek unions. Their formation turned on the English decision to trade guns to various perceived allies, leading to raids as far south as Georgia and Florida by the early eighteenth century.[94]

If we view, and even reframe, these shatter narratives from the perspective of subsistence and nutrition, we can see how the destabilization of indigenous food systems and the destruction of ecological buffer zones was central to the slow—but steady—demographic decline in the Southeast. We have seen that newly introduced diseases decimated European populations during the Black Death, yet did not necessarily result in their demographic destruction in the long term, as defined by outcomes measured after a century. Similar demographic recovery failed to occur in the Southeast after the first century of extended European contact, in part because of nutritional degradation among individuals who were already suffering from the sudden concentration of diseases in shattered societal frameworks. In precontact Mississippian cultures that experienced the greatest intensification of maize agriculture, such as the Dickson Mounds in lower Illinois, immunological health was compromised in the most nucleated communities, as distinct from those that remained more dispersed and less reliant on maize. Diseases flourished due to changed living circumstances, but also because the nutritional profile of communities became less diverse; less able to provide the various micronutrients and macronutrients that aid strong immunity.[95] Throughout the Southeast after extended contact, these phenomena were again apparent. But by this point, they became pan-regional and chronic. And unlike during the previous era, they were not mitigated by any attendant rise in births.

During the first three decades of the seventeenth century, the early wars between Powhatan peoples and English settlers in the Chesapeake Bay region often turned on the trade and storage of maize, corroborating work from other periods and global contexts that suggests a link between storable grains and increased violent competition over its circulation and protection.[96] As English settlers began to disrupt Powhatan subsistence strategies, their communities became more likely to rely on maize as a nutritional source in sedentary defensive settlements. English settlers thus perceived the Native American reliance on maize as more deeply rooted than it in fact was, leading the settlers to expand its role as a market commodity. Relations between English and Powhatan communities soured further as market relations and prices were manipulated by both sides, and as the price of maize fluctuated according to other commodities, including copper and enslaved Native Americans. The English ignored trade treaties and agreements, as Native Americans were forced to rely on the commodity for calories, notwithstanding its nutrient-poor status.[97] Individuals in previously isolated chiefdoms, protected from widespread epidemics by buffer zones, were forced to live in newly concentrated settlements for protection, and to allow reproductive-age men and women to find partners during a period of demographic disruption.[98] Yet in doing so, more people were grouped closely together in sedentary contexts whose nutritional profile compromised immunity and fertility, even before we take into account the greater potential for disease proliferation due to population density.[99]

Greater fortification during the eighteenth century required the further abandonment of seasonal hunting and indigenous subsistence strategies and greater reliance on stored maize. New European animal husbandry techniques allowed diseases to spread more easily, at just the point when nutrient diversity decreased along with immunological health.[100] Slave trade networks became increasingly bound up with other newly defined commodities, particularly deer skin. Hunting expeditions for food became even less frequent, diminishing the opportunity for otherwise sedentary communities to gain nutritional supplementation from animal products—even while deer were slaughtered for skin more than ever before.[101]

The role of European-introduced guns among Native Americans in these exchanges was highly ambiguous and unpredictable. They held an important psychological effect in their perceived ability to protect communities from Europeans or other Native Americans who might be allied with them as raiders. Yet their circulation also reflected a desire to maintain a nutritional advantage in the ability to access hunting animals. As it became evident that European wars and settlement patterns threatened hunting habitats, some communities realized that guns could allow greater efficiency and higher yields to mitigate these otherwise restricted circumstances.[102]

The 1715 Yamasee War at least formally ended the Native American slave trade in the Southeast. Yet a nutritional perspective helps explain why population numbers continued to decline in the following century, accounting for the steady demographic contraction that was so deadly in the long term. Nutritional networks and subsistence strategies were both irrevocably disrupted by the slave trade and allied commodity trades during the previous half-century, and could not simply be reconstructed after the war. Though slavery ostensibly ended in the region, buffer zones were no longer managed as hunting zones, preventing a resurgence of the hybrid between agriculture, horticulture and wild animal nutrition.[103]

More specifically, the sudden decrease in wild animal consumption, coupled with greater reliance on maize as a staple energy source, likely compromised immunity by causing protein, iron and B-12 deficiency. In addition to these deficiencies, which we have already examined in our discussion of Florida settlements, it is worth highlighting other specific micronutrients that were curtailed in Southeastern shatter zones. Decreasing consumption of less well-known micronutrients and minerals also likely affected health, fertility and immune system function, heightening susceptibility to disease and increasing mortality rates among infants and parents. The move away from hunted meats toward grains or toward a reliance on lean muscle meats from newly domesticated European cattle likely compromised immunity through deficiencies in zinc, magnesium, vitamin A, vitamin D, vitamin K2 and iodine; important amino acids such as glutamine; and fatty acids such as DHA. Their deficiency is strongly correlated with poorer outcomes of infectious disease in contemporary studies, allowing us to envision similar problems among Southeastern communities following the Protohistoric era.[104]

Zinc is found in meat and fish, and is particularly apparent in the liver of ruminant animals such as deer as well as in oysters. The latter, as we saw in the previous chapter, were central to the nutritional strategies of many coastal Southeastern communities before contact. Indeed, oysters provide more zinc, proportional to volume consumed, than any other food.[105] Plant sources of zinc are less well absorbed. The mineral is found in maize, for example, but phytates and other anti-nutrients present in the plant inhibit its absorption. Even if zinc remained in the diet of Native Americans thanks to animal consumption, therefore, increasing volumes of maize may have minimized its efficacy.[106]

Zinc's central roles in metabolism, cell synthesis and cell division make its important role for immune cell function unsurprising.[107] It is also required to maintain the integrity of the skin and the epithelial layers in the respiratory and gastrointestinal tract, thereby aiding the body's first line of defense against pathogens. It is required for the activation and differentiation of T lymphocytes, the differentiation of B lymphocytes and for the function of neutrophil and macrophage immune cells.[108] Recent trials have shown that supplementation with zinc reduces incidence of diarrhea, respiratory infections and other diseases as well as decreases the severity of symptoms.[109] Individuals suffering from tuberculosis, pneumonia and other diseases are often deficient in zinc. Several studies have shown a correlation between zinc deficiency and respiratory and diarrheal diseases and infections.[110] Zinc is required for the release of vitamin A from the liver, and so its deficiency may lead to some of the same effects on immunity as deficiency of vitamin A.[111] The curtailment of zinc consumption, therefore, would have been deleterious among individuals in Southeastern communities who required a strong immune response to disease, or among survivors of primary epidemics who wished to avoid secondary infections and thus rebuild demographic strength in the medium to long term.

Vitamin A is immunologically vital on its own terms, separate from its synergy with zinc. According to Scrimshaw, "no nutritional deficiency is more consistently synergistic with infectious disease than vitamin A."[112] The vitamin is supplied by biologically active retinoids such as retinol palmitate, both of which are found in animal foods such as animal liver, eggs and marine oils, whose consumption diminished in the Southeast in favor of vitamin A-deficient maize. First, it is required to maintain epithelial integrity, thereby helping prevent the invasion of pathogens through barriers such as the gut and respiratory tract.[113] Low levels of the vitamin are associated with decreased mucus production in epithelial linings and the loss of cilia.[114] Due to decreased mucus and cilia, pathogens are more likely to adhere to the epithelial tissues and subsequently establish an infection, rather than being cleared.[115] Secondly, vitamin A is required for the innate immune response and the adaptive immune response following any possible infection. It affects cell differentiation and cell proliferation by influencing gene expression. Both those processes are central in the immune response because gene expression is rapidly altered before and as a precursor to the formation of new immune cells. Vitamin A binds to retinoic acid and retinoid receptors in the cell nucleus, and causes transcription of target genes.[116] Moreover, the production and differentiation of T and B cells as part of the adaptive response depends on vitamin A status.[117] In the innate response, vitamin A deficiency affects the functions of several immune cell types, including natural killer cells, macrophages and neutrophils.[118] Many studies have thus concluded that adequate vitamin A decreases risk of the contraction of diarrhea, malaria and measles, respiratory disease, and chronic ear infections, and decreases overall mortality from several infectious diseases.[119]

The precursor carotenoids to vitamin A, including alpha-carotene, beta-carotene and beta-cryptoxanthin, are contained in plant and animal sources. Cleavage of their molecules occurs in the small intestine and liver, to release the active form.[120] However, the conversion factor for carotenoids has been estimated from a range of studies to be 26:1 from vegetable sources and 12:1 from fruits. Thus, the curtailment of animal sources for the vitamin would have been particularly problematic for Southeastern communities during the era of colonial disruption.[121]

The consumption of several essential amino acids, most commonly obtained from animal products, was likely curtailed by colonial disruption in the Southeast. They are increasingly thought to be linked to sound working immunity and the reduction of chronic inflammatory symptoms—both necessary in populations under stress from invading pathogens. Glutamine, for example, is a conditionally essential amino acid that is required for the optimal function of lymphocytes, macrophages and neutrophils as well as lymphoid organs. The enzyme glutaminase, which converts glutamine into the biologically useful form glutamate, is present in all these immune cells.[122] During sepsis and injury, plasma glutamine levels become lowered, likely a result of increased demand by the immune system, liver, kidney and gut in response to the injury. Providing supplementary glutamine to patients following various treatments for infection, as well as among those who have received new organs or bone marrow, has been shown to decrease further risk of infection. These studies have therefore concluded that glutamine may often be a limiting factor in immune function. Its role in reducing secondary infections is particularly important when we recall the need to focus on the ability of affected populations to recover from primary epidemics rather than merely examine their initial population losses without reference to potential demographic recovery in the medium to long term.[123]

In addition to the potential immunological effects of curtailed animal products in the Southeast, it is important to remind ourselves that the region incorporated a rich tapestry of plant agriculture and horticulture during the precontact era, which also contributed to the nutritional building blocks for working immunity. After the Protohistoric era, conversely, Native American farming and plant-gathering practices were increasingly defined by English settlers as public acts on public lands, allowing them to move into those zones with jurisdictional impunity. Even the Virginia Grand Assembly noted the perceived subjugation of Native American land and food resources in these activities, while failing to act to prevent them in any meaningful way. In November 1652 the Assembly met and passed an act highlighting "Complaints" that had "been brought to this Assemblye touching wrong done to the Indians in takeinge away theire lands, fforceinge them into such narrow Streights, and places That they Cannot Subsit, Either by plantinge, or hunting."[124] As English livestock threatened existing agricultural settlements and hunting lands, and encouraged zoonotic pathogens, the growth of tobacco monoculture further enclosed and shut out buffer zones, indigenous agriculture and long-established horticultural spaces.[125] By the eighteenth century, matrilineally focused horticulturalists such as the Cherokee lost further ground as pathogenic stressors required all the building blocks for immunity—including nutritional diversity—to be in place.[126] The nutrients found in the leafy greens, beans and squash that were marginalized by English settlers included magnesium; folate; zinc; antioxidants; vitamins A, C and E; bioflavonoids; and phytochemicals.[127] Antioxidants and vitamins, particularly vitamin C, are well known to be vital for immune function and for protection against chronic diseases. Let us therefore consider the potential effects of their curtailment in more detail.[128]

Oxidative stress, as described in Chapter 1, is decreased by dietary antioxidants such as vitamin E, vitamin C, beta-carotene, selenium, copper and flavonoids. Their consumption in leafy plants, berries and fruits has been suggested to improve immune function and the response to pathogens, and to reduce chronic inflammation.[129] It is known, after all, that the immune response involves the production of oxidizing molecules, including superoxide radicals and hydrogen peroxide, by immune cells such as macrophages and neutrophils, intended to aid in destruction of invading pathogens.[130]

Accumulation of these oxidizing molecules can result in damage to host immune cells and thereby adversely affect their function.[131] To prevent such damage from occurring, mechanisms have evolved to prevent the accumulation of oxidizing molecules, which involve activity by enzymes such as glutathione peroxidase, and antioxidants, which can prevent or inhibit oxidation by neutralizing oxidizing molecules.[132] Dietary antioxidants have a particularly important role in preventing the accumulation of oxidizing molecules, and thereby preserving the function of immune cells.[133] It is thought that deficiency in antioxidants adversely influences the cytokine profile of T cells, and has been suggested to allow increased virulence of viruses through alterations in the viral genome.[134]

Much scientific work has focused on the antioxidant capacity of vitamin C, which protects against oxidative damage in immune cells.[135] Vitamin C can neutralize oxidants secreted by phagocyte immune cells to prevent tissue damage because of the immune response.[136] Vitamin C is found in a huge array of plant sources, particularly in fresh fruits and vegetables, though storage and high heat are thought to damage the bioavailability of the vitamin. It affects immune function by several mechanisms, including the regulation of gene expression in immune T cells, stimulation of inflammatory cytokine production, stimulation of neutrophil immune cell activity and antibody synthesis.[137] Some studies have found evidence of an anti-inflammatory effect, though further research is needed to determine the role of vitamin C in this regard. Two recent meta-analyses found small benefits of vitamin C supplementation in protecting against infection, including a "50% reduction in risk of developing a cold" in one epidemiological study.[138] Some studies have even suggested beneficial effects of vitamin C supplementation in infections of *H.pylori*, *Herpes simplex* and other maladies.[139] Specifically, studies have shown that supplementation improves the proliferation and antimicrobial activity of several types of immune cells.[140]

Vitamin E is an antioxidant that has an important role in preventing peroxidation (oxidative damage) of lipids in the cell membrane and thereby maintaining the integrity of immune cell membranes.[141] Consequently, vitamin E has been shown to improve immune functions in several ways, including increasing the activity of natural killer cells and macrophages, cytokine production and mediated responses.[142] Supplementation with vitamin E has been shown to reduce the incidence of respiratory tract infections in the elderly and to decrease the duration of common colds.[143]

Selenium has also been shown to decrease oxidative damage of immune cells.[144] Consequently, it is thought to increase proliferation of immune cells, improve natural killer cell function and modulate the Th1/Th2 response.[145] Selenium has been shown to protect against hepatitis B and hepatitis C infections.[146] Though we have already discussed many benefits of zinc, it is worth underlining its contribution to antioxidant activity in immune cells.[147] Beta-carotene and other carotenoids can enhance immune function through antioxidant activity independently from their role as a vitamin A precursor.[148] Beta-carotene has been shown to increase natural killer cell activity.[149] The antioxidant activity of copper has also been shown to be important for immune function. Deficiency of copper decreases neutrophil numbers and phagocytotic activities, which increases host susceptibility to infection.[150] One study has shown that copper supplementation reduced the incidents of respiratory tract infections in malnourished infants.[151]

Though magnesium can be found in animal sources, particularly in the brains of ruminant animals, its constituency in plant sources is important to note, as it was likely the most common source of the mineral in indigenous North American communities before European contact. Magnesium, after all, is present at high levels in sunflower, pumpkin and squash seeds, beans and green vegetables—all foods that were consumed readily following the development of Mississippian plant cultures in the centuries before colonization, but which became less accessible as more land was cultivated by Europeans. Indigenous communities in the Southeast moved from point of contact toward the Great Plains and elsewhere, losing traditional horticultural and plant-gathering patterns as they did so, including as an important means to supply nutritional magnesium.[152] The mineral is recognized to have a central role in human well-being, affecting cardiovascular, neurological and immunological health. It is synergistic with the fat-soluble vitamins A and D, and so its deficiency is likely to affect health even further alongside their restriction, particularly in relation to the maintenance of robust immunity.[153] Magnesium is vital during pregnancy, reducing the risk of complications such as preeclampsia and preterm birth. Both would have been particularly problematic in Native American communities that were trying to rebuild their demography after disease epidemics.[154] Diminished access to magnesium is thus likely to have exacerbated the decline in health and fertility.[155]

Through its synergistic role with vitamin D, indeed, magnesium is known to affect skeletal health. Recent research thus shows a strong link between magnesium deficiency and osteoporosis.[156] Females may suffer from poor pelvic development, which can have serious implications for childbearing. Due to their profound role in skeletal health, we also hypothesize that deficiencies of magnesium and fat-soluble vitamins may affect the growth and vitality of children. Children without sufficient vitamin D, for example, may develop serious disorders such as rickets.[157] Diminished access to magnesium, then, likely exacerbated the decline in health and fertility following the exchange of infectious diseases after contact and contributed to problematic skeletal markers that recall the effects of maize intensification in precontact history. Even if such a phenomenon only affected a few individuals enough to make a difference to birth outcomes, such an association becomes relevant when scaled up over decades.

Curtailed access to nutrient-dense plants and animals in favor of maize thus became a key contingent factor in compromising immunity and fertility, and in hastening demographic decline, among the indigenous communities of the Southeast. Yet some neighboring populations could maintain a degree of separation from English trade and settlement, including its increased focus on maize, either through choice or conditional circumstance. In either context, their relative demographic stability in comparison to other communities further demonstrates the role of contingency, rather than immutable biology, in the ability to withstand epidemics—particularly in their ability to maintain indigenous nutritional frameworks. The Choctaws, for example, who were often separated by forests, became raiders rather than victims, and relied on a hybrid between plant horticulture, agriculture and hunting animals to a far greater extent than their neighbors.[158] Some Cherokees and Creeks were more protected than those such as the Pee Dees, Cape Fears, Santees, Winyaws, Cusabos and Etiwans. They suffered greatly from diseases such as smallpox, malaria and typhus as their societal contexts shattered, including their subsistence strategies.[159]

Those who suffered most in the Southeast witnessed the degradation of lands that might have provided mixed subsistence strategies, combining hunted animals on their outskirts and plants cultivated at their center. New markets inspired European settlers to focus on monocultured cash crops, most notably tobacco and maize, at the expense of these mixed uses. Native American subsistence strategies were compromised at just the point when their populations ought to have strengthened their immunity and increased their fertility, in order to recover demographically from diseases that had been present for more than a century.

As white colonial Americans increasingly attached their conception of liberty to the free settlement of western lands—whether in conflict with French forces during the Seven Years War or with British Redcoats during the American Revolution—Native Americans lost further control of their cultural and societal autonomy in the Southeast. In the Declaration of Independence of the United States, patriots defined their own liberty in distinction to tyrannous British attempts to support Native Americans ("savages") on the frontier. Thus, the move from unity with Britain against France to war with the British state encompassed a degree of continuity in the continued expression of American liberty at the expense of Native American landed autonomy, including in relation to indigenous subsistence strategies in the Great Plains.[160]

Having opposed the British for restricting their movements into south-eastern Native American lands during the imperial crisis, newly emboldened American patriots flooded into inland Native American zones, destroying what remained of the ecological balance between sedentary agriculture and hunting across buffer zones. One observer noted of Albermarle County in the Virginia Piedmont at the end of the eighteenth century, "a scene of desolation that baffles description—farm after farm [...] worn out, washed and gullied, so that scarcely an acre could be found [...] fit for cultivation." Indigenous subsistence and nutrition continued to be curtailed—a contingent factor that slowed demographic recovery following the earlier effects of epidemics and pandemics, and which can also be understood in light of the latest literature on the relationship between micronutrients and immunity.[161]

Nutritional Degradation in the Postcontact Southwest, the Great Plains and the Great Basin: Essential Amino Acids, Folate and the Contingent Threat to Demographic Recovery

The shattering of societal frameworks in the Southwest, the Great Plains and the Great Basin followed a similar pattern to the Southeast, with regional nuances. Nutritional degradation and serious demographic decline followed the first prolonged contact with Europeans, rather than during the initial encounters of the protohistoric period. A hybrid between agriculture, horti-culture, and hunting and gathering was shattered by new markets, rivalries, crop systems and an increasing demand for enslaved people. These histor-ical disruptions provide a framework to reveal the role of micronutrient con-sumption as a key contingent factor in immunity and fertility. Having already highlighted the specific importance of iron, protein, B-12, antioxidants, amino acids and myriad other vitamins and minerals from plants and animals, it is not necessary to return to them in this section, notwithstanding their obvious role in many of the nutritional frameworks that were threatened in the Southwest. Rather, we highlight the role of several other important micronutrients, not-ably folate. Extrapolating evidence from modern experimental data, we define their likely contribution to demographic growth and, conversely, the prob-lematic consequences of their restriction among populations that sought to recover their birthrate to counter the effects of disease epidemics. Once again, we expand the causal definition of demographic decline to focus on those contingent nutritional factors that may have prevented population recovery as well as prior immunity.

Following Juan de Oñate y Salazar's 1598 entry into the Rio Grande Valley, indigenous land use patterns were disrupted, as large tracts were taken and guarded by Spanish soldiers and encomenderos.[162] Rather than immediately altering the dietary frameworks of Native Americans in the region, Protohistoric Spanish entradas into the Southwest heralded gradual nutritional depriv-ation, while immediately encouraging isolated instances of zoonotic disease. Spanish missions contributed to these phenomena by constructing European-style fields and agricultural settlements near friaries and churches, often using forced Native American labor.[163] Spanish friars pressured Pueblo commu-nities, including through force, to stay in Pueblos all year round, rupturing deeply rooted migratory patterns that had allowed dispersed hunting and gathering during the summer and more sedentary occupation in the winter.[164] Situating communities in the same space throughout the entire year disrupted hybrid subsistence strategies and required inhabitants to cultivate maize more intensely and to consume it more regularly.[165] Paleoethnobotanical and archaeological data has suggested a relatively sudden increase in maize con-sumption through the disruptions of the seventeenth century, when other more nutritionally diverse sources that had once supplemented maize were restricted.[166]

These disruptions to subsistence provide an often overlooked context to understand the disharmony that characterized the move toward the historic era, preceding the 1680 Pueblo Revolt in which 400 Spanish settlers were killed near present-day Santa Fe, New Mexico. Through the seventeenth cen-tury, and certainly by the revolt, indigenous nutritional health had decreased in ways that likely reduced immunity in the face of disease. Once again, we note communities becoming more sedentary and less reliant on nutrient-diverse and nutrient-dense foods.[167] Skeletal evidence demonstrates that peri-odontal disease and caries rates increased in these contexts, particularly among the Gran Quivira and the Pecos. Those whose deaths preceded the increase in maize consumption show less decay and less isotopic evidence of maize substrates.[168] The decline in nutrient diversity and density, moreover, was con-tiguous with the increasing concentration of people in sedentary defensive settlements, just as in the Southeast.[169]

Long before European contact, as we have seen, Ancient Pueblo communi-ties of the Southwest responded to the depletion of wild game among maize cultivators by developing turkey farming systems. Maize allowed populations to increase due to the sheer volume of calories provided, yet required nutri-tional supplementation with animal products. Sustaining those requirements from larger game became untenable given the population increase that had been fueled by maize intensification, leading southwestern communities to domesticate birds such as turkeys to mitigate against dietary deficiencies from maize that "lowered fertility, increased infant mortality, and made everyone susceptible to infectious disease."[170] Before the Pueblo Revolt against Spanish authority in 1680, and through the eighteenth century, turkey rearing and consumption declined, without any attendant increase in nutrient availability from other animals.[171]

As well as supplying vitamin B-12, iron and protein, turkey products likely provided precontact communities in the Southwest with arginine. Found in the turkey meat and pumpkin seeds that were popular on the eve of European contact, the amino acid's importance for growth, injury recovery and immunity is often overlooked.[172] In fact, the synthesis of nitric oxide by macrophage immune cells—a central process in the working immune system—depends on arginine. Nitric oxide is involved in regulating formation of various proteins involved in the recognition of specific pathogenic molecules and in the destruction of host cells infected with pathogens.[173] Arginine also affects the immune response through increasing the secretion of hormones such as prolactin and insulin-like growth factor 1 (IGF-1). Supplementation with the amino acid has been shown to improve immune function in patients suffering from a range of conditions. A recent meta-analysis found that infections were reduced and several measures of immune function improved with arginine supplementation.[174] That which had once mitigated maize's nutrient-poor status—turkey—became less apparent as the grain's intensification accompanied the arrival of new diseases. Here we note yet another contingency that may have contributed to demographic decline.

The potential effects of other amino acids on immune function can be discussed in similar ways. Methionine and cysteine, for example, are amino acids that are found in the wild game that was restricted in many sedentary communities. They are required for the synthesis of glutathione and taurine, which in turn act as antioxidants to neutralize reactive oxidizing molecules produced during the immune response. Glutathione has been shown to increase the activity and numbers of several immune cells and to increase cytokine secretion (necessary for the temporary inflammatory response associated with an acute immune reaction, rather than leading to chronic inflammation and autoimmunity).[175] A recent study has even shown that glutathione is vital in the activity of natural killer cells in fighting mycobacterium tuberculosis in vitro.[176]

Deficiencies in the amino acid glycine may have been similarly problematic for populations that faced pressures from infectious diseases, or that sought to recover from epidemics to restore population numbers. Glycine, which would have been obtained from organ meats that were prized by many Native American hunter-gatherers, likely decreased due to disrupted hunts and diminished access to full animal carcasses following European colonization. Glycine has recently been suggested to be a semi-essential amino acid. Analysis of metabolic pathways indicates that the body may not be able to synthesize adequate amounts of the amino acid to maintain long-term health, and that inadequate glycine consumption may lead to premature aging and suboptimal health. It is thought that pregnant women may suffer from glycine deficiency if inadequate glycine is consumed in the diet, due to the demands placed by the growing fetus. Given the requirement of glycine for immune function, expectant mothers in Native American shatter zones, including in parts of the Southwest, likely suffered further decreased immunity as sources for the amino acid were curtailed.[177]

That arginine (and other amino acids) was present in sunflower seeds should remind us that indigenous communities in the Southwest, like most precontact Native Americans, rarely relied solely on animal fats and proteins as a nutritional source. Across North America, as we have seen, the gathering and consumption of plants began earlier than 8,500 years ago, including forms of land management that we can comfortably describe as gardening or even horticulture. Native Americans in the Southwest increased their consumption of maize to counteract calorie deficits following their diminished access to hunted animals after European colonization. But they also sought to fill the nutritional gap created by the loss of nonmaize plant sources, which they had gathered and cultivated for centuries. In the Southwest, as Adams and Fish have summarized, these plant products included yucca, beargrass, acorns, piñon nuts, juniper berries, and manzanita and sumac berries. Lowland areas provided mesquite pods, walnuts, wild grapes, cattails and various edible cactus and cactus flower sources.[178] Populations in the region thus resented European agriculture because it was associated with zoonotic diseases and because it disrupted seasonal hunting of meat and fish. But as elsewhere in North America, they also perceived the imposition of European farming as a physical and ecological disruption to their gathering—and cultivating—seeds, tubers, plants and acorns, especially from spring to fall, separate from the consumption of maize.

Let us consider one example, which is particularly pertinent to the Southwest, but which may also apply to other regions: the potential costs to immunological health and fertility after female-centered bean cultivation declined in favor of maize intensification or increasing concentration on women's roles in skinning animals for sale to colonial markets.

Contingent market forces shattered the gendered subsistence strategies of Osage communities between the Mississippi and the Great Plains, who numbered around 10,000 people in 1700. Thanks to newly introduced European horses and guns, Osage men could slaughter animals for skins and fur in increasingly high numbers. Osage women, as a result, were required to decrease their diverse agricultural activities in favor of skinning and processing the animals for sale to new colonial markets. Female-centered Osage agriculture and horticulture, which focused on beans, squash and myriad other plants, in addition to maize, thus declined through the eighteenth century. The supply of nutritious plant products such as beans to their community waned, as did the supply of those products to those further afield who wished to supplement their nutritional profile.[179]

The cultivation and consumption of beans was also compromised by the presence of European livestock in the Southwest. Native Americans in the region became suspicious of European settlers whose ranches and farms threatened plant gathering and horticultural practices, including their gathering mesquite pods and growing beans.[180] Spanish cattle threatened bean patches and mesquite trees by grazing them continuously, as distinct from swift migrations of buffalo that tended to leave the plants intact or bypass them entirely.[181]

It is particularly pertinent to focus on declining bean consumption because it may have reduced the availability of folate in communities whose unstable demography required solid fertility to enable population recovery in the medium to long term. Though folate is most available in the liver of ruminant animals, beans also provide a good plant source of what is known more formally as pteroylglutamate, and often referred to as vitamin B9. When fertility and demography were already ravaged by infectious diseases among some communities in the Southwest, the ability to recover population numbers during the eighteenth century may have been threatened by a reduction in folate among women of childbearing age. In addition to minerals such as magnesium, zinc and iron, folate is known to be important for fetal development and maternal health during pregnancy. Folate is required for early embryonic development and the maturation of important cells in the ovary.[182] Folate deficiency is a well-known cause of neural tube defects, and low maternal folate levels may increase risk of spontaneous abortion (miscarriage). Lack of folate during pregnancy is correlated with other complications including low birth weight, placental abruption, fetal growth retardation and preeclampsia.[183] Some studies have also highlighted the importance of folate in male fertility.[184] Thus, a decrease in the consumption of beans, squash and other fresh vegetables at the expense of less folate-rich calorie sources could be expected to have had a large impact on the health of the population through effects on fertility, maternal health during pregnancy and child development (both during fetal growth and during subsequent breastfeeding and weaning).

The contingent importance of folate during periods of demographic stress is further illustrated by research among those who suffer from genetic mutations such as C677T in the gene methylenetetrahydrofolate reductase (MTHFR), which is prevalent among many different human populations, including among Native Americans, and which has been associated with effects on health such as increased rates of miscarriage. The enzyme MTHFR plays a vital role in the human methylation cycle, which requires the conversion of folate into more usable forms to synthesize signaling molecules, support embryo development and remove toxins or heavy metals from the body. If these processes are reduced through mutations in methylation pathways, levels of intercellular folate become insufficient, making its ready consumption potentially more vital.[185] Those who are homozygous holders of the mutation thus require far more folate to offset the enzyme's reduced ability to convert it to usable form at the outset.[186] Having familiarized ourselves with the role of such enzymatic activity, including the role of folate in facilitating bodily detoxification through methylation pathways, we can form the following hypothesis: reduced folate intake from plants such as beans would have diminished the ability of postcontact Native Americans—particularly women of childbearing age—to respond through reproduction to demographic pressures caused by disease.

With these discussions of compromised fertility and infant health in mind, it is also worth recalling our discussion of the potential compromise to infant immunity in agricultural societies, in comparison to hunter-gathering or more traditional horticultural contexts, because of early weaning onto foods such as wheat and maize. Such a comparison informs another important working hypothesis: the potential nutrient deficiencies outlined in this chapter may well have compromised the nutritional status of breast milk and reduced the term of breastfeeding altogether. If Native American hunting and gathering practices were disrupted by European interventions, both physically and culturally, their nutritional degradation likely reduced the quality of breast milk, while also encouraging earlier weaning on poorer nutritional sources such as maize and wheat, which are easily ground into pastes that infants without teeth can consume. Because of these related phenomena, infant immunity may well have suffered, further raising susceptibility to infectious diseases in communities that sought to recover from earlier pandemics.[187]

To be sure, the restriction of micronutrients from plants and animals was not uniformly experienced in the Southwest and in the Great Plains. As in the case of the Southeastern Choctaws, some populations experienced relative demographic stability, or even population growth, in comparison to other regional communities. Their experience hinged on the maintenance of indigenous nutritional frameworks, or even the expansion of animal consumption to mitigate the loss of those frameworks—contingencies of the colonial era, rather than aspects of immutable biology. After the Pueblo Revolt, for example, Hidatsa, Mandan and a few Pueblo communities began to use and breed Spanish horses to protect themselves, but also to hunt more widely and provide greater nutritional supplementation after the degradations of the previous century. However, they were less successful than communities such as the Apaches, as well as peoples who lived in or moved to the Great Plains and became part of the Cheyenne, Navajo and Comanche nations. The extended hunting zone of those who took advantage of horses and guns allowed their expansion during the period of European colonization, while other groups suffered demographic losses. Algonquian groups in the Northwest Plains, for example, interacted with other tribes that had adopted Spanish horses to hunt for new food sources, to some success.[188] In the medium term, similarly, Comanche communities were particularly successful in generating nutrient density from animal products, while remaining geographically isolated from sites of epidemics in more sedentary zones.[189] The relative demographic success of the Comanche and others further highlights the role of contingency and cultural context, particularly with regard to nutritional resources, rather than innate or inherited immunity, in determining the fate of indigenous peoples.[190]

Previously horticultural Cheyenne communities entered the Plains during the early eighteenth century, coming to rely on hunted buffalo and bison. Some Siouan and Caddoan horticulturalists also switched to horse-nomadic hunting-gathering practices after their traditional forms of plant cultivation and hunting were threatened by the disruptive forces of independent American settlers streaming into the region as well as by new Native American populations fleeing the same population movements. Pawnee groups, as well as some Hidatsas on the upper Missouri, moved toward horse-mounted nomadism. In most of these cases, as Snow has pointed out, "people were not just responding to the attraction of nomadic hunting. There were by this time [after 1700] also strong direct and indirect pressures from the east, brought on by European settlement and expansion."[191]

Yet the introduction of horses and guns set up disruptive social forces that would further diminish the hybrid between agriculture and hunting-gathering systems in various populations on the Great Plains. Some communities abandoned subsistence strategies to hunt more widely or to raid slaves themselves. Others suffered losses from slave raids and disease, and formed defensive sedentary settlements without reconfiguring earlier subsistence strategies.[192] Having reached such a high volume by the end of the seventeenth century, the demand for enslaved people and animal skins across the Great Plains saw networks of nutritional exchange transform into separate rival producers of captive labor and animal skin products for European markets.[193] As they hunted more widely, and less seasonally, Osage and Comanche communities disrupted other groups that sought to maintain their hybrid between seasonal agriculture and hunting and gathering. Wichita and Caddo peoples had previously used trade networks to supplement their own food economies and to provide more nutrient diversity. By the late eighteenth century, their nutrient diverse trade networks were disrupted, their seasonal hunting and gathering patterns were ruptured, and their ecological frameworks were replaced by a shattering slave-raiding impetus.[194]

As American settlement continued to move west of the Appalachian Mountains, moreover, migration routes often bisected hunting grounds. Disease epidemics became more likely as buffer zones broke down and as indigenous peoples were more prone to live in concentrated sedentary communities. Following the American Revolution, concentrated population settlements formed in the American West, as Native Americans were displaced, dispersed or forcibly removed due to the expansion of American settlers following independence from Britain. From the 1760s to the 1790s, indigenous peoples experienced an extension and intensification of their earlier disruption. Native American communities that lived east of the Mississippi River and west of the Appalachian Mountains suffered because of growing American settlement and political power.[195]

Among those who had initially prospered demographically due to increased hunting capability, the mortality rate from the 1780 smallpox epidemic is not sufficient to explain the eventual population decline of Native Americans in the Great Plains, when groups such as the Comanche began to experience levels of population loss that had hitherto been associated with horticultural communities in the region. Although all Plains communities were affected by the 1780 smallpox epidemic, as Ostler has pointed out, "horticultural people, living in relatively densely populated towns and villages, were hit especially hard."[196] They had increasingly focused on the cultivation of maize, above other plants and hunted animals, in a disrupted context that required defensive settlements. Those settlements, unfortunately, allowed the quicker movement of disease and encouraged a nutrient-poor diet—another case study that suggests the link between nutrition, societal context and immunity. Plummeting population numbers required contingent factors—including the likely association between disrupted subsistence and lowered immunological function—to become chronic and irreversible. Those such as the Comanche, who had prospered demographically before the American Revolutionary era, faced increasing difficulties, as American settlers expressed their vision of liberty at cross-purposes with indigenous land sovereignty over the following half-century.[197] Between 1780 and 1820, over the course of merely two generations, it is estimated that the Comanche population dropped by over 50 percent to around 20,000—a reversal of their fortunes after initial contact, when they took advantage of the contingencies of European settlement.[198]

As Plains communities adopted ever more efficient forms of hunting, competition with European settlers in the region led to unsustainable stress on animal resources by the mid-nineteenth century. Initial health profiles, measured through average height, seemed to increase among recent Plains communities due to their new proximity to nutrient-dense bison and other animals, which they hunted with greater efficiency to counteract European Americans who did the same during the first half of the nineteenth century.[199] After the Civil War, the decline of bison increased markedly as non-Native Americans began to use large-bore rifles in ever more lethal and efficient ways. By the 1880s, the requirement to "civilize" reduced their traditional means of subsistence, after epidemics had already diminished their numbers.[200] They and others lost access to micronutrients and macronutrients from fast-diminishing populations of bison. Relative to other European settlers, indeed, their height advantage somewhat diminished. Their activities before that point demonstrated their adaptive agency during the second extended period of European contact, rather than the supposedly inevitable effects of differing immunity. Their demographic decline through the mid to late nineteenth century demonstrated the role of contingency once again. The Mandan people, along with Hidatsas, showed similar population decline during the postrevolutionary period, as increased American settlement combined with overhunting to rupture cultural and ecological norms beyond the colonial frontier.[201] Those such as the Lakotas, who continued to live in more mobile and dispersed populations, were better off than more static populations in fending off diseases during the 1780 epidemic and during subsequent epidemics.[202]

In the Great Basin, the historical synthesis between horticulture and seasonal hunting, fishing and gathering was similarly disrupted by European settlement. Horsebound communities on the Great Plains responded to European market pressures, including from as far away as South and Central America. They raided Great Basin communities, preventing their exchange of niche nutrient sources from land and aquatic animals and plants such as grass seeds and pine nuts. Given the seasonal nature of many nutrient-dense plant and animal resources in the region, communities in the Great Basin required a high degree of mobility. When seasonal movement were disrupted by Euro-Americans, the decline in nutritional diversity was immediately apparent.[203] The demographically successful Utes used European horses to hunt, unlike the less successful Paiutes, who were not able to incorporate horses into their zone of influence due to a lack of grass supplies. Shoshones, similarly, achieved a comparative advantage over other groups that did not develop horse economies, allowing them to travel widely in search of salmon and pine nut resources. Their relative demographic success, despite new diseases in the region, further underscores the role of contingency and context in allowing some communities to gain a demographic advantage over others. Their nutritional diversity was less compromised than other groups, whose societal mechanisms were shattered by colonial markets, wars and slave raids.[204]

Through the eighteenth century, British colonists even encouraged the destruction of beaver populations by overhunting, to slow American expansion into the Great Basin. They sought to claim the region for their own investors by reducing its perceived attraction to other groups, whether European or Native American. Scattering into sedentary horticultural subsistence zones, rather than relying on traditional seasonal hunting expeditions, some Shoshone communities became even more vulnerable to horse-bound slave raiders. They and others declined as a population by the nineteenth century, not because of "virgin soil" epidemics but due to the gradual disruption of ecological and subsistence strategies, living contexts and the greater propensity for periodic diseases to impact individuals whose immunity was compromised by declining access to micronutrients.[205]

Nutritional Degradation in the Postcontact Northeast, New England and Iroquois Country: Zoonotic Diseases and the Interaction between Plant Micronutrients and Animal Fats

Basque, French and English fish trade expeditions in seventeenth-century North America centered on the St. Lawrence River. They eventually linked the region to the Chesapeake Bay area via the upper Potomac and lower Susquehanna Rivers, bringing Native Americans into contact with diseases associated with Spanish and English settlers and explorers farther south.[206] They disrupted aquatic food resources and seasonal hunting patterns while introducing new diseases into the region. Among the Micmac, a move to full-time and non-seasonal hunting of a few prized animals to supply European fishermen diminished the more balanced subsistence systems that had developed over previous centuries. Those systems incorporated cultivated plants as well as a far greater diversity of wild animal and plant sources than scholars once assumed. Concentrating "exclusively on the hunt," as Salisbury has shown, "they abandoned other food-producing activities of the winter months while over-killing the formerly adequate supply of fur-bearing animals."[207] Systematic overhunting of fur-producing animals was sometimes justified according to indigenous precepts, which centered on the reciprocity of animal-human relationships.[208] Nonetheless, the Micmac came to rely on outside markets for food, rather than their own subsistence mechanisms, as the arrival of European markets altered their nutritional balance and weakened the societal frameworks that underlay their food production strategies.[209]

By the second decade of the seventeenth century, other groups such as the Abenaki experienced a similar phenomenon, as "an indigenous pattern of reciprocal exchange by self-sufficient peoples was being transformed into one in which groups engaged in specialized production were dependent on outside sources for at least part of their food supplies."[210] Trade networks were increasingly oriented toward maize and fur. They brought new people into contact with the Abenaki community, whose members could no longer rely on buffer zones to separate them from pathogens in other regions. Their nutritional density, and likely their immunological health, declined at just the point when societal frameworks made their contact with new diseases more likely. Many decades after their first contact with Europeans, epidemics began to decimate their coastal settlements. Between 1616 and 1618, as English settlers such as John Smith surveyed the Northern Atlantic coastal region from Acadia and Penobscot south toward Cape Cod, they noted that those such as the Abenakis who had changed their subsistence strategies and traded more with coastal regions over the previous decade seemed to suffer most.[211]

European markets—including for enslaved Native Americans—also disrupted the subsistence strategies and nutritional profile of Iroquois communities north and west of New England, to the eventual detriment of their health, immunity and demography. Initially, the Iroquois prospered in the wake of European settlement. Their lands stretched from the Atlantic Northeast to the southern, eastern and midrange of the Great Lakes region. A series of wars fought over beaver pelt resources between 1648 and 1657 ruptured relations between indigenous people in the region.[212] By 1680, the Iroquois Confederacy was successful in interceding to control slave raids from the Great Lakes to the North Atlantic coast, and even as far as the Southeast. Yet as in other regions of North America, the transformation of confederal networks and trade zones into captivity trails through the eighteenth century ruptured their earlier role in circulating nutritional resources from one group to another, reducing food availability at just the point that numbers began to suffer from periodic disease epidemics.[213]

The steep indigenous demographic decline associated with "virgin soil" epidemics rarely occurred during the first era of contact in New England, the Atlantic Northeast and Iroquois country. Rather, communities remained partially autonomous and regionally isolated, even after these initial phases of settlement and economic integration. Communities such as the Abenaki and even the Iroquois experienced isolated epidemics, which followed an extended period of localized nutritional, ecological and societal disruption. Their experience, however, offered a model of that which would become more prevalent following mass English settlement.[214]

The disastrous demographic decline among New England and Iroquois Native Americans followed the intensification of English settlement through the seventeenth century and into the eighteenth century. In a 1583 report on the potential colonization of the eastern seaboard of North America, the English colonizer Sir George Peckham suggested, "I doo verily think that God did create lande, to the end that it shold by Culture and husbandrie, yield things necessary for mans lyfe."[215] Over the following decades of English colonization, biblical motifs described holy settlement in association with agriculture—particularly grain farming surrounded by domesticated animals.[216] Indigenous people in the region witnessed a growing mismatch between their long-evolved ecological frameworks and English cattle pens, free-grazing animals and agricultural enclosures. These new farming settlements exacerbated the spread of diseases that Native American communities were already struggling to fight off due to their impaired micronutrient status.[217] Bovine strains of tuberculosis arrived in present-day New England with European cattle, as did tuberculosis bacilli and influenza strains in swine, and the trichina worm.[218] Native Americans, according to one 1674 colonial report, thus perceived English cattle as "Unwholsom for their Bodies, filling them with sundry Diseases." Human diseases seemed to correlate with outbreaks of diseases among cattle so that as Anderson has suggested, those "who survived an initial bout of disease often emerged in a weakened state, vulnerable to subsequent ailments that would not necessarily have imperiled a healthy individual."[219]

Unsurprisingly, then, the earliest negative responses to English settlement during the seventeenth century often incorporated attacks on domesticated animal husbandry rather than against the armed men who suddenly surrounded indigenous communities. These activities continued into the latter part of the seventeenth century, when communities caught up in King Philip's War (1675–78) often "began their hostilities with plundering and destroying cattle," according to one witness. Large-scale killings of domestic animals continued throughout the war, and Native American hostility to the animals—and their owners—extended to the mutilation and torture of cows.[220] Many Native Americans in New England drew an immediate connection between their changed ecological context and the proliferation of diseases. Having lived in communities that tended to separate plant agriculture from animal nutritional sources, they suddenly found their buffer zones filled with settlers, and animals living and defecating near to the places in which they had farmed, gardened and lived.

Native Americans were aware of a phenomenon that has since been corroborated by scholars of agricultural intensification, who as we have seen, describe the spread of zoonotic diseases from animals to human beings following the relatively sudden proximity to domesticated animals and to human and animal waste in Neolithic farming societies. Such proximity has tended to increase the spread of parasitic and eventually pathogenic disease. In hunter-gatherer populations, as we have noted, frequent migrations limited the contact of individuals with human waste. In more sedentary populations, concentrated around grain production and domesticated animals, human and animal waste became more likely to contaminate drinking water. In pre-agricultural societies, zoonotic disease disproportionately affected those who encountered animals and their products during hunting and gathering. In Neolithic and post-Neolithic European and Middle Eastern societies, conversely, a greater proportion of individuals came into close contact with concentrated animal pens and therefore became more liable to infection from diseases that stemmed from their byproducts.[221] The domestication of animals, as we have noted, has historically increased the spread of zoonotic diseases including anthrax, tuberculosis and even types of influenza.[222]

These paleoarchaeological and paleoanthropological insights help us understand why Native Americans in New England were often so vehement in their immediate opposition to European agricultural models. The concentration of cattle in farms and the storage of grain in newly constructed warehouses often accompanied the growth of disease outbreaks among Native Americans from the 1500s. Assessing the imposition of domesticated agriculture by Europeans during early contact, Thornton has thus suggested that "the reasons for the relatively few infectious diseases in this [western] hemisphere [prior to European contact] surely include [...] the existence of fewer domesticated animals, from which many human diseases arise"—unlike those that later grew up due to grain storage and transit patterns, which departed from indigenous settlement models that combined hunting, gathering, horticulture and agricultural settlements surrounded by buffer zones.[223] Rather than highlighting a simple—and abstract—biological exchange of disease, then, we can point to the specific interventions of European enclosure and domesticated cattle raising, which made infectious maladies even more potent and widespread in New England.[224]

The narrative above raises further implications, beyond the issue of zoonotic disease and the greater likelihood of disease vectors in concentrated settlements: as hunting and gathering and indigenous forms of crop cultivation were disrupted by the imposition of European agriculture in New England, the curtailment of micronutrients would have weakened immunity and increased the likelihood of primary or secondary infections, even before zoonotic diseases became apparent. Throughout the seventeenth century, during the period of first prolonged contact between Native Americans and English settlers in Pennsylvania and New England, indigenous communities became aware that depasturing sheep, gathering hay and expanding maize monoculture impacted the ecology of grasses, tubers and squash as well as the wild animals that roamed among them.[225] In summer 1642, Miantonomi, Narrangansett sachem, wrote to the Montauk communities of eastern Long Island and offered an acute summary of the ways in which micronutrient diversity and subsistence strategies had been curtailed by English agricultural colonization: "For so are we all Indians as the English are, and say brother to one another; so must we be one as they are, otherwise we shall all be gone shortly, for you know our fathers had plenty of deer and skins, our plains were full of deer, as also our woods, and of turkies, and our coves full of fish and fowl. But these English having gotten our land, they with scythe cut down the grass, and with axes fell the trees; their cows and horses eat the grass, and their hogs spoil our clam banks, and we shall all be starved." Miantonomi described the role of wild animals and cultivated plants in the hybrid subsistence system that English settlers had ruptured.[226]

The specific micronutrient deficiencies that affected other regional case studies were therefore also present in New England and Iroquois country, and do not bear repeating. Nonetheless, it is worth highlighting one aspect of the contingent association between micronutrient status and immunity that we have not discussed so far: the societal and biological importance of the *interaction* between plant nutrition and animal products in the same meal. Many of the fatty acids and nutrients detailed up to this point can be found in wild animal sources, to a greater degree than in those animals raised on farms with new feed sources that alter their metabolism and biochemical constitution.[227] Plant sources were often important on their own terms, irrespective of their combination with animal fats. Still, we ought to consider recent research that has shown the extent to which some vitamins found in plants are better absorbed by humans in the presence of fats, most likely from animal products.[228] We are becoming increasingly aware that some nutrients found in plants, including essential vitamins as well fat-soluble carotenoid compounds such as lutein, lycopene and zeaxanthin, become less bioavailable if consumed in the absence of fat. As horticulture declined after contact, so therefore did the consumption of plant nutrients *in combination* with fats from animal sources, which may have increased their ability to be processed and absorbed in humans. The precursors to several vitamins are found in plants. But their absorption depends on their aggregation in lipid globules inside the intestine, where they can be enzymatically digested.[229]

Such a nutritional paradigm supports our attempt to reduce the dichotomy between indigenous hunting methods and precontact horticulture. It also allows us to understand one of the nutritional roles of animal products in New England (and elsewhere). Where climate, season and ecology permitted the consumption of calories from cultivated or foraged plants, their nutritional benefits might have been maximized through their combination with animal sources. The latter were gained from hunting practices that continued much later in Native American history than among Neolithic and post-Neolithic European populations. Thus, the susceptibility of Native Americans to European diseases may have been further amplified by their disrupted access to certain meats and fishes, as well as a diminished opportunity to consume them in combination with cultivated plants, thereby decreasing health, immunity and fertility even prior to infection. As horticulture declined after contact, so therefore did the consumption of plant nutrients in combination with fats from animal sources, which may have decreased their ability to be processed and absorbed in humans.[230]

Some New England horticulturalists tried to revert to what Anderson has described as "full time hunting and gathering" as a means for sustenance following the disruption of their agricultural lands.[231] Others were forced to increase their focus on maize intensification to account for lost hunting resources as well as curtailed access to other plants, inspiring European settlers to construct new maize markets to profit from the perceived importance of the resource.[232] In both cases, European colonists in New England tended to overlook the possibility for symbiosis between hunter-gathering and horticultural methods of sustenance, which often oscillated in relative importance according to the season. Instead, some assumed that Native Americans solely engaged in nomadic hunting patterns, erroneously perceiving a deeply rooted indigenous framework when in fact those patterns represented a defensive response to European disruption of diverse nutritional resources. This attitude eventually "contributed to the notion that removal of eastern nations to Midwestern reservations would solve problems of conflict between expanding Euro-American populations and the Indians' loss of hunting lands." Among English colonizers in the eastern seaboard, moreover, the view that Native Americans refrained from land cultivation became key in their attempt to define the territory as *res nullious*—empty of privately managed land and thus legitimate for colonial settlement.[233] Among those communities that chose to intensify maize rather than hunting and gathering, conversely, English settlers chose to overlook the importance of hunting lands in providing biodiverse nutritional supplements. They became comfortable occupying lands that had once constituted ecologically important buffer zones, where hunting occurred outside sedentary agricultural settlements. The nutritionally and immunologically beneficial hybrid between hunting and gathering, and agriculture and horticulture was ruptured, despite many Native Americans remaining keen to maintain private control over their land.[234]

Gendered English notions of domesticity further undermined the hybrid between agriculture and hunting and gathering in New England and Iroquois country. Where Native American women worked in plant cultivation, their physical labor was perceived by English settlers as uncivilized, and discouraged or even sabotaged. English settlers replaced gendered physical spaces with new animal lots or wheat fields. Moreover, although the relative incorporation of English gender norms into Iroquois culture remains a contentious issue, their slave raids on Delaware communities south of Iroquois country further ruptured the delicate dynamic linking female-centered horticulture and agriculture to male-centered hunting and gathering. Women were often removed from the land, while men lost hunting grounds.[235]

From the late seventeenth century through the eighteenth century, some Northeastern Native Americans moved—or fled—to the Great Lakes region and present-day Canada, placing stress on land and resources and forcing other groups to move even further west into the Plains or into the South. In settlements between the northern Mississippi River and the Great Lakes, French traders, missionaries and military personnel met in what White has described as a "middle ground" where neither Europeans nor Native Americans necessarily held the upper hand. In that context, tellingly, demography remained more stable than in eastern shatter zones, which lost autonomy in their subsistence hybrids. Ojibwes found themselves situated between Assiniboine and Sioux communities in the West and the French in the East, allowing their role as middlemen between the two groups, providing some independence in their nutritional strategies. The Assiniboine and Sioux were more connected to Atlantic trade, but were less affected by it during the eighteenth century, also maintaining a degree of autonomy that coincided with greater demographic stability in the medium term.[236]

During the second half of the eighteenth century, American settlers targeted Native Americans in New England and Iroquois country whom they perceived to have been allied with the French during the Seven Years' War or with the British during the American Revolution. These charges were convenient, giving them greater confidence to curtail indigenous access to hunting grounds, buffer zones and female-centered planting fields through the 1770s and 1780s.[237] Like the Comanche in the Great Plains, many Iroquois groups in particular had been able to take advantage of contingent technologies and political alliances to increase their nutritional diversity through hunting and trade, avoiding the population decline that others suffered. By the late eighteenth century, however, they became more reliant on nutrient-poor maize in sedentary defensive settlements, while suffering from (often unfounded) accusations of disloyalty to the patriot cause. Those accusations catalyzed the dispossession of their subsistence frameworks and hunting zones.[238]

The Indian Trade and Intercourse Act (1790) in the Northwest was designed to prevent wholesale loss of land among Native American communities. Yet it was largely ignored by settlers and their state and regional governments.[239] By the 1840s, the Iroquois lost most of their agricultural, horticultural and hunting lands to New York State, whose civic leaders adopted nefarious methods to facilitate such dispossession.[240]

After the Revolution

The disruption of Native American land use—and subsistence—during the revolutionary era set the tone for the following decades, as the United States expanded west, and as individual American settlers gained the support of state and federal authorities in their appropriation of indigenous agricultural lands and hunting zones. Through dissimulation, deliberately ambiguous treaties or even outright theft by American government agents, Native Americans ceded thousands of square miles. The process was not always passive, but Native American armed resistance was usually met with armed militias or federal forces. In the War of 1812, under the pretense of liquidating remaining British forces from the Ohio Country to the Gulf of Mexico, American government forces also removed thousands of Native Americans from their farmland and hunting grounds—easy to do when they could be accused of alliance with the British, as was the case with the Shawnees, who were led by representatives such as Tenskwatawa and his brother Tecumseh, and among those Creeks whom Andrew Jackson's regiments defeated in Alabama in March 1814.[241]

Led by President Andrew Jackson, the 1830 Indian Removal Act prevented the development of Native American homesteads, further decreasing the ability to hunt and cultivate foods. A series of allied acts, spearheaded by United States treaty commissioners, further reduced land access and removed Southeastern Native Americans into western lands. Most had been promised "allotment" options, yet violence, dispossession and fraud prevented them from recovering from the effects of disease epidemics through the continuation of cultural mechanisms, including nutritional frameworks.[242] Federal officials refused to intervene when state actors in Georgia ignored the Supreme Court decision in *Worcester v. Georgia* that the state had no jurisdiction over the Cherokee nation.[243]

The 1838 smallpox epidemic, which took place among surviving Great Plains communities such as the Mandans, was followed by further disruptions to Native American life. The federal government moved Native Americans from the Ohio Valley and the Southeast to the west, forcing other groups to move west so that, in the words of federal government agents, new arrivals could be "civilized" by the adopting of European-style models of agricultural settlement. They were forced to live in even closer proximity, on reservations. As Ostler has pointed out, the "idea was that these tribes could make a transition to 'civilization' through farming, but without hunting to supplement growing crops, these groups had a hard time supporting themselves"—at which point nutritional depravation heightened susceptibility to disease. Mandans, Arikaras and Hidatsas had seen a slight demographic stabilization since the epidemics of 1780. The 1837 epidemic, likely brought on by the arrival of smallpox on a steam ship, had a far higher mortality rate. Echoing earlier instances of disruption that followed the revolutionary wars, their placement in concentrated settlements, their loss of mobility, their increasing inability to trade and exchange nutritionally diverse foods and their declining hybrid between agriculture and hunting offered a perfect storm, reducing immunological health and provided a setting for the rapid movement of diseases through populations.[244]

A healthy immune system—supported by optimal nutrition—ought to have provided at least some defense against total demographic collapse following the biological exchange of diseases during the first period of extended contact between Europeans and Native Americans in North America, between the sixteenth century and the eighteenth century. Neolithic Europeans and ancient Native Americans adapted to or mitigated the consequences of agricultural intensification. In Europe and the Middle East, new agricultural products provided calories to more people so that they might then reach reproductive age without starving. The decline in health of individuals born in such populations was offset by the overall increase in people born. The effects of colonization, however, prevented similar adaptive measures among postcontact Native Americans, as their subsistence systems were ruptured more than ever before.

In many regions of North America, as we have seen, the regular consumption of bison, deer, fish and other animals prevented protein and iron deficiencies that initially accompanied the move toward maize in communities such as Cahokia.[245] Notwithstanding communities such as the Comanche, who used European technologies to consolidate bison consumption, many Native Americans found their meat consumption restricted in favor of maize as Europeans expanded the jurisdiction of their imperial power—a restriction of important micronutrients that coincided with the greater proximity of domesticated European animals to Native American dwellings, and the increasing population density of Native communitie that sought defensive settlement. Societal circumstances that heightened the proliferation of disease increased and thus required the immune system to be functioning as best as it possibly could—particularly among those individuals who had survived initial epidemics and might then have contributed to demographic recovery in the long term.[246]

The arrival of new diseases and pathogens coincided with a sudden increase in consumption and production of maize in some regions, or overhunting of animals in other spheres. These phenomena responded to new markets and colonial impositions that were rapid and far reaching. Contingent factors and contexts, which were associated with the political, military and cultural effects of European colonization, were central to compromising Native

American immunity and fertility at just the point when they were faced with new diseases and epidemics. The Neolithic and ancient Native American examples demonstrated the reproductive value of energy-dense but nutrient-poor grains, notwithstanding declining health outcomes. In many parts of postcontact Native America, conversely, nutritional degradation accompanied the arrival of new diseases, preventing individuals from reaching reproductive age and increasing infant mortality. Nutrition and immunity declined as nutrient-poor foods replaced nutritionally diverse sources at just the point when pathogenic diseases invaded the same sphere. The environmental mismatch was so sudden and marked that any adaptive response was less likely in the medium term. Moreover, warfare, enslavement and other forms of colonial disruption prevented individuals from finding a mate to reproduce—at the point when other stressed populations in other historical periods could recover demographically.

Disrupted access to macronutrients and micronutrients—whether derived from hunted and gathered animals and plants, from indigenous agricultural practices or from a combination of both—should therefore be defined as a cofactor alongside specifically predetermined genetic loci and the biological exchange of diseases. Some infectious diseases began to ravage Native American populations in the decades after extended contact began. But the inability to recover population numbers was exacerbated by declining access to ancestral sources of food. The change to Native American subsistence was often so sudden that its accompaniment by new diseases provided a perfect storm. The inability to enhance nutrition in the medium term, combined with the shattering of social contexts, prevented individuals from achieving the fertility levels that were required for populations to recover from disease during the first period of extended European contact.

Chapter 4

METABOLIC HEALTH AND IMMUNITY IN NATIVE AMERICA, 1750–1950

This chapter considers the disruption to nutritional frameworks among indigenous populations in California, the Pacific Northwest and Alaska during an era of extended contact with Europeans that began in the mid-eighteenth century, and which also heralded the proliferation of pathogens in the regions. Examining a later period of contact than that which is usually implied in general discussions of Native American demographic stress, the chapter also assesses the experience of indigenous communities in the Great Plains and the Southwest during the nineteenth and twentieth centuries, such as the Pima, comparing the nutritional status of populations that maintained their ancestral food traditions with those who were obliged to live in reservation communities. In their adoption of nutritional frameworks that were increasingly dependent on Anglo American intervention, they too suffered in new ways, making their degraded health outcomes analogous to those experienced by their forebears during an earlier period of extended contact.

The discussion of micronutrients in the previous chapter drew case studies from earlier contact history to consider them in light of the most recent work in nutritional science. Using a similar framework, with similar aims, this chapter examines the role of metabolic health in enhancing or decreasing immunity. The changing metabolic role of fat, protein and carbohydrate is vital to examine in Native American communities during these later periods of European contact—including the possible effects on immunity, fertility and overall demographic stability. We highlight a new way of understanding the relative metabolic importance of fat in comparison to carbohydrate as an optimal form of energy in historical context, while also attending to the potential importance of starch and other carbohydrates for immunity and overall health, particularly as defined by the fast-developing literature on the role of gut bacteria in broader human well-being. Disruption to metabolic health is defined as a contingent societal factor, alongside micronutrient restriction. Both are necessary to frame our assessment of the inability of populations to recover from epidemics and their propensity to reach a demographic nadir—as distinct from any supposed immutable genetic predisposition to diseases and syndromes, or to certain metabolic conditions such as diabetes.

Thus we distinguish between micronutrient health effects and those associated with the metabolic effects of various macronutrient profiles, as defined by their relationship with energy utilization and storage in the human body. A central aspect of the metabolic profile of food is the resulting effect on blood sugar level and the concomitant production of the hormone insulin, often associated with problematic health markers including diabetes, chronic inflammation of blood and tissues, and lowered immunity to infectious diseases.[1] Any discussion of metabolism, whether historically or in reference to contemporary scientific literature, should encompass the catabolism of food for energy, the storage of energy from food (for example, in the liver and muscle as glycogen, and in fat cells as triglycerides), and the catabolism of these storage molecules.

Metabolic function depends on the types of food consumed (on the ratios of the macronutrients protein, fat and carbohydrate) and on the frequency of food consumption. In chronic diseases such as cancer, heart disease, diabetes and even in obesity, metabolism is altered in ways that the current literature is beginning to characterize. These alterations in metabolism, in turn, have a profound influence on immune function.[2] The immune system requires a wealth of metabolic resources, including macronutrients and micronutrients. Immune activity in sick patients can increase metabolic rate (consumption of energy by the body) by 40 percent, indicating its intense energy demands.[3] As immunity is such a metabolically costly activity, which diverts energy away from other body systems, its diminishment during times of nutrient deprivation is even considered as an evolutionary adaptation. Organisms risk the consequences of decreasing immune activity to prioritize more vital functions, including those in the heart and brain.[4] Thus, individuals suffering from malnutrition have been shown to have a compromised immune response.[5]

In order to understand how disruptions to optimal metabolic function might influence health and immunity, and its implications for our discussion of Native American epidemiology and demography after European contact, it is necessary to explore several interrelated phenomena: the burning of different macronutrients for energy; the potentially positive metabolic effects of fasting and autophagy (redundant cell clearance); the influence of the gut microbiome on our metabolism; and the interaction between metabolism and the immune system, mediated in part by endocrine signaling pathways and adipocytes (fat cells). We consider metabolic distinctions between previously cultivated plant sources, hunted animals and the grains that some Native American came to rely on more greatly following colonization; whether any correlation can be drawn between forced changes in starch and fat consumption and declining health markers in postcontact Native America; and whether these changes in the metabolic nutritional profile of their food can be said to have compromised Native American immunological health with respect to infectious diseases.

There remains much controversy in both popular and scholarly discussions of the ideal source of energy for the human metabolism. Some suggest that it is not objectively possible to isolate an ideal metabolic system for all humans. Nonetheless much research, documented in popular bestsellers and narrower periodical literature, has recently reasserted the importance of dietary fat— including saturated fat—in regulating the appetite, in providing an adequate transfer of energy at the cellular level and in reducing blood inflammation and a range of related inflammatory syndromes, some of which can be linked to suboptimal human immunity. Recent work, particularly in research into athletic performance, has gone as far has highlighting the potential benefits of burning blood ketones, through a high fat, or "ketogenic," diet, rather than utilizing glucose via a higher intake of carbohydrates. The chapter is informed by these cutting-edge debates. But it also seeks to influence those debates through a nuanced examination of the historical macronutrient profile among indigenous communities in California, the Pacific Northwest and Alaska as well as populations in the expanding American West and Southwest—including those that had used carbohydrate sources (for example, forms of resistant starch) to the potential benefit of their immunity, and that suffered restricted access to those sources as the independent United States expanded.

We have chosen to introduce the contingent link between metabolic health and immunity in this penultimate chapter because case studies from the later era of European American colonization provide the richest material to aid such a discussion. But, of course, our assessment of the problematic role of chronically raised blood sugar, or the curtailed ability to burn fatty acids for energy, might be applied to the historical frameworks examined in the previous chapter—particularly those in which the consumption of protein and fat gave way to the intensification of maize, which is known to raise blood sugar levels to a far greater extent. The discussion of metabolic health in this chapter provides a framework that should apply to communities discussed in the previous chapter, just as our earlier discussion of micronutrient deficiencies ought to apply to many of the disrupted nutritional frameworks examined below.

It is important to avoid replacing a problematic form of genetic determinism, associated with the "virgin soil" thesis, with a different sort of determinism, which uses broad conclusions from modern scientific data on metabolic health to define the exact causal indicators of demographic decline. In assessing metabolic health as a contingent factor in determining working immunity, therefore, we distinguish between broad speculation and stronger causal mechanisms. To this end, we include speculations that are strongly supported by work carried out among postcontact populations that have maintained a good degree of their precontact nutritional frameworks, such as Inuit and Pima communities that were studied during the twentieth century. These examples allow us to draw direct assessments of the positive metabolic effects of indigenous low-glycemic starch sources, for example, or of fat-adapted food patterns that may have enabled the burning of fatty acids or ketones rather than glucose in some populations, and to draw comparisons with control communities that moved away from those beneficial metabolic frameworks, and that are known to have experienced problematic health outcomes as a direct result, including a greater propensity to suffer from infectious disease. Those assessments, in turn, provide solid grounding to speculate regarding the effects of disrupted metabolic frameworks in other historical communities, when such data was not obviously collected, but which experienced demographic decline following disease epidemics.

We do also include discussions of contingent metabolic health that are even more speculative, relying on recent research on the association between energy use and immunological function, and extrapolating their conclusions to pertinent historical contexts. In these instances, we do not have corresponding data from twentieth-century populations that maintained their ancestral traditions versus those that did not. Here, we are sure to signpost our discussions as a broader working hypothesis, nonetheless still useful.

The Insulin Hypothesis and Immunity in Native America after Contact

We have questioned and qualified the notion that Native American communities were predisposed to near-total demographic collapse solely due to their relative lack of immunity in virgin soils. We have suggested that contingent factors, particularly nutritional disruption, contributed to demographic decline and disrupted fertility in the medium to long term, rather than focusing entirely on short-term epidemics. It is now worth raising, and interrogating, a separate example of biological determinism in the history of Native American health, which is equally problematic. Many scholars and health practitioners have noted the startlingly high levels of type 2 diabetes in Native American communities since the mid-twentieth century, and have sought to find genetic loci for diabetes that are unique to those communities. In doing so, they have eschewed the role of colonial and postcolonial interventions in Native American food patterns, which have affected their insulin sensitivity, and thus their likelihood to suffer from type 2 diabetes, distinct from any supposed genetic predisposition. These studies, and their drawbacks, are important for us to consider, as they raise broader questions regarding the metabolic role of high glucose in the diet: its occurrence among those who have turned away from ancestral diets toward higher-carbohydrate diets (confounding examples of high-carbohydrate precontact diets will also be considered); its likely association with inflammation and compromised immunity in historical communities; and how recent reassessments of diabetes and prediabetes causation can inform any association between the intensification of insulinogenic maize and wheat consumption after European contact and compromised health and immunity.

A continuously disrupted metabolic state is associated with chronic inflammation, caused in part by contingent choices and external nutritional changes, rather than immutable genetic predispositions. Such a state is often designated as "metabolic syndrome."[6] It describes a characteristic set of disruptions to energy use, including insulin resistance, obesity, high blood pressure and dyslipidaemia (hypotriglyceridemia, elevated non-esterified fatty acids and decreased high-density lipoprotein (HDL) cholesterol).[7] A diet high in refined starches and sugar, low in antioxidants, low in omega-3 fatty acids and proportionally higher in omega-6 fatty acids (particularly when oxidized through the burning of seed and vegetable oils), and low in vegetable fiber, is increasingly thought to promote a state of chronic inflammation and to increase the likelihood of the development of metabolic syndrome. Our understanding of the role of saturated fat in this process is still ambiguous, and it may potentially even be anti-inflammatory in certain ratios with other macronutrients.[8]

The relative availability or preponderance of macronutrients, most commonly fatty acids and carbohydrates, may act as a limiting factor in certain immune cell functions. From an evolutionary perspective, we can therefore see that the ability of the body to regulate the behavior of immune cells according to macronutrient availability is beneficial.[9] Endocrine (hormone) signaling pathways can sense macronutrient availability, such as the relative availability of glucose or fatty acids in the blood, and can communicate to the immune system to affect the immune response.[10] Sensory proteins also respond to changes in macronutrient availability. This information is communicated by cell-signaling proteins (including hormones such as leptin and insulin), which cause changes in cell behavior by activating receptor proteins.[11] Several proteins and peptide hormones involved in such signaling pathways have been found to affect the immune response, including leptin, insulin, mTOR, double-stranded RNA-activated protein kinase (PKR) and the aryl hydrocarbon receptor (AHR) pathways.[12] Signaling via these pathways therefore enables immune cells to sense nutrient levels and incorporate this information into their response to infection, thereby allowing immune cells to act in the most effective way given the local nutrient status.[13] As a specific example, the AHR protein is activated by kynurenine (a product of tryptophan metabolism) and affects immune cell differentiation and activity. Hence, the amount of tryptophan in the diet may influence immune activity through this pathway—which is particularly important to consider given the centrality of turkey rearing to several Native American communities before contact, the birds being particularly rich in tryptophan.[14]

The diminishment of immunity in a metabolically deranged state is thus unsurprising when we consider the associated role of chronic inflammation with both phenomena—particularly when we incorporate the effects of constantly raised blood sugar and insulin in more detail. A new consensus suggests that the overconsumption of high-glycemic carbohydrates, and the declining effectiveness of the hormone insulin in removing blood sugar, are one of the primary causes of obesity and type 2 diabetes, which are often highly prevalent within the inflammatory state defined as metabolic syndrome.[15] Glucose usage by immune cells increases massively during infection, and glucose availability affects immune activity via several hormonal and signaling pathways.[16] Insulin resistance following chronically raised blood sugar levels results in decreased glucose uptake in muscle and fat cells, decreased uptake of lipids and increased hydrolysis of stored triglycerides in fat cells, and decreased glycogen synthesis and glucose production in the liver. A state of chronic inflammation, partially caused by excessively high blood sugar, can contribute to the development of type 2 Diabetes. The hyperglycaemia that results from diabetes promotes inflammation, so that the chronic inflammatory state and symptoms of metabolic syndrome are progressively worsened.[17] Several studies have suggested that the immune response might thus be impaired in individuals with diabetes mellitus, or even among those who have chronically raised fasting glucose and insulin levels without such a diagnosis.[18]

Adipocytes, more commonly known as fat cells, are involved in the innate immune response. Scholars have begun to speculate that their dysfunction following a high-glucose diet, linked to the onset of type 2 diabetes, might lead to increased inflammation.[19] Adipocytes contribute to the immune response via the secretion of pro-inflammatory cytokines (proteins involved in communication between immune cells that promote the inflammatory response) and hormones such as leptin.[20] Immune cells residing in the adipose tissue also secrete pro-inflammatory cytokines.[21] Particular stressors can contribute to adipocyte dysfunction and increase this secretion of pro-inflammatory molecules.[22] Stressors present in metabolic syndrome include oxidative stress (the accumulation of oxidizing molecules during the metabolism of macronutrients for energy, particularly when burning glucose), high levels of circulating fatty acids, and increased levels of inflammatory cytokines. Such stressors have been shown to affect cell signaling in adipocytes.[23] The dysfunction of adipocytes eventually results in their inability to take up excess nutrients, leading to an accumulation of very low-density lipoprotein (VLDL) and triglycerides in the blood as well as a failure to provide the micronutrients necessary to optimal function of the immune system.[24] Other organs such as the liver and heart are then used for lipid accumulation, which can result in lipotoxicity of organs that are unsuited to storage of lipids. A scholarly consensus has now emerged suggesting that such lipotoxicity can lead to insulin resistance in other parts of the body including the muscle, liver and pancreas, potentially further compromising immunity as a knock-on effect.[25]

It should be apparent, then, why attention to metabolic health, rather than merely micronutrient deficiencies, ought to feature in discussions that account for the effect of disrupted nutrition on the ability of Native American populations to withstand or recover from newly introduced infectious diseases, or from an increasing preponderance of familiar diseases. As a factor that was contingent on external contexts and colonial disruptions to subsistence frameworks, its importance should not be understated.

Notwithstanding the problematic effects of chronically raised blood glucose from grains and other carbohydrates, however, it has been suggested that Europeans have at least undergone a level of genetic adaptation to those effects since their adoption of agriculture.[26] Populations in which the agricultural transition occurred later, including Native American populations, may therefore show greater genetic susceptibility to diabetes, having had less experience with insulin-raising carbohydrates, and becoming even more likely to suffer from metabolic derangements relating to chronically raised insulin (and other hormones). The high concordance rate for diabetes onset between monozygotic (genetically identical) twins compared with dizygotic (nonidentical) twins indicates that there is a genetic aspect to the condition.[27] Indeed, some recent scientific research has located specific loci in the DNA of some Native Americans that affect their insulin sensitivity. Individuals with certain genetic variants at these loci—"susceptibility genes"—would be more likely to develop diseases such as diabetes following a move toward a higher carbohydrate diet, such as that which has taken place among some communities in the postcontact era.[28]

Native American populations have also often featured in discussions that use a "thrifty gene hypothesis" to explain why some people are prone to diabetes and obesity as well as other diseases (and, it is to be assumed, why their immunity might have been further compromised after European contact, given the link between diabetes and compromised immunity). A "thrifty" genotype, it is suggested, may have been evolutionarily successful for individuals descended from hunter-gatherer populations. Its occurrence would have allowed those populations, particularly childbearing women, to gain fat more easily during times of food abundance (particularly starch during summer, which would have been converted into triglycerides and stored in fat cells). Those with more fat may have better survived times of food scarcity, by releasing fat back into their bloodstream, and thus passed on their genes. In post–hunter-gathering populations the thrifty genotype may have appeared among those who had "undergone positive selection for genes that favored energy storage as a consequence of the cyclical episodes of famine and surplus after the advent of farming 10,000 years ago." But according to the hypothesis, during times of nutritional abundance, those same individuals would be more likely to develop metabolic syndromes such as obesity and diabetes.[29]

Yet it is important to avoid necessarily deterministic conclusions when assessing the correlation between recent genetic studies and epidemiological data from Native American communities (whether historic or contemporary). First, more research is still needed to assess whether genetic variants for insulin sensitivity are present exclusively or at a higher frequency in Native American populations compared to other populations, or whether they are equally prevalent in other ethnic communities that were not included in present studies. Despite retaining the same genetic variants, those other communities might not suffer from diabetes to the extent of Native Americans.

Second, greater genetic susceptibility to insulin insensitivity or any other medical condition need not predetermine the actual onset of diabetes or other disorders, as is evidenced by the relatively positive health markers among Native American communities before increasing their consumption of processed and high-sugar foods.[30] After all, there are no records of type 2 diabetes in Native American communities before 1940, when dietary changes became more apparent on reservations. To be sure, there may have been undocumented instances of diabetes before that point, including during the period of agricultural intensification among communities such as those in Cahokia. Notwithstanding a genetic predisposition for diabetes, however, we are increasingly aware that environmental factors are crucial in the development of diabetes and other metabolic conditions. Though genetics may load the gun, environmental factors are required to pull the trigger.[31] Such a pattern is evident in epidemiological studies of other populations living traditional lifestyles. Diabetes and other metabolic conditions develop with the incorporation of Western foods, particularly those high in carbohydrates, into the diet (see the final chapter of this book).[32]

With these distinctions and caveats in mind, it is worth considering the contingent nutritional factors that affect metabolic health, including the onset of type 2 diabetes and other syndromes, and their association with inflammation and immunity. The relative proportions of carbohydrate and fat consumed, and the periodicity of food consumption, can affect metabolism. Understanding such an association allows us to focus on potential changes and disruptions to metabolic frameworks that had been apparent among Native Americans before contact, and their exacerbation during the modern era. It allows us to consider the role of metabolic disruption in the medium to long term, and its contribution to demographic decline, further modifying the notion that Native Americans reached their population nadir due to immutable biological distinctions at contact, or that surviving populations then became more prone to diseases such as diabetes solely because of innate genetic differences.

Consider, for example, work that has been carried out among the Pima Native American populations in present-day southern Arizona, which demonstrate the importance of insulin sensitivity and the reduction of blood glucose levels even in traditional diets that incorporated high levels of starchy plants. Ethnobotanic assessments suggest that precontact nutritional strategies minimized the risk of metabolic degradation—including diabetes or prediabetes—that might otherwise have compromised immunity. Alarmed by the sudden prevalence of diabetes among the Pima since their adoption of an American diet during the 1940s (at nearly half the adult population during the 1990s), Arizona ethnobotanist Gary Nabhan has scrutinized ancestral Pima diets from anthropological sources, initially working on behalf of the Tucson-based Native Seeds/SEARCH foundation. Nabhan and others have noted a contrast between the starches traditionally gathered and cultivated by the community during at least the last several hundred years, which promote a much lower insulin response, and postcontact era grains, newer strains of maize and white potatoes, whose higher glycemic indexes thereby promote much higher levels of insulin production. Such a distinction was correlated by selecting six starchy foods traditionally eaten by the Pimas during the last millennium, and particularly prior to first European contact: mesquite pods, acorns, white and yellow tepary beans, lima beans and a traditional strain of corn. The blood insulin level following consumption of these foods was measured in healthy, nondiabetic subjects and compared to newer starch sources consumed by the same subjects. Some of the traditional foods have been shown to contain higher-than-average proportions of amylose starch, which takes longer to break down into simple sugars than amylopectin, the predominant starch found in white potatoes and bread, thereby explaining the lower rises in blood sugar after consumption of these starch sources.[33] Before contact, Pima populations also consumed a cereal containing the grain-like seeds of psyllium, sometimes known as plantago, which more recent studies have linked to the potential lowering of fasting blood sugar levels. Another study has even suggested that the phytochemical composition and metabolic performance of some "dietary berries traditionally used by Native Americans" can be associated with positive health markers, including the regulation of blood sugar levels and lipid metabolism.[34]

Pima and other Native American communities do not seem prepared for the high-glycemic consumption patterns introduced by Western interventions since the eighteenth century. Even in communities that incorporated maize intensification, as we have seen, hunting and gathering animals and less insulinogenic plants continued long after that phenomenon. "For Native American and other recently Westernized indigenous people," according to Nabhan, "a return to a diet similar to their traditional one is no nostalgic notion; it may, in fact, be a nutritional and survival imperative."[35] From such an analysis, indeed, we can draw a related hypothesis: following Spanish and Anglo American colonization of the Southwest, the Southeast and elsewhere, reduced access to lower-glycemic starches, intensification of insulinogenic maize and curtailed access to less insulinogenic sources of animal fat and protein could well have heightened the susceptibility of indigenous communities to infectious diseases or raised their mortality after infection.[36]

This hypothesis can be applied to the case studies discussed in the previous chapter, which focused on the diminishment of micronutrients due to intensified maize consumption during the postcontact era. We can now add metabolic disruption to these narratives. For example, Native Americans on Long Island, as in several mid-Atlantic and southern New England populations, only began sustained agricultural practices after European contact, when they were forced into concentrated communities for defense, or simply because Europeans had curtailed their hunting lands. After this point, and not before, they were obliged to maintain a more sedentary settlement concentrated on carbohydrates rather than hunted animal fats and protein as a core element of subsistence. Such a paradigm could also be linked to discussions of problematic Spanish missionary zones in Florida during the seventeenth century, when some Native Americans found themselves restricted to sedentary agricultural settlements that relied on wheat and maize as a primary source of calories; or to the story of the Powhatan confederacy in seventeenth- and eighteenth-century Virginia, whose members became enmeshed in European rivalries and trade wars, and who increasingly relied on maize in defensive sedentary villages. Greater sedentism, of course, would have compounded metabolic disruption by burning less glucose through movement, heightening the problematic effects of consuming maize and other storable grains—including in compromising immunity due to chronic inflammation.

Consider also the historical trajectory of the Micmac communities of present-day Nova Scotia and New Brunswick. European trade foods accompanied the consolidation of transatlantic fur markets during the sixteenth century and suddenly replaced traditional subsistence items. Dried peas, beans,

wheat, corn and biscuits replaced animal and plant foods that were one
cultivated, gathered, hunted and preserved for winter before the period of
market contact. Animals previously hunted for consumption were preserved
for fur, reducing adequate winter stores of nutrient-dense meat and fish, and
forcing communities to rely on carbohydrate-rich and nutrient-poor storable
trade foods. According to Miller's ethnographic assessment of this sixteenth-
century phenomenon, "the Indians themselves, as well as European observers,
noted the effects of dietary change on health and the fact that lung, chest, and
intestinal disorders were increasingly common."[37] A French priest noted in
1611 that, "since the French have begun to frequent their country [...] they
do nothing all summer but eat; and the result is that, adopting an entirely
different custom and thus breeding new diseases, they pay for their indulgence
during the autumn and winter by pleurisy, quincy, and dysentery, which kill
them off."[38] In 1613, Jesuits noted that Micmac populations "are astonished
and often complain that since the French mingle and carry on trade with
them they are dying fast, and the population is thinning out. For they assert
that before this association and intercourse, all their countries were very popu-
lous and they tell how one by one the different coasts, according as they have
begun to traffic with us, have been more reduced by disease."[39] Though, as
we have suggested, direct causation is always tricky to discern in discussing
contingent disruptions and mortality from disease, it is likely that the Micmac
transition away from nutrient-dense to nutrient-poor insulinogenic foods at
least exacerbated the compromise to immunity in these contexts, as suggested
by ethnographic accounts of the link between dietary change and disease in
Native American perceptions.

Having discussed the role of carbohydrate sources in Native America in
relation to insulin sensitivity, we should also consider the related question of
their seasonality, and whether disruption of their consumption at *certain times*
of the year contributed to a decline in health, immunity and even fertility,
due to problematic metabolic effects. In New England through the 1600s, as
Anderson has shown, European farming enclosures clashed with the summer
gathering of tubers and squash, while tending European domesticated animals
in the winter conflicted with itinerant winter hunting for fats and proteins. The
historical record there and elsewhere thus suggests that in the precontact era,
during summer and early fall, starches were consumed in far greater number
than during the winter, when protein and fat consumption increased proportionally.[40] By 1600, as another example, Western Apache communities had
developed a "seasonal cycle" that veered between food gathering, horticulture and winter hunts.[41] Similarly, on the Texas plains before European contact, Apache communities spent spring and summer in agricultural villages,
moving toward hunting-dominated nutrition in the winter.[42]

While surveying indigenous communities that had avoided the level of European contact suffered by their southern neighbors, Weston A. Price's early twentieth-century *Nutrition and Physical Degeneration* suggested that similar practices were maintained during the early twentieth century among communities living inside the Rocky Mountain Range in far northern Canada. As Price noted, they cycled between the summer cultivation of starches and fruits and far greater reliance on fats from animals (particularly organ meats and marrow) during winter:

> The successful nutrition for nine months of the year was largely limited to wild game, chiefly moose and caribou. During the summer months the Indians were able to use growing plants. During the winter some use was made of bark and buds of trees. I found the Indians putting great emphasis upon the eating of the organs of the animals, including the wall of parts of the digestive tract. Much of the muscle meat of the animals was fed to the dogs. It is important that skeletons are rarely found where large game animals have been slaughtered by the Indians of the North. The skeletal remains are found as piles of finely broken bone chips or splinters that have been cracked up to obtain as much as possible of the marrow and nutritive qualities of the bones. These Indians obtain their fat-soluble vitamins and also most of their minerals from the organs of the animals. An important part of the nutrition of the children consisted in various preparations of bone marrow, both as a substitute for milk and as a special dietary ration.[43]

When assessing the health and vitality of precontact communities in more southerly regions, we should not discount the possibility of seasonal gains and loss in fat mass, due to the greater consumption of carbohydrates in summer and fall, or the strenuous exertions and fat-adapted metabolic state that may have accompanied long winter hunts. During summer months, when carbohydrate sources were more abundant in many regions outside the Arctic, consumption likely increased. Gains in weight, and even fertility, made communities more likely to conceive children at the end of summer, often leading to spring births. Seasonal rather than year-round consumption of carbohydrates may have limited the overall production of insulin in the bloodstream, reducing the potential for diabetes, obesity and certain cardiovascular diseases. Indeed, we might even consider historical case studies that support these seasonal distinctions in light of recent scientific research on the interaction between vitamin D from sunshine at lower latitudes and the greater ability to process carbohydrates in a more optimal metabolic state (requiring less production of insulin).[44]

Of course, we should not discount confounding evidence, such as that shown in the historical record for Tarahumara communities in northwestern Mexico, who ran great distances through the colonial era while eating comparatively few animal meat products even during winter. A similar association can be found with historic Apaches and Hopis, both of whom ran for long distances with a diet dominated by maize, squash and beans. Yet even here, other analytical indicators are relevant. The problematic effects of high blood glucose, for example, might have been mitigated by intense exercise burning the substance for fuel rather than raising insulin to a suboptimal level.[45]

The Tarahumara case study allows us to examine a further set of questions, which speak to recent research by O'Keefe and others on the burning of glucose during periods of aerobic endurance activity. Compared to long-distance aerobic activity in a potentially fat-adapted state, scholars ought to consider the long-term consequences of burning glucose for fuel in a high state of oxidative stress, such as long-distance running and hunting among historical communities. Exercise may have prevented glucose from being stored as fat among Tarahumaras as well as lowered inflammatory markers. Yet oxidative damage due to their metabolic state during exercise may have portended problematic cardiovascular health outcomes in addition to other problematic health consequences.[46]

Such a hypothesis rests on what we know about the distinctions between a healthy cellular metabolism and a disrupted cellular metabolism, which in turn depends on the role of mitochondria, the energy-producing organelles within cells. Mitochondria are abundant in immune cells and those that are connected to the immune system signaling pathways.[47] Memory t cells have a particularly large number of mitochondria, for example, and this increases their capacity for energy production and provides "a bioenergetic advantage for survival."[48] Most studies of the importance of mitochondria for the metabolic health of cells have focused on their dysfunction in respect to cancer.[49] Tumor cells often show a decreased ability to metabolize fatty acids as a result of decreased numbers of healthy mitochondria, resulting in the increased fermentation of glucose for energy and the consequent increased production of lactate—a hallmark of many tumor cells.[50]

An unhealthy cellular metabolism, such as that seen in cancer cells, can result in increased oxidative stress, disrupting cell signaling pathways, including those related to the immune system. Oxidizing molecules known as reactive oxygen species (ROS) are generated as byproducts of normal metabolism. In a healthy cell these molecules exist at low concentrations, preventing them from causing significant damage to cellular components. When a cell is under oxidative stress, however, such as in the state of hyperglycemia, reactive oxygen species accumulate inside the cell, exposing cellular components to damage that can in some cases lead to cell death.[51] As well as being harmful to cell health directly, the effect of oxidative stress on the metabolism of glucose and fatty acids has recently been found to have a profound role in cell signaling. This has consequences for cell metabolism and behavior, including the acute immune response by immune cells during periods of exposure to pathogens.[52] Indeed, recent studies have begun to show how ROS signaling affects the immune response to infectious pathogens and the development of chronic metabolic diseases such as diabetes.[53] The production of ROS has been shown to disrupt the acute immune response by activating several cell signaling pathways, particularly those involved in the inflammatory response.[54]

In light of the above, we can speculate that health declined as Native Americans were forced to consume maize and other starches during the winter months, having lost access to ancestral winter hunting grounds. Seasonal rather than year-round consumption of carbohydrates could have improved health by limiting the overall production of insulin in the bloodstream. In assessing such a hypothesis, the above discussion of ROS in the presence of excess glucose metabolism becomes more relevant. As we have noted, the move toward all-year-round abundance of food in many populations may have caused overconsumption at times when the human metabolism may otherwise have benefited from calorie reduction and greater insulin sensitivity. The latter has been linked to reduced carbohydrate and protein access in comparison to fat, often during winter. Moreover, several studies have shown a correlation between blood vitamin D levels and insulin sensitivity. Thus, from an evolutionary perspective, it can be postulated that some human populations may be adapted to consume more starch during those months when insulin sensitivity is higher due to raised blood vitamin D levels from available sunshine.[55]

Shattered Subsistence in California and the Pacific Northwest in the Eighteenth and Nineteenth Centuries: Acorns, Resistant Starch and the Assault on the Indigenous Microbiome

So far, we have focused on the importance of metabolic fueling for the human body in general and the human immune system in particular. But we should also attend to the importance of the bacteria that reside in the human gut, where a large percentage of immune cells are present. Disruption to the optimal fuel source for gut bacteria can be defined as a related contingent factor in our discussion of the association between metabolic health and the history of postcontact Native American subsistence. The "gut microbiome" is increasingly outlined as a community of commensal, or "friendly," nonpathogenic microorganisms, such as bacteria, archaea, viruses and eukaryotic microbes, which live within the human digestive tract.[56] The relationship between the gut microbiome and host is described as symbiotic, or mutually beneficial: the microorganisms gain a warm, nutrient-dense environment, while the host gains the benefit of nutrients derived from the metabolism of the microorganisms, which may aid in the defense against pathogens and reduce the likelihood of a chronic inflammatory response, often described as an "autoimmune" condition.[57] Colonization of the gut with microbial organism begins at birth when the neonate is exposed to microbes in the birth canal, and changes over time according to diet and exposure to microbes from the external environment.[58] Some aspects of the gut microbiome are highly conserved between individuals, but at the level of individual species, there is immense variation. Recent studies suggest that such individual variation may have profound implications for health.[59]

Modern biological scholarship thus allows us to frame the effects of European settlement using a new language: colonization likely altered the microbiota of Native Americans in problematic ways. In many regions, a mismatched microbial context in affected individuals may have further contributed to the decline in overall health and immunity among those who sought to rebuild population numbers following epidemics. Colonial disruption of subsistence strategies may have unsettled the type and proportion of carbohydrate sources provided to individuals, changing not only the metabolic fuel of Native Americans but also the microbes in their guts. Altering the metabolic state of the gut may have allowed some bacteria to flourish too greatly and others to suffer losses. Either phenomenon could be linked to increasing inflammatory markers inside and outside the digestive tract, as food came to be partially digested in a suboptimal environment. That which affected the gut microbiome can be defined as a further contingent factor in the ongoing threat to Native American immunological health after contact.

Nutritional disruption among indigenous people in California from the late-eighteenth century to the mid-nineteenth century provides an appropriate case study to frame our discussion of the microbiome's potential contribution to metabolic health and broader immunity in disrupted societal contexts. Indigenous communities in California resented colonial Spanish missions because their settlers curtailed access to nutrient-dense plant and animal sources. Their health and immunity were also threatened by the sedentary and grain-centered aspect to Mission zones, given the likelihood that those who were forced to subsist in such zones experienced raised blood sugar levels and declining insulin sensitivity over a more extended period. Disruption of ground acorn products in their subsistence complexes, moreover, likely affected the metabolic state of their microbiota. Ground up into powders, acorns provided a source of resistant starch in the indigenous California diet—a form of starch, we are now beginning to realize, which provides a metabolic source for beneficial gut bacteria, and which may therefore have an outsized role in facilitating an optimal context to reduce chronic inflammation and maintain working immunity. Let us therefore consider the case of California more closely.

In California, indigenous people experienced isolated encounters with Spanish missionaries several centuries before the period of extended contact that began in the late eighteenth century. Among other communities, Chumash people in California lived in villages that were loosely confederated, exchanging marine, land and plant resources to maintain food diversity. Between September 1542 and January 1543, the first skirmishes between Spanish imperial agents and Native American communities—likely Chumash representatives—centered on food resources. Indigenous people near present-day San Diego Bay perceived an immediate threat to the sustainability of their fishing in the area. Ipai men fired arrows at Spanish arrivals who intruded in their fishing waters. On Santa Catalina Island, Chumash guards did the same. Such instances were isolated, however, as Spanish movements in the region remained sporadic.[60]

In 1595, Sebastian Rodriguez Cermeno traveled to coastal California under instruction from Luis de Velasco II, viceroy of New Spain, and encountered Chumash representatives. He also reported that the "soil will return any kind of seed that may be sown, as there are trees which bear hazelnuts, acorns, and other fruits of the country, madrones and fragrant herbs like those in Castile [...] There are also in the country a quantity of crabs and wild birds and deer, with which the people maintain their existence." Yet these reports failed to encourage much further Spanish settlement in California. Chumash and other indigenous peoples were thus able to retain autonomy in their subsistence methods, long into the eighteenth century.[61]

Only by the late eighteenth century did Spanish settlers arrive with a consolidated presence in California. They heralded the so-called mission period that continued into the early nineteenth century, which altered Native American subsistence strategies and nutritional density in serious ways. As in other regions and eras, intensified European settlement shattered the indigenous hybrid between cultivated staple products (often acorns, in the case of California Native Americans) and hunted and gathered animals and plants. Using ethnohistorical and archaeological evidence, Cook and others have estimated that the precontact Native American population in California of around 310,000 people declined to fewer than 25,000 by 1900. Here, as elsewhere, "virgin soil" epidemics were not required to account for such a loss. Intensification of settlement and the disruption of societal and nutritional mechanisms, all necessary for sound immunity, fertility and demographic recovery, was more than enough to account for the gradual but steady decline in population from the late eighteenth century through the nineteenth century.[62]

Spanish priests, for example, removed Chumash people from their villages in a policy of *reducción* that intensified by the early nineteenth century. Coerced to live in missions, often through the threat of force, as "agricultural laborers, the Chumash were required to adopt a work schedule that was more regimented and probably also more time consuming than the one they followed as hunter gatherers." Some, as Walker and Johnson summarize, were openly "deprived of meat" either due to necessity, disruption or as punishment for protesting the mission system. By the late eighteenth century, as a result, the "diverse native diet was gradually replaced by one composed mainly of corn, wheat, barley, beans, and beef [where] [t]ypically a corn gruel was served for breakfast and dinner."[63] According to Anderson, in the mission systems, "deficient diets consisting of starchy cereal soup and a little meat predisposed Indians to infectious diseases and malnutrition."[64] Indeed, California missions only began to experience disease epidemics in the period between 1806 and 1833, when they became more entirely controlling of Native American living circumstances, movements and subsistence strategies.[65] It is thus unsurprising that several estimates have suggested a relatively sudden increase in Chumash mortality rates during these new stages in Spanish colonization—long after initial first contact, belying the "virgin soil" paradigm, and providing another case study to consider the likely link between nutrition, fertility and immunity.[66]

Conversely, Native Americans who lived near Spanish missions that respected the autonomy of their land tended to demonstrate lower rates of demographic loss. In Santa Barbara Mission, for example, a priest noted in 1812 that in addition to the maize and wheat provided by the Spanish settlers, "the Indians are also very fond of the food they enjoyed in their pagan state: those from the mountains, venison, rabbits, rats, squirrels or any small animal they can catch; those from the seashores enjoy every species of sea food." Such a description, of course, may have reflected European bias, or more recent Native American adaptations, rather than a model of precontact subsistence. Yet it is corroborated by ethnographic and archaeological evidence for ancient California communities.[67] An important 1820 history of the Luiseño community, which lived among Franciscan missions, demonstrated their ability to maintain subsistence traditions when Spanish settlers avoided constructing year-round farms.[68] As a consequence, they maintained traditional gendered distinctions between those who gathered and processed acorns, and those who hunted and fished. Where missions incorporated European agriculture as a year-round endeavor, in contrast, ecologies were altered and subsistence strategies suffered.[69] Those who lived in Spanish mission communities modified European layouts to transform irrigation ditches into tacit boundaries that protected their horticultural and hunting grounds, their oak trees and their medicinal plants. When epidemics finally arrived in these communities, mortality rates were significantly lower than those whose members lost greater autonomy in their subsistence methods.[70]

Elsewhere, over the course of the nineteenth century, attempts to maintain precontact nutritional cultures tended to dissipate as mission agriculture appropriated hunting and gathering zones and disrupted Native American gardens. Traditional burning practices, which allowed soil to become more mineral dense, were prevented.[71] Communally protected high-ranking game were hunted more than before, largely to supply the nutritional needs of new Spanish markets. The traditional Native American focus on low-ranking animals was abandoned, as Spanish missions ruptured the cultural mechanisms and traditions that underlay such practices.[72] From 1810, the movement for independence from Madrid among colonists in New Spain isolated missions in California from Mexico, leading them to increase agricultural output as well as the domestication of animals in and around their settlements. The products of the missions included European cattle, alcohol, maize and wheat—all nutrient poor but energy dense. Grain production increased to provide products for exchange with British forces in the Eastern United states, rupturing local food networks and indigenous horticulture even further.[73]

The discovery of California gold in 1848 marked a sudden turn toward the encouragement of private property rights in horticultural and hunting centers—similar to the situation in New England two centuries earlier. Much remaining Native American agricultural land and hunting zones were bifurcated. As Bauer has pointed out, "domesticated livestock, such as cattle, pigs, and sheep, consumed Native food sources, such as acorns, while farmers prevented California Indians from hunting and harvesting on what they suddenly announced was private property."[74] Even in the 1840s, to be sure, some California Native American communities, such as those in the San Joaquin Valley, attempted to maintain farms in ways that adapted earlier nutritional and ecological traditions.[75]

In the inner coastal California ranges from Sonoma to San Diego, Spanish-introduced grazing animals and grain agriculture disrupted traditional ecologies and subsistence methods. As Anderson has shown, "coastal prairies, oak savannahs, prairie patches in coastal redwood forests, and riparian habitats, all rich in plant species diversity and kept open and fertile through centuries of Indian burning, became grazing land for vast herds of cattle, sheep, goats, hogs, and horses owned by Spanish missions and rancheros. By 1832 the California missions had more than 420,000 head of cattle, 320,000 sheep, goats, and hogs, and 60,000 horses and mules." Meanwhile, as missions stepped up production of wheat and maize through the eighteenth century, "agricultural fields replaced native ecosystems." In mid and northern coastal California, Spanish cattle, hogs and horses began devouring nuts, acorns, seeds and grasses by the late eighteenth century, leaving Native Americans without valuable sources of micronutrients and macronutrients, which they had hitherto developed extraction techniques and trade networks to maintain.[76]

California indigenous communities regularly complained to Spanish missionaries that settler livestock destroyed their acorn supplies. Their raids on European livestock in the region were often motivated by this specific grievance. By the nineteenth century, surviving California communities of hunters and gatherers found themselves shut out by Euro-American fences, which enabled cattle and sheep to consume wild grass seeds and acorns. According to an 1856 European settler account, Native American "spring and summer food [...] [has] been this season, and will hereafter be, consumed by cattle, horses, and hogs"—a final act of colonization that prevented the consumption of ancestral sources of starches and seeds, particularly acorns. Native Americans resented the advancement of nonindigenous seeds and livestock into regions where ancestral acorn starch sources had hitherto been gathered, just as they also resented the loss of habitats to hunt animals for their fat and protein.[77]

Interior missions that retained an agricultural focus were thus deadlier for Native Americans than those which confined their communities to religious instruction. As in other missions, they subjected the nutritional lives of Native Americans to more change, and forced people to live in dense settlements.[78] Unsurprisingly, archaeological evidence comparing Chumash populations before and after contact demonstrates that colonial-era skeletons were significantly smaller than their predecessors—a difference that "may in part be a result of nutritional deficiencies of the mission diet, [alongside infectious diseases and psychological stress]."[79] These changes could be measured over several generations—more than a century in cases—rather than solely deriving from specific short-term epidemics. California Native Americans experienced an extended contact era, and demographic decline in the medium to long term, mirroring other regions in earlier periods, which also suffered disrupted subsistence patterns.

During the 1850s and 1860s, indeed, California communities experienced ecological disturbances that were similar to those which took place two centuries earlier in New England. Farmers and squatters used the imposition of Euro-American agricultural methods to curtail indigenous foods and hunting sources, leading to a series of California Native American revolts and attempts to destroy the perceived source of disease epidemics: the new proximity between people and animals in sedentary contexts. Native Americans targeted settler livestock sources, mirroring their counterparts two centuries earlier in

New England, who had targeted European animals before any retaliation against people.[80]

As federal authorities forced Native Americans into reservations and allotments during the late nineteenth and the early twentieth century, some Native Americans adapted landholding patterns to reassert precontact subsistence strategies. They positioned allotments so that members of the community retained communal access to supposedly private segments, each of which was placed next to the other. Though designated as private allotments, they were treated as conduits to public land and resources, such as fishing rivers, hunting lands and grazing sites. In 1895, however, the federal government revised the nature of the reservation, making sure to deny access to those communal resources. Such a multiuse land system, and its attempt to reconfigure earlier ways of linking horticulture with fishing and hunting, was ruined. Though famously admitted to the United States as a free state, Californian freedom in these contexts centered on land privatization at the expense of Native American societal frameworks, including their food production and subsistence networks.[81]

The contingency of nutritional frameworks was likely as important for health and immunity in California, therefore, as in the shatter zones examined in the previous chapter. But rather than focusing on micronutrient deficiencies, let us assess the potential threat to metabolic health as California's indigenous acorn complex was destroyed. Precontact acorn production, as we have seen, was facilitated by a familiar gendered vision: women gathered acorns and leached them of tannic acid by soaking ground nut flour, while men hunted and fished animals. Fires were also used to control insects that might threaten acorn crops.[82] Though ground up into flour-like powders and baked in bread-like patties, acorns (and other nuts) were in fact far higher in fat and protein than traditional grain flours made from maize or wheat.[83] The centrality of acorn powder in subsistence systems before contact need not have suggested a high glycemic load nor any comparable loss of insulin sensitivity—as distinct from the eras of European colonial disruption. Given our discussion in the previous section of this chapter, it is thus worth raising the potentially problematic effects of raised blood glucose in compromising health and immunity among California communities that turned from ground acorn powder as a consumed staple to higher-glycemic wheat and maize.

But rather than merely focusing on the potentially negative outcomes of excess carbohydrate consumption, as demonstrated by the link between raised blood sugar and compromised health and immunity, we ought also to consider the positive metabolic effects of some starches—particularly in the form of acorn powder—and the negative effects of their curtailment. Aside from their greater reliance on less-nutritional and higher-glycemic starches after colonization, Native Americans in California might also have suffered from reduced access to resistant starch (RS) as their preparation and consumption of its primary source—ground acorns—gave way to wheat and corn.[84] The gut contains a vast array of bacterial species, many of which are thought to depend in part on fermentable carbohydrates, including RS, to provide metabolic fuel.[85] Most fermentable carbohydrates are obtained from dietary sources from plants, though some are synthesized by the host and by other microbes (such as yeast) in the digestive tract, or are obtained from meat in the form of glycans.[86] As a beneficial substrate for fermentation, instead of being digested by amylases in the upper digestive tract, RS tends to pass through to the bowel, where it is fermented by bacteria into short-chain fatty acids (SCFA) such as butyrate, which as we will see, are particularly beneficial to the development and function of the immune system.[87] SCFAs provide energy for the host, at up to 70 percent of the host energy needs.[88] Butyrate, we should point out, is the "preferred energy source for the colon epithelial cells, contributes to the maintenance of the gut barrier functions, and has immunomodulatory and anti-inflammatory properties."[89] It has therefore been suggested that RS is important in aiding the digestion of accompanying proteins and fats, thanks to its contribution to fueling bacteria in the gut microbiome.[90]

Understanding the association between RS intake and the production of short-chain fatty acids in the microbiome is particularly important for our purposes because it is also correlated with the optimal function of the human immune system. We are concerned with the contingent factors that might have reduced Native American immunological health when destructive pathogens and secondary infections were more prevalent than ever before. Inulin and other prebiotics, such as isomalto-oligosaccharide and lactulose, have been found to increase the concentration of immunologically beneficial bifidobacteria in the human gut, both in vitro and in human studies.[91] A lack of RS in the diet has been suggested to result in increases in species that are adapted to feeding on mucins in the intestinal mucus layer.[92] This may result in depletion of gut mucus and loss of integrity of the intestinal barrier, which may further compromise immunity, given the gut's role as a mediator between outside pathogens (in foods) and the rest of the body.[93] The potential association between RS intake, the production of SCFAs by gut bacteria and optimal immunity thus requires further analysis at the deepest biological level.

As well as being directly involved in the digestion of food, and acting as a mediator between external pathogens and the bloodstream, the microbiome is involved in signaling between commensal bacteria and the body's immune cells. Such communication is vital in allowing the immune system to distinguish between pathogenic and commensal (beneficial) bacteria, so that the immune response is mounted against the former but not the latter. As well as maintaining a healthy microbiotal composition, this communication affects aspects of the immune response such as intestinal inflammation and the response to pathogens.[94] Various signaling pathways are involved in communication between the immune system and the microbiota, including the toll-like receptor pathway and the nod-like receptor pathway.[95] All involve pattern recognition of commensal bacterial proteins by the immune cells, encouraging the growth of commensal bacteria and inhibiting invasion by pathogenic organisms, in an important feedback loop.[96] Mononuclear phagocytes, a class of immune cells, are also affected by microbiota signaling. Those in the lymphoid organs of germ-free mice (which lack a microbiome) have been shown to display aberrant gene expression, resulting in a decreased response from natural killer cells, which are important in their ability to destroy host cells infected with pathogens.[97] The intestinal microbiome influences immune function in several other ways, all of which are thought to affect aspects of the immune response such as intestinal inflammation and the response to pathogens.[98] Commensal bacteria secrete antimicrobial compounds that can kill pathogenic bacteria directly.[99] Due to the profound influence that the microbiome exerts on immune function, therefore, perturbations in the number or types of species present in the microbiome would be expected to increase chronic inflammation and thus affect the acute immune response to diseases in problematic ways.[100] Fermentation of RS improves the integrity of the intestinal epithelium, which can help prevent infection and aberrant inflammation.[101]

Healthy gut bacteria, moreover, facilitate the bioavailability and even synthesis of many important vitamins that, as we saw in the previous chapter, are required for immunological health. Several vitamins are synthesized by the gut microbiota, including vitamin B12 (cobalamin), vitamin B6 (pyridoxal phosphate), vitamin B3 (niacin), vitamin B5 (pantothenic acid), biotin, tetrahydrofolate and vitamin K. These micronutrients play a role in the metabolism of the host.[102] The absorption of some minerals, such as iron, is also affected by the microbiota.[103] The effect of the microbiome on the host's absorption of iron is illustrated by experiments in rats. Germ-free rats become iron deficient when fed a diet low in iron, which is lost in their feces, whereas rats with a normal gut biome do not.[104] Similarly, in a mouse model of Crohn's disease, iron supplementation changes the composition of the gut microbiome.[105] These effects may well be echoed in the human organism.[106] As we have seen, evidence of iron and vitamin B12 deficiency in communities that came to rely on grains at the expense of animals and other plants shows that they were also likely to suffer immunological degradation. Furthermore, it has been suggested that certain species of bacteria may be involved in the absorption of vitamin A in the intestine—another nutrient that we have already discussed in relation to immune function.[107]

The fast-developing biological literature on the microbiome, and the potential contribution of RS sources such as acorn powder to gut health and immunity, thus illuminates our discussions in previous chapters of the importance of what might at first glance seem to have been relatively niche food products that were cultivated or gathered in Native American communities in western North America, particularly the Pacific Northwest: artichokes, rhizomes, corms and tubers.[108] The first period of serious contact between indigenous people and Europeans in the Pacific Northwest can also be traced from the late eighteenth century. Mirroring the situation in California, European settlers ruptured Native American nutritional diversity, and its delicate ecological basis, before United States federal institutions then cemented those disruptions in legal statutes.[109] The importance of RS should remind us that most scholarly accounts of Native American life in the region have underestimated the role of starchy plant sources, including as stored in powders for winter use—and the resulting problems faced by communities that were eventually restricted in their consumption of RS. That restriction may well have contributed to the nutritional disruptions that in turn exacerbated the demographic decline in the Pacific Northwest through the nineteenth century.

The availability of fibrous tubers, roots and rhizomes had once determined the nature of sedentary occupation in sites where hunting and fishing also took place. Historical communities in the precontact British Columbia Plateau, such as the Thompson (Nlaka'pmx) and Lillooet (Stl'atl'imx), spent between one week and a month every late-summer season gathering and processing lance leaf spring beauty, often known as "wild potatoes," which they then consumed in the same meal as animal products. Regional languages often determined the names for seasons according to plants—often relatively rich in starch—that were harvested or gathered to supplement animal fats and protein. The Shuswap people named April, for example, as "the month when yellow glacier lilies sow growth."[110] Roots and tubers tended to be cooked in late summer through early winter, in earth ovens that consisted of deeply dug fire pits filled with hot rocks that were then covered with cooler vegetation. The RS in harvested camas, onions and balsam roots was likely made more bioavailable by slow-cooking them in this way.[111]

Many of the plants in these Pacific Northwest examples contain inulin and oligofructose. Those non-fermentable carbohydrate RS sources, often classed as fructans, are stored in the roots, tubers and bracts of many flowering plant species as an energy reserve, and act in a similar way to ground acorn powder when prepared appropriately.[112] As with other nondigestible carbohydrates that can be classed as RS, inulin has been linked to several health-promoting effects, including lowering of blood glucose levels and improvements in lipid metabolism. Recent medical literature has shown that RS may reduce the potential for type 2 diabetes in populations that eat carbohydrates.[113] Experiments in humans suggest that fructans can lower blood sugar levels following ingestion of starch and can improve fasting blood glucose levels.[114] In healthy human subjects, for example, 10g artichoke inulin added to a meal of 50g wheat starch resulted in a lower blood glycemic response.[115] Another experiment in humans showed that inclusion of inulin in the diet for eight weeks reduced fasting insulin concentrations.[116] Consumption of inulin has also been shown to affect lipid metabolism, potentially reducing triglyceride levels in the blood and liver (which are potentially inflammatory in effect).[117] Given our discussions of the possible link between chronically raised blood sugar, diminished insulin sensitivity and compromised immunity among postcontact Native American communities, the association between RS, enhanced microbiome diversity and increased insulin sensitivity seems even more pertinent.

Thus we should not underestimate the role of plant carbohydrates in the Pacific Northwest, or elsewhere, particularly as harvested and cultivated by women. They often provided energy sources for men and women to hunt for animal products. That hunting and plant horticulture were synergistic is further underscored by our discussions of the relationship between RS, microbiome quality and optimal digestion. If communities were to digest the nutrient-dense animal products they required, RS may well have provided the optimal gut flora to facilitate that process. The restriction of RS collection by European disruptions, conversely, likely prevented optimal micronutrient absorption from the gut to the wider body.[118]

In our hypothesis, then, Native American communities that moved rapidly toward European-imposed diets likely found their RS intake declining, their microbiome altered in problematic ways and thus their immunity compromised at just the point when new pathogens required the strongest possible immune response. While aspects of the "virgin soil" paradigm are salient, therefore, contingent external nutrition factors may have reduced further the possibility of survival or recovery in affected populations. The hypothesis is supported by recent studies of microbiome distinctions between Western and hunter-gatherer populations in the contemporary era. Scientists have supplemented Western populations with fermentable carbohydrates to match those consumed by contemporary hunter-gatherer communities, and have shown the microbiome to become more diverse, better able to digest food and potentially more likely to discourage inflammatory markers from developing in subjects.[119] A comparison between non-Western indigenous diets and Western diets has suggested that acellular carbohydrates may change the gut microbiotal species to those that promote greater inflammation.[120]

Accordingly, studies that show that the ingestion of Western meals (high in refined carbohydrates and lower in fermentable fiber) results in increased circulating levels of lipopolysaccharides, which closely correlates with inflammation levels and a chronically raised immune response (raising the likelihood of autoimmune conditions rather than sound working immunity to pathogens).[121]

Aside from the influence of RS on the functioning of the microbiome, and the threat to optimal micronutrient absorption and immunity following its restriction by colonial disruption, we should also consider the role of societal stress in Native American life and its similar effects. At the biological level, particularly in relation to the interaction between gut health and immunity, psychological stress is often overlooked in accounts of the assault on Native America after contact. External stress can be defined as the "physiological disruption of an organism resulting from environmental perturbation."[122] The gastrointestinal tract is known to be sensitive to stress, most obviously in instances of the onset of irritable bowel syndrome.[123] The outcome of enteric infections also depends on levels of stress.[124] The concept of the gut-brain axis describes the "bidirectional communication" between the gut and brain.[125] It involves communication through the vagus nerve (which directly links the gut to the brain) and the secretion of hormones by the hypothalamic-pituitary-adrenal (HPA) axis, a response system that responds to stress.[126] Such communication is thought to regulate GI function, appetite and weight control.[127]

Recently, the term "microbiota-gut-brain axis" has been applied, implicating the role of the microbiome in both the response to stress and the regulation of stress.[128] The microbiota may in turn influence stress levels. Such an effect is suggested by separation experiments with germ-free mice: unlike wild-type mice, germ-free mice were found not to demonstrate stress behaviors when separated from their mothers. Rather, the commensal bacteria were required for the exhibition of stress.[129] Scholars have even outlined the effect of the gut bacteria in the depressive response in mice studies. Depressive response was measured using the forced swimming test, in which mice are placed in water and forced to swim to exhaustion. Maternal separation before the forced swimming test caused a decreased duration of swimming, but this effect was reversed after introducing the probiotic *Bifidobacterium infantis*, suggesting that this bacteria decreased the depressive response.[130] The production of catecholamine neurotransmitters by bacteria suggests that bacteria may influence stress levels directly through the secretion of neurotransmitters into the host.[131] *Eshcherichia* and *Enterococcus* produce serotonin, and *Bacillus* and *Serratia* produce dopamine.[132] Gut microbes may also affect stress levels by influencing inflammation of the gut.[133] The inflammatory response involves the secretion of cytokines, which cross the blood-brain barrier and affect mood and behavior, sometimes referenced through the exhibition of well-documented "sickness behaviors" in individuals suffering from infections.[134]

The interaction between the microbiome and stress has obvious relevance in the case of Native Americans in the Pacific Northwest, California, and elsewhere, who would have presumably experienced much higher levels of the emotional state during the period of colonization that witnessed whole-sale threats to societal structures, new diseases, uprooted subsistence strategies, destabilization of spiritual confidence, unknown bellicose enemies, the constant threat of enslavement and a general state of eerie uncertainty.

Shattered Subsistence in Alaska in the Eighteenth and Nineteenth Centuries: Seasonal Vitamin D, Fatty Acids, Ketosis and Autophagy

On the eve of Western contact, the indigenous population of present-day Alaska numbered around 80,000. They included the Alutiiq and Unangan communities, more commonly defined as Aleuts, Iñupiat and Yupiit, Athabaskans, and the Tinglit and Haida groups.[135] Most groups suffered a stark demographic decline from the mid-eighteenth century to the mid-nineteenth century, during the period of extended European—particularly Russian—contact. Oral traditions among indigenous groups in Alaska described whites as having taken hunting grounds from other related communities, warning of a similar fate to their own.[136] The Unangan community, numbering more than 12,000 at contact, declined by around 80 percent by 1860. By as early as the 1820s, as Jacobs has described, "the rhythm of life had changed completely in Unangan villages, now based on the exigencies of the fur trade rather than the subsistence cycle, meaning that often villages were unable to produce enough food to keep them through the winter." Here, as elsewhere, societal disruption was most profound in the nutritional sphere, helping account for the failure to recover population numbers following disease epidemics.[137]

In many parts of Alaska, Native American nutritional strategies and ecological niches were suddenly disrupted by the arrival of Spanish and Russian settlers. "Because," as Saunt has pointed out "it was extraordinarily difficult to extract food from the challenging environment," in Alaska and other Pacific coastal communities, "any disturbance was likely to place enormous stress on local residents."[138] One of indigenous Alaska's most important ecological niches centered on salmon access points. They became steadily more important between the Paleo-Eskimo era around 4,200 years ago and the precontact period, but were increasingly threatened by Russian and American disruptions from the 1780s through the nineteenth century.[139] Dependent on nutrients and omega fatty acids such as DHA from marine resources such as salmon, Aleut and Alutiiq communities also required other animal products, such as intestines, to prepare tools and waterproof clothing to take advantage of fishing seasons. Through the later part of the eighteenth century, however, Russian fur traders and settlers began to force them away from the coast with ruthless efficiency, even destroying their hunting tools and waterproof apparatus. The Russians were clear in their objectives here, with one of their men observing that Native American fishing boats were "as indispensable as the plow and the horse for the farmer."[140]

Here we are provided with another tragic case study, which allows us to consider the likely association between disrupted access to omega-3 fatty acids such as DHA and compromised immunity. We have already noted the link between DHA, reduced inflammation and enhanced immunity in the millennia following the evolution of the small human gut and the comparatively large human brain. Wild animals, but particularly wild fish, have been shown to contain far higher proportions of omega-3 fatty acids than the food sources that apparently became more abundant in Native American diets after European contact, including in Alaska.[141] Fat-soluble vitamins and DHA are abundantly found in fish eggs and fish fats, which were prized by Native Americans in the Northwest and Great Lakes regions, in the marine life used by California communities, and perhaps more than anywhere else, in the salmon products consumed by indigenous Alaskan communities.

Restriction of DHA likely accompanied the curtailment of dietary vitamin D, given their duel occurrence in animal products, particularly marine animals such as salmon. Any discussion of the comparison between demographically successful communities and those that were unable to recover from epidemics should therefore incorporate the contingency of dietary vitamin D access alongside DHA. As we have seen, we can track the decline of nitrogen stable isotope ratios—an indicator of declining marine food consumption—in comparison to increasing carbon maize indicators after European contact in coastal regions of the Southeast and Florida, such as the Guale province. We would likely be able to find similar indicators elsewhere, including in Alaska.[142] It is certainly possible that Arctic indigenous communities have evolved genetic mutations that allow them to require less vitamin D for optimal health. Yet it is increasingly suggested that their requirements before European contact were met through dietary sources—animal meat in the interior region, and salmon in coastal region—and that the disruption of those sources has indeed resulted in vitamin D deficiencies.[143]

The nutritional source of vitamin D in animals, so vital for health and immunity, is often overlooked in favor of its synthesis from the action of sunlight on the skin.[144] Vitamin D3 is synthesized from 7-dehydrocholestrol on the exposure of many organisms to UVB radiation.[145] Activation of the vitamin

D receptor, a nuclear steroid hormone, can alter the expression of more than 200 genes, indicating the profound role that vitamin D has on cellular function.[146] Most importantly, for the purposes of our discussion, the discovery of the VDR in several types of immune cells—including B cells and T cells—illustrates the central role of vitamin D in immunity.[147] The VDR is present on most immune cells and in most tissues involved in the immune response, regulating the expression of many genes necessary for that response.[148] Following activation of the VDR, several immune responses are activated, including the production of cytokines and antimicrobial peptides.[149] Much recent research has thus outlined the mechanisms through which vitamin D affects immune function and reduces chronic inflammation.[150] It has been found to affect the activity of immune cells including macrophages, phagocytes and dendritic cells, and to reduce inflammatory cytokine production.[151] Unsurprisingly, then, low blood serum levels of vitamin D are strongly correlated with susceptibility to infectious diseases as well as the development of autoimmune conditions, which result from chronically raised inflammatory markers, and which in turn reduce working immunity to invading pathogens.[152]

Several studies have focused on the link between vitamin D and the health outcomes of individuals infected with tuberculosis, taking care to discount other causal factors and to avoid determining causation merely through association. Given the historical occurrence of the disease among indigenous people after contact, including in Alaska, those studies that have isolated the contingency of immunity on active vitamin D are particularly pertinent to note. In biochemical experiments, the presence of the active form of vitamin D has been shown to have a crucial role in the destruction of *Mycobacterium tuberculosis* by macrophages.[153] A recent review has found that tuberculosis patients tend to retain a lower-than-average vitamin D status, and that supplementation of the nutrient improved outcomes in most cases.[154]

In our discussion of the potential interaction between nutritional context and the evolution of genetic traits after the Neolithic transition, we suggested that some European communities may have developed lighter skin to generate greater vitamin D from light after nutritional sources for the vitamin diminished in favor of nutrient-poor grains in intensified agricultural contexts.[155] What, then, of those Native American communities that required dietary vitamin D for optimal immune function, particularly those such as the indigenous peoples of Alaska, who lived in far northern latitudes? Even south of Alaska, many communities likely achieved vitamin D status from food: other than among Florida Native American communities, after all, vitamin D was likely consumed through dietary sources from late fall to late spring. After European contact, when Native Americans sought to prevent the outbreak of infectious diseases, or at least to allow surviving individuals to reproduce without suffering from secondary diseases or infections, declining vitamin D levels from curtailed access to foods such as salmon, and other vitamin D-rich foods, likely posed a significant problem.

The association between curtailed dietary vitamin D and DHA, and compromised immunity can also be understood in relation to metabolic health, given the importance of both micronutrients in enhancing insulin sensitivity (the efficiency of glucose removal from the blood). Exceptional glucose tolerance, due to insulin sensitivity, was noted in seminal early twentieth-century studies that were conducted among Alaskan "Eskimo" communities that were determined to maintain precontact nutritional traditions. In an often-cited 1928 paper, blood glucose was found to rise to lower levels than expected following carbohydrate consumption, illustrating efficient uptake into other tissues, or insulin sensitivity.[156] Subsequent researchers noticed that diabetes mellitus prevalence was particularly low in Eskimos.[157] Low diabetes rates, to be sure, likely derive from the low-carbohydrate diet in ancestral Inuit communities, whose focus on fat and protein has traditionally prevented the chronic insulin spikes that are now linked to the development of type 2 diabetes in global populations. But insulin sensitivity may well have been enhanced further by vitamin D and DHA-rich food sources, such as wild salmon. Recent research has highlighted the potential for omega-3 fatty acids to improve glucose and insulin sensitivity.[158] Several studies have shown that the glucose tolerance of Alaskan indigenous people is improved with greater consumption of omega-3 fatty acids. They suggest that high glucose tolerance may in part be a result of their high consumption of omega-3 fatty acids, coupled with their low-glycemic diet.[159] Studies of Alaskan Inuits in contemporary populations have demonstrated an inverse relationship between consumption of plasma omega-3 concentrations and plasma glucose concentrations as well as an inverse relationship between plasma omega-3 concentrations and plasma insulin concentrations.[160] A high intake of omega-3 fatty acids is important in allowing glucose homeostasis, which as we have seen, is vital for healthy immune function. A similar scholarly consensus now suggests the link between vitamin D, enhanced insulin sensitivity and optimal immunity.[161] That the two micronutrients are often found synergistically in food sources, particularly marine animals, underlines their likely contribution to nutritional frameworks for immunity among populations that consumed those foods for thousands of years.

Aside from the metabolic advantages provided by DHA and vitamin D in salmon and wild animals, it is worth considering a separate unique aspect of the indigenous Alaskan metabolic profile, which was disrupted by European contact. Though some plants were available to precontact Arctic and Alaskan communities, they subsisted almost entirely on animal products, including animals such as walrus, which were comparatively high in fat content. Historically, up to and including the late twentieth century, adult "Eskimos" are thought to have consumed around four to eight pounds of meat every day. The only carbohydrates consumed have likely included the glycogen within meat, and occasionally kelp or berries.[162] Such a low-carbohydrate diet may have allowed communities in the region to burn fatty acids, or even ketones, rather than glucose as a primary metabolic fuel. Cellular metabolism can be affected detrimentally by the overconsumption of glucose, which can decrease the metabolism of fatty acids and ketones.[163] The metabolic state of ketosis is defined as the elevation of the ketone bodies D-beta-hydroxybutyrate (R-3hydroxybutyrate) and acetoacetate in the body in response to the consumption of a diet low in glucose and high in fats.[164] Healthy cells can use ketone bodies and fatty acids for energy when the supply of glucose is limited, thereby conserving glucose.[165] In mammals, ketones are required for the brain, which, unlike other tissues, cannot use fatty acids as a fuel in the absence of glucose.[166] In the metabolic state of ketosis, therefore, the use of ketones by the brain replaces most of the glucose it would otherwise use.[167]

The metabolism of ketones is thought to have several health benefits, potentially including increased longevity, which again are related to beneficial effects on cellular metabolism.[168] The metabolic pathway allowing cells to use ketones may have arisen very early in evolution. It has been suggested that an "alternate metabolic program"—akin to ketosis—originally evolved in microorganisms.[169] Hence, the metabolic pathway involving the use of ketones as fuel is distinct from that used in the metabolism of other nutrients, and has profound consequences for the health of the organism. Ketosis can thus be defined as an evolutionary adaptation to limited nutrient availability, which also has several positive effects on health.[170]

As an illustration of the health-promoting effects of the metabolic state of ketosis, let us explore some of the specific medical uses of ketosis, and the mechanisms responsible for the beneficial effects. Ketosis induced by calorie restriction or high-fat diets has shown to be beneficial in specific situations, including as a therapy for epilepsy, and potentially in relation to other neurological problems, including brain cancer.[171] Attempts have been made to treat cancer with a diet low in glucose and high in fat. It has tentatively been suggested that this treatment may deprive some cancer cells of glucose, while allowing other cells to use ketone bodies to fuel their metabolism.[172] It is thought that several mechanisms are involved in the therapeutic benefits of ketosis: the reduction in oxidative stress, increased numbers of mitochondria in cells and reduced inflammation, potentially due to the decrease in glucose and the increase in blood ketone levels.[173] Given that some cancers are thought to result from disrupted cellular metabolism, the potential therapeutic benefits of ketogenic diets in cancer patients suggests that the use of ketones as a metabolic substrate may be beneficial for cellular metabolic health—including in immune cell health, so vital for communities threatened by new pathogens or in new contexts in which diseases are more likely to proliferate.

Given the potential health benefits of periodic ketosis, rather than glucose burning, it is worth considering potential disruption to this metabolic state among communities such as the Inuit, who may have been more likely to have spent part of their lives in ketosis, and who might even have been genetically adapted to cold climates where low-glucose-producing animal products were consumed. Several recent studies have suggested that the metabolic use of ketones may benefit long periods of medium-intensity movement by reducing the need for regular consumption of carbohydrates. They have focused on the ability of endurance athletes to maintain or perhaps even increase performance while consuming a high-fat diet.[174] Endurance exercise, such as long hunts, may incorporate adaptations that increase fat-burning capacity while preserving glycogen breakdown.[175]

We ought to consider the possibility that some indigenous communities before European contact would at least have cycled between periods of keto-adaptation and of glucose-burning, depending on the season. Communities in the northernmost parts of Canada and Alaska have historically utilized fat-adapted diets, burning fat obtained from meat and fish rather than glucose as a primary fuel for many months of the year.[176] Even if they could manufacture glucose from animal protein, via the process of gluconeogenesis, communities in the region might still have remained metabolically flexible thanks to the likelihood of fasted periods between hunting or fishing, which would have removed glucose from the blood and encouraged individuals to burn fatty acids from their own body. Whether from exogenous or endogamous sources of fatty acids, therefore, precontact Alaskan communities may have been well placed to burn ketones for fuel. If we recall the link between chronically raised blood glucose and compromised immunity, any disruption to the ketotic metabolic state by European interventions in indigenous subsistence strategies takes on new meaning, as a further contingency in the association between nutritional consumption, immunity and demographic collapse.

A few scholars have indeed considered the role of fat-adapted metabolic states among indigenous communities in Alaska and Arctic North America, given the likelihood that they relied on animal fats to a far greater extent than carbohydrates as an adaptation to their difficult context. They caution against assuming that they or indeed any other historical community would have been in continual ketosis simply because of their greater propensity to consume animal products rather than plant-derived carbohydrates.[177] In 1928, Heinbecker measured levels of acetoacetate (a ketone) in the urine of

"Eskimos" over three days of fasting. The levels of urinary ketones were lower than expected, suggesting only a mild level of ketosis. Glucose tolerance was found to be normal, also supporting the conclusion that subjects were in only a mild state of ketosis, given that glucose tolerance is expected to decrease in the state of ketosis.[178] Studies in 1972 measuring ketone levels in the urine of "Eskimos" using the strip paper technique also found no evidence of ketosis.[179] Some researchers suggest that the high protein content of the diet prevents ketosis in Eskimos, whether historically or during the present date, given the potential to produce excess glucose from protein through gluconeogenesis.[180]

Rather than being in deep ketosis, precontact indigenous peoples in Alaska and the North American Arctic interior region may have evolved increased ability to fully oxidize fat in the absence of carbohydrate. Therefore, although they may not have experienced deep ketosis historically, their metabolism was highly efficient in using fat to fuel metabolism. Subsequent studies have supported the hypothesis that the metabolism of Eskimos is more efficient at oxidizing fat.[181] Indeed, the diet of some Native Americans may have been higher in fat and lower in protein than that of the Eskimos, and may have therefore been more conducive to the metabolic state of ketosis. However, it is not possible to verify whether the Native Americans experienced high levels of ketosis. We can certainly hypothesize, however, that the lower consumption of glucose and the higher consumption of fat, combined with higher levels of fasting that accompany a hunting lifestyle, would have had favorable metabolic effects on the health and immunity of Native Americans, and that the disruption of animal fat sources in favor of European grains would have had the same negative effects detailed in other case studies, or perhaps even worse effects, given the lack of historical adaptation to higher-carbohydrate diets in Alaska.

Recent assessments in exercise physiology suggest that burning of fatty acids rather than glucose during extended moderate-tempo exercise is thought to reduce inflammatory markers associated with oxidative stress.[182] Immunity, we hypothesize, was likely also affected by proinflammatory metabolic interventions. If winter hunts were disrupted in favor of year-round grain reliance, or if activities on short-range hunts were fueled by maize and other grains rather than fatty acids from animal consumption or from bodily stores, then greater oxidative stress might have become apparent in affected Native American populations. Thus, we ought to consider how cellular metabolism might have been affected by the changing availability of macronutrients and the changing regularity of food consumption after European contact.

Though much more research is needed to determine the nature of fat burning during physical activity, or even in a resting state, we should also recall that fat adaptation (the efficient use of fatty acids as an energy source, including but not confined to the subsequent production of ketone bodies) may have resulted from what indigenous Alaskan (and other communities) refrained from eating, rather than merely what they consumed. Ketosis, after all, is entered by all human beings in the absence of any food, rather than merely through the consumption of high-fat and very low-carbohydrate diets. Fasting requires the body to provide energy from its own fat stores by releasing them into fatty acids, which when concentrated in the blood in the absence of glucose, leads to the beta-oxidation of fatty acids, to be converted into ketone bodies by the liver.[183]

A useful hypothesis can be gleaned by noting that precontact Alaskan communities, like many Native Americans, undertook long hunts over several hours at just the point in the season when they may have benefited from increased endurance due to their fat-adapted metabolic states and high fat consumption. Particularly during the winter, as we have seen, many Native American communities relied on hunting and gathering fatty cuts of meat for optimal nutritional health, long after Neolithic-era Europeans had moved toward domesticated animal husbandry and grain production. After European contact, many communities were forced to consume maize and other starches during the winter months, having lost access to ancestral winter hunting grounds.[184] European disruption to winter hunts threatened ancestral metabolic patterns that incorporated seasonal fat adaptation, or even seasonal ketosis. Evidence of the potential health-promoting benefits of fat-adapted diets, at least in periodic cycles, supports the hypothesis that disruption to ancestral metabolic cycles prevented other benefits that are as yet unknown, pending further scientific research—thus potentially exacerbating Native American susceptibility to infectious diseases following European contact. Here, therefore, the case study entails far broader implications for our understanding of human metabolic health in the past and present.[185]

The disruption of seasonal hunting and subsistence patterns led many communities to rely on year-round grain stores in ways that reduced the role of "autophagy" in problematic ways—particularly with regard to working immunity. Like ketosis, autophagy is associated with the fat-adapted metabolic state, during periods of low glucose consumption or even during fasting.[186] Literally translated as "self-eating," autophagy is defined as the digestion of protein aggregates and damaged cellular material.[187] Constitutive autophagy eliminates damaged organelles such as mitochondria, ribosomes (organelles inside cells that facilitate protein synthesis) and portions of the endoplasmic recticulum, a membrane system within cells in which specific metabolic reactions occur.[188] The process prevents accumulation of dysfunctional molecules and organelles that would otherwise inhibit the metabolic efficiency of cells, including immune cells.[189]

Autophagy is upregulated in a state of starvation: the recycling of nutrients during the starved state frees up material to allow the maintenance of cellular metabolism.[190] Due to the role of autophagy in survival during conditions of food restriction, it has been hypothesized that it initially arose early in evolution as a stress response to starvation, subsequently offering beneficial metabolic effects—particularly in reducing chronic inflammation and in providing the context for the function of immune cells.[191] The anti-inflammatory benefits of short-term fasting, as distinct from chronic malnutrition and calorie restriction, are thought to be a result of the beneficial effects on cellular metabolism, including decreased blood glucose levels and a switch from glucose to ketone bodies and fatty acids as an energy source.[192] Given the potential for autophagy to reduce chronic inflammation, indeed, scholars are increasingly confident that it is also associated with the optimal function of innate and adaptive immunity.[193] It is now known that the degradation of pathogens inside cells requires the autophagy pathway, as illustrated by the demonstration that mutations in autophagy genes increase susceptibility to infection "in organisms ranging from plants to flies to worms to mice, and possibly to humans."[194] Studies have recently discovered other novel autophagy pathways that are necessary for the immune response to function at its most optimal state.[195] Research has now begun to investigate the role of autophagy in several inflammatory diseases, many of which are known to interfere with the immune system more generally.[196]

The effects of increased glucose consumption, decreased fat consumption and decreased periods of autophagy are vital to consider when discussing the potential threat to immunological health in historical populations, including in Alaska. European interventions disrupted indigenous subsistence strategies that had once allowed seasonal periods of calorie restriction, low-insulin states and autophagy. A similar analysis could apply to dozens of other examples we have noted, where indigenous communities came to reside in year-round sedentary settlements that relied on storable grains rather than foods that had once been sourced during winter hunts, thereby preventing methods that may well have encouraged periodic autophagy or even ketosis, to the benefit of the immune system.

In Alaska, where DHA and vitamin D-rich salmon consumption was central to precontact subsistence strategies, alongside the consumption of nutrient-dense animal products and the regulation of metabolic hormones through periods of fasting or even through the efficient use of fatty acids or ketones for energy, disruptions to those strategies compromised immunity among those who suffered greater incursions from Russian and other European settlers through the first half of the nineteenth century.

A collapse in sustainable subsistence practices among the Aleuts of Alaska exacerbated population decline during the period of Russian contact. The

Russian colonial regime from the 1740s to the 1840s destroyed Aleut communities through open warfare and by attacking and curtailing their nutritional resources, such as sea otters, which Russians plundered to supply the Chinese market for animal skins. Aleuts were often forced into labor, and threatened by the regular occurrence of Aleut women being taken as hostages. Curtailed by armed force, Aleuts were often relocated to the Pribilof Islands or to California to collect seals and sea otters. The same process occurred as Aleuts were co-opted into Russian expansion through the Aleutian Islands, Kodiak Island and into the southern coast of Alaska. Suffering murder and other atrocities, Aleuts provided only one use to Russian settlers: their perceived expertise in hunting local marine animals. They were removed from their communities, disrupting demography further and preventing those who remained from accessing vital nutritional resources due to the discontinuation of hunting frameworks. Colonial disruption, warfare, captivity and disease were accompanied by the degradation of nutritional resources. Aleut population numbers declined from 18,000 to 2,000 during the period of Russian occupation in the first half of the nineteenth century. A lag between the first period of contact and the intensification of colonial disruption demonstrates the role of contingent interventions in framing the deleterious effects of epidemics, including the 1837–38 smallpox epidemic in the region.[197] Compounding these problems, communities used to a relatively high-fat and low-fructose diet were introduced to alcohol by the Russians, to the immediate detriment of their health and well-being.[198]

The initial demographic distinction of Tlingits from Aleuts and Alutiiqs underscores our focus on nutrition and subsistence as important contingent factors in the ability of communities to withstand or recover from disease epidemics. Notwithstanding their first contact with Russian traders in 1783, Tlingits maintained their supply of marine animals and their sources of meat and waterproof mammal parts from the interior. Unlike Aleuts and Alutiiqs in other Russian-Native American zones of contact, or indeed many Spanish-Native American contact zones in northern California, they retained their cultural autonomy, nutritional subsistence strategies and their population numbers through the nineteenth century. Their societal frameworks isolated their community members from diseases elsewhere in the region. Combined with the continuation of nutrient-dense consumption patterns, these factors reduced the likelihood of disease epidemics.[199] During the first half of the nineteenth century, similarly, Athabaskan communities were isolated from European contact due to their interior position along major rivers. Elsewhere in the region, Yupiit and Iñupiat maintained a good degree of isolation. Contingencies and context mattered above and beyond relative immunity to diseases brought by Europeans, particularly on the northern Pacific coast where communities were most often very small, autonomous and isolated. Those communities could not rely on new networks of exchange if and when their ecological systems were altered, or even sabotaged.[200]

As the seminal work of Burch has shown, European whalers placed great stress on hitherto sustainable supplies of marine animals among Iñupiaq people in northern Alaska. They also threatened supplies of caribou, which were already experiencing a natural dip in their reproductive cycle. Diverse animal products were restricted at just the point that indigenous populations became more sedentary and reliant on whaling ships for processed foods. Through the latter part of the nineteenth century their population numbers dropped drastically, as they suffered from both infectious diseases and metabolic conditions. Underscoring the role of contingency in the ability of these communities to withstand demographic decline, the latter was halted during the first half of the twentieth century when Iñupiaq populations chose to stress the importance of large families, departing from their historical norm, in order to rebuild their population numbers. As we have seen, a similar response was prevented in many other indigenous communities in North America, due to the ongoing effects of European disruption, including in the subsistence frameworks that contributed to optimal immunity. As whaling expeditions declined, European settlers lost interest in the region and enabled indigenous people to rebuild their demography.[201]

This chapter has reasserted the evolutionary and dietary importance of fat without discounting the role of carbohydrates in and beyond Native America. We have sought to offer a new interpretation of the seasonal nature of metabolic health, reading Native American hunting and agricultural patterns from previous chapters in light of the burgeoning scientific literature on the positive aspects of metabolic flexibility, as defined by the ability to store fat during some periods of higher carbohydrate intake, before then mobilizing that fat for energy during subsequent periods of fasting or during seasons when dietary carbohydrates are restricted.[202]

Changes in macronutrient intake—particularly an increase in glucose-producing foods –significantly influenced a deterioration health in general, and immunity in particular, in the centuries after European colonial disruption began. The process of autophagy, upregulated at times of food scarcity and low blood glucose, has been implicated in reducing chronic inflammation by clearing dead or damaged cells and protein aggregates and allowing new cells to be formed.[203] The metabolic state of ketosis, which occurs during times of fasting or because of a very low carbohydrate diet that relies on the burning of fatty acids for energy, may also influence levels of inflammation. Periodic disruption of both interlinked processes may have portended negative health consequences in Native American communities, particularly if they became more likely to rely on refined carbohydrates such as maize, whose high glycemic load, constant consumption and association with greater sedentism may have further reduced the likelihood of those biological processes acting in order to facilitate optimal working immunity.[204]

But as we have also noted, it is unrealistic to suggest that most human diets, including those in indigenous North America, evolved without carbohydrates (other than in certain extreme contexts such as the Arctic). In the previous chapter we examined the micronutrient benefits of many indigenously cultivated plants, including starch sources, and the problems that may have followed their curtailment by colonial disruption. In this chapter, we have noted the likely benefits of Resistant Starch sources among Native Americans, including in providing optimal conditions for immune signaling. Their restriction, therefore, may have been particularly deleterious at a time when diseases became more prevalent. The intake of glucose and fermentable fibers alters the composition of the bacteria that constitute the gut microbiome. These changes, we are now beginning to realize, have a potentially profound influence on immune function and inflammation. We can reread the assault on Native American subsistence, then, also as an assault on the delicate microbial environment of individuals in affected communities, as well as an assault on what was previously a more fat-adapted metabolism.[205]

Epilogue

DECOLONIZING THE DIET: FOOD SOVEREIGNTY AND BIODIVERSITY

The history of Native American health and demography in the three centuries after extended European contact shows that external interventions in indigenous food systems contributed to heightened susceptibility to infectious diseases, problematic metabolic syndromes and population decline. Multiple nutritional and ecological changes accompanied the introduction of infectious diseases: a greater threat from zoonotically spread pathogens in new European farming practices, mirroring the situation during the initial stages of the Neolithic transition in Europe and the Middle East; diminished access to fats, vitamins, proteins, and essential vitamins and minerals from animal and plant sources; an increasing inability to gather potentially beneficial indigenous starches and fermentable carbohydrate sources; and a growing threat to seasonal oscillations of the ratio between consumed fat and carbohydrate sources.

A growing scientific consensus on the problematic inflammatory effects of excess blood glucose, decreased micronutrients, proinflammatory foods, and restricted omega-3 fatty acid intake informs our understanding of bioarchaeological evidence of compromised immunity in Europe and the Middle East through the Neolithic transition. By synthesizing the latest historical, archaeological and bioanthropological assessments of Neolithic health in those regions with recent biological literatures on nutrition, inflammation and immunity, we have provided a conceptual framework to inform a strong working hypothesis: following the intensification of maize consumption in precontact Native American settlements such as Cahokia, or due to subsequent European disruptions, Native American immunological health was affected in the short to medium term by divergences from the micronutrient and macronutrient requirements that most human populations developed from around 2.4 million years ago. After European contact, furthermore, post-epidemic demographic recovery was inhibited by continuing nutrient poverty and metabolical derangement, which compromised health and fertility even further.

Following the Neolithic transition in Europe, and the later era of maize intensification in areas of North America, dietary changes were gradual enough to allow a level of adaptation to and mitigation of initially negative health consequences. Notwithstanding the problematic health markers and compromised immunity evidenced in both contexts, relative demographic stability or even growth became contingent on gradual adaptations such as improved sanitation, increasing access to nutrient-dense plant and animal products to supplement grains and a new understanding of the need to separate living settlements from zoonotic disease vectors. New disease epidemics occurred, to be sure, especially in Europe and elsewhere in the Old World. But nutritional density and diversity became a key contingent factor in providing general health after those initial epidemics, including by strengthening immunity and preventing secondary infections, and supporting fertility, thereby allowing demographic recovery in the medium to long term.

Problematic health effects of grain intensification were also mitigated by higher birth rates, and even, potentially, in the natural selection of genetic mutations of individuals within communities. In Neolithic Europe and the Middle East, and in Native America after maize intensification, new grains provided energy to reach reproductive age without starving, and early weaning that allowed less birth spacing. The decline in health of individuals born in such populations was offset by the overall increase in births.

The recovery of Neolithic, post-Neolithic and medieval European agricultural populations from disease epidemics, and the ability of maize-intensifying Native American communities to avoid population instability, has provided a salient counterpoint to the inability of Native American demography to stabilize in the centuries after European contact. Neolithic and post-Neolithic adaptation, and the precontact Native American avoidance of mass epidemics, can be contrasted with the later inability of Native American populations to counter sudden nutritional changes during periods of infectious disease proliferation.

The delay between first contact and demographic nadir after 1492, whether in the protohistoric periods of Spanish colonization of the Southeast or the early period of Russian contact in Alaska, demonstrates the role of contingent circumstances, including nutritional challenges, in encouraging population decline. Contrary to the "virgin soil" paradigm, new disease vectors or differing immunities did not affect immediate epidemics or sudden population loss. More gradual losses, interspersed with time-delayed epidemics, provide a more accurate picture. Within this framework, postcontact Native American populations were unable to implement adaptations to nutritional degradation, leading their health and immunity to suffer, without requiring innate immunological differences to act as a key determinant of population loss or recovery.

Though the sudden threat to nutrient diversity in many communities certainly compromised immunity in the short term, affected individuals might well have died even with the most optimal nutrition and the strongest immune system—particularly when responding to deadly diseases such as smallpox. But in the medium to long term, in the decades *after* initial infections and epidemics, nutrition was a key scalable factor in the subsequent ability of populations to recover their demographic stability. We have therefore suggested a broader explanation of the epidemiological effects of disease on demography at a time of continued colonial disruption of indigenous subsistence frameworks.

Nutrient poverty, moreover, likely increased infant mortality for generations after epidemics, either among weaning infants or because breast milk was compromised or less abundant, due to nutritional restrictions, thereby removing yet another immunological building block from communities already suffering demographic stress.

That communities such as the Comanche enjoyed an initial population increase after contact further underscores the contingent contribution of nutrition to population growth, given their ability to use European technologies to hunt and then supply nutrient-dense animal products, despite their biological contact with Europeans in supposed virgin soils. Their experience highlights the contrast with those who found their meat consumption curtailed in favor of maize—a nutrient-poor and insulinogenic food source whose abundance coincided with the greater proximity of domesticated animals and greater population density in defensive communities. Colonial settlement brought new diseases and heightened the proliferation of disease vectors, requiring the immune system to be functioning optimally—at just the point when the nutritional requirements for immunity were compromised. This paradigm is further supported by bioarchaeological evidence for compromised immunity, and even autoimmune diseases, among precontact maize-intensifying cultures.

Even if nutritional factors only directly compromised mortality outcomes for a small percentage of individuals during primary epidemics, the scaled effects within populations would have been enough to affect later demographic recovery. Moreover, if the inability to enhance nutrition in the medium term, combined with the shattering of social contexts, even prevented a small percentage of individuals from achieving the health and fertility levels that were required for populations to recover after epidemics, such a phenomenon would have been enough to disrupt demography in the long term, contributing to the eventual population nadir in Native America.

From Compromised Immunity to Autoimmunity in the Modern Era

We have noted the problematic effects of the mismatch between evolved nutritional requirements and available food sources, including in the association between disrupted metabolic health and compromised immunity to infectious diseases. In an era of antibiotics, vaccination and greater sanitation, however, the latter effects are less prevalent. Rather, just as in the United States more broadly, Native Americans have become more likely to suffer from the effects of metabolic derangement in producing autoimmune conditions, rather than infectious disease. Among Native American populations that survived the first era of European disruption from the sixteenth century to the early nineteenth century, subsequent government interventions and local settlement treaties have exacerbated nutritional degradation and compromised indigenous health in new ways. Rather than affecting demography through compromised immunity to infectious disease or through disrupted recovery following epidemics, the problematic effects of modern interventions have increasingly centered on conditions with an inflammatory and autoimmune component, particularly type 2 diabetes.

Autoimmunity, as we have noted, is defined by the problematic reconfiguration of the body's response to external infectious vectors toward its own structural components, often due to the inflammatory response becoming chronic rather than acute and specific. Type 1 diabetes has long been defined, in part, as an autoimmune disease due to the role of the immune system attacking and compromising the pancreas's insulin-producing beta cells.[1] Type 2 diabetes has also begun to be categorized as an inflammatory condition with an autoimmune component, due in part, or at least in some cases, to the determination of insulin resistance by an association between chronic exogenous glucose consumption and the overactivity of immune cells in attacking the body's own tissues.[2]

We have suggested that the problematic effects of type 2 diabetes or prediabetes might have been apparent among some Native American communities that were forced to rely on maize rather than a more diverse diet immediately following European settlement. But as far the condition has been diagnosed more formally in Native America, as a widespread condition, an emerging scholarly consensus has suggested that "diabetes is a 'new' disease among Native Americans," that has developed "from a rarity before World War II to [become] an 'epidemic' in recent years."[3]

Through the first half of the twentieth century, reservation communities were more susceptible to certain problems that are associated with the modern Western diet, as broadly defined during the second half of the twentieth century—particularly its reliance on refined carbohydrates in packaged and processed goods. From the 1960s to the 1970s, for example, medical researchers began to define a clear correlation between the appearance of obesity and type 2 diabetes in Native American communities before that era and their adoption of processed foods in federal welfare programs that targeted newly formed reservations. Reports of type 2 diabetes among Oklahoma communities increased after their move into federally mandated reservations through the 1940s. A review of literature from 1832 to 1939 by the epidemiologist Kelly West found no reports of diabetes among the Kiowa, Comanche or Apache communities living in the region.[4]

To be sure, we should be careful not to exclude the possibility that undiagnosed symptoms were present long before the era delineated by West, due to earlier Euro-American disruption of Native American subsistence strategies. As Mihesuah has recently pointed out, "Historical and ethnobotanical data reveals that Indians in Indian Territory (made the state of Oklahoma in 1907) began suffering from food-related illnesses, including diabetes or prediabetes, before the Civil War"—thus demonstrating "the importance of utilizing ethnohistorical data in medical studies dealing with indigenous health, as well as understanding the connection between the loss of traditional foodways and the modern health crisis."[5] What is certain is that by the 1960s diabetes had reached epidemic proportions. Discussing the epidemiological work of West, one more recent review has suggested that the condition "in the Native American population was virtually unknown in 1940. Diabetes started in the 1950's and its increasing frequency was noted in the mid-1960's literature."[6]

Notwithstanding the likelihood that type 2 diabetes became prevalent during earlier periods of disrupted subsistence, the greater proliferation of type 2 diabetes after the 1940s is clearly contextualized by federally mandated interventions among Native American communities during the previous 80 years, which cemented the disruption of indigenous subsistence strategies and encouraged greater reliance on energy-dense and nutrient-poor processed foods. Let us consider these interventions, and their likely effects on what we are increasingly defining as a disease with an autoimmune component, in more detail.

In 1867the Treaty of Medicine Lodge required Southern Plains Native Americans to give up land in return for government annuities. The federal government then began supplying them with food handouts, using the industrial and transportation systems developed to supply troops with grains during the Civil War.[7] The 1887 United States Dawes Act divided reservations into segments, or "allotments," where "surplus" land could be used by white settlers. The 1928 federal Meriam Report showed the failure of the 1887 Act to provide autonomous spaces that could replicate indigenous subsistence methods. Rather than allowing semiautonomy in food production and societal governance, the act bifurcated lands, turning them into unsustainable Bantustans that encouraged food insecurity and an increasing reliance on nutrient-poor grains supplied by wider markets rather than local economies.[8]

Indeed, the proliferation of cures, tonics and "snake-oil" medicines for digestive problems in Indian Territory newspapers during the century after the Civil War era provides clues to problematic dietary changes among Native Americans, changes that resulted in part from disruptive state and federal policies, which were contiguous with challenging interventions that took place during the earlier colonial era.[9]

The containment of Native Americans on reservations severely limited the physical activity to which their communities had grown accustomed over previous centuries, and also allowed federal institutions greater control in food provisions provided to the areas. By the second and third decades of the twentieth century, it has been suggested, decreased energy expenditure made many Native Americans less likely to burn increasing volumes of glucose in their diet, contributing to the development of diabetes and other immune disorders through the twentieth century.[10]

Commissioned nutritional assessments, such as the 1902 *Physiological and Medical Observations among the Indians of Southwestern United States and Northern Mexico*, and the *Annual Reports of the Commissioner of Indians Affairs*, which provide evidence from Indian Territory (Oklahoma) between the 1820s and the 1930s, show the degradation of health among communities placed in government-initiated reservations. They demonstrate the increase in processed starches and high-sugar beverages among reservation communities, in contrast to those who lived away from those communities. The *Indian and Pioneer Papers*, which details thousands of interviews of residents in Oklahoma in the 1930s, describes similarly problematic nutritional changes, diseases, perceived health problems and ecological and agricultural developments. Many of those residents were elderly and recalled nutritional, agricultural and health developments that took place during the previous century. *Physiological and Medical Observations* reported that obesity and associated "grave disease[s] of the liver" were "exclusively" found among Pima Indians on new reservations, rather than among those who relied on a more traditional system of hunting meats and gathering or cultivating fibrous seeds, chenopods, plants and starchy tubers. Over the following half-century, most physicians and researchers among the Pima Indians avoided the conclusion that a more sedentary lifestyle was the decisive factor in the degradation of health on communities. Instead, many drew a correlation with the increase in processed starches and high-sugar beverages among reservation Pima communities, in contrast to those who lived away from those regions that came to rely on federally sanctioned processed foods.[11]

As Goetz notes, sugar, corn and flour became far more abundant—even dominant—as a calorie source as hunting and gathering patterns were fully erased during the reservation era, and as communities continued to suffer poverty that required access to cheap, processed and high-carbohydrate foods that American manufacturers began to market to the public at large during the second half of the twentieth century: "In 1830s and 1840s, under the Indian

Removal Act, Native American tribes signed treaties with the U.S. government that relegated them to reservations. This relocation also removed Native people from their usual food sources and the active lifestyle that hunting and gathering required. By 1890 the government decreed that Native Americans were not allowed to leave their lands to fish, hunt or gather in their usual territories. Instead, they were given government rations of commodities such as flour, lard and sugar." "Those original commodities were not healthy for the people," noted the Community Nutritionist for the Suquamish Tribe on Puget Sound in Washington State, in 2012: "They moved to a lot of highly processed foods really quickly. At the same time, they lost that physically active lifestyle that was practiced because they had to be active to hunt and gather and fish. That's why we've seen a rapid increase in obesity and diabetes within the last 150 years or so."[12]

The health of reservation Native Americans, then, was impacted by new federal food and land policies, just as earlier colonial interventions impacted Native American nutritional lives in problematic ways. "On many reservations," as one review notes, "malnutrition and nutritional deficiencies were endemic. Despite recommendations to improve Native American diets, food aid provided to the tribes was usually insufficient and of low quality. Also, the food aid did not include traditional foods, leading to further deterioration in health. The history of food insecurity for Native Americans that began with the establishment of reservations continues today. Until the 1950s, malnutrition and hunger were the primary food issues facing tribes [...] After the 1950s, Native American dietary patterns were increasingly dictated by 'the arrival of welfare checks and the distribution of government commodities' [...] [But] [t]o the contrary, despite the increase in federal food aid, Native American diets remained inadequate to their needs."[13]

Myriad problematic effects of micronutrient deficiencies likely continued in these circumstances, while the proliferation of metabolic diseases increased markedly. As we have already noted, diabetes seems to have been much less prevalent among Pima Indian populations that lived away from reservations in the American Southwest before 1940. Since the turn of the twenty-first century, however, around half of all Pima Indians have been reported to suffer from diabetes. There is a clear correlation between the appearance of obesity and type 2 diabetes in Native American communities and their adoption of processed and highly insulinogenic foods in federal welfare programs up to the present day.[14] Poor health among more recent Native American populations, and disparities between those on reservations and those who have managed to maintain subsistence strategies closer to precontact history, demonstrate that external context is often more important than genetic susceptibility to diseases and syndromes, or biologically immutable genetic differences such as those defined in the "thrifty gene" hypothesis.[15] As Hill has argued, surveying the sudden growth of diabetes from the mid-twentieth century, "[t]he difference is that smallpox killed swiftly, but diabetes 'kills softly, one fry bread at a time'."[16]

From the 1970s to the early 2000s, the influential lipid hypothesis implicated excess fat consumption in diabetes epidemiology. More recently, scholars have made a convincing claim that such an association has muddled effect (obesity) with cause (anything that might cause obesity, including calorie-dense fats), thereby overlooking specific metabolic changes wrought by overconsumption of carbohydrates, including the disruption of insulin hormone signaling, one of whose effects is often (but not always) obesity, and which can result in the onset of type 2 diabetes.[17]

Indeed, an inability to distinguish effect from cause has led federal organizations such as the Indian Health Service (IHS) to ignore the relatively sudden dominance of processed carbohydrates in Native American communities as a primary culprit in the exponential growth of type 2 diabetes levels from the mid-twentieth century, as described in the context above. Rather than focusing on inflammation caused by chronically raised blood glucose and declining insulin sensitivity, the IHS and similar institutions have until very recently defined the outcome of excess sugar consumption—obesity—as the culprit in type 2 diabetes epidemics, without highlighting the exact cause, often suggesting instead that high calories from dietary fat causes obesity, which in turn somehow leads to the metabolic derangement associated with type 2 diabetes in Native American communities.[18]

Yet despite what we are beginning to realize regarding the epidemiology of type 2 diabetes, and the importance of nutrient-dense, anti-inflammatory and low-glycemic foods more generally, federal welfare initiatives continue to promote the food pyramid model and allied low-fat nutritional frameworks to Native American populations. Having recognized its own earlier role in sanctioning the destruction of Native America, the government has promised welfare to assist communities that remain on reservations, and outside those zones. But in doing so, its food delivery system continues to bring processed foods into communities that already suffer from poor health associated with diabetes and other syndromes. According to relatively recent federal statistics, Native American communities suffer from diabetes, cirrhosis, influenza, pneumonia and perinatal and early infancy diseases at greater rates than the general American population.[19] Yet as the US Department of Agriculture (USDA) nutritional guidelines for the Food Distribution Program on Indian Reservations (FDPIR) program demonstrate, Native American populations continue to receive food welfare in the form of packaged and processed starches, industrial seed and vegetable oils that are far too high in inflammatory omega-6 fatty acids rather than anti-inflammatory omega-3 fatty acids, and low-fat animal sources (a reversal of the focus on lard in the early twentieth century)—foods that have potentially contributed to increasing metabolic syndrome in the US population more generally).[20]

From Native America to North America: Compromised National Nutritional Guidelines

Determining the contingent effects of nutrition on health and immunity in historical Native American populations does not negate the possibility that individuals in those same populations were more genetically predisposed to metabolic disorders or to compromised immunity than those in other global communities. It is perfectly logical, for example, to suggest that some communities were (or are) less insulin sensitive, and thus more prone to prediabetes, given their ancestors' greater relative historical reliance on fat and protein than post-Neolithic agricultural communities. Over thousands of years, selective pressures, epigenetic changes and selective mutations may well have allowed distinctive genetic heritages to develop in contexts that retained less access to insulinogenic grains than in other societal frameworks. Similarly, modifying the "virgin soil" paradigm does not repudiate the notion that ancestral Native Americans may have developed differences over time in their inherited or acquired immune response. In the expression of these autoimmune diseases, genetic factors may load the gun, requiring contextual interventions to pull the trigger. Yet even where genetic predispositions are not present, if contingent factors such as nutritional degradation become strong and sudden enough, then the same problematic effects are likely to follow.

Indeed, the experience of Native Americans since the early twentieth century is even more meaningful because the triggering of potential genetic predispositions offered a portent of that which would become more widely apparent in North America by the end of the twentieth century. Contingent dietary factors have made type 2 diabetes an epidemic, irrespective of genetic differences, even if some among the affected populations also demonstrate greater genetic susceptibility to metabolic derangement and insulin dysregulation. A reliance on refined carbohydrates and processed foods is likely to affect most human populations in problematic ways.[21] Though these effects reached epidemic proportions in Native America in large part due to sudden nutritional changes and declining physical activity, their onset was potentially more rapid due to genetic predispositions. But the latter need not have expressed themselves if individuals were able to continue a broadly anti-inflammatory diet in which blood glucose was not chronically raised. In the present era, a similar mismatch between evolved metabolic requirements and nutritional consumption has become starkly apparent. As we continue to note these correlations between history and nutritional science, therefore, we can begin to think about problematic nutritional interventions and paradigms outside the Native American community, among the American public more generally. The study of early American history, and the problematic European intervention in Native American nutritional life, can inform public health discussions more broadly.

Our synthesis thus provides a framework to approach contemporary health dilemmas, both inside and outside Native America. Using nutritional and immunological science to understand the shocking history of postcontact Native American health and ecology also provides a lens to comprehend the health crisis that has faced Europe, the United States and the wider world since the 1960s. Many developed nations now face a medical crisis: so-called "diseases of civilization" have been linked to an evolutionary mismatch between our ancient genetic heritage and our present social, nutritional and ecological environments. The disastrous European intervention in Native American life after 1492 brought about a similar—though of course far more destructive—mismatch between biological needs and societal context.

To be sure, it is important to avoid what might seem like an egregious comparison between the problematic health effects of the modern food pyramid and the horrific decimation of Native Americans due to the combination of newly introduced diseases with compromised immunity and fertility, a phenomenon that was exacerbated by nutritional degradation within a violent colonial context that prevented any adaptation to, or mitigation of, its problematic consequences. Nonetheless, there are salient associations to be made that are not egregious, and which can inform both contemporary Native American health strategies as well as other communities struggling with compromised metabolic health, nutritional status and immunity.

Proposing that many of the problems that followed the move toward European agriculture in Native America, and which bedevil populations both inside and outside Native America today, are somehow "diseases of Western civilization" should not somehow suggest that Native Americans without those diseases prior to contact were somehow "uncivilized." Rather, their own separate civilizations incorporated ecological frameworks whose positive health outcomes can help us all overcome the problematic health and ecological effects of the global move toward the consumption of corn, soy, wheat and factory-farmed animals, at the expense of more nutrient-dense plants and animals, since the 1960s.[22]

We ought to consider these more recent phenomena in light of modern scientific literature on metabolic syndrome, inflammatory conditions and compromised immunity to diseases. Reservation communities have been more susceptible to certain problems that are more broadly associated with the modern Western diet, as defined during the second half of the twentieth century—particularly its reliance on refined carbohydrates in packaged and processed goods. We can trace the problematic development of the modern food pyramid in Europe and the United States since the late-1950s, when scientists allied their scientific and nutritional research with new policies that came to be promoted by various governments. Ancel Keys and other scientists famously sought a new research agenda to question the health benefits of fats from animals, fish and dairy. Contrary to those who highlighted the problematic medical implications of foods that were readily converted into glucose, as well as the potential inflammatory effects of oxidized omega-6 polyunsaturated fats, Keys and others used their mandate to promote research that supported the governments of the day in their stated desire to increase agricultural output in soy, wheat, corn and seed oils.[23]

A new generation of scholars, scientists, public policy analysts and journalists have recently begun to suggest that the resulting food pyramid recommendations have worsened certain aspects of American public health, particularly through the associated growth of metabolic disorders such as diabetes, and even in the prevalence of certain forms of heart disease (though the exact effects of the "diet-heart hypothesis" on public health are still currently being debated).[24] Beginning in the 1970s, as Ludwig has recently summarized, "the US government and major professional nutrition organizations recommended that individuals in the United States eat a low-fat/high-carbohydrate diet, launching arguably the largest public health experiment in history." The effects, according to Ludwig's review of the literature, have been dramatic: "Throughout the ensuing 40 years, the prevalence of obesity and diabetes increased several-fold, even as the proportion of fat in the US diet decreased by 25%. Recognizing new evidence that consumption of processed carbohydrates—white bread, white rice, chips, crackers, cookies, and sugary drinks—but not total fat has contributed importantly to these epidemics, the 2015 USDA Dietary Guidelines for Americans essentially eliminated the upper limit on dietary fat intake. However, a comprehensive examination of this massive public health failure has not been conducted. Consequently, significant harms persist, with the low-fat diet remaining entrenched in public consciousness and food policy. In addition, critical scientific questions have been muddled."[25]

The cluster of chronic diseases that are generally categorized under the framework of metabolic syndrome are often manifested as inflammatory autoimmune conditions due to a mismatch between what humans are broadly evolved to eat and what many now consume. Whether inside or outside Native America, the association between dysregulated immunity and compromised health has become internalized. After European contact, as we have seen, the acute immune response to external pathogens was compromised in part by nutritional scarcity, long before autoimmune conditions could become chronic. Today, as we can rely on antibiotics and vaccines to reduce the danger of infectious disease, autoimmunity has become a chief determinant of poor health and even mortality. The body's internal immune response has become chronically overactive, due to inflammation following nutritional and metabolic derangement, leading it to attack its own tissues and hormonal pathways.[26]

Conditions such as diabetes are thus often associated with heart disease and other syndromes, given their inflammatory component. They now make up a huge proportion of treatment and spending in health services on both sides of the Atlantic. Yet policy makers and researchers in those same health services often respond to these conditions reactively rather than proactively—as if they were solely genetically determined, rather than arising due to external nutritional factors. A similarly problematic pattern of analysis, as we have noted, has led scholars to ignore the central role of nutritional change in Native American population loss after European contact, focusing instead on purportedly immutable genetic differences.[27]

Modern Tribal Sovereignty as a Model for American Biodiversity and Public Health

Many of the debilitating metabolic and autoimmune conditions detailed above derive in part from an overreliance on refined grains, particularly wheat and corn, industrialized seed and vegetable oils, and soy beans. Much of the latter, moreover, underpins the factory farming of animals in industrialized feed lots. Scholars and activists have begun to highlight the ecological problem—some say catastrophe—that has followed the conversion of biodiverse grasslands, forests, prairies, small farms and lakes into vast monocultured agricultural zones, with nutrient-poor topsoil and an overreliance on antibiotics and pesticides that increase the yields of products that are nonetheless detrimental to the evolved needs of human health.[28]

When combined with government regulation through subsidies, market capitalism has proved to be highly efficient in converting biodiverse regions into single-crop zones that produce cheap sources of energy for humans, cattle and machines. As shown by the continued degradation of the Great Plains and Midwest, money has been shifted from taxpayers to farmers, who have been encouraged to produced single crops, to the degradation of local diverse ecologies, where animals, plants and agricultural products once complemented each other and offered a relatively diverse ecological environment.[29] These Midwestern zones, moreover, are increasingly blanketed in pesticides and herbicides such as glyphosate, which are designed to be synergistic with genetically modified plants, potentially to the detriment of surrounding bees, animals, indigenous plants and even people.[30]

Farmers and activists inside and outside Native America are renewing the call for biodiverse farming practices, which allow a natural cycle where pasture-raised roaming animals convert grass into nutrient-dense meat, while also fertilizing the soil and providing the context for other plants and crops to grow, and other smaller animals to reproduce. In an era of increasing population density and vested agribusiness and biochemical interests, which treat soil as a conduit or receptacle for chemicals, rather than a living organic entity, these efforts may continue to face strong headwinds.[31]

The struggle for Native American land sovereignty, and its association with the protection of sustainable nutrient-dense food systems, offers ecological and nutritional models that broader populations might follow, despite the inevitable headwinds from professional interest groups, lobbyists, agribusiness, and their growing partnership with university science and engineering programs. These headwinds threaten to bias research on nutrition, ecology and public health in order to obscure the clear causes of metabolic and autoimmune conditions in North America, and the unambiguous degradation of ecological health and nutrient diversity by industrialized agricultural methods.

Even before the Great Plains and Midwest were turned toward industrialized monoculture in the second half of the twentieth century, new markets in and out of the region were prone to threaten biodiversity and the subsistence strategies that such an ecological state supported—particularly as had been developed by Native Americans, who had formed a relatively sustainable hybrid between hunting and gathering and horticulture/agriculture. To use reasoning developed by Worster and Moore in a more general world systems context, new colonial markets since the sixteenth century have demonstrated their ability to "mobilize capital and labor quickly and efficiently in order to seize resources in distant lands and make them available to consumers living far from the site of extraction"—a "metabolic rift [...] [reflecting] displacement in the cyclical flows of resources and wastes from the local to the global."[32] Long before the degradation of fertile grasslands, as we have seen, mixed-use subsistence economies became shatter zones that relied on maize or a few overhunted animals, at just the point when new diseases followed the same market trajectories and required Native American immunity to be stronger than ever.

During Franklin Roosevelt's New Deal administration, a few analysts used the 1928 *Meriam Report* to understand the failure of the Dawes Act regarding the nutritional health of Native American communities. The 1934 Indian Reorganization Act ended the encouragement of allotment spaces and allowed an updated notion of tribal government, including in relation to ancestral sub-sistence practices, at least in principle. Such a policy was expanded in Richard Nixon's administration during the early 1970s, as tribes throughout Oklahoma demanded even more self-determination.[33] Since then, tribal sovereignty has underpinned a call to return to mixed-use subsistence frameworks, breaking down ecological barriers that have prevented nutrient-dense food systems from feeding populations and maintaining ecological balance.

We are reminded of the legacy of the "Red Power" movement of the 1960s and 1970s, when "fish-ins" in the Pacific Northwest and the Great Lakes region coincided with the civil rights movement, showing how subsistence autonomy is central to cultural survival and communal health.[34] Since the 1960s and 1970s, Mi'kmaqs have called for the restoration of fishing rights lost to corrupt treaties and land seizures following the American Revolution. Other tribes have also gained federal acknowledgment of their lost land, cultures and nutritional systems, if not any material gain. They include the Narrangansetts and Mashantucket Pequots, the Aquinna Wampanoags and the Mohegans.[35]

We are reminded of those on our own campus in the University of Minnesota system, who are challenging the threat to Native American autonomy in Minnesota wild rice production from multinational agribusinesses.[36] As Kalt and Singer have argued, and as Doerfler and Redix have corroborated in their discussion of the relationship between contemporary gaming revenue and Native American sovereignty in Minnesota, "tribal self-rule—sovereignty—has proven to be the only policy that has shown concrete success in breaking debilitating economic dependence on federal spending programs and replenishing the social and cultural fabric that can support vibrant and healthy communities and families."[37] The Shakopee Mdewakanton Sioux Community (SMSC), near Minneapolis and St. Paul, Minnesota, is descended from the Mdewakanton Dakotas, who survived the conflict with United States settlers in Minnesota in 1862. The SMSC, with around 300 members in the commu-nity, has been the largest recent employer in surrounding Scott County (as of 2015). With over 4,000 employees, the SMSC has established gaming as its central economic strategy, running the Little Six Bingo Palace and the Mystic Lake Casino. Yet this case represents more than merely the harnessing of sov-ereignty to gain economic power through gambling. Even in these relatively urban circumstances, sovereignty has positively impacted the local ecological and nutritional balance. The SMSC, it should be noted, "works to continue the Dakota tradition of caring for the earth through several initiatives, including establishing organic gardens, opening a natural food market," and several other initiatives. Of course, like most initiatives, the nutritional paradigms are never perfect, and could always use more updated scientific guidelines. Given our earlier discussion of the problematic effects of industrial seed oils, which produce inflammatory oxidized omega-6 fatty acids, the use of vegetable oil in tribal restaurants might be replaced by more traditional—and biologically stable—fats from animals, butter or other sources such as olive oil (the use of vegetable oils in tribal transport seems less problematic).[38]

Yet biodiversity in Native American lands, ironically, can also be threatened by ostensibly benevolent federal conservation efforts. Many Native American groups object to national park systems that prevent what they view as indigenous land management measures designed to maintain, rather than threaten, ecological balance. Those same groups, and others, also object to private enterprise destroying habitats. In the last two decades in Death Valley, for example, the Timbisha Shoshone Tribe has requested "comanagement" of its former resources on National Park Service Land, as well as nearby lands controlled by the Bureau of Land Management, the US Forest Service, and the US Fish and Wildlife Service. The Timbisha community, as Fowler has explained, "feels that it has never lost its custodial obligation to its homeland and that it would be seriously remiss if it did not push for a say in its future. Members would like to trim and manage the mesquite, whip the pinyon trees, burn the marshes now choked with cattail, and conduct limited small and large game hunts. They feel that the philosophy of benign neglect has not contributed to the health of the land and resources and that something must be done." Since the 1990s, similar demands have been made by the Western Shoshone National Council in Nevada and California, succeeding in various attempts to regulate fishing and hunting grounds on ostensibly public lands. They continue to be concerned that commercial pine nut farmers damage trees and alter ecological systems to the future detriment of those resources.[39]

Analogous claims have been made in other very different regions of North America, such as British Columbia, where local indigenous groups have called for the resumption of indigenous burning practices and the reduction of pesticides that have halted the growth of native species of plants and animals. In 1971, as the conservation movement took off more widely in the United States, indigenous peoples in British Columbia lamented the curtailment of their own ecological management techniques, such as burning, which had earlier provided biodiversity. According to Baptiste Ritchie in 1971, "because the white man really watches us, we don't burn anything. We realize already, it seems the things that were eaten by our forefathers have disappeared from the places where they burned. It seems that already almost everything has disappeared. Maybe it is because it's weedy. All kind of things grow and they don't burn. If you go to burn then you get into trouble because the white men want to grow trees."[40] Plant-rich regions such as the Gary Oak savannah around Southern Vancouver Island and Puget Sound have markedly declined as a result of lost management techniques since European contact, including the use of fire to encourage growth and mineral availability at the ground level.[41] According to Chambers and Turner, indeed, during the modern postcontact era the growth of these important plants—vital to Native American food sovereignty—"has been suppressed by forest policy in both Canada and the United States, and the resulting reduction of fire, along with urbanization and agricultural development, has resulted in a decrease of prairie and early successional habitats that produce important traditional plant sources such as thinleaf huckleberry."[42]

Yet tribal governance remains a contested concept, not least insofar as local state actors and corporate organizations often stand accused of disrupting indigenous sovereignty over fishing, hunting and agricultural practices—often in full view of the federal government. As we write this final chapter, indeed, we note the standoff at Standing Rock in North Dakota, only a few hours west of our university campus. Federal agents and private corporations continue to disrupt the societal governance and food sovereignty of Native Americans in the region. We are reminded, in the full glare of this conflict, that modern diseases of civilization are most prevalent in regions where the legacy of political and economic inequality has ruptured ancestral food practices and made communities more likely to rely on highly insulinogenic and inflammatory foods. This is even the case at Standing Rock, where disruption by corporate industrial activity has led communities to rely on problematic processed foods more than ever before.[43]

The positive effects of Native American and First Nation sovereignty over subsistence ecologies therefore highlights the broader issue of biodiversity and provides a potential model for our collective response to the degradation of once fertile lands in the face of agribusiness, subsidized crop monocultures, and factory animal farming. The move toward tribal sovereignty can be integrated with a return to locally specific food systems, as defined by those that underlay the myriad regional hybrids between hunting, gathering, horticulture and agriculture before European contact.

"Decolonizing the diet" in this way need not reflect a romanticized attempt to return to a premodern lifestyle. Rather, it incorporates what we now realize are better practices in ecological science, which in turn supply diverse micronutrients and reduce the reliance on nutrient-poor and energy-dense foods, which have contributed to metabolic syndromes in and out of Native America during the last half-century. Native Americans continue to suffer from societal inequalities that are embedded in centuries of colonial disruption, which has included nutritional dysregulation. Thus, they often live in so-called "food deserts" or rely on highly insulinogenic and nutrient-poor processed foods. Economic inequality has translated into food consumption patterns that are at cross-purposes with the evolved biological needs of all humans.[44]

To be sure, it would be problematic to suggest that only specific foods cultivated during the precontact era offer nutritionally optimal profiles to Native Americans (or any other population in North America, for that matter). To do so would be to supplant the biological determinism of the "virgin soil" paradigm with another sort of determinism, focused on connecting health outcomes to very specific foods. Rather, public health authorities would be wise to focus more broadly on the nutrient density and the insulinogenic effects of foods, whether or not they appeared in Native America. In doing so, of course, they would likely come far closer to those that were consumed before contact, in comparison to that which has dominated industrial food frameworks and even the food pyramid in the last few decades.

A desire to return to specific indigenous foods, nonetheless, has important cultural meanings, which should not be downplayed. Decolonizing the diet more specifically, therefore, is a worthy endeavor within Native American communities, even if those outside Native America only use the model as an example of the broader importance of foods that encourage immunity and discourage autoimmunity and inflammation. Inspired by the political frame-work provided by tribal sovereignty, and the health problems suffered by Native American communities, several contemporary initiatives have indeed begun to speak of the need to "decolonize" dietary habits within their local and specific contexts. Aware of disproportionate instances of diabetes, heart disease, depression, fertility problems and chronic inflammatory conditions, various projects have studied and then simulated pre-European contact Native American diets, using historical and anthropological methods. They have begun to suggest an association between mixed land use (rather than industrialized monocultures) and the positive health outcomes that follow the consumption of foods provided by biodiverse zones.

The Decolonizing Diet Project at Northern Michigan University, for example, has enabled students and local community members to learn how the move away from ancestral nutritional principles has been detrimental to the health of Native Americans and the wider ecology of the Great Lakes region. A similar project, the American Indian Health and Diet Project (AIHDP), has been inspired by the work of Devon Abbott Mihesuah, a Choctaw historian and writer. Through her teaching and writing, Mihesuah has used the study of history, anthropology and literature to inform contemporary health and nutritional practices—coming a little closer to the diets that many Native American communities consumed before European contact. The Centre for Indigenous Peoples' Nutrition and Environment (CINE) at McGill University has begun to offer an institutional context to study these intersecting ideas. Besides attempts to protect endangered Native American plants, Cherokee communities have endeavored to revive small farming and preserve traditional plant varieties.

In Oklahoma, the work of the Mvskoke (Muskogee Creek) Food Sovereignty Initiative has done the same. The Center for Disease Control (CDC) has also supported Traditional Foods Program grantee partner programs, which have incorporated some of these concerns in positive ways. The Traditional Foods Project seeks to "illustrate tribally driven solutions, built on traditional eco-logical knowledge, to reclaim foods systems for health promotion and preven-tion of chronic illnesses, including diabetes."[45]

We have already noted the work of Gary Nabhan among the Pima com-munities of southern Arizona, which has engaged in similar objectives in and around the Sonoran Desert bioregion north of the United States-Mexico border. Nabhan has worked with Seri Indian "para-ecologist" trainees who act as an interchange between their elders and visiting conservation biologists to protect native species and cultivation techniques. As Nabhan has argued, such an endeavor should "provide a model for other indigenous communi-ties, for it honors both Western scientific and traditional ecological knowledge about biodiversity." Wiedman has encouraged similar paradigms in his own work on discriminatory activities against Native American communities, the development of metabolic syndromes among those communities and the new possibilities open to them by evolutionary nutritional principles.[46]

We can learn much from these efforts, and we hope they can be inspired by our own attempt to synthesize contact history and the latest work in biological science and evolutionary studies. The science of nutrition and immunity can benefit from a broader historical and evolutionary framework. Historical narrative, in turn, can benefit from the most recent developments in biological science and bioarchaeology. Such an interpretative template is necessary to understand the effects of the mismatch between environmental context and evolved nutritional needs in and out of indigenous North America.

NOTES

Introduction. Nutrition and Immunity in Native America: A Biological and Historical Controversy

1 Alfred W. Crosby, *Ecological Imperialism: The Biological Expansion of Europe, 900–1900* (Cambridge and New York: Cambridge University Press, 1986); Alfred W. Crosby, *The Columbian Exchange: Biological and Cultural Consequences of 1492* (Westport, CT: Greenwood Publishing Group, 1972); Francesco Di Castri, "History of Biological Invasions with Special Emphasis on the Old World," in *Biological Invasions: A Global Perspective*, ed. J. A. Drake et al. (Oxford: John Wiley & Sons, 1989), 1–30.

2 Bruce G. Trigger and William R. Swagerty, "Entertaining Strangers: North America in the Sixteenth Century," in *The Cambridge History of the Native Peoples of The Americas*, vol. 1, *North America*, part 1, ed. Bruce G. Trigger and Wilcomb E. Washburn (Cambridge: Cambridge University Press, 1996), 363.

3 For a discussion of these scholarly changes in emphasis see Russell Thornton, "Health, Disease, and Demography," in *A Companion to American Indian History*, ed. Philip J. Deloria and Neal Salisbury (Malden, MA: Wiley-Blackwell, 2002), 70–75.

4 William H. McNeill, *Plagues and Peoples* (New York: Anchor Press, 1996), 150. See Thornton's discussion of

5 Robert S. Gottfried, *The Black Death: Natural and Human Disaster in Medieval Europe* (New York: Free Press, 1985), xv–xvi, 129–35 and 156–59.

6 D. A. Herring., "There Were Young People and Old People and Babies Dying Every Week: The 1918 Influenza Pandemic at Norway House," *Ethnohistory* 41, no. 1 (1994): 73–105. See also Thornton's discussion of these scholarly paradigms in Thornton, "Health, Disease, and Demography," 72–73.

7 David S. Jones, "Population, Health, and Public Welfare," in *The Oxford Handbook of American Indian History*, ed. Frederick E Hoxie (New York: Oxford University Press, 2016), 414; David S. Jones, *Rationalizing Epidemics: Meanings and Uses of American Indian Mortality Since 1600* (Cambridge, MA: Harvard University Press, 2004), 21–28; David S. Jones, "Virgin Soils Revisited," *William and Mary Quarterly* 60, no. 4 (2003): 740–42; Catherine M. Cameron, Paul Kelton and Alan C. Swedlund, eds., *Beyond Germs: Native Depopulation in North America.* (Phoenix, AZ: University of Arizona Press, 2015); Paul Kelton, *Epidemics and Enslavement: Biological Catastrophe in the Native Southeast, 1492–1715* (Lincoln: University of Nebraska Press, 2007). On the debated differences between European and Native American immune systems at the time of contact see F.L. Black, "Why Did They Die?" *Science* 11, vol. 258, no. 5089 (December 1992): 1739–40.

8 Jones, *Rationalizing Epidemics*, 21–28; Jones, "Virgin Soils Revisited," 740–42; Kelton, *Epidemics and Enslavement*, 1–20.

9   Mark Nathan Cohen and George J. Armelagos, eds., *Paleopathology at the Origins of Agriculture* (New York: Academic Press, 1984); Mark Nathan Cohen *Health and the Rise of Civilization* (New Haven, CT: Yale University Press, 1989), 61–62 and 115–17; David Wiedman, "Native American Embodiment of the Chronicities of Modernity: Reservation Food, Diabetes, and the Metabolic Syndrome among the Kiowa, Comanche, and Apache," *Medical Anthropology Quarterly* 26 (2012): 599–600. For more on the density of micro and macro nutrients from animals, particularly in the eastern coastal area prior to contact, see Timothy Silver, *A New Face on the Countryside: Indians, Colonists, and Slaves in South Atlantic Forests, 1500–1800* (New York: Cambridge University Press, 1990), 35–39; Cronon, *Changes in the Land*, 39–45; Stephen R. Potter, *Commoners, Tribute, and Chiefs: The Development of Algonquian Culture in the Potomac Valley* (Charlottesville, VA: University of Virginia Press, 1993), 101; Virginia Anderson, *Creatures of Empire: How Domestic Animals Transformed Early America* (New York: Oxford University Press, 2004), 32–35.

10 For a recent overview, see Russell Thornton, "Health, Disease, and Demography," 70–75.

11 Dean R. Snow, "The First Americans and the Differentiation of Hunter Gatherer Cultures" in *The Cambridge History of the Native Peoples of The Americas:* vol. 1, *North America: Part I*, ed. Bruce G. Trigger and Wilcomb E. Washburn (Cambridge: Cambridge University Press, 1996), 194.

12 On the population nadir, see Suzanne A. Alchon, *A Pest in the Land: New World Epidemics in a Global Perspective* (Albuquerque: University of New Mexico Press, 2003), 147–72; Douglas H. Ubelaker, "Population Size, Contact to Nadir," in *Handbook of North American Indians*, vol. 3, *Environment, Origins and Population*, ed. Douglas H. Ubelaker and William C. Sturtevant (Washington, DC: Smithsonian Institution Scholarly Press, 2007), 694–701.

13 Carolyn Merchant, *Ecological Revolutions: Nature, Gender and Science in New England* (Chapel Hill: University of North Carolina Press, 1989).

14 Pekka Hämäläinen, "The Politics of Grass: European Expansion, Ecological Change, and Indigenous Power in the Southwest Borderlands," *William and Mary Quarterly* 67, no. 2 (2010): 173–208.

15 Elizabeth H. Simmons, "Humanities Strengthen Science," *Inside Higher Education*, August 14, 2014. https://www.insidehighered.com/views/2014/08/14/humanities-strengthen-study-science-essay.

16 On the lectures, see John De La Mother, *C. P. Snow and the Struggle of Modernity* (Austin: University of Texas Press, 1992).

17 Simmons, "Humanities Strengthen Science."

18 On the potential for these new interdisciplinary links, see the 2014 *American Historical Review* Roundtable "History Meets Biology," particularly John L. Brooke and Clark Spencer Larsen, "The Nurture of Nature: Genetics, Epigenetics, and Environment in Human Biohistory," *American Historical Review* 119, no. 5 (2014): 1500–1513.

19 See the excellent contributions in C. S. Larsen, ed. *Bioarchaeology of La Florida: The Impact of Colonialism* (Gainesville: University Press of Florida, 1997).

20 Russel Thornton, *American Indian Holocaust and Survival: A Population History since 1492* (Norman: Norman: University of Oklahoma Press, 1987)

21 Colin Fisher, "Race and US Environmental History," in *A Companion to American Environmental History*, ed. Douglas Cazaux Sackman (Oxford: Blackwell Press, 2014), 99; J. Donald Hughes, *American Indian Ecology* (El Paso: Texas Western Press, 1983). In addition to Hughes, for studies that suggested Indians were pristine ecologists who

offered examples for modern society to follow (and thus a model for countercultural environmentalists), see Wilbur Jacobs, "The Indian and the Frontier in American History: A Need for Revision," *Western Historical Quarterly* 4, no. 1 (1973): 43–56; Michael P. Cohen, *The Pathless Way: John Muir and American Wilderness* (Madison: University of Wisconsin Press, 1984); Roderick Nash, *Wilderness and the American Mind* (New Haven, CT: Yale University Press, 1967).

22 David Rich Lewis, "American Indian Environmental Relations," in *A Companion to American Environmental History*, 194–95; Paul Nadasky, "Transcending the Debate over the Ecologically Noble Indian: Indigenous Peoples and Environmentalism," *Ethnohistory* 52, no. 2 (2005): 291–331; Shepard Krech III, *The Ecological Indian: Myth and History* (New York: W. W. Norton, 1999), 23–27.

23 Shepard Krech III, "Beyond the Ecological Indian," in *Native Americans and the Environment: Perspectives on the Ecological Indian*, ed. Michael E. Harkin and David Rich Lewis (Lincoln: University of Nebraska Press, 1994), 3.

24 See, for example, Gary Nabham, *Enduring Seeds: Native American Agriculture and Wild Plant Conservation* (San Francisco: North Point Press, 1989); T. C Blackburn and M. K. Anderson, *Before the Wilderness: Environmental Management by Native Californians* (Menlo Park, CA: Ballena Press, 1993).

25 For an outline of this problematic tendency among those who justify environmentally problematic interventions of governments and corporations, see the essays in Harkin and Lewis, eds., *Native Americans and the Environment*.

26 Stephen Devries et al., "A Deficiency of Nutrition Education in Medical Training," *American Journal of Medicine* 127, no. 9 (2014): 804–6.

27 On the problematic nature of these assumptions in light of new data, see for example, R. Barazzoni et al., "Carbohydrates and Insulin Resistance in Clinical Nutrition: Recommendations from the ESPEN Expert Group," *Clinical Nutrition* 36, no. 2 (April 2017): 355–63; C. E. Ramsden et al., "N-6 Fatty Acid-Specific and Mixed Polyunsaturate Dietary Interventions Have Different Effects on CHD Risk: A Meta-Analysis of Randomised Controlled Trials," *British Journal of Nutrition* 104, no. 11 (December 2010): 1586–600; W. E. Lands, "Dietary Fat and Health: The Evidence and the Politics of Prevention: Careful Use of Dietary Fats Can Improve Life and Prevent Disease," *Annals of the New York Academy of Sciences* 1055 (December 2005): 179–92; Philip C. Calder, "n−3 Polyunsaturated Fatty Acids, Inflammation, and Inflammatory Diseases," *American Journal of Clinical Nutrition* 83, no. 6 (June 2006): S1505–S1519.

28 Z. Harcombe, J. Baker and B. Davies, "Food for Thought: Have We Been Giving the Wrong Dietary Advice?" *Food and Nutrition Sciences* 4, no. 3 (2013): 240–44.

29 For a most recent summary of this paradigm, see Jacob C. Eaton and Lora L. Iannotti, "Genome–Nutrition Divergence: Evolving Understanding Of The Malnutrition Spectrum," *Nutrition Reviews* 75, no. 11 (2017): 934–50.

30 For a useful discussion of these distinctions in experimental procedure, see Shobha Misra, "Randomized Double Blind Placebo Control Studies, the 'Gold Standard' in Intervention Based Studies," *Indian Journal of Sexually Transmitted Diseases* 33, no. 2 (2012): 131–34. *PMC*, "Reading Epidemiological Reports," in *Epidemiology for the Uninitiated*, ed. D. Coggon et al., ch. 12 (online ed.): http://www.bmj.com/about-bmj/resources-readers/publications/epidemiology-uninitiated/12-reading-epidemiological-reports; Alice Ottoboni and Fred Ottoboni, "Low-Fat Diet and Chronic Disease Prevention: The Women's Health Initiative and Its Reception," *Journal of American Physicians and Surgeons* 12, no. 1 (Spring 2007): 10–13.

31   L. Cordain et al., "Plant-Animal Subsistence Ratios and Macronutrient Energy
      Estimations in Worldwide Hunter-Gatherer Diets," *American Journal of Clinical Nutrition*
      71, no. 3 (March 2000): 682–92; L. Cordain et al., "The Paradoxical Nature of
      Hunter-Gatherer Diets: Meat-Based, Yet Non-Atherogenic," *European Journal of Clinical
      Nutrition* 56, suppl. 1 (2002): S42–S52; S. J. Nicholls et al., "Consumption of Saturated
      Fat Impairs the Anti-Inflammatory Properties of High-Density Lipoproteins and
      Endothelial Function," *Journal of the American College of Cardiology* 15, no. 48 (August
      2006): 715–20. For more nuance on insulin, notwithstanding the misleading title, see
      the recent hypothesis put forward by Christopher Masterjohn: "Sugar is the Ultimate
      Antioxidant and Insulin Will Make You Younger." http://blog.cholesterol-and-health.
      com/2016/05/sugar-is-ultimate-antioxidant-and.html.

32   Clark Spencer Larsen, "Supplement: Animal Source Foods to Improve Micronutrient
      Nutrition in Developing Countries: Animal Source Foods and Human Health during
      Evolution," *Journal of Nutrition* 133, no. 11 (2003): 3893S–3897S.

33   Some communities, such as those in subarctic Alaska or those whose seasonal hunting
      patterns relied on animal fats and protein to a far greater extent than carbohydrate,
      may sometimes have lived in a metabolic state of ketosis (though there is now even
      debate on this issue in discussions of Alaskan subsistence, as discussed in Chapter 4.)

34   Rosário Monteiro and Isabel Azevedo, "Chronic Inflammation in Obesity and the
      Metabolic Syndrome," *Mediators of Inflammation* 2010 (2010): 289645; Jaspinder Kaur,
      "A Comprehensive Review on Metabolic Syndrome," *Cardiology Research and Practice*
      2014 (2014): 943162.

35   M. K. Bennet, "The Food Economy of the New England Indians, 1605–75," *Journal
      of Political Economy* 63 (1955): 369–87.

1. The Evolution of Nutrition and Immunity: From the Paleolithic Era to the Medieval European Black Death

1   According to the Expensive Tissue Hypothesis, which we believe is supported by
     strong evidence, the small human gut has evolved to require nutrient-dense foods that
     do not need as much digestion to provide important micronutrients and fatty acids.
     Minimizing the digestive process has allowed energy to be diverted elsewhere, such as
     to the larger brain, without forgoing the nutrients that the body needs. Among other
     animals with large guts and smaller brains, less nutrient- and energy-dense foods such
     as grass are required, as the animal can afford to spend a greater proportion of its
     energy processing the plant material and converting it into nutrient-rich sources of
     food, in its own tissue. See Leslie C. Aiello and Peter Wheeler, "The Expensive-Tissue
     Hypothesis: The Brain and the Digestive System in Human and Primate Evolution,"
     Current Anthropology 36, no. 2 (1995): 199–221.

2   For a discussion of the potential role of omega-3 fatty acids in the evolution of the
     modern human brain, see M.A. Crawford et al. "Evidence for the unique function of
     docosahexaenoic acid during the evolution of the modern hominid brain," *Lipids* 34,
     (1999): S39–S47. For a review of the role of omega-3 fatty acids in inflammation, see
     Philip C. Calder, "Polyunsaturated Fatty Acids, Inflammation, and Immunity," *Lipids*
     36, no. 9 (2001): 1013–17. doi:10.1007/s11745-001-0812-7.

3   On the debate regarding the nature of immune system evolution, including the so-called
     immunological Big Bang and the divergence between vertebrates and invertebrates, see
     G. W. Litman et al., "The Origins of Vertebrate Adaptive Immunity," *Nature Reviews*

Immunology 10 (2010): 543–53; Flajnik and Kasahara, "Origin and Evolution of the Adaptive Immune System," 47–59; M. Hirano et al., "The Evolution of Adaptive Immunity in Vertebrates," *Advances in Immunology* 109 (2011): 125–57; M. F. Flajnik, "Reevaluation of the Immunological Big Bang," *Current Biology* 24, no. 21 (2014): R1060–65; V. Müller et al., "An Evolutionary Perspective on the Systems of Adaptive Immunity," *Biological Reviews of the Cambridge Philosophical Society*, July 26, 2017 (Epub ahead of print).

4   On Neolithic health decline, see the discussions below. For the later literature on Native American health and contingent external factors, such as nutrition, see David S. Jones, "Population, Health, and Public Welfare," in *The Oxford Handbook of American Indian History*, ed. Frederick E. Hoxie (New York: Oxford University Press, 2016), 414; David S. Jones, *Rationalizing Epidemics: Meanings and Uses of American Indian Mortality since 1600* (Cambridge, MA: Harvard University Press, 2004), 21–28; David S. Jones, "Virgin Soils Revisited," *William and Mary Quarterly* 60, no. 4 (2003): 740–42; Catherine M. Cameron, Paul Kelton and Alan C. Swedlund, eds., *Beyond Germs: Native Depopulation in North America* (Phoenix: University of Arizona Press, 2015); Paul Kelton, *Epidemics and Enslavement: Biological Catastrophe in the Native Southeast, 1492–1715* (Lincoln: University of Nebraska Press, 2007).

5   David W. K. Acheson and Luccioli Stefano, "Mucosal Immune Responses," *Best Practice & Research Clinical Gastroenterology* 18, no. 2 (2004): 387–89.

6   See L. Cordain, "Cereal Grains: Humanity's Double-Edged Sword," *Evolutionary Aspects of Nutrition and Health (World Review of Nutrition and Dietetics)* (1999), 21. Proteins present in grains, such as gluten, may trigger an aberrant immune response, involving autoimmunity or allergy. For a description of the autoimmune response, which involves an adaptive immune response against the body's own tissues, see Charles Janeway et al., eds., *Immunobiology: The Immune System in Health and Disease*. 5th ed. (New York: Garland Science, 2001), chap. 13. For a description of the immune response that occurs in response to allergens from food, see S. Sicherer and H. Sampson, "Food Allergy," *Journal of Allergy and Clinical Immunology* 117, no. 2 (2006): S470–71. Such aberrant activation of immune cells by proteins in grains may decrease the immune response to pathogens (see discussion below).

7   A state of chronic inflammation (e.g., in the states of obesity and diabetes) is associated with disrupted immune function. Immune responses usually employed in the defense against pathogens are activated, including the secretion of inflammatory cytokines and activation of immune cells. Thus, immune cells may be misdirected from attacking potential pathogens. See Rosário Monteiro and Isabel Azevedo, "Chronic Inflammation in Obesity and the Metabolic Syndrome," *Mediators of Inflammation* (2010): 2; Dana T. Graves and Rayyan A. Kaya, "Diabetic Complications and Dysregulated Innate Immunity," *Frontiers in Bioscience* 13 (2011): 1227–39; H. Loe, "Periodontal Disease: The Sixth Complication of Diabetes Mellitus," *Diabetes Care* 16, no. 1 (1993): 329–34; R. H. Drachman et al., "Studies on the Effect of Experimental Nonketotic Diabetes Mellitus on Antibacterial Defense: I. Demonstration of a Defect in Phagocytosis," *Journal of Experimental Medicine* 124, no. 2 (1966): 227–40; Jan Evans Patterson and Vincent T. Andriole, "Bacterial Urinary Tract Infections in Diabetes," *Infectious Disease Clinics of North America* 11, no. 3 (1997): 735–50; Joshi et al., "Infections in Patients with Diabetes Mellitus," *New England Journal of Medicine* 341, no. 25 (1999): 1906–12.

8   Katharine Milton, "The Critical Role Played by Animal Source Foods in Human (Homo) Evolution," *Journal of Nutrition* 133, no. 11, suppl. 2 (2003): 3886–92S; Clark Spencer Larsen, "Animal Source Foods and Human Health during Evolution," *Journal of Nutrition* 133, no. 11, suppl. 2 (2003): 3893–97S.

9   C. Stanford, "Chimpanzee Hunting Behavior and Human Evolution," *American Scientist* 83 (1995): 256–61; Larsen, "Animal Source Foods and Human Health," 3893–94S.

10 M. P. Richards, "A Brief Review of the Archaeological Evidence for Palaeolithic and Neolithic Subsistence," *European Journal of Clinical Nutrition* 56, no. 12 (2002): 1273; Mary C. Stiner, *Honor among Thieves: A Zooarchaeological Study of Neandertal Ecology* (Princeton, NJ: Princeton University Press, 1994).

11 Begoña Ruiz-Núñez et al., "Lifestyle and Nutritional Imbalances Associated with Western Diseases: Causes and Consequences of Chronic Systemic Low-grade Inflammation in an Evolutionary Context," *Journal of Nutritional Biochemistry* 24, no. 7 (2013): 1184.

12 Aiello and Wheeler, "The Expensive-Tissue Hypothesis," 199–221.

13 Ruiz-Núñez et al., "Lifestyle and Nutritional Imbalances," 1184; William R. Leonard et al., "Effects of Brain Evolution on Human Nutrition and Metabolism," *Annual Review of Nutrition* 27, no. 1 (2007): 311–27.

14 Karen Hardy et al., "The Importance of Dietary Carbohydrate in Human Evolution," *Quarterly Review of Biology* 90, no. 3 (September 2015): 252; N. L. Conklin-Brittain, R. W. Wrangham and C. C. Smith, "A Two-Stage Model of Increased Dietary Quality in the Early Hominid Evolution: The Role of Fiber," in *Human Diet: Its Origins and Evolution*, ed. P. S. Ungar and M. F. Teaford (Westport, CT: Praeger Press, 2002), 61–76.

15 M. A. Crawford and C. L. Broadhurst, "The Role of Docosahexaenoic and the Marine Food Web as Determinants of Evolution and Hominid Brain Development: The Challenge for Human Sustainability," *Nutrition and Health* 21, no. 1 (2012): 23; Crawford et al., "Evidence for the Unique Function of Docosahexaenoic Acid," S39–S47; C. Broadhurst et al., "Brain-Specific Lipids from Marine, Lacustrine, or Terrestrial Food Resources: Potential Impact on Early African Homo Sapiens," *Comparative Biochemistry and Physiology Part B: Biochemistry and Molecular Biology* 131, no. 4 (2002): 653–73.

16 Jack G. Chamberlain, "The Possible Role of Long-Chain, Omega-3 Fatty Acids in Human Brain Phylogeny," *Perspectives in Biology and Medicine* 39, no. 3 (1996): 438.

17 Crawford et al., "Evidence for the Unique Function of Docosahexaenoic Acid," S39–S47; Joane Bradbury, "Docosahexaenoic Acid (DHA): An Ancient Nutrient for the Modern Human Brain," *Nutrients* 3, no. 12 (2011): 530. Broadhurst et al., "Brain-Specific Lipids," 653–73; M. A. Crawford, "Cerebral Evolution," *Nutrition and Health* 16, no. 1 (2002): 29–34; Crawford et al., "Docosahexaenoic Acid and Cerebral Evolution," *Fatty Acids and Lipids—New Findings World Review of Nutrition and Dietetics* (2000), 6–17.

18 Crawford et al., "Evidence for the Unique Function of Docosahexaenoic Acid," S39–S47. DHA from marine animals, and to a lesser extent from terrestrial sources (particularly bone marrow and ruminant brains), may have been linked to the evolution of an increasingly large brain during the last 200,000 years. See also L. Cordain et al., "Fatty Acid Composition and Energy Density of Foods Available to African Hominids: Evolutionary Implications for Human Brain Development," *World Review of Nutrition and Dietetics* 90 (2001): 144–61; Chamberlain, "The Possible Role of Long-Chain, Omega-3 Fatty Acids," 436–45.

19 Crawford et al., "Evidence for the Unique Function of Docosahexaenoic Acid." S39–S47.

20   Curtis W. Marean, "The Origins and Significance of Coastal Resource Use in Africa and Western Eurasia," *Journal of Human Evolution* 77 (2014): 20; Michael D. Gumert et al., "The Physical Characteristics and Usage Patterns of Stone Axe and Pounding Hammers Used by Long-tailed Macaques in the Andaman Sea Region of Thailand," *American Journal of Primatology* 71, no. 7 (2009): 594–608; Michael D. Gumert et al., "Sex Differences in the Stone Tool-use Behavior of a Wild Population of Burmese Long-tailed Macaques (Macaca Fascicularis Aurea)," *American Journal of Primatology* 73, no. 12 (2011): 1239–49; Suchinda Malaivijitnond et al., "Stone-Tool Usage by Thai Long-Tailed Macaques (Macaca Fascicularis)," *American Journal of Primatology* 69, no. 2 (2007): 227–33. doi:10.1002/ajp.20342.

21   Curtis W. Marean, "Coastal South Africa and the Coevolution of the Modern Human Lineage and the Coastal Adaptation," *Trekking the Shore: Interdisciplinary Contributions to Archaeology* 77 (2011): 421–40. See also Marean, "The Origins and Significance of Coastal Resource Use," 18; Curtis W. Marean, "Pinnacle Point Cave 13B (Western Cape Province, South Africa) in Context: The Cape Floral Kingdom, Shellfish, and Modern Human Origins," *Journal of Human Evolution* 59, no. 3–4 (2010): 425–43.

22   Bradbury, "Docosahexaenoic Acid (DHA): An Ancient Nutrient," 529. doi:10.3390/nu3050529.

23   Artemis Simopoulos, "An Increase in the Omega-6/Omega-3 Fatty Acid Ratio Increases the Risk for Obesity," *Nutrients* 8, no. 3 (2016): 128.

24   Bradbury, "Docosahexaenoic Acid (DHA): An Ancient Nutrient," 534; J. Thomas Brenna and Norman Salem, "Workshop Proceedings: DHA as a Required Nutrient," *Prostaglandins, Leukotrienes and Essential Fatty Acids* 81, nos. 2–3 (2009): 97. DHA is metabolized into EPA, which is then converted into DPAn-3 (22:5n-3 or docosapentaenoic acid). DPAn-3 is then converted into DHA in several further steps. In addition to Bradbury's definition of this association, see also W. W. Christie, "Fatty Acids: Methylene-Interrupted Double Bonds: Structures, Occurrence and Biochemistry," 2010. Available online: http://lipidlibrary.aocs.org/Lipids/fa_poly/index.htm. The amount of DHA that can be produced from ALA in the human body is currently not known, though the consensus is that the amount is insufficient for normal physiology. Isotope studies generally suggest that the biosynthesis of DHA from ALA in humans is extremely low. See Graham C. Burdge et al., "Eicosapentaenoic and Docosapentaenoic Acids Are the Principal Products of α-linolenic Acid Metabolism in Young Men," *British Journal of Nutrition* 88, no. 4 (2002): 355–63. R. H. M. De Groot et al., "Effect of α-linolenic Acid Supplementation during Pregnancy on Maternal and Neonatal Polyunsaturated Fatty Acid Status and Pregnancy Outcome," *American Journal of Clinical Nutrition* 79 (2004): 251–60; Thomas A. B. Sanders, "DHA Status of Vegetarians," *Prostaglandins, Leukotrienes and Essential Fatty Acids* 81, no. 2–3 (2009): 137–41. Several studies show that supplementation with preformed DHA increases DHA content of serum phospholipids and tissues, suggesting that dietary intake of DHA is necessary, or at least beneficial, to health. In addition to Sanders, see Julia Geppert et al., "Microalgal Docosahexaenoic Acid Decreases Plasma Triacylglycerol in Normolipidaemic Vegetarians: A Randomised Trial," *British Journal of Nutrition* 95, no. 4 (2006): 779; Jay Whelan et al., "Docosahexaenoic Acid: Measurements in Food and Dietary Exposure," *Prostaglandins, Leukotrienes and Essential Fatty Acids* 81, no. 2–3 (2009): 133–36; Brenna and Salem, "Workshop Proceedings: DHA as a Required Nutrient," 97.

25   Broadhurst et al., "Brain-Specific Lipids," 662; Bradbury, "Docosahexaenoic Acid (DHA): An Ancient Nutrient," 534; Burdge, "Eicosapentaenoic and Docosapentaenoic

Acids," 355–63; De Groot, "Effect of α-linolenic Acid Supplementation," 251–60; Thomas Sanders, "DHA Status of Vegetarians," *Prostaglandins, Leukotrienes and Essential Fatty Acids* 81, nos. 2–3 (2009): 137–41. Crawford and Broadhurst, "The Role of Docosahexaenoic and the Marine Food Web," 23; M. A. Crawford et al., "Evidence for the Unique Function of Docosahexaenoic Acid,"

26   Ruiz-Núñez et al., "Lifestyle and Nutritional Imbalances," 1184; C. Broadhurst et al., "Rift Valley Lake Fish and Shellfish Provided Brain-specific Nutrition for Early Homo," *British Journal of Nutrition* 79, no. 1 (1998): 3–21; Broadhurst et al., "Brain-Specific Lipids," 653–73; A. Gibbons, "Becoming Human: In Search of the First Hominids," *Science* 295, no. 5558 (2002): 1214–19; F. A. J. Muskiet and R. S. Kuipers, "Lessons from Shore-Based Hunter-Gatherer Diets in East Africa," in *Human Brain Evolution: The Influence of Freshwater and Marine Food Resources*, ed. Stephen C. Cunnane, and Kathlyn Moore (Hoboken, NJ: Wiley-Blackwell, 2010), 77–104.

27   Crawford and Broadhurst, "The Role of Docosahexaenoic and the Marine Food Web," 23; Crawford et al., "Evidence for the Unique Function of Docosahexaenoic Acid," S39–S47; Broadhurst et al., "Brain-Specific Lipids," 653–73.

28   Marean, "The Origins and Significance of Coastal Resource Use," 18–19.

29   Curtis W. Marean, "Early Human Use of Marine Resources and Pigment in South Africa during the Middle Pleistocene," *Nature* 449, no. 7164 (2007): 907; Robert C. Walter, "Early Human Occupation of the Red Sea Coast of Eritrea during the Last Interglacial," *Nature* 405, no. 6782 (2000): 65–69.

30   On the controversy over the marine coastal thesis, including several rebuttals, as well as attempts to integrate some of its claims while also attending to other overlooked aspects of brain evolution, see B. A. Carlson, "Docosahexaenoic Acid, the Aquatic Diet, and Hominin Encephalization: Difficulties in Establishing Evolutionary Links," *American Journal of Human Biology* 19, no. 1 (2007): 132–41; S. C. Cunnane et al., "Docosahexaenoic Acid and Shore-Based Diets in Hominin Encephalization: A Rebuttal," *American Journal of Human Biology* 19, no. 4 (2007): 578–81; K. Stewart et al., "Special Issue: The Role of Freshwater and Marine Resources in the Evolution of the Human Diet, Brain and Behavior," *Journal of Human Evolution* 77 (2004): 1–216; J. C. Joordens et al., "A Fish Is Not a Fish: Patterns in Fatty Acid Composition of Aquatic Food May Have Had Implications for Hominin Evolution," *Journal of Human Evolution* 77 (December 2014):107–16.

31   For the latest synthesis on DHA and immune receptor function, see Elisa Alvarez-Curto and Graeme Milligan, "Metabolism Meets Immunity: The Role of Free Fatty Acid Receptors in the Immune System," *Biochemical Pharmacology* 114 (August 2016): 3–13. In 1989, a NATO Advanced Research Workshop stated that current research showed that omega-3 fatty acids have important effects on health, including anti-inflammatory effects, the lowering of triglycerides and cholesterol, and a decrease in thrombosis and platelet aggregation. See A. P. Simopoulos, "Summary of the NATO Advanced Research Workshop on Dietary Omega 3 and Omega 6 Fatty Acids: Biological Effects and Nutritional Essentiality," *Journal of Nutrition* 119 (1989): 521–28. Subsequently, research has emphasized the importance of dietary intake of omega-3 fatty acids, offering further support for the workshop findings. Dozens of studies on patients with insufficient intakes of AHA, EPA and DHA provide support for the hypothesis that dietary intake of these fatty acids is vital for normal physiological function. See Bradbury, "Docosahexaenoic Acid (DHA): An Ancient Nutrient," 533; S. K. Gebauer et al., "n-3 Fatty Acid Dietary Recommendations and

Food Sources to Achieve Essentiality and Cardiovascular Benefits," *American Journal of Clinical Nutrition* 83 (suppl.) (2006): S1526–S35; Hau D. Le et al., "The Essentiality of Arachidonic Acid and Docosahexaenoic Acid," *Prostaglandins, Leukotrienes and Essential Fatty Acids* 81, no. 2–3 (2009): 165–70. Several studies show physiological effects arise when patients suffer from deficiency of omega-3 fatty acids. For example, Holmon and colleagues observed a six-year old girl who had lost a large proportion of her intestine and therefore relied on total parental nutrition suffered from ALA deficiency: symptoms including blurry vision, numbness, paresthesia, and an inability to walk were reversed when her diet included a large increase in ALA. Elderly patients also requiring parental nutrition were observed to have dermatological symptoms (nervous system pathology could not be observed in these studies) when the quantities of EPA, DHA and ALA were low in the diet. See Bradbury, "Docosahexaenoic Acid (DHA): An Ancient Nutrient," 533 and 543; R. T. Holman et al., "A Case of Human Linolenic Acid Deficiency Involving Neurological Abnormalities. *American Journal of Clinical Nutrition* 35 (1982): 616–23. Further studies suggest that omega-3 fatty acids are important in cognitive development. See Bradbury, "Docosahexaenoic Acid (DHA): An Ancient Nutrient," 543; A. R. Lucas, "Breast Milk and Subsequent Intelligence Quotient in Children Born Preterm," *The Lancet* 339, no. 8788 (1992): 261–64.

32 Elena Tomasello and Sammy Bedoui, "Intestinal Innate Immune Cells in Gut Homeostasis and Immunosurveillance," *Immunology and Cell Biology* 91 (2013): 201–3.

33 Animals such as ruminants can synthesize omega-3 and omega-6 from their precurors ALA and LA, respectively. See E. Abedi and A. Sahir, "Long-Chain Polyunsaturated Fatty Acid Sources and Evaluation of Their Nutritional and Functional Properties," *Food Science and Nutrition* 2, no. 5 (2014): 119. These omega-3 and omega-6 fatty acids are then incorporated into their tissues. See Cynthia A. Daley et al., "A Review of Fatty Acid Profiles and Antioxidant Content in Grass-Fed and Grain-Fed Beef," *Nutrition Journal* 9, no. 10 (2010), 1–12. Therefore, ruminants can gain enough omega-3 and omega-6 fatty acids by consuming plant foods. Humans, however, likely cannot synthesize adequate omega-3 fatty acids from the precursor ALA. See Brenna and Salem, "Workshop Proceedings: DHA as a Required Nutrient," 97.

34 Prakash Shetty, *Nutrition Immunity Infection* (Wallingford, Oxfordshire, UK: CABI, 2010), 6–10; Ian R. Mackay et al., "The Immune System: First of Two Parts," *New England Journal of Medicine* 343, no. 1 (2000): 37–49.

35 Shetty, *Nutrition Immunity Infection*, 8–10.

36 Mackay, "The Immune System: First of Two Parts," 37–49; Shetty, *Nutrition Immunity Infection*, 11–21.

37 For example, "Specific MHC alleles have been associated with infection by hepatitis B, hepatitis C, dengue, and HIV." See Jones, "Virgin Soils Revisited," 727.

38 Mackay, "The Immune System: First of Two Parts," 37–49; Shetty, *Nutrition Immunity Infection*, 11–21.

39 Shetty, *Nutrition Immunity Infection*, 11–21; Mackay, "The Immune System: First of Two Parts," 37–49

40 Shetty, *Nutrition Immunity Infection*,19–21.

41 On differentiation into subclasses, such as T helper 1 (Th1) or T helper 2 (Th2) cells, see P. Kidd, "Th1/Th2 Balance: The Hypothesis, Its Limitations, and Implications for Health and Disease," *Alternative Medicine Review* 8, no. 3 (2003): 223–46.

42 Mackay, "The Immune System: First of Two Parts," 37–49.

43   Ian R. Mackay et al., "The Immune System: Second of Two Parts," *New England Journal of Medicine* 343, no. 2 (2000): 108–17.

44   Shetty, *Nutrition Immunity Infection*, 15–21.

45   Mackay, "The Immune System: First of Two Parts," 37–49.

46   Ibid; Susumu Tonegawa, "Somatic Generation of Antibody Diversity," *Nature* 302, no. 5909 (1983): 575–81.

47   Monteiro and Azevedo, "Chronic Inflammation," 2; M. Qatanani and M. A. Lazar, "Mechanisms of Obesity Associated Insulin Resistance: Many Choices on the Menu," *Genes and Development* 21, no. 12 (2007): 1443–55; B. Henderson et al., "Mediators of Rheumatoid Arthritis," *British Medicine Bulletin* 43 (1987): 415–28.

48   Shetty, *Nutrition Immunity Infection*, 166.

49   Janeway et al., *Immunobiology*, 503–9.

50   The inactive immune system consumes almost one-quarter of the body's metabolic fuel, the majority of which is glucose. Immune activity results in substantial increases in the metabolic demands of the immune system. See Ruiz-Núñez, "Lifestyle and Nutritional Imbalances," 1185. For an excellent recent overview, see Rainer H. Straub and Carsten Schradin, "Chronic Inflammatory Systemic Diseases: An Evolutionary Trade-Off between Acutely Beneficial But Chronically Harmful Programs," *Evolution, Medicine, and Public Health*, 2016, no. 1 (January 2016): 37–51; Rainer H. Straub, "Evolutionary Medicine and Chronic Inflammatory State—Known and New Concepts in Pathophysiology," *Journal of Molecular Medicine*, 90, no. 5 (2012): 523.

51   J. M. Milner and M. A. Beck, "Micronutrients, Immunology and Inflammation: The Impact of Obesity on the Immune Response to Infection," *Proceedings of the Nutrition Society* 71, no. 2 (2012): 298–306; D. C. Nieman et al., "Influence of Obesity on Immune Function," *Journal of the American Dietetic Association* 99, no. 3 (March 1999): 294–99; H. Ghanim et al., "Circulating Mononuclear Cells in the Obese Are in a Proinflammatory State," *Circulation* 110, no. 12 (September 2004):1564–71; E. Falagas and M. Kompoti, "Obesity and Infection," *Lancet Infectious Diseases* 6, no. 7 (July 2006): 438–46; M. E. Falagas and M. Kompoti, "Obesity and Infection," *Lancet Infectious Diseases* 6, no. 7 (July 2006): 438–46; D. Vilar-Compte et al., "Surgical Site Infections at the National Cancer Institute in Mexico: A Case-Control Study," *American Journal of Infection Control* 28, no. 1 (February 2000): 14–20; P. Ylöstalo et al., "Association between Body Weight and Periodontal Infection," *Journal of Clinical Periodontology* 35, no. 4 (April 2008): 297–304; W. Jedrychowski et al., "Predisposition to Acute Respiratory Infections among Overweight Preadolescent Children: An Epidemiologic Study in Poland," *Public Health* 112, no. (May 1998): 189–95. These studies suggest that obese patients have an increased risk of infection, proposing that adiposity may dampen the immune response to pathogens.

52   I. A. Myles, "Fast Food Fever: Reviewing the Impacts of the Western Diet on Immunity," *Nutrition Journal* 13 (2014): 616; Milner and Beck, "Micronutrients, Immunology and Inflammation," 298–306; A. M. Wolf et al., "Adiponectin Induces the Anti-inflammatory Cytokines IL-10 and IL-1RA in Human Leukocytes," *Biochemical and Biophysical Research Communications* 323 (2004): 630–35; K. Kim et al., "Adiponectin Is a Negative Regulator of NK Cell Cytotoxicity," *Journal of Immunology* 176 (2006): 5958–64; H. Ziegler-Heitbrock et al., "Tolerance to Lipopolysaccharide Involves Mobilization of Nuclear Factor Kappa B with Predominance of p50 Homodimers," *Journal of Biological Chemistry* 269 (1994): 17001–4.

53   For reviews of the role of leptin in immunity and specific studies, see A. La Cava and
     G. Matarese, "The Weight of Leptin in Immunity," *Nature Reviews Immunology* 4, no. 5
     (May 2004): 371–79; P. Mancuso et al., "Leptin-Deficient Mice Exhibit Impaired
     Host Defense in Gram-Negative Pneumonia," *Journal of Immunology* 168 (2002): 4018–
     24; F. Caldefie-Chezet et al., "Leptin: A Potential Regulator of Polymorphonuclear
     Neutrophil Bactericidal Action?" *Journal of Leukocyte Biology* 69 (2001): 414–18; Y. Zhao
     et al., "Expression of Leptin Receptors and Response to Leptin Stimulation of Human
     Natural Killer Cell Lines," *Biochemical and Biophysical Research Communications* 300
     (2003): 247–52; T. Gainsford et al., "Leptin Can Induce Proliferation, Differentiation,
     and Functional Activation of Hemopoietic Cells," *Proceedings of the National Academy of
     Sciences of the United States of America* 93 (1996): 14564–65.
54   They note an increase in the production of IL-10 and IL-1RA, and a decrease in the
     production of the cytokine IFN γ. See Wolf et al., "Adiponectin Induces," 630–35.
55   Milner and Beck, "Micronutrients, Immunology and Inflammation," 298–306; Myles,
     "Fast Food Fever," 61.
56   Myles, Fast Food Fever," 6. For studies showing the down-regulation of the steroid
     response in steroid users, see A. Buttner and D. Thieme, "Side Effects of Anabolic
     Androgenic Steroids: Pathological Findings and Structure-Activity Relationships,"
     Handbook of Experimental Pharmacology 195 (2010): 459–84.
57   Ian Spreadbury, "Comparison with Ancestral Diets Suggests Dense Acellular
     Carbohydrates Promote an Inflammatory Microbiota, and May Be the Primary
     Dietary Cause of Leptin Resistance and Obesity," *Diabetes, Metabolic Syndrome
     and Obesity: Targets and Therapy* (2012): 182; Carey N. Lumeng and Alan R. Saltiel,
     "Inflammatory Links between Obesity and Metabolic Disease," *Journal of Clinical
     Investigation* 121, no. 6 (2011): 2111–17; Claudia Sanmiguel et al., "Gut Microbiome
     and Obesity: A Plausible Explanation for Obesity," *Current Obesity Reports* 4, no. 2
     (2015), 254; Gökhan S. Hotamisligil, "Inflammation and Metabolic Disorders,"
     Nature 444, no. 7121 (2006): 860–67; J. Choi et al., "Obesity and C-reactive Protein
     in Various Populations: A Systematic Review and Meta-analysis," *Obesity Reviews* 14,
     no. 3 (2013): 232–44; P. Marques-Vidal et al., "Association between Inflammatory and
     Obesity Markers in a Swiss Population-Based Sample (CoLaus Study)," *Obesity Facts* 5,
     no. 5 (2012): 734–44; M. D. Bahceci et al., "The Correlation between Adiposity and
     Adiponectin, Tumor Necrosis Factor α, Interleukin-6 and High Sensitivity C-reactive
     Protein Levels. Is Adipocyte Size Associated with Inflammation in Adults?" *Journal of
     Endocrinological Investigation* 30, no. 3 (2007): 210–14.
58   For example, the overexpression of a glucose uptake protein in mouse T cells in
     vitro (which allowed increased uptake of glucose into the T cells) resulted in altered
     cell metabolism and cytokine production. See Milner and Beck, "Micronutrients,
     Immunology and Inflammation," 298–306; F. B. Tentz and A. E. Kitabchi,
     "Hyperglycemia-Induced Activation of Human T-Lymphocytes with De Novo
     Emergence of Insulin Receptors and Generation of Reactive Oxygen Species,"
     Biochemical and Biophysical Research Communications 335 (2005):491–95; S. R. Jacobs et al.,
     "Glucose Uptake Is Limiting in T Cell Activation and Requires CD28-Mediated Akt-
     Dependent and Independent Pathways," *Journal of Immunology* 180 (2008): 4476–86.
59   For example, the exposure of human immune cells to increasing concentrations of
     the saturated fatty acid palmitate was found to cause activation of T cells and an
     increase in the production of cytokines and reactive oxygen species generation and
     lipid peroxidation in vitro. See Milner and Beck, "Micronutrients, Immunology and

Inflammation," 298–306; F. B. Stentz and A. E. Kitabchi, "Palmitic Acid-Induced Activation Of Human T-Lymphocytes and Aortic Endothelial Cells With Production of Insulin Receptors, Reactive Oxygen Species, Cytokines, and Lipid Peroxidation," *Biochemical and Biophysical Research Communications* 46, no. 3 (August 2006): 721–26.

60   For example, fatty acids have been shown to activate the toll-like receptors TLR-2 and TLR-4 in vitro, inducing expression of inflammatory markers. See J. Y. Lee et al., "Saturated Fatty Acids, But Not Unsaturated Fatty Acids, Induce the Expression of Cyclooxygenase-2 Mediated Through Toll-Like Receptor 4," *Journal of Biological Chemistry* 276 (2001): 16683–89

61   Graves and Kaya, "Diabetic Complications and Dysregulated Innate Immunity," 1227–39; H. Vlassara, "Recent Progress in Advanced Glycation End Products and Diabetic Complications," *Diabetes* 46, no. Supplement 2 (1997): S19–25; George L. King and Michael Brownlee, "The Cellular And Molecular Mechanisms of Diabetic Complications," *Endocrinology and Metabolism Clinics of North America* 25, no. 2 (1996): 255–70.

62   Graves and Kaya, "Diabetic Complications and Dysregulated Innate Immunity," 1227–39; A. M. Schmidt et al., "Regulation of Human Mononuclear Phagocyte Migration by Cell Surface-binding Proteins for Advanced Glycation End Products," *Journal of Clinical Investigation* 91, no. 5 (1993): 2155–68; Roweba Brandt and Sven Krantz, "Glycated Albumin (Amadori Product) Induces Activation of MAP Kinases in Monocyte-like MonoMac 6 Cells," *Biochimica Et Biophysica Acta (BBA)—General Subjects* 1760, no. 11 (2006): 1749–53; Margo P. Cohen et al., "Glycated Albumin Increases Oxidative Stress, Activates NF-κB and Extracellular Signal-regulated Kinase (ERK), and Stimulates ERK-dependent Transforming Growth Factor-β1 Production in Macrophage RAW Cells," *Journal of Laboratory and Clinical Medicine* 141, no. 4 (2003): 242–49; G. Rashid et al., "The Effect of Advanced Glycation End-Products and Aminoguanidine on Tnfalpha Production by Rat Peritoneal Macrophages," *Peritoneal Dialysis International* 21 (2001): 122–29; Z. Alikhani et al., "Advanced Glycation End Products Enhance Expression of Pro-Apoptotic Genes and Stimulate Fibroblast Apoptosis through Cytoplasmic and Mitochondrial Pathways," *Journal of Biological Chemistry* 280 (2005): 12087–95; Mani Alikhani et al., "Advanced Glycation End Products Stimulate Osteoblast Apoptosis via the MAP Kinase and Cytosolic Apoptotic Pathways," *Bone* 40, no. 2 (2007): 345–53.

63   Graves and Kaya, "Diabetic Complications and Dysregulated Innate Immunity," 1227–39; Marc A. Mazade and Morven S. Edwards, "Impairment of Type III Group B Streptococcus-Stimulated Superoxide Production and Opsonophagocytosis by Neutrophils in Diabetes," *Molecular Genetics and Metabolism* 73, no. 3 (2001): 259–67; Sung-Hee Ihm et al., "Effect of Tolrestat, an Aldose Reductase Inhibitor, on Neutrophil Respiratory Burst Activity in Diabetic Patients," *Metabolism* 46, no. 6 (1997): 634–38; S. E. Tebbs et al., "The Influence of Aldose Reductase on the Oxidative Burst in Diabetic Neutrophils," *Diabetes Research and Clinical Practice* 15, no. 2 (1992): 121–29; O. M. Boland et al., "Effects of Ponalrestat, an Aldose Reductase Inhibitor, on Neutrophil Killing of Escherichia Coli and Autonomic Function in Patients with Diabetes Mellitus," *Diabetes* 42, no. 2 (1993): 336–40; J. R. K. Williamson, "Hyperglycemic Pseudohypoxia and Diabetic Complications," *Diabetes* 42, no. 6 (1993): 801–13; Pedro Carrera-Bastos et al., "The Western Diet and Lifestyle and Diseases of Civilization," *Research Reports in Clinical Cardiology* 2

(2011): 24; A. W. Barclay et al., "Glycemic Index, Glycemic Load, and Chronic Disease Risk: A Meta-Analysis of Observational Studies," *American Journal of Clinical Nutrition* 87, no. 3 (2008): 627–37; C. K. Roberts and S. Liu, "Effects of Glycemic Load on Metabolic Health and Type 2 Diabetes Mellitus," *Journal of Diabetes Science and Technology* 3, no. 4 (2009): 697–704. Aside from the effects of oxidative stress and inflammation, a further potential mechanism for the effect of hyperglycemia on innate immune function has been proposed. According to Kiselar, levels of the dicarbonyls methylgloxal (MGO) and glyoxal (GO), metabolic products of glycolysis, the metabolism of glucose to pyruvate, become elevated in hyperglycemia. These dicarbonyls affect the structure and activity of Human β-defensin-2 (hBD-2), which is active against gram-negative bacteria, and "chemoattracts immature dendritic cells, thus regulating innate and adaptive immunity." The altered structure of hBD-2 has been found to correspond with lower chemotactic and antimicrobial activity of hBD-2. See Janna G. Kiselar, "Modification of β-Defensin-2 by Dicarbonyls Methylglyoxal and Glyoxal Inhibits Antibacterial and Chemotactic Function In Vitro," *Plos One* 10, no. 8 (2015).

64   Dean P. Jones, "Redefining Oxidative Stress," *Antioxidants & Redox Signaling* 8, nos. 9–10 (2006): 1865. doi:10.1089/ars.2006.8.1865.

65   Recent research highlights the strong association between oxidative stress and chronic inflammatory diseases such as diabetes. See Jones, "Redefining Oxidative Stress," 1865–79; Graves and Kaya, "Diabetic Complications and Dysregulated Innate Immunity," 1227–39; Timothy M. Millar, "ROS Generation in Endothelial Hypoxia and Reoxygenation Stimulates MAP Kinase Signaling and Kinase-Dependent Neutrophil Recruitment," *Free Radical Biology and Medicine* 42, no. 8 (2007): 1165–77; Sanchayita Mitra and Abraham Edward, "Participation of Superoxide in Neutrophil Activation and Cytokine Production," *Biochimica Et Biophysica Acta (BBA)—Molecular Basis of Disease* 1762, no. 8 (2006): 732–41; Michael D. Buck, "T Cell Metabolism Drives Immunity," *Journal of Cell Biology* 210, no. 4 (2015): 1348–49.

66   The most commonly disrupted immune cell pathway is the MAP kinase pathway. See Graves and Kaya, "Diabetic Complications and Dysregulated Innate Immunity," 1227–39; Timothy M. Millar et al., "ROS Generation in Endothelial Hypoxia and Reoxygenation," 1165–77; Sanchayita Mitra and Edward Abraham, "Participation of Superoxide in Neutrophil Activation and Cytokine Production," *Biochimica Et Biophysica Acta (BBA)—Molecular Basis of Disease* 1762, no. 8 (2006): 732–41; Geoffrey Gloire et al., "NF-κB Activation by Reactive Oxygen Species: Fifteen Years Later," *Biochemical Pharmacology* 72, no. 11 (2006): 1493–505.

67   Maria A. Puertollano et al., "Dietary Antioxidants: Immunity and Host Defense," *Current Topics in Medicinal Chemistry* 11, no. 14 (2011): 1755.

68   Ibid., 1754–55.

69   Jones, "Redefining Oxidative Stress," 1865.

70   Jones, "Redefining Oxidative Stress," 1865–79; Monteiro and Azevedo, "Chronic Inflammation," 3; Qatanani and Lazar, "Mechanisms of Obesity Associated Insulin Resistance," 1443–55.

71   Ruiz-Núñez et al., "Lifestyle and Nutritional Imbalances," 1183; M. Stumvoll et al., "Type 2 Diabetes: Principles of Pathogenesis and Therapy," *The Lancet* 365, no. 9467 (2005): 1333–46.

72   Ruiz-Núñez et al., "Lifestyle and Nutritional Imbalances," 1185.

73   Ibid.

74   F. de Carvalho Vidigal et al., "The Role of Hyperglycemia in the Induction of Oxidative
      Stress and Inflammatory Process," *Nutrición Hospitalaria* 27, no. 5 (2012): 1391–98.
75   Graves and Kaya, "Diabetic Complications and Dysregulated Innate Immunity,"
      1227–39; Loe, "Periodontal Disease: The Sixth Complication of Diabetes Mellitus,"
      329–34; Drachman et al., "Studies on the Effect of Experimental Nonketotic Diabetes
      Mellitus," 227–40; Patterson and Andriole, "Bacterial Urinary Tract Infections
      in Diabetes," 735–50; Joshi et al., "Infections in Patients with Diabetes Mellitus,"
      1906–12.
76   Graves and Kaya, "Diabetic Complications and Dysregulated Innate Immunity,"
      1227–39; Rayyan A. Kayal, "Diminished Bone Formation during Diabetic Fracture
      Healing Is Related to the Premature Resorption of Cartilage Associated With
      Increased Osteoclast Activity," *Journal of Bone and Mineral Research* 22, no. 4 (2007): 560–
      68; Eric M. Kagel et al., "Effects of Diabetes and Steroids on Fracture Healing,"
      Current Opinion in Orthopaedics 6, no. 5 (1995): 7–13.
77   F. M. Wensveen, "The 'Big Bang' in Obese Fat: Events Initiating Obesity-Induced
      Adipose Tissue Inflammation," *European Journal of Immunology* 45 (2015): 2446–56; F. M.
      Wensveen et al., "NK Cells Link Obesity-Induced Adipose Stress to Inflammation and
      Insulin Resistance," *Nature Immunology* 16, no. 4 (April 2015): 376–85; Case Western
      Reserve University, "High Blood Sugar of Diabetes Can Cause Immune System
      Malfunction, Triggering Infection: Scientists Show How Sugar-Derived Molecules
      Can Weaken Infection-Fighting Antimicrobial Beta-Defensin Peptides," *ScienceDaily*,
      August 6, 2015, www.sciencedaily.com/releases/2015/08/150806151354.htm;
      Kiselar et al., "Modification of β-Defensin-2 by Dicarbonyls Methylglyoxal and
      Glyoxal," e0130533; Oregon State University, "Immune System Uses Gut Bacteria
      to Control Glucose Metabolism," *ScienceDaily*, November 14, 2016, www.sciencedaily.
      com/releases/2016/11/161114105642.htm; Greer et al., "Akkermansia Muciniphila
      Mediates Negative Effects of Ifnγ on Glucose Metabolism," *Nature Communications* 7
      (2016): 13329; Washington University in St. Louis, "Tumors Disable Immune Cells
      by Using Up Sugar," *ScienceDaily*, June 6, 2013, www.sciencedaily.com/releases/2013/
      06/130606140452.htm; Chang Chih-Hao et al., "Posttranscriptional Control of T
      Cell Effector Function by Aerobic Glycolysis," *Cell* 153, no. 6 (2013): 1239; D. E. Moller
      and K. D. Kaufman, "Metabolic Syndrome: A Clinical and Molecular Perspective,"
      Annual Review of Medicine 56 (2005): 45–62; L. P. Bharath et al., "Adaptive Immunity and
      Metabolic Health: Harmony Becomes Dissonant in Obesity and Aging," *Comprehensive
      Physiology* 7, no. 4 (September 2017): 1307–37; T. J. Guzik and F. Cosentino,
      "Epigenetics and Immunometabolism in Diabetes and Aging," *Antioxidants & Redox
      Signaling* September 11, 2017. (Epub ahead of print); D. Frasca and B. B. Blomberg,
      "Adipose Tissue Inflammation Induces B Cell Inflammation and Decreases B Cell
      Function in Aging," *Frontiers in Immunology* 8 (August 2017): 1003; A. Harusato and
      B. Chassaing, "Insights on the Impact of Diet-Mediated Microbiota Alterations on
      Immunity and Diseases," *American Journal of Transplantation* 2017 (August 2017): 1–6;
      D. A. de Luis et al., "Gene Expression Analysis Identify a Metabolic and Cell Function
      Alterations as a Hallmark of Obesity without Metabolic Syndrome in Peripheral
      Blood, A Pilot Study," *Clinical Nutrition*, June 10, 2017, pii: S0261-5614(17)30217-0;
      J. Pindjakova et al., "Gut Dysbiosis and Adaptive Immune Response in Diet-induced
      Obesity vs. Systemic Inflammation," *Frontiers in Microbiology* 8 (June 2017): 1157; T. J.
      Guzik, "The Role of Infiltrating Immune Cells in Dysfunctional Adipose Tissue,"
      Cardiovascular Research 113, no. 9 (July 2017): 1009–23; P. Matafome and R. Seiça,

"Function and Dysfunction of Adipose Tissue," *Advances in Neurobiology* 1, no. 9 (2017): 3–31; E. Vergadi et al., "Akt Signaling Pathway in Macrophage Activation and M1/M2 Polarization," *Journal of Immunology* 198 no. 3 (February 2017): 1006–14; P. Bullon, "AMPK/Mitochondria in Metabolic Diseases," *EXS* 107 (2016): 129–52; C. Münz, "Autophagy Proteins in Phagocyte Endocytosis and Exocytosis," *Frontiers in Immunology* 8 (September 2017): 1183; E. Liu et al., "Endoplasmic Reticulum Stress Is Involved in the Connection between Inflammation and Autophagy in Type 2 Diabetes," *General and Comparative Endocrinology* 210 (January 2015): 124–29.

78   Simopoulos, "An Increase in the Omega-6/Omega-3 Fatty Acid Ratio," 128. ALA is metabolized to the biologically active omega-3 fatty acids DHA and EPA. However, the conversion of ALA to DHA and EPA is inefficient. Therefore, the amount of DHA and EPA that can be obtained from conversion of ALA from plant sources may not be sufficient for optimal health. See H. Gerster, "Can Adults Adequately Convert Alpha-Linolenic Acid (18:3n-3) to Eicosapentaenoic Acid (20:5n-3) and Docosahexaenoic Acid (22:6n-3)," *International Journal for Vitamin and Nutrition Research* 68, no. 3 (1998): 159–73; F. Ottoboni and M. Alice Ottoboni, *The Modern Nutritional Diseases: Heart Disease, Stroke, Type-2 Diabetes, Obesity, Cancer: And How to Prevent Them* (Sparks, NV: Vincente Books, 2002), 178; Michael J. James et al., "Dietary Polyunsaturated Fatty Acids and Inflammatory Mediator Production," *American Society for Clinical Nutrition* 71, no. 1 (2000): S343.

79   The inflammatory eicosanoids include including prostaglandin E2 and leukotiend B4. See James et al., S343.

80   Ibid., S344.

81   Ibid., S344; B. Henderson et al., "Mediators of Rheumatoid Arthritis," *British Medicine Bulletin* 43 (1997): 415–28.

82   The anti-inflammatory molecules include leukotriene B$_3$ See Ottoboni and Ottoboni, *The Modern Nutritional Diseases*, 178–85; James et al. "Dietary Oolyunsaturated Fatty Acids," S344; M. J. James et al., "Interaction between Fish and Vegetable Oils in Relation to Rat Leucocyte Leukotriene Production," *Journal of Nutrition* 121 (1881): 631–37; D. W. Goldman et al., "Human Neutrophil Chemotactic and Degranulating Activities of Leukotriene B5 (LTB5) Derived from Eicosapentaenoic Acid," *Biochemical and Biophysical Research Communications* 117, no. 1 (1983): 282–88.

83   Philip C. Calder, "Omega-3 Fatty Acids and Inflammatory Processes," *Nutrients* 2, no. 3 (2010): 355–74. Parveen Yaqoob et al., "Influence of Cell Culture Conditions on Diet-induced Changes in Lymphocyte Fatty Acid Composition," *Biochimica Et Biophysica Acta (BBA)—Lipids and Lipid Metabolism* 1255, no. 3 (1995): 333–40; J. Palombo et al., "Cyclic vs. Continuous Enteral Feeding with Omega-3 and Gamma-linolenic Fatty Acids: Effects on Modulation of Phospholipid Fatty Acids in Rat Lung and Liver Immune Cells," *Journal of Parenteral and Enteral Nutrition* 21, no. 3 (1997): 123–32; M. Careaga-Houck and H. Sprecher, "Effect of a Fish Oil Diet on the Composition of Rat Neutrophil Lipids and the Molecular Species of Choline and Ethanolamine Glycerophospholipids," *Journal of Lipid Research* 30 (1989): 77–87; R. Vázquez et al., "Effects of Different Dietary Oils on Inflammatory Mediator Generation and Fatty Acid Composition in Rat Neutrophils," *Metabolism* 53, no. 1 (2004): 59–65.

84   The molecules required to produce further anti-inflammatory molecules include COX-2 and vascular cell adhesion molecule-1. See Frederic Gottrand, "Long-Chain Polyunsaturated Fatty Acids Influence the Immune System of Infants," *Journal of Nutrition* 138, no. 9 (2008): S1808; Harini Sampath and James M. Ntambi,

"Polyunsaturated Fatty Acid Regulation of Genes of Lipid Metabolism," *Annual Review of Nutrition* 25, no. 1 (2005): 317–40.

85 Gottrand, "Long-Chain Polyunsaturated Fatty Acids Influence," S1808.

86 The less biologically active molecules include leukotrienes and prostaglandins. See H. K. Grimm et al., "Regulatory Potential of N-3 Fatty Acids in Immunological and Inflammatory Processes," *British Journal of Nutrition* 87, no. S1 (2002): S59–67.

87 Gottrand, "Long-Chain Polyunsaturated Fatty Acids Influence," S1808; M. Zeyda and T. Stulnig, "Lipid Rafts & Co.: An Integrated Model of Membrane Organization in T Cell Activation," *Progress in Lipid Research* 45, no. 3 (2006): 187–202; D. Ma et al., "3 PUFA and Membrane Microdomains: A New Frontier in Bioactive Lipid Research," *Journal of Nutritional Biochemistry* 15, no. 11 (2004): 700–6.

88 Such a phenomenon has been noted in contemporary populations whose omega-6 intake, often from industrially produced seed and vegetable oils, vastly outweighs omega-3 consumption, contributing to a chronic inflammatory response. See Calder, "Omega-3 Fatty Acids and Inflammatory Processes," 355–74; Simopoulos, "An Increase in the Omega-6/Omega-3 Fatty Acid Ratio," 1–17.

89 During human evolution, the ratio of omega-3 to omega-6 consumed was around 1:1. A. P. Simopoulos, "Evolutionary Aspects of Diet and Essential Fatty Acids," in *Fatty Acids and Lipids—New Findings*, ed. T. Hamazaki et al. (Karger: Basel, Switzerland, 2001): 18–27. A higher ratio of omega-6: omega-3 fatty acids in the diet increase risk of obesity and cardiovascular disease. See Simopoulos, "An Increase in the Omega-6/Omega-3 Fatty Acid Ratio," 1–17; A. P. Simopoulos, "The Importance of the Omega-6/Omega-3 Fatty Acid Ratio in Cardiovascular Disease and Other Chronic Diseases," *Experimental Biology and Medicine* 233 (2008): 674–88.

90 G. J. Armelagos et al., "The Origins of Agriculture: Population Growth during a Period of Declining Health," *Population and Environment: A Journal of Interdisciplinary Studies* 13, no. 1 (Fall 1991): 9–22. See also C. M. Cassidy, "Nutrition and Health in Agriculturalists and Hunter-Gatherers: A Case Study of Two Prehistoric Populations," in *Nutritional Anthropology: Contemporary Approaches to Diet & Culture*, ed. N. W. Jerome et al. (Pleasantville, NY: Routledge, 1980), 117–45.

91 Carrera-Bastos et al., "The Western Diet and Lifestyle," 19; Mark Nathan Cohen, *Health and the Rise of Civilization* (New Haven, CT: Yale University Press,1989): 118–19; L. S. Cordain et al., "The Paradoxical Nature of Hunter-Gatherer Diets: Meat-Based, Yet Non-atherogenic," *European Journal of Clinical Nutrition* 56, no. S1 (2002); L. Cordain et al., "Plant-Animal Subsistence Ratios and Macronutrient Energy Estimations in Worldwide Hunter-Gatherer Diets," *American Journal of Clinical Nutrition* 71 (2000): 682–92.

92 Clark Spencer Larsen, "Biological Changes in Human Populations with Agriculture," *Annual Review of Anthropology* 24, no. 1 (1995): 186.

93 Clark Spencer Larsen, "The Agricultural Revolution as Environmental Catastrophe: Implications for Health and Lifestyle in the Holocene," *Quaternary International* 150, no. 1 (2006): 12; George J. Armelagos and John R. Dewey, "Evolutionary Response to Human Infectious Diseases," *BioScience* 20, no. 5 (1970): 271–75; Edward S. Deevey, "The Human Population," *Scientific American* 203, no. 3 (1960): 194–98.

94 Larsen, "The Agricultural Revolution as Environmental Catastrophe," 12; B. D. Smith, *The Emergence of Agriculture* (New York: W. H. Freeman, 1998); K. Neumann, "Anthropology: Enhanced: New Guinea: A Cradle of Agriculture," *Science* 301, no. 5630 (2003): 180–81.

95   Larsen, "Biological Changes in Human Populations with Agriculture," 186; Gayle
     J. Fritz, "Are the First American Farmers Getting Younger?" *Current Anthropology* 35,
     no. 3 (1994): 305–9. doi:10.1086/204280.
96   Larsen, "The Agricultural Revolution as Environmental Catastrophe," 12; Smith,
     The Emergence of Agriculture n.p.; Bruce Winterhalder and Carol Goland, "On
     Population, Foraging Efficiency, and Plant Domestication," *Current Anthropology* 34,
     no. 5 (1993): 710–15.
97   Richard B. Lee and Irven DeVore, *Man the Hunter* (Chicago: Aldine, 1969), 35.
98   Armelagos et al., "The Origins of Agriculture," 9–11; V. Gordon Childe, *Man Makes
     Himself* (New York: New American Library, 1951).
99   The increase in population size following the Neolithic move to agriculture was
     accompanied by the declining health of individual members in the relevant societies.
     See Larsen, "Biological Changes in Human Populations with Agriculture," 185–
     213; Larsen, "The Agricultural Revolution as Environmental Catastrophe," 12–20;
     Armelagos et al., "The Origins of Agriculture," 9–22; Mark Nathan Cohen and
     George J. Armelagos, *Paleopathology at the Origins of Agriculture* (New York: Academic
     Press, 1984).
100 Larsen, "Biological Changes in Human Populations with Agriculture," 185–213;
     Richards, "A Brief Review of the Archaeological Evidence," 1270–78.
101 Richards, "A Brief Review of the Archaeological Evidence," 1271–72.
102 Larsen. "Biological Changes in Human Populations with Agriculture," 187.
103 Ibid.
104 Larsen, "The Agricultural Revolution as Environmental Catastrophe," 12.
105 Aubrey Sheiham, "Dietary Effects on Dental Diseases," *Public Health Nutrition* 4,
     no. 2b (2001): 569–91; Clark Spencer Larsen, *Bioarchaeology: Interpreting Behavior
     from the Human Skeleton* (New York: Cambridge University Press, 1997), 71; Larsen,
     "Biological Changes in Human Populations with Agriculture," 188; David Lubell
     et al., "The Mesolithic-Neolithic Transition in Portugal: Isotopic and Dental
     Evidence of Diet," *Journal of Archaeological Science* 21, no. 2 (1994): 201–16.
106 Larsen, "Biological Changes in Human Populations with Agriculture," 189;
     G. Wolf, "Vitamin A," in *Human Nutrition*, ed. R. B. Alfin-Slater and D. Kritchevsky
     (New York: Plenum Press, 1980), 97–201.
107 Larsen, *Bioarchaeology*, 67.
108 E. Newbrun, "Sugar and Dental Caries: A Review of Human Studies," *Science* 217,
     no. 4558 (1982): 418–23; Larsen, "Biological Changes in Human Populations with
     Agriculture," 188.
109 Larsen, "Biological Changes in Human Populations with Agriculture," 188;
     P. Hartnady and Je Rose, "Abnormal Tooth-Loss Patterns among Archaic-Period
     Inhabitants of the Lower Pecos Region, Texas," in *Advances in Dental Anthropology*,
     ed. Marc A. Kelley and Clark Spencer Larsen (New York: Wiley-Liss, 1991), 267–
     78; K. D. Sobolik, "Paleonutrition of the Lower Pecos region of the Chihuahuan
     Desert," in *Paleonutrition: The Diet and Health of Prehistoric Americans* (Carbondale: Center
     for Archaeological Investigations, Southern Illinois University at Carbondale,
     1994), 247–64; D. W. Frayer, "Caries and Oral Pathologies at the Mesolithic Sites
     of Muge: Cabe o da Arruda and Moita do Sebastiao," *Trabalhos de Antropologia e
     Etnologia* 27 (1988): 9–25; David Lubell et al., "The Mesolithic-Neolithic Transition
     in Portugal: Isotopic and Dental Evidence of Diet," *Journal of Archaeological Science* 21,
     no. 2 (1994): 201–16; C. Meiklejohn et al., "Caries as a Probable Dietary Marker

in the Western European Mesolithic," in *Diet and Subsistence: Current Archaeological Perspectives*, ed. Genevieve M. LeMoine and Brenda V. Kennedy (Calgary: University of Calgary, 1988), 273–79. Lubell and colleagues suggest that the increased number of caries observed in Mesolithic populations is likely a result of consumption of non-domesticated cariogenic plants.

110   Larsen, *Bioarchaeology*, 69; Christy G. Turner, "Dental Anthropological Indications of Agriculture among the Jomon People of Central Japan. X. Peopling of the Pacific," *American Journal of Physical Anthropology* 51, no. 4 (1979): 619–36; Daniel H. Temple and Clark Spencer Larsen, "Dental Caries Prevalence as Evidence for Agriculture and Subsistence Variation during the Yayoi Period in Prehistoric Japan: Biocultural Interpretations of an Economy in Transition," *American Journal of Physical Anthropology* 134, no. 4 (2007): 501–12; P. L Walker et al., "Diet, Dental Health, and Cultural Change among Recently Contacted South American Indian Hunter-Horticulturalists," in *Human Dental Development, Morphology, and Pathology: A Tribute to Albert A. Dahlberg*, ed. John R. Lukacs (Eugene: University of Oregon, 1998), 355–86.

111   Larsen, *Bioarchaeology*, 69; Larsen, "Biological Changes in Human Populations with Agriculture," 187–89; Peter S. Ungar and Mark Franklyn Teaford, *Human Diet: Its Origin and Evolution* (Westport, CT: Bergin & Garvey, 2002), 22.

112   Larsen, "Biological Changes in Human Populations with Agriculture," 189; Clark Spencer Larsen, "Behavioural Implications of Temporal Change in Cariogenesis," *Journal of Archaeological Science* 10, no. 1 (1983): 1–8; C. S. Larsen et al., "Dental Caries Evidence for Dietary Change: An Archaeological Context," in *Advances in Dental Anthropology*, ed. Marc A. Kelley and Clark Spencer Larsen (New York: Wiley-Liss, 1991), 179–202.

113   Larsen, "Biological Changes in Human Populations with Agriculture," 189; Clark Spencer Larsen, *The anthropology of St. Catherines Island 3. Prehistoric human biological adaptation* (New York: Anthropological Papers of the American Museum of Natural History, Volume 57, part 3, 1982)..

114   W. J. Loesche and N. S. Grossman, "Periodontal Disease as a Specific, Albeit Chronic, Infection: Diagnosis and Treatment," *Clinical Microbiology Reviews* 14, no. 4 (2001): 727–52; Larsen, *Bioarchaeology*; C. F. Hildebolt and S. Molnar, "Measurement and Description of Periodontal Disease in Anthropological Studies," in *Advances in Dental Anthropology*, ed. Marc A. Kelley and Clark Spencer Larsen (New York: Wiley-Liss, 1991), 225–40.

115   Larsen, *Bioarchaeology*, 79.

116   Ibid., 82–83; J. C. Rose et al., "Dental Anthropology of the Nile Valley," in *Biological Anthropology and the Study of Ancient Egypt*, ed. W. V. Davies and Roxie Walker (London: British Museum Press, 1993), 61–74.

117   Larsen, *Bioarchaeology*, 81–83.

118   Ibid., 302; Robert E. Hedges and Linda M. Reynard, "Nitrogen Isotopes and the Trophic Level of Humans in Archaeology," *Journal of Archaeological Science* 34, no. 8 (2007): 1240–51; Robert Hedges et al., "Collagen Turnover in the Adult Femoral Mid-shaft: Modeled from Anthropogenic Radiocarbon Tracer Measurements," *American Journal of Physical Anthropology* 133, no. 2 (2007): 808–16.

119   Larsen, *Bioarchaeology*, 302.

120   Ibid., 316; M. L. Murray and M. J. Schoeninger, "Diet, Status, and Complex Social Structure in Iron Age Central Europe: Some Contributions of Bone Chemistry,"

in *Tribe and Polity in Late Prehistoric Europe: Demography, Production, and Exchange in the Evolution of Complex Social Systems*, ed. D. Blair Gibson and Michael N. Geselowitz (New York: Plenum Press, 1988), 155–76; E. A. Pechenkina et al., "Diet and Health in the Neolithic of the Wei and Middle Yellow River Basins, Northern China," in *Ancient Health: Skeletal Indicators of Agricultural and Economic Intensification*, M. N. Cohen and G. M. M. Crane-Kramer (Gainesville: University Press of Florida, 2010), 255–72.

121 For example, adult stature declined during the transition from foraging to farming in the Eastern Mediterranean and in the Mesolithic to Neolithic transition in Western Europe. See Larsen, *Bioarchaeology*; C. Meiklejohn et al., "Socioeconomic Change and Patterns of Pathology and Variation in the Mesolithic and Neolithic of Western Europe: Some Suggestions," in *Paleopathology at the Origins of Agriculture*, 75–100; J. L. Angel, "Health as a Crucial Factor in the Changes from Hunting to Developed Farming in the Eastern Mediterranean," in *Paleopathology at the Origins of Agriculture*, 51–73.

122 Larsen, "Biological Changes in Human Populations with Agriculture," 191; Stanley M. Garn, *The Earlier Gain and the Later Loss of Cortical Bone, in Nutritional Perspective* (Springfield, IL: Thomas, 1970); S. M. Garn et al., "Compact Bone Deficiency in Protein-Calorie Malnutrition," *Science* 145, no. 3639 (1964): 1444–45; J. H. Himes et al., "Patterns of Cortical Bone Growth in Moderately Malnourished Preschool Children," *Human Biology* 47, no. 3 (1975): 337–50.

123 S. M. Garn et al., "Malnutrition and Skeletal Development in the Preschool Child," in *Preschool Child Malnutrition* (National Academy of Sciences, National Research Council, Washington, DC, 1966), 43–62

124 Larsen, "Biological Changes in Human Populations with Agriculture," 191; Larsen, *Bioarchaeology*, 57–63.

125 Larsen, *Bioarchaeology*, 196–97 and 256–57; E. A. Carson, "Maximum-Likelihood Variance Components Analysis of Heritabilities of Cranial Nonmetric Traits," *Human Biology*, 78, no. 4 (2006): 383–402; B. Johannsdottir et al., "Heritability of Craniofacial Characteristics between Parents and Offspring Estimated from Lateral Cephalograms," *American Journal of Orthodontics and Dentofacial Orthopedics*, 127, no. 2 (2005): 200–7; M. Calcagno, "Mechanisms of Human Dental Reduction: A Case Study from Post-Pleistocene Nubia," *University of Kansas Publications in Anthropology* 18 (1989); D. S. Carlson and D. P. Van Gerven, "Masticatory Function and Post-Pleistocene Evolution in Nubia," *American Journal of Physical Anthropology* 46 (1977): 495–506; D. S. Carlson, "Diffusion, Biological Determinism, and Biocultural Adaptation in the Nubian Corridor," *American Anthropologist* 81 (1979): 561–80; G. Edynak, "Culture, Diet, and Dental Reduction in Mesolithic Forager-Fishers of Yugoslavia," *Current Anthropology* 19 (1978): 616–18; G. Edynak and S. Fleisch, "Microevolution and Biological Adaptability in the Transition from Food-Collecting to Food-Producing in the Iron Gates of Yugoslavia," *Journal of Human Evolution* 12 (1983): 279–96; M. T. Newman and C. E. O. Snow, "Preliminary Report on the Skeletal Material from Pickwick Basin, Alabama," in *An Archeological Survey of Pickwick Basin in the Adjacent Portions of the States of Alabama, Mississippi and Tennessee*, ed. William S. Webb et al. (Washington, DC: US GPO, 1942): 393–507; C. Larsen, "Bioarchaeological Interpretations of Subsistence Economy and Behaviour from Human Skeletal Remains," in *Advances in Archaeological Method and Theory*, ed. Michael B. Schiffer (Orlando: Academic Press, 1987): 339–445; M. Anderson, "The Human

Skeletons," in *The Prehistory of the Tehuacan Valley: Vol. 1: Environment and Subsistence*, ed. Douglas S. Byers (Austin: University of Texas Press, 1967), 91–113.

126 Larsen, "Biological Changes in Human Populations with Agriculture," 193; M. E. Guagliardo, "Tooth Crown Size Differences between Age Groups: A Possible New Indicator of Stress in Skeletal Samples," *American Journal of Physical Anthropology* 58 (1982): 383–89; S. W. Simpson et al., "Coping with Stress: Tooth Size, Dental Defects, and Age-At-Death ," in *The Archaeology of Mission Santa Catalina De Guale*, vol. 2, *Biocultural Interpretations of a Population in Transition*, ed. Clark Spencer Larsen (New York: American Museum of Natural History, 1990), 66–77; Larsen, *Bioarchaeology*, 26.

127 Larsen, "Biological Changes in Human Populations with Agriculture," 193; G. A. Clark et al., "Poor Growth Prior to Early Childhood: Decreased Health and Life-Span in the Adult," *American Journal of Physical* Anthropology 70 (1986): 145–60; A. H. Goodman and G. J. Armelagos, "Childhood Stress, Cultural Buffering, and Decreased Longevity in a Prehistoric Population," *American Anthropologist* 90 (1988): 936–44.

128 Larsen, *Bioarchaeology*, 26; M. V. Apps et al., "The Effect of Birthweight on Tooth-Size Variability in Twins," *Twin Research*, 7, no. 5 (2004): 415–20; W. Seow and A. Wan, "Research Reports Clinical: A Controlled Study of the Morphometric Changes in the Primary Dentition of Pre-term, Very-Low-Birthweight Children," *Journal of Dental Research* 79, no. 1 (2000): 63–69; M. N. Cohen et al., "Crown-size Reduction in Congenital Defects," in *Orofacial Growth and Development*, ed. T. M. Graber and A. A. Dahlberg, (Berlin: De Gruyter Mouton, 1977): 119–26.

129 See the arguments in M. Calcagno, *Mechanisms of Human Dental Reduction: A Case Study from Post-Pleistocene Nubia* (Lawrence: University of Kansas, Department of Anthropology, 1989)

130 Larsen, *Bioarchaeology*, 273; D. E. Lieberman, *The Evolution of the Human Head* (Cambridge, MA: Belknap Press of Harvard University Press, 2011).

131 Larsen, "Biological Changes in Human Populations with Agriculture," 199.

132 Ibid; D. L. Martin, "Health Conditions before Columbus: Paleopathology of Native North Americans," *Western Journal of Medicine* 176, no. 1 (2002): 66.

133 Larsen, "The Agricultural Revolution as Environmental Catastrophe," 14.

134 P. L. Stuart-Macadam, "Porotic Hyperostosis: Representative of a Childhood Health Condition," *American Journal of Physical Anthropology* 66 (1985): 391–98.

135 P. L. Walker et al., "The Causes of Porotic Hyperostosis and Cribra Orbitalia: A Reappraisal of the Iron-Deficiency-Anemia Hypothesis," *American Journal of Physical Anthropology*, 139, no. 2 (2009): 109–25.

136 Ibid., 115.

137 Ibid.

138 Ibid. 114; R. J. Turner et al., "Infantile Megaloblastosis Secondary to Acquired Vitamin B12 Deficiency," *Pediatric Hematology and Oncology* 16, no. 1 (1999): 79–81; E. B. Casella et al., "Vitamin B12 Deficiency in Infancy as a Cause of Developmental Regression," *Brain and Development* 27, no. 8 (2005): 592–94; F. Cetinkaya et al., "Nutritional Vitamin B 12 Deficiency in Hospitalized Young Children," *Pediatric Hematology and Oncology* 24, no. 1 (2007): 15–21.

139 Rebecca Huss-Ashmore et al., "Nutritional Inference from Paleopathology," *Advances in Archaeological Method and Theory* 5 (1982): 413; H. A. Harris, "The Growth of Longbones in Children, with Special Reference to Certain Bony Striations of the Metaphysic and to the Role of the Vitamins," *Archives of Internal Medicine 38*

(1925): 785–806; H. A. Harris, "Bone Growth in Health and Disease: The Biological Principles Underlying the Clinical, Radiological, and Histological Diagnosis of Perversions of Growth and Disease in the Skeleton," *JAMA: The Journal of the American Medical Association* 101, no. 27 (1933): 2143.

140   R. M. Acheson, "The Effects of Starvation, Septicaemia, and Chronic Illness on the Growth Cartilage Plate and Mataphysis of the Immature Rat," *Journal of anatomy* 93 (1959): 123–30.

141   Huss-Ashmore et al., "Nutritional Inference from Paleopathology," 413.

142   Cohen and Armelagos. *Paleopathology at the Origins of Agriculture*, 22–24.

143   Armelagos et al., "The Origins of Agriculture," 13.

144   Larsen, "Biological Changes in Human Populations with Agriculture," 198–99; Cohen and Armelagos, *Paleopathology at the Origins of Agriculture*, 586.

145   C. Meiklejohn et al., "Socioeconomic Change and Patterns of Pathology and Variation in the Mesolithic and Neolithic of Western Europe: Some Suggestions," in *Paleopathology at the Origins of Agriculture*, 75–100.

146   On declining meat consumption in many regions after the adoption of agriculture, to be replaced by nutrient-poor grains, see Larsen, "Biological Changes in Human Populations with Agriculture," 199; Walker et al., "The Causes of Porotic Hyperostosis and Cribra Orbitalia," 114. Individuals who lived through the transition to agriculture, according to Larsen, are likely to have suffered much lower intakes of micronutrients and minerals such as iron and vitamin B12, including serious deficiency. See Larsen, "The Agricultural Revolution as Environmental Catastrophe," 12–13; L. Cordain et al., "The Paradoxical Nature of Hunter-Gatherer Diets: Meat-Based, Yet Non-Atherogenic," *European Journal of Clinical Nutrition 56* (suppl. 1) (2002): S42-S52; L. Cordain et al., "Plant-Animal Subsistence Ratios," 682–92; Larsen, "Animal Source Foods and Human Health," 3893S and 3895S. Since meat is a rich source of protein and several micronutrients including iron, zinc and fat-soluble vitamins, a decrease in meat consumption may have led to deficiencies in these nutrients in some populations. See Milton, "The Critical Role Played by Animal Source Foods," 3890S.

147   V. Herbert, "Staging Vitamin B-12 (cobalamin) Status in Vegetarians," *American Journal of Clinical Nutrition* 59 (suppl.) (1994): 1213S–22S; V. Herbert, "Vitamin B-12: Plant Sources, Requirements, and Assay," *American Journal of Clinical Nutrition* 48 (1988): 857; I. Chanarin et al., "Megaloblastic Anaemia in a Vegetarian Hindu Community," *The Lancet* 326, no. 8465 (1985): 1168–72.

148   N. E. Scrimshaw, C. E. Taylor, and J. E. Gordon, *Interactions of Nutrition and Infection* (Geneva: World Health Organization, 1968); Larsen, "Animal Source Foods and Human Health," *Journal of Nutrition* 133, no.11, suppl. 2 (2003): 3895S.

149   Sicherer and Sampson, "Food Allergy," S470–1.

150   Ibid; Mirna Chehade and Lloyd Mayer, "Oral Tolerance and Its Relation to Food Hypersensitivities," *Journal of Allergy and Clinical Immunology* 115, no. 1 (2005): 3–12; K. Y. Hsieh et al., "Epicutaneous Exposure to Protein Antigen and Food Allergy," *Clinical Experimental Allergy* 33, no. 8 (2003): 1067–75; Gideon Lack, "Factors Associated with the Development of Peanut Allergy in Childhood," *New England Journal of Medicine* 348, no. 11 (2003): 977–85; E. Untersmayr et al., "Anti-ulcer Drugs Promote IgE Formation toward Dietary Antigens in Adult Patients," *FASEB Journal*, 19 (2005):656–58; Allan Mowat, "Anatomical Basis of Tolerance and Immunity to Intestinal Antigens," *Nature Reviews Immunology* 3, no. 4 (2003): 331–41.

151 Sicherer and Sampson, "Food Allergy," S470–1.

152 Cordain, "Cereal Grains: Humanity's Double-Edged Sword," 47–49.

153 Karin De Punder and Leo Pruimboom, "The Dietary Intake of Wheat and Other Cereal Grains and Their Role in Inflammation," *Nutrients* 5, no. 3 (2013): 772; A. Pusztai et al., "Antinutritive Effects of Wheat-Germ Agglutinin and Other *N*-acetylglucosamine-specific Lectins," *British Journal of Nutrition* 70 (1993): 313–21. See also Eugenia Lauret and Rodrigo Luis, "Celiac Disease and Autoimmune-Associated Conditions," *BioMed Research International* 2013 (2013): 1–17; De Punder and Pruimboom, "The Dietary Intake of Wheat," 771–87; Loren L. Cordain et al., "Modulation of Immune Function by Dietary Lectins in Rheumatoid Arthritis," *British Journal of Nutrition* 83, no. 03 (2000): 207–17; Cordain, "Cereal Grains: Humanity's Double-Edged Sword," 19–73; P. Collin and M. Mäki, "Associated Disorders in Coeliac Disease: Clinical Aspects," *Scandinavian Journal of Gastroenterology* 29, no. 9 (1994): 769–75; De Punder and Pruimboom, "The Dietary Intake of Wheat," 772; P. R. Shewry, "Wheat," *Journal of Experimental Botany* 60, no. 6 (2009): 1537–53; A. S. Tatham and P. R. Shewry, "Allergy to Wheat and Related Cereals," *Clinical & Experimental Allergy*, 38 (2008): 1712–26; A. Sapone et al., "Spectrum of Gluten-Related Disorders: Consensus on New Nomenclature and Classification," *BMC Medicine* 10 (2012): 13. For wheat as insulinogenic, see F. W. Scott, D. Daneman and J. M. Martin, "Evidence for a Critical Role of Diet in the Development of Insulin-Dependent Diabetes Mellitus," *Diabetes Research* 7 (1988): 153–57; F. W. Scott and E. B. Marlss, "Conference Summary: Diet as an Environmental Factor in Development of Insulin-Dependent Diabetes Mellitus," *Canadian Journal of Physiology and Pharmacology* 69 (1991): 311–19.

154 Isabel Comino et al., "Role of Oats in Celiac Disease," *World Journal of Gastroenterology* 21, no. 41 (2015): 11825–31; Juan Ortiz-Sánchez et al., "Maize Prolamins Could Induce a Gluten-Like Cellular Immune Response in Some Celiac Disease Patients," *Nutrients* 5, no. 10 (2013): 4174–83; Elide A. Pastorello et al., "The Maize Major Allergen, Which Is Responsible for Food-induced Allergic Reactions, Is a Lipid Transfer Protein," *Journal of Allergy and Clinical Immunology* 106, no. 4 (2000): 744–51; De Punder and Pruimboom, "The Dietary Intake of Wheat," 776.

155 Punder and Pruimboom, "The Dietary Intake of Wheat," 774; S. Drago et al., "Gliadin, Zonulin and Gut Permeability: Effects on Celiac and Non-Celiac Intestinal Mucosa and Intestinal Cell Lines," *Scandinavian Journal of Gastroenterology* 41 (2006): 408–19; Karen M. Lammers et al., "Gliadin Induces an Increase in Intestinal Permeability and Zonulin Release by Binding to the Chemokine Receptor CXCR3," *Gastroenterology* 135, no. 1 (2008): 194–204.

156 Punder and Pruimboom, "The Dietary Intake of Wheat," 774–75; Alessio Fasano, "Leaky Gut and Autoimmune Diseases," *Clinical Reviews in Allergy & Immunology* 42, no. 1 (2011): 71–78; Alessio Fasano, "Zonulin, Regulation of Tight Junctions, and Autoimmune Diseases," *Annals of the New York Academy of Sciences* 1258, no. 1 (2012): 25–33; A. Fasano, "Zonulin and Its Regulation of Intestinal Barrier Function: The Biological Door to Inflammation, Autoimmunity, and Cancer," *Physiological Reviews* 91, no. 1 (2011): 151–75.

157 Fasano, "Zonulin, Regulation of Tight Junctions," 25–33; Punder and Pruimboom, "The Dietary Intake of Wheat," 775.

158 Punder and Pruimboom, "The Dietary Intake of Wheat," 778; C. Dalla Pellegrina et al., "Effects of Wheat Germ Agglutinin on Human Gastrointestinal

Epithelium: Insights from an Experimental Model of Immune/Epithelial Cell Interaction," *Toxicology and Applied Pharmacology* 237 (2009):146–53.

159 Punder and Pruimboom, "The Dietary Intake of Wheat," 774; Fasano, "Leaky Gut and Autoimmune Diseases," 71–78; Cordain et al., "Modulation of Immune Function," 207–17; Å. V. Keita and J. D. Söderholm, "The Intestinal Barrier and Its Regulation by Neuroimmune Factors," *Neurogastroenterology & Motility* 22, no. 7 (2010): 718–33.

160 Punder and Pruimboom, "The Dietary Intake of Wheat," 775; Sicherer and Sampson, "Food Allergy," S470; Untersmayr, "Anti-ulcer Drugs Promote," 656–58.

161 Punder and Pruimboom, "The Dietary Intake of Wheat," 773; R. Troncone and B. Jabri, "Coeliac Disease and Gluten Sensitivity," *Journal of Internal Medicine* 269, no. 6 (2011): 582–90.

162 The inflammatory cytokines include IL-23, IL-1beta and TNF-alpha. See Punder and Pruimboom, "The Dietary Intake of Wheat," 773; K. M. Harris et al., "Cutting Edge: IL-1 Controls the IL-23 Response Induced by Gliadin, the Etiologic Agent in Celiac Disease," *Journal of Immunology* 181, no. 7 (2008): 4457–60: Karen M. Lammers et al., "Identification of a Novel Immunomodulatory Gliadin Peptide That Causes Interleukin-8 Release in a Chemokine Receptor CXCR3-dependent Manner Only in Patients with Coeliac Disease." *Immunology* 132, no. 3 (2011): 432–40.

163 The relevant cytokines include IL-4 and IL-13 from basophils. The activity of T cells and natural killer cells include increased secretion of IFN-γ. See Punder and Pruimboom, "The Dietary Intake of Wheat," 777; A. Karlsson, "Wheat Germ Agglutinin Induces NADPH-oxidase Activity in Human Neutrophils by Interaction with Mobilizable Receptors," *Infection and Immunity* 67 (1999): 3461–68; Helmut Haas et al., "Dietary Lectins Can Induce in Vitro Release of IL-4 and IL-13 from Human Basophils." *European Journal of Immunology* 29, no. 3 (1999): 918–27; Eric Muraille et al., "Carbohydrate-Bearing Cell Surface Receptors Involved in Innate Immunity: Interleukin-12 Induction by Mitogenic and Nonmitogenic Lectins," *Cellular Immunology* 191, no. 1 (1999): 1–9.

164 Graves and Kayal, "Diabetic Complications and Dysregulated Innate Immunity," 1227–39; Cordain, "Cereal Grains: Humanity's Double-Edged Sword," 47–49.

165 Graves and Kayal, "Diabetic Complications and Dysregulated Innate Immunity," 1227–39.

166 Armelagos and Dewey, "Evolutionary Response to Human Infectious Diseases," 271–75.

167 Armelagos et al., "The Origins of Agriculture," 11.

168 Ibid., 15; A. Papathanasiou. "Health Status of the Neolithic Population of Alepotrypa Cave, Greece," *American Journal of Physical Anthropology* 126, no. 4 (2005): 377–90.

169 Armelagos et al., "The Origins of Agriculture," 119–22; V. Eshed et al., "Paleopathology and the Origin of Agriculture in the Levant," *American Journal of Physical Anthropology* 143, no. 1 (2010): 121–33.

170 Larsen, "Animal Source Foods and Human Health," 3894S.

171 Armelagos and Dewey, "Evolutionary Response to Human Infectious Diseases," 273; C. A. Hoare, "The Spread of African Trypanosomes beyond Their Natural Range," *Zeitschrift Fur Tropenmedizin Und Parasitologie* 8 (1957): 1–6.

172 Armelagos and Dewey, "Evolutionary Response to Human Infectious Diseases," 273; S. Polgar, "Evolution and the Ills of Mankind," in *Horizons of Anthropology*, ed. S. Tax (Chicago: Aldine Publishing Company, 1964), 200–11.

173 Armelagos and Dewey, "Evolutionary Response to Human Infectious Diseases," 273.

174 Ibid; J. R. Audy, "The Ecology of Scrub Typhus," in *Studies in Disease Ecology*, ed. Jacques M. May (New York: Hafner, 1961), 387–433.

175 Cohen and Armelagos, *Paleopathology at the Origins of Agriculture*, 586.

176 S. J. Ulijaszek et al., "Human Dietary Change [and Discussion]," *Philosophical Transactions of the Royal Society B: Biological Sciences* 334, no. 1270 (1991): 271–79.

177 Armelagos et al., "The Origins of Agriculture," 9–22.

178 Ibid. See also C. M. Cassidy, "Nutrition and Health in Agriculturalists and Hunter-Gatherers: A Case Study of Two Prehistoric Populations," in *Nutritional Anthropology: Contemporary Approaches to Diet & Culture*, ed. N. W. Jerome et al. (Pleasantville, NY: Routledge, 1980), 117–45.

179 Armelagos et al., "The Origins of Agriculture," 17–20; George L. Cowgill, "On Causes and Consequences of Ancient and Modern Population Changes," *American Anthropologist* 77, no. 3 (1975): 505–25.

180 Armelagos et al., "The Origins of Agriculture," 15–20.

181 Ibid., 18–20.

182 Mary Jackes, David Lubell and Christopher Meiklejohn, "Healthy but Mortal: Human Biology and the First Farmers of Western Europe," *Antiquity* 71, no. 273 (1997): 639.

183 Lars Å. Hanson, "Breast-Feeding and Protection against Infection," *Scandinavian Journal of Food & Nutrition* 50, no. 1 (2006): 33; Lars Å. Hanson et al., "Breast Feeding Is a Natural Contraceptive and Prevents Disease and Death in Infants, Linking Infant Mortality and Birth Rates," *Acta Paediatrica* 83, no. 6 (2008): 626.

184 Lars Å. Hanson. *Immunobiology of Human Milk: How Breastfeeding Protects Babies* (Amarillo, TX: Pharmasoft, 2004); Hanson, "Breast-Feeding and Protection against Infection," 33. It has been shown to provide protection against numerous diseases, including diarrhea-causing pathogens such as *Shigella*, *V. cholerae* and *E. coli*, which are a major cause of infant mortality.

185 Breast milk contains SIgA antibodies, immune cells such as macrophages, T and B lymphocytes, lactoferrin, lysozyme, oligosaccharides, glycoconjugates, nucleotides, hormones, cytokines and growth factors. SIgA antibodies bind to microbes on the mucosal membranes and prevent attachment of pathogens to mucosal epithelium and infection in underlying tissue. Lactoferrin is able to kill gram-negative bacteria by interacting with bacterial lipopolysaccharide (LPS) and thereby create holes in the cell membrane, and by binding iron. In doing so, it has been shown to kill viruses and candida. Oligosaccharides and glycoconjugates prevent the binding of microbes to cells lining the gut and the respiratory and urinary tracts. For example, oligosaccharides conjugated with the protein K-casein and have been shown to prevent attachment of *H. pylori* to human gastric mucosa. See Katona and Katona-Apte, "The Interaction between Nutrition and Infection"; Hanson, "Breast-Feeding and Protection against Infection," 32–34; Bo Lönnerdal, "Bioactive Proteins in Human Milk: Health, Nutrition, and Implications for Infant Formulas," *Journal of Pediatrics* 173 (2016): S4; Kelly M. Jackson and A. M. Nazar, "Breastfeeding, the Immune Response, and Long-term Health," *Journal of American Osteopathic Association* 106, no. 4 (2006): 203–7; B. Andersson et al., "Inhibition of Attachment of Streptococcus Pneumoniae and Haemophilus Influenzae by Human Milk," *Journal of Infectious Disease* 153 (1986): 232–7; D. S. Newburg et al., "Human Milk Glycans Protect Infants against Enteric Pathogens," *Annual Review of Nutrition 25* (2005):37–58; Mats

Strömqvist et al., "Human Milk K-Casein and Inhibition of Helicobacter Pylori Adhesion to Human Gastric Mucosa," *Journal of Pediatric Gastroenterology and Nutrition* 21, no. 3 (1995): 288–96.

186 Jackson and Nazar, "Breastfeeding, the Immune Response, and Long-term Health," 203.

187 Ibid., 203–4; A. E. Wold and I. Adlerberth, "Does Breastfeeding Affect the Infant's Immune Responsiveness?" *Acta Paediatrica SPAE* 87, no. 1 (1998): 19–22; L. Jain et al., "In Vivo Distribution of Human Milk Leucocytes after Ingestion by Newborn Baboons," *Archives of Disease in Childhood* 64, no. 7 Spec No (1989): 930–33. Leonard Seelig and Judith R. Head, "Uptake of Lymphocytes Fed to Suckling Rats: An Autoradiographic Study of the Transit of Labeled Cells through the Neonatal Gastric Mucosa," *Journal of Reproductive Immunology* 10, no. 4 (1987): 285–97.

188 Lars Å. Hanson, "Breastfeeding Provides Passive and Likely Long-Lasting Active Immunity," *Annals of Allergy, Asthma & Immunology* 81, no. 6 (1998): 525–29. doi:10.1016/s1081-1206(10)62704-4; Jackson and Nazar, "Breastfeeding, the Immune Response, and Long-Term Health," 204–6. The mechanism by which milk stimulates development of the infant's own immune system is not fully understood, but is likely to involve actions of immunoregulatory substances such as hormones and cytokines (such as such as IFN-γ and TGF-β). It is also thought to incorporate chemokines and growth factors. All prime the infant's immune system through the stimulation and production of antibodies. It also encourages the vital process of T cell maturation, increasing the size of the thymus gland, and increases the number of CD8+ cells. See Hanson, "Breast-Feeding and Protection against Infection," 33; H. Hasselbalch et al., "Decreased Thymus Size in Formula-fed Infants Compared with Breastfed Infants," *Acta Paediatrica* 85, no. 9 (1996): 1029–32; Dorthe L. Jeppesen, "T-lymphocyte Subsets, Thymic Size and Breastfeeding in Infancy," *Pediatric Allergy and Immunology* 15, no. 2 (2004): 127–32.

189 Armelagos et al., "The Origins of Agriculture," 17–20; Cowgill, "On Causes and Consequences," 505–25.

190 M. Inhorn, "The Anthropology of Infectious Disease," *Annual Review of Anthropology* 19, no. 1 (1990): 91.

191 Jones, "Virgin Soils Revisited," 726; Mackay et al., "The Immune System: First of Two Parts," 37–49.

192 Jones, "Virgin Soils Revisited," 732.

193 Ibid., 703–33.

194 Ibid., 729; Celia M. T. Greenwood et al., "Linkage of Tuberculosis to Chromosome 2q35 Loci, Including NRAMP1, in a Large Aboriginal Canadian Family," *American Journal of Human Genetics* 67, no. 2 (2000): 405–16.

195 They refer to class I and class II MHC molecules. See Francis L. Black, "An Explanation of High Death Rates among New World Peoples When in Contact with Old World Diseases," *Perspectives in Biology and Medicine* 37, no. 2 (1994): 296. In support of this hypothesis, it has been shown that measles is more virulent when passed between two hosts with similar MHC molecules, and that HIV and Hepatitis B are more virulent in hosts with limited diversity of MHC molecules. See Jones, "Virgin Soils Revisited," 732; Hill, "Defence by Diversity," *Nature* 398 (1999): 668–69.

196 For a discussion of these distinctions, see Jones, "Virgin Soils Revisited," 729.

197 J. L. Brooke and C. S. Larsen, "The Nurture of Nature: Genetics, Epigenetics, and Environment in Human Biohistory," *American Historical Review* 119, no. 5 (2014): 1500.

198   Carrera-Bastos et al., "The Western Diet and Lifestyle," 16.

199   See Brooke and Larsen, "The Nurture of Nature," 1501; K. Ye and Z. Gu, "Recent
       Advances in Understanding the Role of Nutrition in Human Genome Evolution,"
       Advances in Nutrition: An International Review Journal 2, no. 6 (2011): 486–96; Carrera-
       Bastos et al., "The Western Diet and Lifestyle," 15–35.

200   Carrera-Bastos et al., "The Western Diet and Lifestyle," 18; George Chaplin and
       Nina G. Jablonski, "Vitamin D and the Evolution of Human Depigmentation,"
       American Journal of Physical Anthropology 139, no. 4 (2009): 451–61.

201   Genome sequencing of DNA from European hunter-gatherers shows that the
       evolution of light skin pigmentation is more complex than previously thought,
       involving many different genetic loci in different geographical locations. See Iain
       Mathieson et al., "Genome-Wide Patterns of Selection in 230 Ancient Eurasians,"
       Nature 528, no. 7583 (2015): 499–503; Iñigo Olalde et al., "Derived Immune and
       Ancestral Pigmentation Alleles in a 7,000-Year-Old Mesolithic European," *Nature*
       507, no. 7491 (2014): 225–28. Sequencing of a preagricultural Mesolithic European
       genome discovered at the La-Braña-Arintero site in León, Spain, has revealed that
       lighter skin likely evolved later than previously thought in this region. Genome
       sequencing revealed that an examined individual retained the ancestral allele for
       lactose intolerance, and five copies of AMY1, a genetic marker expected from a
       preagricultural period. However, variants in other markers, which are the "strongest
       known loci affecting light skin pigmentation in Europeans," were absent, suggesting
       that this individual was still dark-skinned. Analysis of genetic loci responsible for
       skin tone in Eurasian hunter-gatherers by Mathieson and colleagues revealed that
       the genetic variants responsible for light skin were present at very low frequency
       in Eurasian hunter-gatherers, suggesting that the light skin pigmentation did not
       evolve in many hunter-gatherer populations until after the adoption of agriculture.
       See Olalde et al., "Derived Immune and Ancestral Pigmentation Alleles," 228;
       R. L. Lamason, "SLC24A5, a Putative Cation Exchanger, Affects Pigmentation
       in Zebrafish and Humans," *Science* 310, no. 5755 (2005): 1782–86; H. L. Norton
       et al., "Genetic Evidence for the Convergent Evolution of Light Skin in Europeans
       and East Asians," *Molecular Biology and Evolution* 24, no. 3 (2006): 710–22; Richard
       A. Sturm, "Human Pigmentation Genes under Environmental Selection," *Genome
       Biology* 13, no. 9 (2012): 248.

202   Brooke and Larsen, "The Nurture of Nature," 1504; I. Lazaridis et al., "Ancient
       Human Genomes Suggest Three Ancestral Populations for Present-Day Europeans,"
       Nature 513, no. 7518 (September 2014): 409–13.

203   Ye and Gu, "Recent Advances in Understanding the Role of Nutrition," 492.
       Analysis of individuals from seven populations that have historically consumed more
       starch has found an average of one more copy of the salivary amylase gene, AMY1,
       among population members. See George H. Perry et al., "Diet and the Evolution
       of Human Amylase Gene Copy Number Variation," *Nature Genetics* 39, no. 10
       (2007): 1256–60. The low level of nucleotide variations in this region of the genome
       suggests a recent origin to these copy number variations. See Ye and Gu, "Recent
       Advances in Understanding the Role of Nutrition," 492.

204   Ye and Gu, "Recent Advances in Understanding the Role of Nutrition," 491; A. M.
       Hancock et al., "Human Adaptations to Diet, Subsistence, and Ecoregion Are Due
       to Subtle Shifts in Allele Frequency," *Proceedings of the National Academy of Sciences* 107
       (suppl. 2) (2010): 8924–30.

205 Lactase expression persisting into adulthood, known as lactase persistence, exists in over 90% of Swedish and Danish individuals; in around 50% of Southern Europeans and Middle Eastern communities; in 5–20% of West African populations; and only in around 1% of Chinese populations. Environmental correlation analyses concur with the hypothesis that lactase persistence evolved with increasing milk consumption of populations after the Paleolithic. It is associated with different mutations in different populations. The origins of those various mutations correlate with the period in which milk consumption is thought to have originated in the regions. See Ye and Gu, "Recent Advances in Understanding the Role of Nutrition," 491; Sarah A. Tishkoff et al., "Convergent Adaptation of Human Lactase Persistence in Africa and Europe," *Nature Genetics* 39, no. 1 (2006): 31–40; Todd Bersaglieri et al., "Genetic Signatures of Strong Recent Positive Selection at the Lactase Gene," *American Journal of Human Genetics* 74, no. 6 (2004): 1111–20; Nabil Sabri Enattah et al., "Independent Introduction of Two Lactase-Persistence Alleles into Human Populations Reflects Different History of Adaptation to Milk Culture," *American Journal of Human Genetics* 82, no. 1 (2008): 57–72.

206 We have seen that the adaptive immune response is triggered by specific major histocompatability (MHC) proteins, which are encoded by a set of genes referred to as the human leucocyte antigen (HLA) system. Genetic variations in HLA genes therefore affect the immune response to different antigens and pathogens. Certain HLA genes have a high affinity for gliadin fragments, and therefore trigger a stronger immune response. Some HLA haplotypes confer a greater susceptibility to autoimmune diseases (a haplotype refers to a variant of a specific DNA sequence in a particular chromatic region). Notably, different HLA haplotypes have been implicated in susceptibility to celiac disease. HLA haplotypes follow a similar gradient with the most susceptible haplotypes existing at higher levels in northern Europe and the lowest in the Middle East. See F. J. Simoons, "Celiac Disease as a Geographic Problem," *Food, Nutrition, and Evolution: Food as an Environmental Factor in the Genesis of Human Variability*, ed. Dwain N. Walcher and Norman Kretchmer (New York: Masson, 1981): 179–99.

207 Cordain, "Cereal Grains: Humanity's Double-Edged Sword," 19–73; Simoons, "Celiac Disease as a Geographic Problem," 179–199; B. McNicholl et al., "History, Ggenetics and Natural History of Celiac Disease—Gluten Eenteropathy," in *Food, Nutrition, and Evolution*, 169–77.

208 Simoons, "Celiac Disease as a Geographic Problem," 179–199; McNicholl et al., "History, Genetics and Natural History of Celiac Disease—Gluten Enteropathy," 169–77.

209 E. T. Wang et al., "Global Landscape of Recent Inferred Darwinian Selection for Homo Sapiens," *Proceedings of the National Academy of Sciences* 103 (2005): 135–40; S. H. Williamson et al., "Localizing Recent Adaptive Evolution in the Hume Genome," *PLOS Genetics* 3, no. 6 (June 2007): e90. Epub 2007 April 20; B. F. Voight et al., "A Map of Recent Positive Selection in the Human Genome," *PLOS Biology* 4, no. 3 (March 2006): e72.

210 K. N. Laland, J. Odling-Smee and S. Myles, "How Culture Shaped the Human Genome: Bringing Genetics and the Human Sciences Together," *Nature Reviews Genetics* 11 (2010): 137–48.

211 Lazaridis et al., "Ancient Human Genomes Suggest," 409–13; Inchley et al., "Selective Sweep on Human Amylase Genes," 37198.

212 Inchley et al., "Selective Sweep on Human Amylase Genes," 37198; Perry et al., "Diet and the Evolution," 1256–60.

213 A. Zhernakova et al., "Evolutionary and Functional Analysis of Celiac Risk Loci Reveals SH2B3 as a Protective Factor against Bacterial Infection," *American Journal of Human Genetics* 86, no. 6 (June 2010): 970–77.

214 C. D. Huff et al., "Crohn's Disease and Genetic Hitchhiking at IBD5," *Molecular Biology and Evolution* 29, no. 1 (2011): 101–11.

215 Ye and Gu, "Recent Advances in Understanding the Role of Nutrition," 490.

216 Huff et al., "Crohn's Disease and Genetic Hitchhiking at IBD5," 101–11.

217 Ibid; Nelli G. Markova et al., "Skin Cells and Tissue Are Capable of Using L-ergothioneine as an Integral Component of Their Antioxidant Defense System," *Free Radical Biology and Medicine* 46, no. 8 (2009): 1168–76.

218 Since the early twentieth century, scholars have proposed that human populations have adapted to infectious disease on a genetic level since the agricultural transition. See Inhorn, "The Anthropology of Infectious Disease," 91; B. S. Haldane, "Disease and Evolution," *La Ricerca Scientifica* 19 (1949): 68–76.

219 While some genetic adaptation to infectious diseases may have taken place before the Neolithic, a number of factors that might show genetic variation and therefore be subject to natural selection could be linked to the post-Neolithic era. Those factors include "efficiency of phagocytosis, levels of complements, antimicrobial factors in tissue, and serum inhibitors of microbial growth" as well as antibody production. See Inhorn, "The Anthropology of Infectious Disease," 91; Haldane, "Disease and Evolution," 68–76; A. G. Motulsky, "Metabolic Polymorphism and the Role of Infectious Diseases," *Human Biololgy* 32 (1960): 28–63.

220 Jones, "Virgin Soils Revisited," 726; R. Medzhitov and C. Janeway Jr., "Innate Immunity," *New England Journal of Medicine* 343, no. 5 (August 2000): 338–39.

221 P. Muehlenbein, *Human Evolutionary Biology* (Cambridge: Cambridge University Press, 2010), 7–8.

222 See Gregory Cochran and Henry Harpending, "Evolutionary Responses to Infectious Disease," in *Genetics and Evolution of Infectious Disease*, ed. Michel Tibayrenc (Amsterdam: Elsevier, 2011): 237; David A. Lomas, "The Selective Advantage of α 1 -Antitrypsin Deficiency," *American Journal of Respiratory and Critical Care Medicine* 173, no. 10 (2006): 1072–77; A. Bashir et al., "Novel Variants of SERPIN1A Gene: Interplay between Alpha1-antitrypsin Deficiency and Chronic Obstructive Pulmonary Disease," *Respiratory Medicine* 117 (2016): 139–49; M. Malerba, "Neutrophilic Inflammation and IL-8 Levels in Induced Sputum of Alpha-1-antitrypsin PiMZ Subjects," *Thorax* 61, no. 2 (2006): 129–33; Magne K. Fagerhol and Diane Wilson Cox, "The Pi Polymorphism: Genetic, Biochemical, and Clinical Aspects of Human A_1-Antitrypsin," *Advances in Human Genetics* 11, 1981, 1–62.

223 In recent sequencing the genomes of Eurasian hunter-gatherers and Anatolian and European Neolithic farmers, Mathieson and colleagues found evidence of selection at the major histocompatibility complex (MHC) on chromosome six. This may indicate selective pressures from infectious disease. Mutations in other gene clusters may also have been selected for due to providing increased resistance to infectious diseases such as leprosy or tuberculosis. See Muehlenbein, *Human Evolutionary Biology*, 8; Jones, "Virgin Soils Revisited," 731; Hill, "Defence by Diversity," 668–69; Mathieson et al., "Genome-Wide Patterns of Selection in 230

Ancient Eurasians," 499–503; Luis B. Barreiro et al., "Evolutionary Dynamics of Human Toll-Like Receptors and Their Different Contributions to Host Defense," *PLOS Genetics* 5, no. 7 (2009); P. Uciechowski et al., "Susceptibility to Tuberculosis Is Associated with TLR1 Polymorphisms Resulting in a Lack of TLR1 Cell Surface Expression," *Journal of Leukocyte Biology* 90, no. 2 (2011): 377–88; S. H. Wong et al., "Leprosy and the Adaptation of Human Toll-Like Receptor 1," PLOS Pathogens 6 (2010): e1000979.

224 Jones, "Virgin Soils Revisited," 732; Hill, "Defence by Diversity," 668–69.

225 Brooke and Larsen, "The Nurture of Nature," 1510–11.

226 N. A. Tchurikov, "Molecular Mechanisms of Epigenetics," *Biochemistry (Moscow)* 70, no. 4 (2005): 406–23; Richard G. Hunter, "Epigenetic Effects of Stress and Corticosteroids in the Brain," *Frontiers in Cellular Neuroscience* 6 (2012): 18.

227 Christopher W. Kuzawa and Zaneta M. Thayer, "Timescales of Human Adaptation: The Role of Epigenetic Processes," *Epigenomics* 3, no. 2 (2011): 221–23; Brooke and Larsen, "The Nurture of Nature," 1510; Day et al., "A Unified Approach to the Evolutionary Consequences of Genetic and Nongenetic Inheritance," *American Naturalist* 178, no. 2 (2011): E18–E36; C. K. Ghalambor et al., "Adaptive versus Non-adaptive Phenotypic Plasticity and the Potential for Contemporary Adaptation in New Environments," *Functional Ecology* 21, no. 3 (2007): 394–407.

228 B. T. Heijmans et al., "Persistent Epigenetic Differences Associated with Prenatal Exposure to Famine in Humans," *Proceedings of the National Academy of Sciences* 105, no. 44 (2008): 17046–49. Recent research has demonstrated the capacity of psychological stress to cause epigenetic changes. See K. Gudsnuk and F. A. Champagne, "Epigenetic Influence of Stress and the Social Environment," *ILAR Journal* 53, no. 3–4 (2012): 279–88; Hunter, "Epigenetic Effects of Stress and Corticosteroids in the Brain," 18; Marta Weinstock, "The Long-Term Behavioural Consequences of Prenatal Stress," *Neuroscience & Biobehavioral Reviews* 32, no. 6 (2008): 1073–86. Maternal separation experiments in rats and mice show that stress induces epigenetic changes resulting in decreased expression of the glucocorticoid receptor and increased expression of corticotrophin-releasing factor (CRF), both affecting levels of hormones involved the stress response. See Ian C. G. Weaver et al., "Epigenetic Programming by Maternal Behavior," *Nature Neuroscience* 7, no. 8 (2004): 847–54; Julia Lehmann and Joram Feldon, "Long-Term Biobehavioral Effects of Maternal Separation in the Rat: Consistent or Confusing?" *Reviews in the Neurosciences* 11, no. 4 (2000): 383–408; Melanie Lippmann et al., "Long-Term Behavioural and Molecular Alterations Associated with Maternal Separation in Rats," *European Journal of Neuroscience* 25, no. 10 (2007): 3091–98.

229 Waterland and colleagues conducted experiments in mice showing that supplementation with vitamin B12, folic acid, choline and betaine during pregnancy altered DNA methylation and consequently the expression of the Agouti gene, thereby showing that a lack of these nutrients could alter gene expression by preventing methylation. See R. A. Waterland and J. L. Jirtle, "Transposable Elements: Targets for Early Nutritional Effects on Epigenetic Gene Regulation," *Molecular and Cell Biology* 23 (2003): 5293–300.

230 J. Lederberg, "Comments on A. Motulsky's Genetic Systems in Disease Susceptibility in Mammal," in *Genetic Selection in Man: Third Macy Conference on Genetics*, ed. William J. Schull (Ann Arbor: University of Michigan Press, 1963), 112–260.

231 Armelagos et al., "The Origins of Agriculture," 17; C. Svenborg-Eden and B. R. Levin, "Infectious Disease and Natural Selection in Human Populations: A Critical Re-Examination," in *Disease in Populations in Transition: Anthropological and Epidemiological Perspectives*, ed. Alan C. Swedlund and George J. Armelagos (New York: Bergin and Garvey, 1990), 531–46.

232 Jo N. Hays, "Historians and Epidemics: Simple Questions, Complex Answers," in *Plague and the End of Antiquity*, ed. Lester K. Little (Cambridge: Cambridge University Press, 2007), 33–56.

233 McNeill, *Plagues and Peoples*, 150 and 161–207.

234 J. N. Hays, *The Burdens of Disease: Epidemics and Human Response in Western History*, rev. ed. (New Brunswick, NJ: Rutgers University Press, 2009), 46–47.

235 Ibid., 41–42; David Herlihy, *Medieval and Renaissance Pistoia: The Social History of an Italian Town, 1200–1430* (New Haven, CT, Yale University Press, 1967), 55–148.

236 Harry A. Miskimin, *The Economy of Early Renaissance Europe, 1300–1460* (Cambridge: Cambridge University Press, 1975), 32–72.

237 Hays, *The Burdens of Disease*, 41–42.

2. More Than Maize: Native American Subsistence Strategies from the Bering Migration to the Eve of Contact

1 On the ecological Indian trope, and for a recent overview of Native American environmental studies, see James D. Rice, "Beyond 'The Ecological Indian' and 'Virgin Soil Epidemics': New Perspectives on Native Americans and the Environment," *History Compass* 12, no. 9 (2014): 745–57.

2 For these associations with chronic metabolic diseases in contemporary studies, in addition to the discussions in the previous chapter, see for example, Rosário Monteiro and Isabel Azevedo, "Chronic Inflammation in Obesity and the Metabolic Syndrome," *Mediators of Inflammation* 289645 (2010): 2.

3 On the potential scholarly overemphasis on the centrality of maize in precontact Native American history, see Gayle J. Fritz, "Levels of Native Biodiversity in Eastern North America," in *Biodiversity and Native America*, ed. Paul E. Minnis and Wayne J. Elisens (Norman: University of Oklahoma Press, 2000), 232–33.

4 Jane E. Buikstra, "The Lower Illinois River Region: A Prehistoric Context for the Study of Ancient Diet and Health," in *Paleopathology at the Origins of Agriculture*, ed. Mark Nathan Cohen and George J. Armelagos (New York: Academic Press, 1984), 226–27; Thomas McKewon, *Origins of Human Disease* (New York: Blackwell, 1988), 61; C. M. Cassidy, "Skeletal Evidence for Prehistoric Subsistence Adaptation in the Central Ohio River Valley," in *Paleopathology at the Origins of Agriculture*, 337; Jane E. Buikstra, "Diseases of the Pre-Columbian Americas," in *Cambridge World History of Human Disease*, ed. Kenneth F. Kiple (Cambridge: Cambridge University Press, 1993), 311–13.

5 John F. Hoffecker et al., "Out of Beringia?" *Science* 343, no. 6174 (February 2014): 979–80; J. F. Hoffecker et al., "Beringia and the Global Dispersal of Modern Humans," *Evolutionary Anthropology* 25 (2016): 64–78.

6 Emma Battel Lowman and Adam Barker, "Indigenizing Approaches to Research," *Sociological Imagination*, October 28, 2010; Jon M. Erlandson et al., "The Kelp Highway Hypothesis: Marine Ecology, the Coastal Migration Theory, and the Peopling of the Americas," *Journal of Island and Coastal Archaeology* 2, no. 2 (2007): 161–74.

7 On the greater proportion of omega-3 fatty acids in relation to saturated fat in wild animals, including in historical populations, see L. Cordain et al., "Plant-Animal Subsistence Ratios and Macronutrient Energy Estimations in Worldwide Hunter-Gatherer Diets," *American Journal of Clinical Nutrition* 71, no. 3 (March 2000): 682–92; L. Cordain et al., "The Paradoxical Nature of Hunter-Gatherer Diets: Meat-Based, Yet Non-Atherogenic," *European Journal of Clinical Nutrition* 56, Suppl. 1 (2002): S42–S52.

8 See, for example, Jacques Cinq-Mars and Richard E. Morlan, "Bluefish Caves and Old Crow Basin: A New Rapport," in *Ice Age Peoples of North America: Environments, Origins, and Adaptations of the First Americans*, ed. Robson Bonnichsen and Karen L. Turnmire, eds. (Corvallis: Oregon State University Press, 1999), 200–12; Christyann M. Darwent, "Archaelogical and Ethnographic Evidence for Indigenous Hunting and Fishing Economies in the North American Arctic and Subarctic," in *The Subsistence Economies of Indigenous North American Societies: A Handbook*, ed. Bruce D. Smith (Washington, DC: Smithsonian Institution Scholarly Press, 2011), 46.

9 Vincas P. Steponaitis, "Prehistoric Archaeology in the Southeastern United States, 1970–1985," *Annual Review of Anthropology* 15 (1986): 363–404.

10 Darwent, "Archaeological and Ethnographic Evidence," 47.

11 George C. Frison, *Survival by Hunting: Prehistoric Human Predators and Animal Prey* (Berkeley: University of California Press, 2004): 18, 99, 116, 127 and 171; George C. Frison, *Prehistoric Hunters of the High Plains*. 2nd ed. (St. Louis, MO: Left Coast Press, 1991).

12 William R. Hildebrandt and K. R. McGuire, "The Ascendance of Hunting during the California Middle Archaic: An Evolutionary Perspective," *American Antiquity* 67 (2002): 231–56; Terry L. Jones and J. A. Ferneau, "Deintensification along the Central Coast," in *Catalysts to Complexity: Late Holocene Societies of the California Coast*, ed. Jon M. Erlandson and Terry L. Jones (Los Angeles: Cotsen Institute of Archaeology, University of California, 2002), 205–32.

13 Sarah K. Campbell and Virginia L. Butler, "Prehistoric Native American Use of Animals on the Northwest Coast and Plateau," in *The Subsistence Economies of Indigenous North American Societies*, 103; Sarah K. Campbell and Virginia L. Butler, "Archaelogical Evidence for Resilience of Pacific Northwest Salmon Populations and the Socio-Ecological System over the Last 7500 Years," Ecology and Society 15, no. 1 (2010): 17.

14 On the difficulty in preserving plant material, see M. Nestle, "Animal vs Plant Foods in Human Diets and Health: Is the Historical Record Unequivocal?" *Proceedings of the Nutrition Society* 58 (1999): 215; M. P. Richards, "A Brief Review of the Archaeological Evidence for Palaeolithic and Neolithic Subsistence," *European Journal of Clinical Nutrition*, 56, no. 12 (2002): 1270–78.

15 Brian Fagan, *Before California: An Archaeologist Looks at Our Earliest Inhabitants* (Walnut Creek, CA: AltaMira, 2003), 39–124.

16 For these phenomena, and the veracity of "stretching" to define gardening as horticulture, see William E. Doolittle, *Cultivated Landscapes of Native North America* (New York: Oxford University Press, 2000), 456–63.

17 See, for example, Harold Hickerson, "The Virginia Deer and Intertribal Buffer Zones in the Upper Mississippi Valley," in *Man, Culture, and Animals: The Role of Animals in Human Ecological Adjustments*, ed. Anthony Leeds and Andrew P. Vayda, eds. (Washington, DC: American Association for the Advancement of Science, 1965), 43–65.

18 Kent V. Flannery, *Guila Naquitz: Archaic Foraging and Early Agriculture in Oaxaca, Mexico* (Walnut Creek, CA: Left Field Press, 2009); D. R. Piperno and K. V. Flannery, "The Earliest Archaeological Maize (Zea Mays L.) from Highland Mexico: New Accelerator Mass Spectrometry Dates and Their Implications," *Proceedings of the National Academy of Sciences USA* 98, no. 4 (2001): 2101–103.

19 Pumpkins, marrows and other gourds were first domesticated in Mesoamerica, while acorn squashes, scallop squashes, fordhooks, crooknecks, curcubita and a variety of gourd species were then cultivated in North America. See Bruce D. Smith, "Origins of Agriculture in Eastern North America," *Science* 246, no. 4937 (December 1989): 1566–71; Wade Roush, "Archaeobiology: Squash Seeds Yield New View of Early American Farming," *Science* 276, no. 5314 (1997): 894–95; Bruce D. Smith, "The Cultural Context of Plant Domestication in Eastern North America," *Current Anthropology* 52, no. S4 (October 2011): S471–S484; T. D. Price, "The Origins of Agriculture: New Data, New Ideas," *Current Anthropology* 52, no. S4 (October 2011): S471–S484.

20 Karen R. Adams and Suzanne K. Fish, "Subsistence through Time in the Greater Southwest," in *The Subsistence Economies of Indigenous North American Societies*, 161–62.

21 Lisa W. Huckell, "Ancient Maize in the American Southwest: What Does It Look Like and What Can It Tell Us? in *Histories of Maize: Multidisciplinary Approaches to the Prehistory, Linguistics, Biogeography, Domestication, and Evolution of Maize*, ed. John E. Staller, Robert H. Tykot, and Bruce F. Benz, (New York: Elsevier, 2006), 100.

22 Though introduced to the Southeast around 2,000 years ago, maize only came to dominate plant production around 950 years ago. See Margaret C. Scarry, "Agricultural Risk and the Development of the Moundville Chiefdom," in *Foraging and Farming in the Eastern Woodlands*, ed. Margaret C. Scarry (Gainesville: University Press of Florida, 1993), 157–81.

23 On the move toward maize, beans and squash as important plant staples cultivated through horticulture in the southeast from AD 900 to AD 1300, see Kelly, "Emergence of Mississippian Culture," 113–52; Cassidy, "Skeletal Evidence for Prehistoric Subsistence Adaptation," 307–45.

24 Linda S. Cordell and Bruce D. Smith, "Indigenous Farmers," in *The Cambridge History of the Native Peoples of the Americas*, vol. 1, *North America*: part 1, ed. Bruce G. Trigger and Wilcomb E. Washburn (Cambridge: Cambridge University Press, 1996), 235.

25 Jane E. Buikstra, "Diet and Disease in Late Prehistory," in *Disease and Demography in the Americas*, ed. John W. Verano and Douglas H. Ubelaker (Washington, DC: Smithsonian Press, 1992), 88.

26 John W. Verano, "Prehistoric Disease and Demography in the Andes," in *Disease and Demography in the Americas*, 21.

27 Smith, "Origins of Agriculture in Eastern North America," 1566–71.

28 Paul Kelton, *Epidemics and Enslavement: Biological Catastrophe in the Native Southeast, 1492–1715* (Lincoln: University of Nebraska Press, 2007), 13. See also Cohen, *Health and the Rise of Civilization*, 14.

29 Clark Spencer Larsen, "The Agricultural Revolution as Environmental Catastrophe: Implications for Health and Lifestyle in the Holocene," *Quaternary International* 150, no. 1 (2006): 15.

30 Kristen J. Gremillion, "The Role of Plants in Southeastern Subsistence Economies," in *The Subsistence Economies of Indigenous North American Societies*, 396.

31 J. E. Buikstra and S. Williams S., "Tuberculosis in the Americas: Current Perspectives," in *Human Paleopathology: Current Syntheses and Future Options*, ed. D. J. Ortner and A. C.

Aufderheide (Washington, DC: Smithsonian Institution Scholarly Press, 1991), 161–72.

32   On research that suggests a health decline in the Eastern Region of North America due to increased sedentism and reliance on maize, see J. E. Buikstra et al., "Fertility and the Development of Agriculture in the Prehistoric Midwest," *American Antiquity* 51, no. 3 (1986): 528–46; Clark Spencer Larsen, *Bioarchaeology: Interpreting Behavior from the Human Skeleton* (Cambridge: Cambridge University Press, 1997), 70–72; Cassidy, "Skeletal Evidence for Prehistoric Subsistence Adaptation," 307–45; Clark Spencer Larsen et al., "Dental Caries Evidence for Dietary Change: An Archaeological Context," in *Advances in Dental Anthropology*, ed. M. Kelley and C. S. Larsen (New York: Wiley-Liss, 1991): 179–202; V. J. Polyak and Y. Asmerom, "Late Holocene Climate and Cultural Changes in the Southwestern United States," *Science* 294, no. 5541 (October 2001): 148–51; L. Benson et al., "Ancient Maize from Chacoan Great Houses: Where Was It Grown?" *Proceedings of the National Academy of Sciences of the United States of America* 100 (2003): 13111–15; P. S. Bridges, "Prehistoric Arthritis in the Americas," *Annual Review of Anthropology* 21 (1992): 67–91. Maize agriculturalists in Georgia have been found to have smaller teeth (indicative of poor health) than their predecessors. See C. S. Larsen, "Deciduous Tooth Size and Subsistence Change in Prehistoric Georgia Coast Populations," *Current Anthropology* 22 (1984): 422–23.

33   G. S. Tansarli et al., "Iron Deficiency and Susceptibility to Infections: Evaluation of Clinical Evidence," *European Journal of Clinical Microbiology & Infectious Diseases* 32 (2013): 1253–58.

34   D. L. Martin and A. H. Goodman, "Health Conditions before Columbus: Paleopathology of Native North Americans," *Western Journal of Medicine* 176, no. 1 (January 2002): 65–68; R. P. Mensforth et al., "The Role of Constitutional Factors, Diet, and Infectious Disease in the Etiology of Porotichyperostosis and Periosteal Reactions in Prehistoric Infants and Children," *Medical Anthropology* 2 (1978): 1–59.

35   J. Lallo et al., "Paleoepidemiology of Infectious Disease in the Dickson Mounds Population," *Medical College of Virginia Quarterly* 14 (1977): 17–23. On detecting maize, see C. S. Larsen, "Biological Changes in Human Populations with Agriculture," *Annual Review of Anthropology* 24 (1995): 185–213.

36   Larsen, "Biological Changes in Human Populations with Agriculture," 185–213. On the link between iron deficiency and maize intensification, see Martin and Goodman, "Health Conditions before Columbus," 66; Robert P. Mensforth et al., "Part Two: The Role of Constitutional Factors, Diet, and Infectious Disease in the Etiology of Porotic Hyperostosis and Periosteal Reactions in Prehistoric Infants and Children," *Medical Anthropology* 2, no. 1 (1978): 1–59; Lallo et al., "Paleoepidemiology of Infectious Disease," 17–23; M. Y. El-Najjar et al., "The Etiology of Porotic Hyperostosis among Prehistoric and Historic Anasazi Indians of the Southwestern U.S.," *American Journal of Physical Anthropology* 44 (1976): 447–88; T. D. Holland and M. J. O'Brien, "Parasites, Porotic Hyperostosis, and the Implications of Changing Perspectives," *American Antiquity* 62 (1997): 183–203. On similar phenomena in Neolithic Middle Eastern communities, see Vered Eshed, "Paleopathology and the Origin of Agriculture in the Levant," *American Journal of Physical Anthropology* 143 (2010): 121–33.

On these aspects of early Mississippian history, see David H. Dye and Cheryl Ann Cox, eds., *Towns and Temples Along the Mississippi* (Tuscaloosa: University of Alabama Press, 1990); Christina Synder, "The South," in *The Oxford Handbook of American*

Indian History, ed. Frederick E Hoxie (New York: Oxford University Press, 2016), 31; Cameron B. Wesson and Mark A. Rees, *Between Contacts and Colonies: Archaeological Perspectives on the Protohistoric Southeast* (Tuscaloosa: University of Alabama Press, 2002); Timothy R. Pauketat, *Cahokia: Ancient America's Great City on the Mississippi* (New York: Penguin, 2009).

37   Martin and Goodman, "Health Conditions before Columbus," 67; Lallo et al., Paleoepidemiology of Infectious Disease," 17–23.

38   S. R. Saunders, "Subadult Skeletons and Growth Related Studies," in *Skeletal Biology of Past Peoples: Research Methods*, ed. S. R. Saunders and M.A Katzenberg (New York: Wiley-Liss, 1992), 1–20; Goodman et al., "Health Changes at Dickson Mounds, Illinois (AD 95–1300)," 271–305; D. C. Cook, "Subsistence and Health in the Lower Illinois Valley: Osteological Evidence," in *Paleopathology at the Origins of Agriculture*, 237–69; Larsen, "Biological Changes in Human Populations with Agriculture," 190–91.

39   See David H. Dye and Cheryl Ann Cox, eds., *Towns and Temples along the Mississippi* (Tuscaloosa: University of Alabama Press, 1990); Christina Synder, "The South," 31; Wesson and Rees, *Between Contacts and Colonies*; Pauketat, *Cahokia: Ancient America's Great City on the Mississippi*.

40   Martin and Goodman, "Health Conditions before Columbus," 67; Lallo et al., "Paleoepidemiology of Infectious Disease," 17–23.

41   Larsen, "Biological Changes in Human Populations with Agriculture," 190; Cook, "Subsistence and Health in the Lower Illinois Valley," 237–69.

42   H. Goodman and G. J. Armelagos, "Disease and Death at Dr. Dickson's Mounds," *Natural History*, September 1985, 12 and 15–16; Goodman, Lallo, Armelagos, and Rose, "Health Changes at Dickson Mounds, Illinois (AD 950–1300)," 271–305.

43   Larsen, *Bioarchaeology*, 59; S. K. Pfeiffer and P. King, "Cortical Bone Formation and Diet among Protohistoric Iroquoians," *American Journal of Physical Anthropology* 60 (1983): 23–28.

44   Clark Spencer Larsen, "Animal Source Foods and Human Health during Evolution," *Journal of Nutrition* 133, no. 11, suppl. 2 (2003): 3893S; C. S. Larsen et al., "Frontiers of Contact: Bioarchaeology of Spanish Florida," *Journal of World Prehistory* 15 (2001): 69–123.

45   Cassidy, "Skeletal Evidence for Prehistoric Subsistence Adaptation," 307–45; Cohen, and Armelagos, *Paleopathology at the Origins of Agriculture*, 592–94.

46   Kelton, *Epidemics and Enslavement*, 12; Kenneth Parham, "Toqua Skeletal Biology: A Biocultural Approach," in *The Toqua Site: A Late Mississippian Dallas Phase Town*, ed. Richard Polhemus, vol. 1 (Report of Investigations No. 41, Department of Anthropology, University of Tennessee, and Publications in Anthropology no. 44, Tennessee Valley Authority, Knoxville, 1987), 431–552; Leslie Eisenberg, "Mississippian Cultural Terminations in the Middle Tennessee: What the Bioarcheological Evidence Can Tell Us," in *What Mean These Bones? Studies in Southeastern Bioarchaeology*, ed. Mary Lucas Powell, Patricia S. Bridges, and Ann Marie Wagner Mires. 3rd ed. (Tuscaloosa: University of Alabama Press, 1991), 86.

47   See, for example, Larsen, *Bioarchaeology*, 308; J. B. Coltrain and T. W. J. R. Stafford, "Stable Carbon Isotopes and Great Salt Lake Wetlands Diet: Towards an Understanding of the Great Basin Formative," in *Prehistoric Lifeways in the Great Basin Wetlands: Bioarchaeological Reconstruction and Interpretation*, ed. B. E. Hemphill and C. S. Larsen (Salt Lake City: University of Utah Press, 1999), 55–83.

48 Larsen, *Bioarchaeology,* 306; J. E. Buikistra and G. R. Milner, "Isotopic and Archaeological Interpretations of Diet in the Central Mississippi Valley," *Journal of Archaeological Science* 18 (1991): 319–29.

49 George Milner, "Health and Cultural Change in the Late Prehistoric American Bottom, Illinois," in *What Mean These Bones?,* 65.

50 Larsen, *Bioarchaeology,* 305–7.

51 Lallo et al., "Paleoepidemiology of Infectious Disease," 17–23; Martin and Goodman, "Health Conditions before Columbus," 67–68. On detecting maize, see Larsen, "Biological Changes in Human Populations with Agriculture," 185–213.

52 Philip L. Walker et al., "The Causes of Porotic Hyperostosis and Cribra Orbitalia: A Reappraisal of the Iron-Deficiency-Anemia Hypothesis," *American Journal of Physical Anthropology* 139, no. 2 (2009): 109–25; Polyak and Asmerom, "Late Holocene Climate and Cultural Changes in the Southwestern United States," 148–51; L. Benson et al., "Ancient Maize from Chacoan Great Houses: Where Was It Grown?" *Proceedings of the National Academy of Sciences of the United States of America* 100 (2003): 13111–15; S. J. Kunitz, Disease and Death among the Anasazi: Some Notes on Southwestern Paleoepidemiology," *Palacio* 76 (1969): 17–22; S. Kent, "The Influence of Sedentism and Aggregation on Porotic Hyperostosis and Anaemia: A Case Study," *Man* 21 (1986): 605–36.

53 P. M. Newberne and V. R. Young, "Marginal Vitamin B 12 Intake during Gestation in the Rat Has Long Term Effects on the Offspring," *Nature* 242, no. 5395 (March 1973): 263–65; D. J. Ortner et al., "Evidence of Probable Scurvy in Subadults from Archeological Sites in North America," *American Journal of Physical Anthropology* 114 (2001): 343–51; G. G. Schollmeyer and C. G. Turner, "Dental Caries, Prehistoric Diet, and the Pithouse-to-Pueblo Transition in Southwestern Colorado," *American Antiquity* 69 (2004): 569–82; Walker et al., "The Causes of Porotic Hyperostosis and Cribra Orbitalia," 109–25; J. L. Olivares et al., "Vitamin B12 and Folic Acid in Children with Intestinal Parasitic Infection," *Journal of the American College of Nutrition* 21 (2002): 109–13; K. J. Reinhard et al., "Helminth Remains from Prehistoric Indian Coprolites on the Colorado Plateau," *Journal of Parisitology* 73 (1987): 630–39; E. Beli et al., "Salmonella Serotypes Isolated from Turkey Meat in Albania," *International Journal of Food Microbiology* 63 (2001): 165–67.

54 Walker et al., "The Causes of Porotic Hyperostosis and Cribra Orbitalia," 109–25.

55 Turkey remains were found to rise substantially after around AD 1100 in several Puebloan regions and were found to reach 17% of the total fauna at Pueblo Alto in Chaco Canyon. See B. E. Beacham and S. R. Durand, "Eggshell and the Archaeological Record: New Insights into Turkey Husbandry in the American Southwest," *Journal of Archaeological Science* 34 (2007): 1610–21; Thomas C. Windes, "The Use of Turkeys at Pueblo Alto Based on the Eggshell and Faunal Remains," in *Investigations at the Pueblo Alto Complex, Chaco Canyon, New Mexico, 1975–1979,* vol. 3, part 2, *Artifactual and Biological Analyses,* ed. Frances Joan Mathien and Thomas C. Windes (Santa Fe, NM: National Park Service, US Department of the Interior, 1997), 679–90; K. A. Spielmann and E. Angstadt-Leto, "Hunting, Gathering and Health in the Prehistoric Southwest," in *Evolving Complexity and Environmental Risk in the Prehistoric Southwest,* ed. J. Tainter and B. B. Tainter (Boston: Addison-Wesley, 1996), 79–106; Walker et al., "The Causes of Porotic Hyperostosis and Cribra Orbitalia," 109–25.

56 R. K. Chandra, "Nutrition and the Immune System: An Introduction," *American Journal of Clinical Nutrition* 66, no. 2 (August 1997): 460S–63S.

57 Larsen, *Bioarchaeology,* 70–71; M.G Hardinge et al., "Carbohydrates in Foods," *Journal of American Dietetic Association* 46 (1965): 197–204.

58 B. J. Schmucker, "Dental Attrition: A Correlative Study of Dietary and Subsistence Patterns," in *Health and Disease in the Prehistoric Southwest,* ed. C. F. Merbs and R. J. Miller (Tempe: Arizona State University Press, 1985): 275–322; Philip L. Walker and Jon M. Erlandson, "Dental Evidence for Prehistoric Dietary Change on the Northern Channel Islands, California," *American Antiquity* 51, no. 2 (1986): 375–83.

59 Cohen and Armelagos, *Paleopathology at the Origins of Agriculture,* 25; Goodnam et al., "Enamel Hypoplasias As Indicators of Stress in Three Prehistoric Populations from Illinois," *Human Biology* 52 (1980): 515–28; Larsen, *Bioarchaeology,* 69–70; C. S. Larsen et al., "Dental Evidence for Dietary Change: An Archaeological Context," in *Advances in Dental Anthropology,* ed. M. A. Kelley and C. S Larsen (New York: Wiley-Liss, 1991), 179–202; G. R. Milner, "Dental Caries in the Permanent Dentition of a Mississippian Period Population from the American Midwest," *Collegium Antropologicum* 8 (1984): 77–91.

60 Cohen and Armelagos, *Paleopathology at the Origins of Agriculture,* 25–27.

61 Larsen, *Bioarchaeology,* 54; Goodman et al., "Health Changes at Dickson Mounds, Illinois (AD 950–1300)," 84.

62 Larsen, *Bioarchaeology,* 46.

63 Ibid., 47

64 G. J. Armelagos et al., "The Origins of Agriculture: Population Growth during a Period of Declining Health," *Population and Environment: A Journal of Interdisciplinary Studies* 13, no. 1 (Fall 1991): 9–11.

65 On the notion that agricultural intensification heightened birth numbers through weight gain and early weaning, see Kelton, *Epidemics and Enslavement,* 6; Cohen, *Health and Rise of Civilization,* 71 and 103; J.E. Kelly, "The emergence of Mississippian culture in the American Bottom" in *The Mississippian Emergence,* ed. Bruce D. Smith (Washington, DC: Smithsonian Institution Scholarly Press, 1990), 113–52; Gillian R. Bentley et al., "Is the Fertility of Agriculturalists Higher Than That of Nonagriculturalists?" *Current Anthropology* 34, no. 5 (December 1993): 778–85.

66 El-Najjarm, "Maize, Malaria, and the Anemias"; Parham, "Toqua Skeletal Biology," 488 and 491; Goodman and Armelagos, "Disease and Death at Dr. Dickson's Mounds," 15–16; Eisenberg, "Mississippian Cultural Terminations in the Middle Tennessee," 86; Larsen, "Health and Disease in Prehistoric Georgia," in Cohen and Armelagos, *Paleopathology at the Origins of Agriculture,* 367–92.

67 Cook, "Subsistence and Health in the Lower Illinois Valley," 184; Buikstra, "Diet and Disease in Late Prehistory," 96.

68 Goodman et al., "Health Changes at Dickson Mounds, Illinois (AD 950–1300)," 271–305; Goodman and Armelagos, "Disease and Death at Dr. Dickson's Mounds," 12–18.

69 K. David Patterson, "Amebic Dysentery," in *Cambridge World History of Human Disease,* 568–71; C. F. Merbs, "A New World of Infectious Disease, *Yearbook of Physical Anthropology* 35 (1992): 10.

70 Goodman and Armelagos, "Disease and Death at Dr. Dickson's Mounds," 15–16; Larsen, "Health and Disease in Prehistoric Georgia," in *Paleopathology at the Origins of Agriculture,* 367–92.

71   Kelton, *Epidemics and Enslavement*, 17; Kenneth Parham, "Toqua Skeletal Biology: A Biocultural Approach," 508.

72   Kelton, *Epidemics and Enslavement*, 18. See also Ann Ramenofsky, "Diseases of the Americas, 1492–1700," in *Cambridge World History of Human Disease*, 323.

73   David S. Jones, "Population, Health, and Public Welfare," in *The Oxford Handbook of American Indian History*, ed. Frederick E. Hoxie (New York: Oxford University Press, 2016), 421; Martin and Goodman, "Health Conditions before Columbus," 68.

74   See the essays in Jane E. Buikstra, ed., *Prehistoric Tuberculosis in the Americas*. (Evanston, IL: Northwestern University Archeological Program, 1981), esp. 7, 85–86 and 91; Robert L. Blakely and David S. Mathews, "What Price Civilization? Tuberculosis for One," in *The Burden of Being Civilized: An Anthropological Perspective on the Discontents of Civilization*, ed. Miles Richardson and Malcolm C. Webb (Athens: University of Georgia Press, 1986), 11–23; Mary Lucas Powell, "Ancient Disease, Modern Perspectives: Treponematotis and Tuberculosis in the Age of Agriculture," in *Bioarchaeological Studies of Life in the Age of Agriculture: A View from the Southeast*, ed. Patricia M. Lambert (Tuscaloosa: University of Alabama Press, 2000) 6–34.

75   William H., McNeill, *Plagues and Peoples* (New York: Anchor Press, 1996), 226–28.

76   Francis L. Black, "Infectious Diseases in Primitive Societies," *Science* 187 (1975): 517.

77   Shelley R. Saunders et al., "Transformation and Disease: Precontact Ontario Iroquoians," in *Disease and Demography in the Americas*, 123.

78   See J. C. Rose et al., "Bioarchaeology and Subsistence in the Central and Lower Portions of the Mississippi Valley," in *What Mean These Bones?*, 7–21; Milner, "Health and Cultural Change in the Late Prehistoric American Bottom, Illinois," in ibid., 52–70.

79   For example, in the Eastern Woodland region, "[t]he exponential increase in the proportion of deer remains on sixteenth and seventeenth century Neutral sites after a fifteenth century lull suggests that hunting might have alleviated two climate-related stresses" to provide an "alternative source of protein" due to the changed growing conditions of the Little Ice Age—a return to "traditional large-game hunting practices." See William R. Fitzgerald, "Contact, Neutral Iroquoian Transformation, and the Little Ice Age," in *Societies in Eclipse: Archaeology of the Eastern Woodlands A.D.1400–1700*, ed. David S. Brose and Robert C. Mainfort Jr. (Tuscaloosa: University of Alabama Press, 2001), 42 and 46.

80   Rose et al. highlight low levels of iron-deficiency indicators in lower and central Mississippi communities from around AD 300 through AD 700, as usually found in maize-intensifying sites, demonstrating "well-balanced diets throughout this cultural sequence, at least with respect to iron intake." The latter was provided by animal products. The authors continue in support of the "archaeologically established dietary reconstruction that suggests an emphasis on aquatic resources, small and large mammals, and the collection of wild plants, fruits, and nuts" in the central and lower Mississippi Valley regions through 700 AD. See J. C. Rose et al., "Bioarchaeology and Subsistence in the Central and Lower Portions of the Mississippi Valley," 17 and 21.

81   Sissel Johannessen, "Farmers of the Late Woodland," in *Foraging and Farming in the Eastern Woodlands*, ed. C.M Scarry (Gainesville: University Press of Florida, 1994), 57–77.

82   On these aspects of early Mississippian history, see David H. Dye and Cheryl Ann Cox, eds., *Towns and Temples Along the Mississippi* (Tuscaloosa: University of Alabama

Press, 1990); Christina Synder, "The South," 31; Wesson and Rees, *Between Contacts and Colonies*; Pauketat, *Cahokia: Ancient America's Great City on the Mississippi.*

83 Fritz, "Levels of Native Biodiversity in Eastern North America," 234.

84 Smith, "Origins of Agriculture in Eastern North America," 1566–71; L. Kistler and B. Shapiro, "Ancient DNA Confirms a Local Origin of Domesticated Chenopod in Eastern North America," *Journal of Archaeological Science* 38, no. 12 (December 2011): 3549–54.

85 Smith, "Origins of Agriculture in Eastern North America," 1566–71; Roush, "Archaeobiology: Squash Seeds Yield New View," 894–95; Smith, "The Cultural Context of Plant Domestication in Eastern North America," S481–S482; Price, "The Origins of Agriculture: New Data, New Ideas," *Current Anthropology* 52, no. S4 (October 2011): S471–S484.

86 According to Gremillion, the "most effective countermeasure to the nutritional shortcomings of a heavily maize-based diet was consumption of alternative sources of vitamins, minerals, fats, and proteins from wild plants and a variety of garden crops." See Gremillion, "The Role of Plants in Southeastern Subsistence Economies," 395–96. On the historic need to supplement nutrient-poor maize with other cultivated and gathered plants, see also Margaret C. Scarry, "Variability in Mississippian Crop Production Strategies," in *Foraging and Farming in the Eastern Woodlands*, ed. Margaret C. Scarry (Gainesville: University Press of Florida, 1993), 78–90.

87 Fritz, "Levels of Native Biodiversity in Eastern North America," 232–33.

88 Ibid., 234–35.

89 Jane E. Buiktra et al., "A Carbon Isotopic Perspective on Dietary Variation in Late Prehistoric Western Illinois," in *Agricultural Origins and Development in the Midcontinent*, ed. William Green, ed. (Iowa City: University of Iowa, 1994), 155–70.

90 Fritz, "Levels of Native Biodiversity in Eastern North America," 235.

91 Richard A. Yarnell and M. Jean Black, "Temporal Trends Indicated by a Survey of Archaic and Woodland Plant Food Remains from Southeastern North America," *Southeastern Archaeology* 4 (1985): 93–106; Paul S. Gardner, "The Ecological Structure and Behavioral Implications of Mast Exploitation Strategies," in *People, Plants, and Landscapes: Studies in Paleoethnobotany*, ed. Kristen J. Gremillion (Tuscaloosa: University of Alabama Press, 1997), 161–78. See also the description of nuts and fruit cultivation in Julia E. Hammet, "Ethnohistory of Aboriginal Landscapes in the Southeastern United States," in *Biodiversity and Native America*, 265.

92 During fall and winter, dried walnuts, chestnuts, acorns and chinquapins were "served as staples" among developing Algonquian cultures, even when maize was also available. See Stephen R. Potter, *Commoners, Tribute, and Chiefs: The Development of Algonquian Culture in the Potomac Valley* (Charlottesville: University Press of Virginia, 1993), 41.

93 Richard A. Yarnell, "A Survey of Prehistoric Crop Plants in Eastern North America," *Missouri Archaeologist* 47 (1986): 47–60.

94 Gremillion, "The Role of Plants in Southeastern Subsistence Economies," 396.

95 Synder, "The South," 315.

96 Loretta Fowler, "The Great Plains from the Arrival of the Horse to 1885," in *The Cambridge History of the Native Peoples of the Americas*, vol. 1, *North America*: part 2, ed. Bruce G. Trigger and Wilcomb E. Washburn (Cambridge: Cambridge University Press, 1996), 2.

97 For all these developing traditions, see the important discussion in Doolittle, *Cultivated Landscapes of Native North America*, 456–63.

98   See the discussion of Smith's observations, and their usefulness, in Hammet, "Ethnohistory of Aboriginal Landscapes in the Southeastern United States," 257.

99   On the varied diet in the Southeast many centuries before European contact, including animals, fish and plants that were gathered as well as cultivated, see Charles M. Hudson, *The Southeastern Indians* (Knoxville: University of Tennessee Press, 1978), 272–89; Timothy Silver, *A New Face on the Countryside: Indians, Colonists, and Slaves in South Atlantic Forests, 1500–1800* (New York: Cambridge University Press, 1990), 36–37; Kelton, *Epidemics and Enslavement*, 5–6; Smith, "Origins of Agriculture in Eastern America," 1566–71; Kelly, "Emergence of Mississippian Culture," 113–52.

100 Cheryl P. Claassen, "Temporal Patterns in Marine Shellfish-Species Use along the Atlantic Coast in the Southeastern United States," *Southeastern Archaeology* 5 (1986): 120–37.

101 Mark A. Reese, "Subsistence Economy and Political Culture in the Protohistoric Central Mississippi Valley," in *Between Contacts and Colonies: Archaeological Perspectives on the Protohistoric Southeast*, 170–98; Evan Peacock, "Shellfish Use during the Woodland Period in the Middle South," in *The Woodland Southeast*, ed. David G. Anderson and Robert C. Mainfort Jr., (Tuscaloosa: University of Alabama Press, 2002), 444–60.

102 Heather A. Lapham, "Animals in Southeastern Native American Subsistence Economies," in *The Subsistence Economies of Indigenous North American Societies*, 415–16.

103 Ibid.

104 John Smith, *Travel and Works of Captain John Smith*. 2 vols., ed. Edward Arber, (Edinburgh: John Grant, 1910), 1: 61.

105 Fritz, "Levels of Native Biodiversity in Eastern North America," 235.

106 Potter, *Commoners, Tribute, and Chiefs*, 41–42 and 153.

107 Ibid., 151–52.

108 Helen C. Rountree, *The Powhatan Indians of Virginia: Their Traditional Culture* (Norman: University of Oklahoma Press, 1989), 149–50; Potter, *Commoners, Tribute, and Chiefs*, 151–52.

109 Smith, *Travel and Works of Captain John Smith*, 1: 68.

110 Ibid.

111 Ibid., 61; Potter, *Commoners, Tribute, and Chiefs*, 42.

112 John Lawson, *A New Voyage to Carolina* (1709), ed. Hugh T. Lefler (Chapel Hill: University of North Carolina Press, 1967), 160.

113 Smith, *Travel and Works of Captain John Smith*, 1: 58.

114 On the preference for dispersal of communities even when maize came to be consumed as a greater proportion of diet, see Bruce D. Smith, "Mississippian Patterns of Subsistence and Settlement," in *Alabama and the Borderlands from Prehistory to Statehood*, ed. R. R. Badger and L. A. Clayton (Tuscaloosa: University of Alabama Press, 1985), 75–77.

115 Kelton, *Epidemics and Enslavement*, 41–42; Russel Thornton et al., "Depopulation in the Southeast after 1492," in *Disease and Demography in the Americas*, 187–88; George R. Milner, "Epidemic Disease in the Postcontact Southeast: A Reappraisal," *Mid-Continental Journal of Archaeology* 5 (1980): 41.

116 Julia E. Hammet, "Ethnohistory of Aboriginal Landscapes in the Southeastern United States," *Southern Indian Studies* 41 (1992): 34.

117 Hickerson, "The Virginia Deer and Intertribal Buffer Zones," 43–65.

118 See, for example, the discussion of Garcilaso de la Vega's *A History of the Conquest of Florida* and *The Florida of the Inca* [1605] and the earlier de Soto observations in

Hammet, "Ethnohistory of Aboriginal Landscapes in the Southeastern United States," 266–67.

119   Ibid., 261.

120   Lucretia S. Kelly, "Patterns of Faunal Exploitation at Cahokia," in *Cahokia: Domination and Ideology in the Mississippian* World, ed. Timothy R. Pauketat and Thomas E. Emerson (Lincoln: University of Nebraska Press, 1997), 69–88; Lucretia S. Kelly, "A Case of Ritual Feasting at the Cahokia Site," in *Feasts: Archaeological and Ethnographic Perspectives on Food, Politics, and Power,* Michael Dietler and Brian Hayden (Washington, DC: Smithsonian Institution Scholarly Press, 2001), 334–67; Timothy R. Pauketat et al., "The Residues of Feasting and Public Ritual at Early Cahokia," *American Antiquity* 67 (2002): 257–79.

121   H. Edwin Jackson and Susan L. Scott, "The Faunal Record of the Southeastern Elite: The Implications of Economy, Social Relations, and Ideology," *Southeastern Archaeology* 14 (1995): 103–19; H. Edwin Jackson and Susan L. Scott, "Patterns of Elite Faunal Utilization at Moundville, Alabama," *American Antiquity* 68 (2003): 552–72; Lapham, "Animals in Southeastern Native American Subsistence Economies," 415.

122   Francis E. Smiley, "Black Mesa before Agriculture: Paleoindian and Archaic Evidence," in *Prehistoric Culture Change on the Colorado Plateau: Ten Thousand Years on Black Mesa,* ed. Shirley Powell and Francis E. Smiley (Tucson: University of Arizona Press, 2002), 21–22.

123   Steven R. James, "Monitoring Archaeofaunal Changes during the Transition to Agriculture in the American Southwest," *Kiva* 56 (1990): 25–43.

124   Huckell, "Ancient Maize in the American Southwest," 100.

125   Karen R. Adams and Suzanne K. Fish, "Subsistence through Time in the Greater Southwest," in *The Subsistence Economies of Indigenous North American Societies,* 161–62.

126   Ibid., 157; Huckell, "Ancient Maize in the American Southwest"; Alan Simmons, "New Evidence for the Early Use of Cultigens in the American Southwest," *American Antiquity* 51 (1986): 73–88.

127   Suzanne K. Fish and Paul R. Fish, "Prehistoric Desert Farmers of the Southwest," *Annual Review of Anthropology* 23 (1994): 83.

128   Lisa W. Huckell and Mollie S. Toll, "Wild Plant Use in the North American Southwest," in *People and Plants in Ancient Western North America,* ed. Paul E. Minnis (Washington, DC: Smithsonian Institution Scholarly Press, 2004), 63–69; Adams and Fish, "Subsistence through Time in the Greater Southwest," 158.

129   On the importance of movement rather than stasis, see James F. Brooks, "The Southwest," in *The Oxford Handbook of American Indian History,* 218; Linda S. Cordell and Maxine E. McBrinn, *Archaeology of the Southwest,* 3rd ed. (Walnut Creek, CA: Left Coast, 2012).

130   Steven R. James, "Prehistoric Hunting and Fishing Patterns in the American Southwest," in *The Subsistence Economies of Indigenous North American Societies,* 206–8.

131   Adams and Fish, "Subsistence through Time in the Greater Southwest," 169.

132   Huckell and Toll, "Wild Plant Use in the North American Southwest," 63–69.

133   Doolittle, *Cultivated Landscapes of Native North America,* 456–63.

134   Tessie Naranjo, "Life as Movement: A Tewa View of Community and Identity," in *The Social Construction of Communities: Agency, Structure, and Identity in the Prehispanic Southwest,* ed. Mark. D. Varien and James M. Potter (Lanham, MD: Altamira, 2008), 252. See also the discussion of Naranjo's movement paradigm in Brooks, "The Southwest," 218.

135   Adams and Fish, "Subsistence through Time in the Greater Southwest," 149.

136   Ibid., 161

137   M. K. Bennet, "The Food Economy of the New England Indians, 1605–75," *Journal of Political Economy* 63 (1955), 369–87.

138   Catherine C. Carlson et al., "Impact of Disease on the Precontact and Early Historic Populations of New England and the Maritimes," in *Disease and Demography in the Americas*, 141. See also E. S. Chilton, "The Origin and Spread of Maize (zea mays) in New England," in *Histories of Maize: Multidisciplinary Approaches to the Prehistory, Linguistics, Biogeography, Domestication, and Evolution of Maize*, ed. in John E. Staller, Robert H. Tykot, and Bruce F. Benz (New York: Elsevier, 2006), 539–47; Gary W. Crawford, "People and Plant Interactions in the Northeast," in *The Subsistence Economies of Indigenous North American Societies*, 431–48.

139   Carlson et al., "Impact of Disease on the Precontact and Early Historic Populations," 142.

140   Neil Salisbury, *Manitou and Providence: Indians, Europeans, and the Making of New England, 1500–1643* (New York: Oxford University Press, 1982), 32–33.

141   Giovaanni da Verrazano, cited in Carlson et al., *Disease and Demography in the Americas*, 142. See also Lawrence C. Wroth, ed., *The Voyages of Giovanni de Verazzano, 1524–1528* (New Haven, CT: Yale University Press, 1970), 139.

142   William Wood, *New England's Prospect* (Boston: University of Massachusetts Press, 1977 [1643]), 106–7; Salisbury, *Manitou and Providence*, 32–33.

143   Calvin Martin, *Keepers of the Game: Indian-Animal Relationships and the Fur Trade* (Berkeley: University of California Press, 1978), 42. See also Peter A. Thomas, "Contrastive Subsistence Strategies and Land Use as Factors for Understanding Indian-White Relations in New England," *Ethnohistory* 23 (1976), 5–11; Melvin L. Fowler, "Agriculture and Village Settlement in the North American East: The Central Mississippi Valley Area, A Case History," in *Prehistoric Agriculture*, ed. Stuart Struever (Garden City, NY: American Museum of Natural History Press, 1971), 391–403.

144   Neal Salisbury, "The Atlantic Northeast," in *The Oxford Handbook of American Indian History*, 337.

145   Gary D. Crites, "Domesticated Sunflower in Fifth Millennium B.P. Temporal Context: New Evidence from Middle Tennessee," *American Antiquity* 58 (1993) 146–48; David L. Asch and Nancy B. Asch, "Prehistoric Plant Cultivation in West-Central Illinois," in *Prehistoric Food Production in North America*, ed. Richard I. Ford (Ann Arbor: University of Michigan Press, 1985), 149–203; Bruce D. Smith, "Eastern North America as an Independent Center of Plant Domestication," *Proceedings of the National Academy of Sciences* 103 (2006): 12223–28. See also the very recent work on Adena/Hopewell communities by Mueller: Natalie G.Mueller, "The earliest occurrence of a newly described domesticate in Eastern North America: Adena/ Hopewell communities and agricultural innovation," *Journal of Anthropological* 49 (March 2018): 39-50.

146   Gary W. Crawford, "People and Plant Interactions in the Northeast," in *The Subsistence Economies of Indigenous North American Societies*, 442–43; Jefferson Chapman et al., "Archaeological Evidence for Precolumbian Introduction of Portulaca oleracea and Mollugo verticililata into Eastern North America," *Economic Botany* 28 (1974): 411–12.

147   Neil Salisbury, *Manitou and Providence*, 38.

148 Kathleen J. Bragdon, *Native People of Southern New England, 1500–1650* (Norman: University of Oklahoma Press, 1996), 81–91; Robert J. Hassenstab, "Fishing, Farming, and Finding the Village Sites: Centering Late Woodland New England Algonquins," in *The Archaeological Northeast*, ed. Mary Ann Levine, Kenneth E. Sassaman, and Michael S. Nassaney (Westport, CT: Bergin and Garvey, 1999), 139–53; Elizabeth Chilton, "Farming and Social Complexity in the Northeast," in Timothy R. Pauketat and Diana DiPaolo Loren, eds., *North American Archaeology* (Malden, MA: Blackwell, 2005), 138–60. On the perceived scholarly consensus that women "replaced" men as primary food producers, see Salisbury, "The Atlantic Northeast," 337–47.

149 C. Margaret Scarry and Richard A. Yarnell, "Native American Domestication and Husbandry of Plants in Eastern North America," in *The Subsistence Economies of Indigenous North American Societies*, 483.

150 Fritz, "Levels of Native Biodiversity in Eastern North America," 223–47; Julia E. Hammett, "Ethnohistory of Aboriginal Landscapes in the Southeastern United States," *Southern Indian Studies* 41 (1992), 1–50; Margaret C. Scarry and John F. Scarry, "Native American 'Garden Agriculture' in Southeastern North America," *World Archaeology* 379 (2005): 259–74; Kristen J. Gremillion, "Adoption of Old World Crops and Processes of Cultural Change in the Historic Southeast," *Southeastern Archaeology* 12 (1993): 15–20.

151 J. L. Fuller et al., "Impact of Human Activity on Regional Forest Composition and Dynamics in Central New England," *Ecosystems* 1 (1998): 76–95; Crawford, "People and Plant Interactions in the Northeast," 442–43.

152 Doolittle, *Cultivated Landscapes of Native North America*, 456–63.

153 Calvin Martin, "Fire and Forest Structure in the Aboriginal Eastern Forest," *Indian Historian* 6, no. 4 (1973): 38–42.

154 Adriaen Van der Donck, *A Description of the New Netherlands* [1656], cited in Hammet, "Ethnohistory of Aboriginal Landscapes in the Southeastern United States," 261.

155 Salisbury, *Manitou and Providence*, 19.

156 Paul Allen Zoch et al. *Bison Hunting at Cooper Site: Where Lightning Bolts Drew Thundering Herds* (Norman: University of Oklahoma Press, 1999), 6–7; Dennis J. Stanford and Bruce A. Bradley, *Across Atlantic Ice: The Origin of America's Clovis Culture* (Berkeley: University of California Press, 2012), 3–4; Troy D. Smith, "Indian Territory and Oklahoma," in *Oxford Handbook of American Indian History*, 360.

157 Geoff Cunfer and Bill Waiser, eds., *Bison and People on the North American Great Plains: A Deep Environmental History* (College Station: Texas A&M University Press, 2016), 3–4; Douglas Bamforth, ed., *The Allen Site: A Paleoindian Camp in Southwestern Nebraska* (Albuquerque: University of New Mexico Press, 2006); Matthew E. Hill Jr., "A Moveable Feast: Variation in Faunal Resource Use among Central and Western North American Paleoindian Sites," *American Antiquity* 72 (2007): 417–38.

158 Joel C. Janetski, "Animal Use in the Great Basin of North America: Ethnographic and Archaeological Evidences," in *The Subsistence Economies of Indigenous North American Societies*, 273–93.

159 Douglas H. Ubelaker and William C. Sturtevant, eds., *Handbook of North American Indians*, vol. 3, *Environment, Origins, and Population* (Washington, DC: Smithsonian Institution Scholarly Press, 2007), 363–64; Edwin Bryant, *What I Saw in California* (Lincoln: University of Nebraska Press, 1985), 162

160 Ubelaker and Sturtevant, eds., *Handbook of North American Indians*, vol. 3, *Environment, Origins, and Population*, 364.

161   Bruce D. Smith, "Introduction: Indigenous North American Societies and the Environment," in *The Subsistence Economies of Indigenous North American Societies*, 6. See also Melinda Zeder, "Archaeological Approaches to Documenting Animal Domestication," in *Documenting Domestication: New Genetic and Archaeological Paradigm*, ed. M. A. Zeder, D. Bradley, E. Emshwiller and B. D. Smith (Berkeley: University of California Press, 2006), 171–80.

162   Mary J. Adair and Richard R. Drass, "Patterns of Plant Use in the Prehistoric Central and Southern Plains," in *The Subsistence Economies of Indigenous North American Societies*, 340–44.

163   Mary J. Adair, "Great Plains Paleoethnobotany," in *People and Plants in Ancient Eastern North America*, 293–94; George C. Frison, "Hunting and Gathering Tradition: Northwestern and Central Plains," in *Handbook of North American Indians*, vol. 13, *Plains*, ed. Raymond J. DeMaillie (Washington, DC: Smithsonian Institution Scholarly Press, 2001), 131–45. See also the essays in B. Leland and Kent Buhker, "MEMOIR 29: Southern Plains Bison Procurement and Utilization from Paleoindian to History," *Plains Anthropologist* 42 (1997): 1–182.

164   Mary J. Adair and Richard R. Drass, "Patterns of Plant Use in the Prehistoric Central and Southern Plains," 341.

165   Douglas K. Boyd, "Prehistoric Agriculture on the Canadian River of the Texas Panhandle: New Insights from West Pasture Sites on the M-Cross Ranch," *Plains Anthropologist* 53 (2008): 33–57; Richard R. Drass, "Corn, Beans, and Bison: Cultivated Plants and Changing Economies of the Late Prehistoric Villagers on the Plains of Oklahoma and Northwest Texas," *Plains Anthropologist* 42 (1997): 183–204.

166   John R. Bozell et al., "Native American Use of Animal on the North American Great Plains," in *The Subsistence Economies of Indigenous North American Societies: A Handbook*, ed. Bruce D. Smith (Washington, DC: Smithsonian Institution Scholarly Press, 2011), 365.

167   Mary J. Adair and Richard R. Drass, "Patterns of Plant Use in the Prehistoric Central and Southern Plains," 341.

168   Jeffrey Ostler, "The Plains," in *The Oxford Handbook of American Indian History*, 235–37.

169   Bozell et al., "Native American Use of Animal on the North American Great Plains," 367. See also Michael J. Quigg, "Bison Processing at the Rush Site, 41TG346, and Evidence for Pemmican Production in the Southern Plains," *Plains Anthropologist* 42 (1997): 145–61; Landon P. Karr et al., "Bone Marrow and Bone Grease Exploitation on the Plains of South Dakota: A New Perspective on Bone Fracture Evidence from the Mitchell Prehistoric Indian Village," *South Dakota Archeology* 26 (2008), 33–62; Susan Vehik, "Bone Fragment and Bone Grease Manufacturing: A Review of Their Archeological Use and Potential," *Plains Anthropologist* 22 (1977): 169–82.

170   Catherine S. Fowler, "Subsistence," in *Handbook of North American Indians*, vol. 11, *Great Basin*, ed. William C. Sturtevant (Washington, DC, Smithsonian Institution Scholarly Press, 1986), 64–66; Ubelaker and Sturtevant, eds., *Handbook of North American Indians*, vol. 3, *Environment, Origins, and Population*, 334; David Rhode and David B. Madsen, "Pine Nut Use in the Early Holocene and Beyond: The Danger Cave Archaeobotanical Record," *Journal of Archaeological Science* 25 (1998): 1199–1210.

171   Linda Scott Cummings, "Great Basin Paleobotany," in *People and Plants in Ancient Western North America*, 205–77; David Rhode and Lisbeth A. Louderback, "Dietary Plant Use in the Bonneville Basin during the Terminal Pleistocene-Early Holocene Transition," in *Paleoindian or Paleoarchaic? Great Basin Human Ecology*

at the Pleistocene-Holocene Transition, ed. Kelly Graf and Dave N. Schmitt (Salt Lake City: University of Utah Press, 2007), 231–47.

172 Fowler and Rhode, "Plant Foods and Foodways among the Great Basin's Indigenous Peoples," 246.

173 Ibid., 249–51.

174 Eugene S. Hunn et al., "Ethnobiology and Subsistence," in *Handbook of North American Indians*, vol. 12, *Plateau*, ed. Deward E. Walker Jr. (Washington, DC: Smithsonian Institution Scholarly Press, 1998), 526–27; Douglas H. Ubelaker and William C. Sturtevant, eds., *Handbook of North American Indians*, vol. 3, *Environment, Origins and Population* (Washington, DC: Smithsonian Institution Scholarly Press, 2007), 343; Fowler and Rhode, "Plant Foods and Foodways among the Great Basin's Indigenous Peoples," 249.

175 James C. Chatters, "Population Growth, Climatic Cooling, and the Development of Collector Strategies on the Southern Plateau, Western North America," *Journal of World Prehistory* 9 (1995), 341–400.

176 Harry W. Lawton et al., "Agriculture among the Paiute of Owens Valley," *Journal of California Anthropology* 3 (1976): 13–50.

177 On the exchange of plants in the Great Basin and beyond, see David B. Madsen and Steven R. Simms, "The Fremont Complex: A Behavioral Perspective," *Journal of World Prehistory* 12 (1998): 255–336; Craig S. Smith, "Seeds, Weeds, and Prehistoric Hunters and Gatherers: The Plant Macrofossil Evidence from Southwest Wyoming," *Plains Anthropologist* 33 (1998): 141–58; Margaret M. Lyneis, "The Virgin Anasazi, Far Western Puebloans," *Journal of World Prehistory* 9 (1995): 199–242; Linda Scott Cummings, "Great Basin Palebotany," 205–77; Joan B. Coltrain and Steven W. Leavitt "Climate and Diet in Fremont Prehistory: Economic Variability and Abandonment of Maize Agriculture in the Great Salt Lake Basin," *American Antiquity* 67 (2002): 453–85.

178 Timothy G. Baugh, "Ecology and Exchange: The Dynamics of Plains-Pueblo Interaction," in *Farmers, Hunters, and Colonists: Interaction between the Southwest and the Southern Plains*, ed. Katherine A. Spielmann (Tucson: University of Arizona Press, 1991), 107–27; John R. Bozell, "Culture, Environment, and Bison Populations on the Late Prehistoric and Early Historic Central Plains," *Plains Anthropologist* 40 (1995): 145–63.

179 Robert L. Bettinger and Eric Wohlgemuth, "Archaeological and Ethnographic Evidence for Indigenous Plant Use in California," in *The Subsistence Economies of Indigenous North American Societies*, 124.

180 On the social context for hunting in California through and after Holocene, see William R. Hildebrandt and K. R. McGuire, "The Ascendance of Hunting during the California Middle Archaic, 231–56. On the interaction between hunting, gathering, and acorn complexes more generally, see Robert F. Heizer and Albert B. Elsasser, *The Natural World of the California Indians* (Berkeley: University of California Press, 2005); M. Kat Anderson, *Tending the Wild: Native American Knowledge and the Management of California's Natural Resources* (Berkeley: University of California Press, 2005); Ken G. Lightfoot, *Indians, Missionaries and Merchants: The Legacy of Colonial Encounters on the Colonial Frontiers* (Berkeley: University of California Press, 2006); Lynn H. Gamble, *The Chumash World at European Contact: Power, Trade and Feasting among Complex Hunter-Gatherers* (Berkeley: University of California Press, 2008); Christopher Chase-Dunn

and Kelly Mann, *The Wintu and Their Neighbors: A Very Small World- System in Northern California* (Tucson: University of Arizona Press, 1998).

181 Henry T. Lewis, ed., *Patterns of Indian Burning in California: Ecology and Ethnohistory* (Ramona, CA: Ballena Press Anthropological Papers 1, 1973): 1–101; Lowell J. Bean and Harry W. Lawton, "Some Explanations for the Rise of Cultural Complexity in Native California with Comments on Proto-Agriculture and Agriculture," in *Patterns of Indian Burning in California.*, v–xvii.

182 Robert L. Bettinger, *Orderly Anarchy: Sociopolitical Evolution in Aboriginal California* (Oakland: University of California Press, 2015), 111; Ubelaker and Sturtevant, eds., *Handbook of North American Indians*, vol. 3, *Environment, Origins, and Population*, 275; Kent Lightfoot and Otis Parrish, *California Indians and Their Environment: An Introduction* (Berkeley and Los Angeles: University of California Press, 2009), 316.

183 On the hunting and consumption of terrestrial birds such as quails and mourning doves, see C. Hart Merriam, *Ethnographic Notes on California Indian Tribes* (Berkeley: University of California Archaeological Survey Reports 68), 1966–67.

184 Ubelaker and Sturtevant, eds., *Handbook of North American Indians*, vol. 3, *Environment, Origins, and Population*, 285. On hunting sea lions during the prehistoric and Holocene eras, see Alfred L. Kroeber and S. A. Barrett, "Fishing Among the Indians of Northwestern California," *University of California Anthropological Records* 21 (1960): 121; William R. Hildebrandt and Terry L. Jones, "Evolution of Marine Mammal Hunting: A View from the California and Oregon Coasts," *Journal of Anthropological Archaeology* 11 (1992): 360–401; Roger H. Colten and Jeanne E. Arnold, "Prehistoric Marine Mammal Hunting on California's Northern Channel Islands," *American Antiquity* 63 (1998): 679–701.

185 Alfred L. Kroeber, "Culture Elements Distributions. XV, Salt, Dogs, and Tobacco," *University of California Anthropological Records* 13 (1939): 1–20; Frank F. Latta, *Handbook of Yokuts Indians* (Oildale, CA: Bear State Books, 1949), 115–18.

186 Hildebrandt and Carpenter, "Native Hunting Adaptations in California: Changing Patterns of Resource Use from the Early Holocene to European Contact," in *The Subsistence Economies of Indigenous North American Societies: A Handbook*, ed. Bruce D. Smith (Washington, DC: Smithsonian Institution Scholarly Press, 2011), 138.

187 Kroeber and Barrett, "Fishing among the Indians of Northwestern California," 99.

188 M. Kat Anderson, *Tending the Wild,* 177.

189 Bettinger and Wohlgemuth, "Archaeological and Ethnographic Evidence for Indigenous Plant Use in California," 116; Bettinger, *Orderly Anarchy*, 110–14.

190 Bettinger, *Orderly Anarchy*, 111; Douglas H. Ubelaker and William C. Sturtevant, eds., *Handbook of North American Indians*, vol. 3, *Environment, Origins, and Population*, 275; Lightfoot and Parrish, *California Indians and Their Environment*, 316.

191 Bettinger and Wohlgemuth, "Archaeological and Ethnographic Evidence for Indigenous Plant Use in California," 116.

192 Glenn Farris, "Quality Food: The Quest for Pine Nuts in Northern California," in *Before the Wilderness: Environmental Management by Native Californians*, ed. T. C. Blackburn and M. K. Anderson (Menlo Park, CA: Ballena Press, 1993), 229–40.

193 Frank R. LaPena, "Wintu," in *Handbook of North American Indians*, vol. 8, *California*, ed. Robert F. Heizer (Washington, DC: Smithsonian Institution Scholarly Press, 1978), 324–40; Hildebrandt and Carpenter, "Native Hunting Adaptations in California," 138.

194 Gamble, *The Chumash World at European Contact*, 235–39 and 223–28; William McCawley, *The First Angelinos: The Gabrielino Indians of Los Angeles* (Banning, CA: Malki Museum Press, 1996), 235–39; Anderson, *Tending the Wild*, 146–48.

195 Hildebrandt and Carpenter, "Native Hunting Adaptations in California," 138.

196 W. R. Goldschmidt, "Nomlaki," in *Handbook of North American Indians,* vol. 8, *California*, 341–49.

197 Hildebrandt and Carpenter, "Native Hunting Adaptations in California," 141.

198 For these figures and an overview, see Andrew H. Fisher, "The Pacific Northwest," in *The Oxford Handbook of American Indian History*, chap. 13; R. G. Matson and Gary Coupland, *The Prehistory of the Northwest Coast* (New York: Academic Press, 1995), 1–36.

199 Fisher, "The Pacific Northwest," 255–56; Eugene S. Hunn, with James Selam and Family, *Nch'i-wána, "the Big River": Mid-Columbia Indians and Their Land* (Seattle: University of Washington Press, 1990), 133–36; Lillian A. Ackerman, *A Necessary Balance: Gender and Power Among Indians of the Columbia Plateau* (Norman: University of Oklahoma Press, 2003), 84–113.

200 Douglas Deur and Nancy J. Turner, eds., *"Keeping It Living": Traditions of Plant Use and Cultivation on the Northwest Coast of North America* (Seattle: University of Washington Press; Vancouver: UBC Press, 2005), 62 and 115.

201 Fiona Hamersley Chambers and Nancy J. Turner, "Plant Use by Northwest Coast and Plateau Indigenous Peoples," in *The Subsistence Economies of Indigenous North American Societies*, 77–78.

202 Ibid., 68–69; H. V. Kuhnlein and N. J. Turner, *Traditional Plant Foods of Canadian Indigenous Peoples: Nutrition, Botany, and Use*, vol. 8, in *Food and Nutrition in History and Anthropology*, ed. S. Katz (Philadelphia: Gordon and Breach Science Publishers, 1991), 54, 80–92, 103, 198 and 227.

203 Hunn with Selam and Family, *Nch'i-wána, "the Big River"*, 135; Ackerman, *A Necessary Balance*, 84–113.

204 Fisher, "The Pacific Northwest," 257; Hunn with Selam and Family, *Nch'i-wána, "the Big River"*, 224–25.

205 Richard Daley, *Our Box Was Full: An Ethnography of the Delgamuukw Plaintiffs* (Vancouver, BC: UBC Press, 2005), 112–14. See also the account in Katherine Czapp, "Native Americans of the Pacific Northwest," *Wise Traditions* (fall 2007). https://www.westonaprice.org/health-topics/in-his-footsteps/native-americans-of-the-pacific-northwest/.

206 Cited in Sally Fallon and Mary G. Enig, "Guts and Grease: The Diet of Native Americans," *Wise Traditions* (spring 2001). https://www.westonaprice.org/health-topics/traditional-diets/guts-and-grease-the-diet-of-native-americans/.

207 For an early critique of the notion that Alaskan indigenous peoples would have been in ketosis, see Peter Heinbecker, "Studies on the Metabolism of Eskimos," *Journal of Biological Chemistry* 80 (1928): 461–68.

208 Darwent, "Archaelogical and Ethnographic Evidence," 47–48.

209 Ibid., 48.

210 Robert E. Ackerman, "Early Maritime Traditions in the Bering, Chukchi and East Siberian Seas," *Arctic Anthropology* 35 (1998): 247–62; Don E. Dumond, *The Eskimos and The Aleuts*. 2nd ed. (London: Thames and Hudson, 1987).

211 Darwent, "Archaelogical and Ethnographic Evidence," 49–50.

212 Bryan C. Gordon, *Of Men and Herds in Barrenland Prehistory* (Ottawa: National Museum of Man, 1975); Bryan C. Gordon, *Migod: 8,000 years of Barrenland Prehistory*

(Ottawa: National Museum of Man, 1976); Bryan C. Gordon, *People of Sunlight, People of Starlight: Barrenland Archaeology in the Northwest Territories* (Ottawa: National Museum of Man, 1996); T. Max Friesen and Andrew M. Stewart, "Inuit Subsistence on the Kazan River, Nunavut," *Canadian Journal of Archaeology*, 28 (2004): 32–50; Darwent, "Archaelogical and Ethnographic Evidence," 54–55.

213   Alestine Andre et al., "Plant Use by Arctic and Subarctic Indigenous Peoples," in *The Subsistence Economies of Indigenous North American Societies*, 11.

214   Ibid., 14.

215   H. M Drury, "Nutrients in Native Foods of Southeastern Alaska," *Journal of Ethnobiology* 5 (1985): 87–100; Andre et al., "Plant Use by Arctic and Subarctic Indigenous Peoples," 15.

216   Deur and Turner, eds., *"Keeping It Living,"* 265–66.

217   Kuhnlein and Turner, "Traditional Plant Foods of Canadian Indigenous Peoples," 9–285; Andre et al., "Plant Use by Arctic and Subarctic Indigenous Peoples," 14.

218   Andre et al., "Plant Use by Arctic and Subarctic Indigenous Peoples," 16.

219   Robin Fisher, "The Northwest from the Beginning of the Trade with Europeans to the 1880s," in *The Cambridge History of the Native Peoples of the Americas:* vol. 1, *North America*: part 2, ed. Bruce G. Trigger and Wilcomb E. Washburn (Cambridge: Cambridge University Press, 1996), 120–24.

220   Samuel Hearne, *A Journal from Prince of Wales's Fort in Hudson Bay to the Northern Ocean (1769–1772)*, ed. J. B. Tyrell (Toronto, CA: The Champlain Society, 1911): 171. See also the discussion of Hearne's testimony in Sally Fallon and Mary G. Enig, "Guts and Grease: The Diet of Native Americans."

221   On the intensification of Caribou hunting after European contact, see Stephen Loring, "On the Trail to the Caribou House. Some Reflections on Innu Caribou Hunters in Northern Ntessinan (Labrador)," in *Caribou and Reindeer Hunters of the Northern Hemisphere*, ed. Lawrence J. Jackson and Paul T. Thacker (Avebury, UK: Aldershot, 1997), 208–9; Ernest S. Burch Jr., "Caribou Eskimo Origins: An Old Problem Reconsidered," *Arctic Anthropology* 15, no. 1 (1978): 1–35.

222   Snow suggests that precontact horticultural communities often "retained hunting and gathering practices as regular supplements and insurance against occasional shortages." As we show, their interaction did not merely respond to the threat of shortage but also provided necessary nutrient diversity outside those periods of food shortage. See Dean R. Snow, "The First Americans and the Differentiation of Hunter Gatherer Cultures," in *The Cambridge History of the Native Peoples of the Americas*, vol. 1, *North America*: part 1, ed. Bruce G. Trigger and Wilcomb E. Washburn (Cambridge: Cambridge University Press, 1996), 125.

3. Micronutrients and Immunity in Native America, 1492–1750

1   On "baseline malnutrition," see David S. Jones, "Virgin Soils Revisited," *William and Mary Quarterly*, 3rd. ser., 60, no. 4 (2003): 703–42.

2   David S. Jones, "Population, Health, and Public Welfare," in *The Oxford Handbook of American Indian History*, ed. Frederick E. Hoxie (New York: Oxford University Press, 2016), 418–19.

3   Dobyns and other scholars suggested that high fertility occurred among populations that took advantage of natural resources without any attendant competition for their differing ecological niches. On these numbers and scholarly trends, see Jones,

"Population, Health, and Public Welfare," 414. See also A. L. Kroeber, "Native American Population," *American Anthropologist*, N.S., 36 (1934): 17; Henry F. Dobyns, "Estimating Aboriginal American Population: An Appraisal of Techniques with a New Hemispheric Estimate," *Current Anthropology* 7, no. 4 (1966): 395–416; Henry F. Dobyns, *Their Number Become Thinned: Native American Population Dynamics in Eastern North America* (Knoxville: University of Tennessee Press, 1983), 18–20 and 264–65.

4 Bruce G. Trigger and William R. Swagerty, "Entertaining Strangers: North America in the Sixteenth Century," in *The Cambridge History of the Native Peoples of The Americas*, vol. 1, *North America*, part 1, ed. Bruce G. Trigger and Wilcomb E. Washburn (Cambridge: Cambridge University Press,1996), 363.

5 Suzanne A. Alchon, *A Pest in the Land: New World Epidemics in a Global Perspective* (Albuquerque: University of New Mexico Press, 2003), 147–72; Douglas H. Ubelaker, "Population Size, Contact to Nadir," in *Handbook of North American Indians*, vol. 3, *Environment, Origins and Population*, ed. Douglas H. Ubelaker and William C. Sturtevant (Washington, DC: Smithsonian Institution Scholarly Press, 2007), 694–701; Michael H. Crawford, *The Origins of Native Americans: Evidence from Anthropological Genetics* (Cambridge: Cambridge University Press, 1998), 33–39; David Henige, *Numbers from Nowhere: The American Indian Contact Population Debate* (Norman: University of Oklahoma Press, 1998); Alchon, *Pest in the Land*; David Henige, "Recent Work and Prospects in American Indian Contact Population," *History Compass* 6, no. 1 (2008): 183–206; Jones, "Population, Health, and Public Welfare," 417.

6 Ubelaker, "Population Size, Contact to Nadir," 699.

7 J. Mausner and A. K. Bahn, *Epidemiology* (Philadelphia: W. B. Saunders, 1974), 27; Shelley R. Saunders et al., "Transformation and Disease: Precontact Ontario Iroquoians," in *Disease and Demography in the Americas*, ed. John W. Verano and Douglas H. Ubelaker (Washington, DC: Smithsonian Institution Scholarly Press, 1992), 117.

8 For these numbers and scholarly trends, and these citations, see Jones, "Population, Health, and Public Welfare," 414.

9 For these and other similar citations, see ibid., 420.

10 Alfred W. Crosby, *The Columbian Exchange: Biological and Cultural Consequences of 1492* (Westport, CT: Greenwood Press, 1972); Alfred W. Crosby, *Ecological Imperialism: The Biological Expansion of Europe, 900–1900* (Cambridge and New York: Cambridge University Press, 1986), 194.

11 Colin Fisher, "Race and US Environmental History," in *A Companion to American Environmental History*, ed. Douglas Cazaux Sackman (Oxford: Blackwell Press, 2014), 100.

12 Steve J. Stern, *Peru's Indian Peoples and the Challenge of Spanish Conquest: Huamanga to 1640*, 2nd ed. (Madison: University of Wisconsin Press, 1993); Jones, "Population, Health, and Public Welfare," 415. For the traditional interpretation of disease laying the way for later Spanish colonization in Peru, see Crosby, *The Columbian Exchange*, 51–52; Jared Diamond, *Guns, Germs, and Steel: The Fates of Human Societies* (New York: W. W. Norton, 1997), 77; Charles C. Mann, *1491: New Revelations of the Americas Before Columbus* (New York: Alfred A. Knopf, 2005), 74–93.

13 Linda A. Newson, "Indian Population Patterns in Colonial Spanish America," *Latin American Research Review* 20, no. 3 (1985): 41–74.

14 Noble David Cook, "Sickness, Starvation, and Death in Early Hispaniola," *Journal of Interdisciplinary History* 32, no. 3 (2002): 349–86; Massimo Livi Bacci, *Conquest: The Destruction of the American Indios*, trans. Carl Ipsen (Cambridge and Malden, MA: Polity Press, 2008); Jones, "Population, Health, and Public Welfare," 418–19.

15 Jones, "Population, Health, and Public Welfare," 410–17.

16 On the early de Soto and Coronado movements into the Southeast and Southwest from 1539, see Charles Hudson, *Knights of Spain, Warriors of the Sun: Hernando de Soto and the South's Ancient Chiefdoms* (Athens: University of Georgia Press, 1997); Richard Flint, *No Settlement, No Conquest: A History of the Coronado Entrada* (Albuquerque: University of New Mexico Press, 2008). On the difficulty of reading the de Soto narratives as accurate historical evidence, including to understand disease origins, see Patricia Galloway, "The Incestuous Soto Narratives," in *The Hernando De Soto Expedition: History, Historiography, and "Discovery" in the Southeast*, ed. Patricia Kay Galloway (Lincoln: University of Nebraska Press, 1997), 11–44; Paul Kelton, *Epidemics and Enslavement: Biological Catastrophe in the Native Southeast, 1492–1715* (Lincoln: University of Nebraska Press, 2007), 52–55. On the complex origins of the Cofitachequi deaths, including the role of famine and malnutrition rather than a virgin soil paradigm, see Randolph J. Widmer, "The Structure of Southeastern Chiefdoms," in *The Forgotten Centuries: Indians and Europeans in the American South, 1521–1704*, ed. Charles M. Hudson and Carmen Chaves Tesser (Athens: University of Georgia Press, 1994), 137–38; Chester DePratter, "The Chiefdom of Cofitachequi," in ibid, 215–16.

17 For evidence of these associations, see Cabeza de Vaca, "Relation," and "Account by a Gentleman from Alvas," cited in Kelton, *Epidemics and Enslavement*, 55–56 and 59.

18 Elinore M. Barrett, *Conquest and Catastrophe: Changing Rio Grande Pueblo Settlement Patterns in the Sixteenth and Seventeenth Centuries* (Albuquerque: University of New Mexico Press, 2002). Disease, as Jones has reminded us, "did not always follow closely on the heels of exploration, let alone precede it" in these regions during the second half of the sixteenth century. See Jones, "Population, Health, and Public Welfare," 415.

19 Kelton, *Epidemics and Enslavement*, xix.

20 See Noble David Cook, *Born to Die: Disease and New World Conquest*, 1492–1650 (Cambridge: Cambridge University Press, 1998), 5. For a critique of this notion, see David S. Jones, *Rationalizing Epidemics: Meanings and Uses of American Indian Mortality Since 1600* (Cambridge, MA: Harvard University Press, 2004), 21–28; Jones, "Population, Health, and Public Welfare," 414.

21 On the early stages of European disease from the north, west and east, see Ann E. Ramenofsky, *Vectors of Death: The Archaeology of European Contact* (Albuquerque: University of New Mexico Press, 1987); Alchon, *Pest in the Land*, 109–46; Karen Ordahl Kupperman, *Indians and English: Facing Off in Early America* (Ithaca, NY: Cornell University Press, 2000).

22 Kelton, *Epidemics and Enslavement*, 30–31. On the demographic disaster of early Chesapeake settlement, at more than 50 percent death rate, see Edmund Morgan, *American Slavery, American Freedom: The Ordeal of Colonial Virginia* (New York: W. W. Norton, 1975), 101–7.

23 Jones, "Virgin Soils Revisited," 735; Ales Hrdlirka, *Tuberculosis among Certain Indian Tribes of the United States* (Washington, DC: Bureau of American Ethnology Bulletins, 1909), 31.

24 Jones, "Virgin Soils Revisited," 730; Gerald Schiffman Black and Pandey P. Janardan, "HLA, Gm, and Km Polymorphisms and Immunity to Infectious Diseases in South Amerinds," *Experimental and Clinical Immunogenetics* 12 (1995): 206–16.

25 Douglas H. Ubelaker, "North American Indian Population Size: Changing Perspectives," in *Disease and Demography in the Americas*, 173.

26 For these figures, see Matthew C. Snipp, "American Indians and Alaska Natives," in *Historical Statistics of the United States, Earliest Times to the Present: Millennial Edition*, ed.

Susan B. Carter et al. (New York: Cambridge University Press, 2006), 715–77; Henry A. Gemery, "The White Population of the Colonial United States, 1607–1790," in *A Population History of North America*, ed. Michael R. Hainesand Richard H. Steckel (Cambridge: Cambridge University Press, 2000), 143–90.

27 Jones, "Population, Health, and Public Welfare," 418–19. As Alchon has argued, "it was the disruption of day-to-day activities so crucial to the survival of any society that seriously undermined the demographic resilience of Native American populations." See Alchon, *Pest in the Land*, 144.

28 Jones, "Population, Health, and Public Welfare," 421; Newson, "Indian Population Patterns in Colonial Spanish America," 41–74; Stephen J. Kunitz, *Disease and Social Diversity: The European Impact on the Health of Non-Europeans* (New York: Oxford University Press, 1994).

29 Kelton, *Epidemics and Enslavement*, xvii–xviii and 3.

30 Crosby, "Virgin Soil Epidemics," 296. Jones discusses the ambiguity in Crosby's discussion of causality in this "vivid" passage. See Jones, "Population, Health, and Public Welfare," 423. See also Paul Kelton, "Avoiding the Smallpox Spirits: Colonial Epidemics and Southeastern Indian Survival," *Ethnohistory* 51, no. 1 (2004): 45–71.

31 Clark Spencer Larsen, "In the Wake of Columbus: Native Population Biology in the Postcontact Americas," *Yearbook of Physical Anthropology* 37 (1994): 110. See also the excellent contributions in C. S. Larsen, ed., *Bioarchaeology of La Florida: The Impact of Colonialism* (Gainesville: University of Florida Press, 1997).

32 Cary W. Meister, "Demographic Consequences of Euro-American Contact on Selected American Indian Populations and Their Relationship to the Demographic Transition," *Ethnohistory* 23 (1976): 165.

33 Anderson, *Creatures of Empire*, 6–7

34 S. K. Kunitz and R. C. Euler, *Aspects of Southwestern Paleoepidemiology* (Prescott, AZ: Prescott College Press, 1972), 39.

35 R. Thornton, *American Indian Holocaust and Survival: A Population History since 1492* (Norman: University of Oklahoma Press, 1987), 51–53.

36 For a description of the immune response of immune cells in the gut, see David W. K. Acheson and Stefano Luccioli, "Mucosal Immune Responses," *Best Practice & Research Clinical Gastroenterology* 18, no. 2 (2004): 387–89.

37 Nevin S. Scrimshaw, Preface to *Nutrition Immunity Infection*, by Prakash Shetty (Wallingford, Oxfordshire, UK: CABI, 2010), xi.

38 Scrimshaw, Preface, ix; N. S. Scrimshaw et al., "Interactions of Nutrition and Infection," *American Journal of the Medical Sciences* 237 (1959): 367–403.

39 Scrimshaw, "Preface," xi.

40 R. K. Chandra, "Symposium on 'Nutrition, Infection and Immunity': Nutrition and Immunology: From the Clinic to Cellular Biology and Back Again," *Proceedings of the Nutrition Society* 58 (1999): 681–83.

41 A. Marcos et al., "Changes in the Immune System Are Conditioned by Nutrition," *European Journal of Clinical Nutrition* 57 (2003) (suppl. 1): S66–S69; P. Bhaskaram, "Micronutrient Malnutrition, Infection, and Immunity: An Overview," *Nutrition Reviews* 60, no. suppl. 5 (2002): S40–S45.

42 R. K. Chandra, "Symposium on 'Nutrition, Infection and Immunity,'" 681–83.

43 Ibid.; R. K. Chandra, "Nutrition and the Immune System: An Introduction," *American Journal of Clinical Nutrition* 66 (1997): S460–S463. Protein energy malnutrition refers to deficiency in protein, or a deficiency of calories from all sources, and usually involves

both. See Ranjit Kumar Chandra, "Protein-Energy Malnutrition and Immunological Responses," *Journal of Nutrition* 122 (1992): 597–600; R. K Chandra, "Nutrition and the Immune System from Birth to Old Age," *European Journal of Clinical Nutrition* 56 (2002) (suppl. 3): S73–S76.

44 J. C. Riley, "Smallpox and American Indians Revisited," *Journal of the History of Medicine and Allied Sciences* 65, no. 4 (2010): 445–46.

45 Ibid.

46 Riley, "Smallpox and American Indians Revisited"; F. Fenner et al., *Smallpox and Its Eradication* (Geneva: World Health Organization, 1988), 176 and 196.

47 Riley, "Smallpox and American Indians Revisited," 463; K. Saha et al., "Undernutrition and Immunity: Smallpox Vaccination in Chronically Starved, Undernourished Subjects and Its Immunologic Evaluation," *Scandinavian Journal of Immunology* 6, nos. 6–7 (1977): 581–89.

48 Riley, "Smallpox and American Indians Revisited," 464; Phillip L. Walker and Russell Thornton, "Health, Nutrition, and Demographic Change in Native California," in *The Backbone of History: Health and Nutrition in the Western Hemisphere*, ed. Richard H. Steckel and Jerome C. Rose (Cambridge: Cambridge University Press, 2002), 506–23, esp. 511–19.

49 Riley, "Smallpox and American Indians Revisited," 464.

50 Ibid., 466.

51 Ramenofsky has suggested that Native American immunological health reduced during the protohistoric era, as nutrition was disrupted. See Ann F. Ramenofsky, "Loss of Innocence: Explanations of Differential Persistence in the Sixteenth-Century Southeast," in *Columbian Consequences*, vol. 2, *Archaeological and Historical Perspectives on the Spanish Borderlands East*, ed. David Hurst Thomas (Washington, DC: Smithsonian Institution Scholarly Press, 1990), 31–48.

52 Elizabeth J. Reitz, "Evidence for Animal Use at the Missions of Spanish Florida," *Florida Anthropologist* 44, no. 2–4 (1991): 295–306.

53 For a most recent and cutting-edge account of these contingencies and ambiguities in the protohistoric Southeast, when indigenous populations were able to adapt to maintain nutritional diversity even while they suffered new constraints, see Heather A. Lapham, "Fauna, Subsistence, and Survival at Fort San Juan," in *Fort San Juan and the Limits of Empire: Colonialism and Household Practice at the Berry Site*, ed. Robin A. Beck, David G. Moore and Christopher B. Rodning (Gainesville: University Press of Florida, 2016), 271–300; Gail Fritz, "The Politics of Provisioning: Food and Gender at Fort San Juan de Juora, 1566–1568," *American Antiquity* 81, no. 1: 3–26; Gail Fritz, "People, Plants, and Early Frontier Food," in *Fort San Juan and the Limits of Empire*, 237–71.

54 For a summary of these Florida missions and their impact on health and demography, see Clark Spencer Larsen et al., "Population Decline and Extinction in La Florida," in *Disease and Demography in the Americas*, 25.

55 Rebecca Saunders, "The Guale Indians of the Lower Atlantic Coast: Historical Archaeology and Ethnohistory," in *Indians of the Greater Southeast During the Historic Period*, ed. Bonnie G. McEwan (Gainesville: University Press of Florida, 2000), 26–56; Rebecca Saunders, "Seasonality, Sedentism, Subsistence, and Disease in the Protohistoric: Archaeological Versus Ethnohistoric Data along the Lower Atlantic Coast," in *Between Contacts and Colonies: Archaeological Perspectives on the Protohistoric Southeast*, ed. Cameron B. Wesson and Mark A. Rees (Tuscaloosa: University of Alabama Press, 2002), 32–48.

56 On the mid-seventeenth-century expansion of Spanish colonialism in the Southeast, including Florida, often through Catholic missions, see Jerald T. Milanich, "Franciscan Missions and Native Peoples in Spanish Florida," in Hudson and Tesser, *Forgotten Centuries*, 276–303; Kelton, *Epidemics and Enslavement*, 99.

57 On the various factors that reduced interaction between chiefdoms and thus the spread of diseases, see James B. Griffin, "Comments on the Late Prehistoric Societies in the Southeast," in *Towns and Temples along the Mississippi*, ed. D. Dye and C. A. Cox (Tuscaloosa: University of Alabama Press, 1990), 10–11; Kelton, *Epidemics and Enslavement*, 40–41.

58 Clark Spencer Larsen et al., "Population Decline and Extinction in La Florida," in *Disease and Demography in the Americas*, 30; Margaret J. Schoeninger et al., "Decrease in Diet Quality between the Prehistoric and Contact Periods," in *The Archaeology of Mission Santa Catalina de Guale*, vol. 2, *Biocultural Interpretations of a Population in Transition*, ed. Clark Spencer Larsen (Anthropological Papers of the American Museum of Natural History 68, 1990), 66–67.

59 Clark Spencer Larsen, *Bioarchaeology: Interpreting Behavior from the Human Skeleton* (New York: Cambridge University Press, 1997), 38. See also *Bioarchaeology of Spanish Florida: The Impact of Colonialism*, ed. Clark Spencer Larsen (Gainesville: University Press of Florida, 2001).

60 As Kelton has summarized, "Native diets in Florida missions during the seventeenth century" became "less diverse, less nutritious, and less abundant. Indigenous converts relied more on the primary staple of maize as they became increasingly sedentary, while the newly introduced foodstuffs failed to compensate for the loss of wild game, fish, vegetables, and fruits." See Kelton, *Epidemics and Enslavement*, 86.

61 Robert C. Galgano, *Feast of Souls: Indians and Spaniards in the Seventeenth-Century Missions of Florida and New Mexico* (Albuquerque: University of New Mexico Press, 2005), 61–87; Robbie Ethridge, "European Invasions and Early Settlement, 1500–1680," in *The Oxford Handbook of American Indian History*, 44.

62 Christopher Stojanowski, *Biocultural Histories in La Florida: A Bioarchaeological Perspective* (Tuscaloosa: University of Alabama Press, 2005), 149.

63 See the discussion of iron and immunity in Chapters 1 and 2.

64 Marianne Reeves, "Dental Health at Early Historic Fusihatchee Town: Biocultural Implications of Contact in Alabama," in *Bioarchaeological Studies of Life in the Age of Agriculture: A View from the Southeast*, ed. Patricia M. Lambert, (Tuscaloosa: University of Alabama Press, 2000), 78–95; C. S. Larsen, "Inferring Iron-Deficiency Anemia from Human Skeletal Remains: The Case of the Georgia Bight," in ibid., 116–33.

65 B. J. Cherayil, "The Role of Iron in the Immune Response to Bacterial Infection," *Immunologic Research* 50, no. 1 (2011): 1–9; A. M. Koorts et al., "Pro- and Anti-Inflammatory Cytokines during Immune Stimulation: Modulation of Iron Status and Red Blood Cell Profile," *Mediators of Inflammation* 2011, Article ID 716301, 11 pages, (2011).

66 Shetty, *Nutrition Immunity Infection*, 40–53.

67 Various other aspects of immune function are clearly altered: the secretion of immunoglobulins such as IgA is often decreased, resulting in a reduced humoral response. Cell-mediated immunity is decreased, as measured by the delayed cutaneous hypersensitivity test. Secretion of complement components is often reduced, suggesting an impairment in complement function. Complement refers to a system

that recognizes antibodies on pathogens, activates other immune cells and causes an inflammatory response. See Shetty, *Nutrition Immunity Infection*, 5–6 and 13–16.

68   Ibid., 40–53.

69   One important study has investigated the effects of a low-protein diet on *M.tuberculosis* in mice. When protein was restricted to 2 percent of calories, immunity was severely impaired and mice died rapidly of infection. Several immune responses were decreased in the lung tissue: expression of the cytokines interferon gamma and tumour necrosis factor alpha were reduced; expression of nitric oxide synthase was reduced; and the formation of granulomas (aggregations of immune cells) was reduced. See J. Chan et al., "Effects of Protein Calorie Malnutrition on Tuberculosis in Mice," *Proceedings of the National Academy of Sciences of the United States of America* 93 (1996): 14857–61.

70   M. Layrisse et al., "Effects of Histidine, Systeine, Glutathione Or Beef on Iron Absorption in Humans," *Journal of Nutrition* 114 (1984): 217.

71   On ascorbic acid and cysteine aiding iron absorption, see L. Hultén et al., "Iron Absorption from the Whole Diet: Relation to Meal Composition, Iron Requirements and Iron Stores," *European Journal of Clinical Nutrition* 49, no.11 (1995): 794–808; C. Martínez-Torres et al., "Effect of Cysteine on Iron Absorption in Man," *American Journal of Clinical Nutrition* 34, no. 3 (1981): 322–27; M. Gillooly et al., "The Effects of Organic Acids, Phytates and Polyphenols on the Absorption of Iron from Vegetables," *British Journal of Nutrition* 49, no. 3 (1983): 331–42; Shetty, *Nutrition Immunity Infection*, 75

72   Shetty, *Nutrition Immunity Infection*, 90; Peter Katona and Judit Katona-Apte, "The Interaction between Nutrition and Infection," *Clinical Infectious Diseases* 46, no. 10 (2008): 1584.

73   Iron is involved in respiration and DNA replication. It is required for cell differentiation (conversion of a cell from a progenitor cell into a specific cell type) in many cells. See James E. Cassat and Eric P. Skaar, "Iron in Infection and Immunity," *Cell Host and Microbe* 13, no. 5 (2013): 509–19.

74   G. S. Tansarli et al., "Iron Deficiency and Susceptibility to Infections: Evaluation of Clinical Evidence," *European Journal of Clinical Microbiology and Infectious Diseases* 32 (2013): 1253–58; Bhaskaram, "Micronutrient Malnutrition, Infection, and Immunity," S43; K. B. Prema et al., "Immune Status of Anaemic Pregnant Women," *BJOG: An International Journal of Obstetrics and Gynaecology* 89, no. 3 (1982): 222–25.

75   Bhaskaram, "Micronutrient Malnutrition, Infection, and Immunity," S43; P. J. Bhaskaram et al., "Anæmia and Immune Response," *The Lancet* 309, no. 8019 (1977): 1000.

76   B. A. Kochanowski and A. R. Sherman, "Decreased Antibody Formation in Iron-Deficient Rat Pups-Effect of Iron Repletion," *American Journal of Clinical Nutrition* 41, no. 2 (1985): 278–84.

77   The white blood cell activity relates to myeloperoxidase activity in neutrophils. Myeloperoxidase is essential for neutrophils' bactericidal activity. See Bhaskaram, "Micronutrient Malnutrition, Infection, and Immunity," S43; J. S. Prasad, "Leucocyte Function in Iron-Deficiency Anemia." *American Journal of Clinical Nutrition* 32, no. 3 (1979): 550–52; Bhaskaram et al., "Anæmia and Immune Response," 1000; Stephen J. Oppenheimer, "Iron and Its Relation to Immunity and Infectious Disease." *American Society for Nutritional Sciences* 131, no. 2 (2001): S616-35.

78   Larsen, *Bioarchaeology: Interpreting Behavior*, 38. Iron, as we have seen, is released by neutrophils in the form of lactoferrin, and zinc is used in the metal-binding protein

metallothionein, an acute-phase protein. Iron and zinc are both consumed by phagocytes and other immune cells. See Shetty, *Nutrition Immunity Infection*, 57–64. Infection decreases vitamin A status, so an original deficiency may be exacerbated. Measles has been shown to decrease vitamin A levels so severely that some individuals suffer blindness, and a skin condition called karatomalacia, as a result. See Katona and Katona-Apte, "The Interaction between Nutrition and Infection," 1582–88; Bhaskaram, "Micronutrient Malnutrition, Infection, and Immunity," S40–S45.

79 Begoña Ruiz-Núñez et al., "Lifestyle and Nutritional Imbalances Associated with Western Diseases: Causes and Consequences of Chronic Systemic Low-Grade Inflammation in an Evolutionary Context," *Journal of Nutritional Biochemistry* 24, no. 7 (2013): 1183–201.

80 Larsen, *Bioarchaeology: Interpreting Behavior*, 38.

81 A. Z. Lalia and I. R. Lanza, "Insulin-Sensitizing Effects of Omega-3 Fatty Acids: Lost in Translation?" *Nutrients* 8, no. 6 (2016): 329; Frédéric Capel et al., "DHA at Nutritional Doses Restores Insulin Sensitivity in Skeletal Muscle by Preventing Lipotoxicity and Inflammation," *Journal of Nutritional Biochemistry* 26, no. 9 (2015): 949–59.

82 Marianne Reeves, "Dental Health at Early Historic Fusihatchee Town, 78–95; Larsen, "Inferring Iron-Deficiency Anemia," 116–33.

83 Larsen, *Bioarchaeology: Interpreting Behavior*, 38; Bonnie G. McEwan, ed., *The Spanish Missions of "La Florida"* (Gainesville: University Press of Florida, 1993); Jerald T. Milanich, *Laboring in the Fields of the Lord: Spanish Mission and Southeastern Indians* (Washington, DC: Smithsonian Institution Scholarly Press, 1999); David Hurst Thomas, "The Spanish Mission of La Florida: An Overview," in *Columbian Consequences*, vol. 2, *Archaeological and Historical Perspectives on the Spanish Borderlands East*, ed. David Hurst Thomas (Washington, DC: Smithsonian Institution Scholarly Press, 1990), 357–97; Brent R. Weisman, *Excavations on the Franciscan Frontier: Archaeology of the Fig Springs Mission* (Gainesville: University Press of Florida, 1992).

84 Robert C. Galgano, *Feast of Souls*, 61–87; Robbie Ethridge, "European Invasions and Early Settlement," 44.

85 Elizabeth J. Reitz, "Evidence for Animal Use at the Missions of Spanish Florida," 295–306; Heather A. Lapham, "Animals in Southeastern Native American Subsistence Economies," in *The Subsistence Economies of Indigenous North American Societies: A Handbook*, ed. Bruce D. Smith (Washington, DC: Smithsonian Institution Scholarly Press, 2011), 417–19.

86 See the account in Arthur S. Aiton and James Alexander Robertson, "True Relation of the Hardships Suffered by Governor Fernando De Soto & Certain Portuguese Gentlemen During the Discovery of the Province of Florida. Now Nearly Set Forth by a Gentleman of Elvas," *Mississippi Valley Historical Review* 20, no. 4 (1934): 556; Robbie Ethridge, *From Chicaza to Chickasaw: The European Invasion and the Transformation of the Mississippian World, 1540–1715* (Chapel Hill: University of North Carolina Press, 2010), 1–59.

87 Kelton, *Epidemics and Enslavement*, 40–41.

88 Other shatter zones have also been identified: among the Navajos, Pueblos and Apache in the Southwest; among the Ojibwes, Miamis and Shawnees in the eastern Great Lakes region; and south of Iroquois territory up to the mid-Atlantic coast. See Ethridge, *From Chicaza to Chickasaw*; Ethridge, "European Invasions and Early Settlement"; Robbie Ethridge, "Creating the Shatter Zone: Indian Slave Traders and the Collapse of the Southeastern Chiefdoms," in *Light on the Path: The Anthropology*

and History of the Southeastern Indians, ed. Thomas J. Pluckhahn and Robbie Ethridge (Tuscaloosa, 2006), 207–18; Robbie Ethridge and Sherie M. Shuck-Hall, eds., *Mapping the Mississippian Shatter Zone: The Colonial Indian Slave Trade and Regional Instability in the American South* (Lincoln: University of Nebraska Press, 2009), 1–62; Patricia Galloway, "Confederacy as a Solution to Chiefdom Dissolution: Historical Evidence in the Choctaw Case," in *The Forgotten Centuries*, 393–420.

89 Kelton, *Epidemics and Enslavement*, 99–100; David J. Silverman, *Thundersticks: Firearms and the Violent Transformation of Native America* (Cambridge, MA: Harvard University Press, 2016), chaps. 1–2.

90 Helen C. Rountree, *The Powhatan Indians of Virginia: Their Traditional Culture* (Norman: University of Oklahoma Press, 1989), 149–50; Stephen R. Potter, *Commoners, Tribute, and Chiefs: The Development of Algonquian Culture in the Potomac Valley* (Charlottesville: University Press of Virginia, 1993), 151–52; Ethridge, "European Invasions and Early Settlement," 42.

91 Kelton, *Epidemics and Enslavement*, 111–12.

92 According to Kelton, English, African and Native American peoples in the Southeast became "linked into what would be a continual chain of infection that stretched from the James River to the Gulf Coast and from the Atlantic Ocean to the Mississippi Valley." Kelton, *Epidemics and Enslavement*, 159. See also Paul Kelton, "The Great Southeastern Smallpox Epidemic: The Region's First Major Epidemic?" in *Transformations of the Southeastern Indians*, 21–37.

93 Kelton, *Epidemics and Enslavement*; Jones, "Virgin Soils Revisited," 703–42; Ethridge and Such-Hall, eds., *Mapping the Mississippian Shatter Zone*, 95–98; Charles Hudson and Carmen Chaves Tesser, eds., *The Forgotten Centuries: Indians and Europeans in the American South, 1521–1704* (Athens: University of Georgia Press, 1994), Christina Snyder, *Slavery in Indian Country: The Changing Face of Captivity in Early America* (Cambridge, MA: Harvard University Press, 2010), chaps. 1–2; Alan Gallay, *The Indian Slave Trade: The Rise of English Empire in the American South, 1670–1717* (New Haven, CT: Yale University Press, 2002), 293–300.

94 Kelton, *Epidemics and Enslavement*, xix, xx and 125. See also Robin Beck, *Chiefdoms, Collapse, and Coalescence in the Early American South* (Cambridge: Cambridge University Press, 2013), which tends to be more positive about the role of maize before these events.

95 Kelton, *Epidemics and Enslavement*, 13; A. H. Goodman and G. J. Armelagos, "Disease and Death at Dr. Dickson's Mounds," *Natural History* 94 (1985): 12–18.

96 See Richard A. Gabriel, *The Culture of War: Invention and Early Development* (New York: Greenwood Press, 1990), 33.

97 Potter, *Commoners, Tribute, and Chiefs*, 180–90.

98 Theda Perdue, *Cherokee Women: Gender and Culture Change, 1700–1835* (Lincoln: University of Nebraska Press, 1998), 67–70; Potter, *Commoners, Tribute, and Chiefs*, 180–90; Ethridge, "European Invasions and Early Settlement," 52.
   Perdue, *Cherokee Women*, 67–70.

99 On communities congregating together as a means of defense against slave raiders, yet also inadvertently as a means of spreading incoming smallpox, see James H. Merrell, *The Indians' New World: Catawbas and Their Neighbors from European Contact through the Era of Removal* (Chapel Hill: University of North Carolina Press, 1989), 22–23; Kelton, *Epidemics and Enslavement*, 144–45. Poor sanitation followed the changed association between human settlement and food subsistence, weakening communal health. See Kelton, *Epidemics and Enslavement*, 159.

100 Kelton, *Epidemics and Enslavement*, xx.

101 Ibid.; Jones, "Virgin Soils Revisited," 703–42; Snyder, *Slavery in Indian Country*, chaps. 1–2.

102 On the use of guns due to the need for greater efficiency in providing food, see R. White, *The Roots of Dependency: Subsistence, Environment, and Social Change among the Choctaws, Pawnees, and Navajos* (Lincoln: Nebraska, 1983), 58–59.

103 Kelton, *Epidemics and Enslavement*, xviii.

104 For a classic account of the importance of zinc and magnesium from nutritional sources on fetal health and overall fertility, see A. Wynn, "Effects of Nutrition on Reproductive Capability," *Nutrition and Health* 1 (1983): 165–78. On vitamin A and immunity, see R. D. Semba, "Vitamin A, Immunity, and Infection," *Clinical Infectious Diseases* 19, no. 3 (September 1994): 489–99.

105 R. S. Hiltner and H. J. Wichmann, "Zinc in Oysters," *Journal of Biological Chemistry* 38 (1919): 205.

106 Prakash Shetty, *Nutrition Immunity Infection* (Wallingford, Oxfordshire, UK: CABI, 2010), 102–3.

107 Zinc is required for the activity of over 300 enzymes involved in gene expression, metabolism, protein synthesis, DNA and RNA synthesis and replication, and heme biosynthesis. It acts as a cofactor for several enzymes involved in DNA synthesis and DNA replication, such as DNA and RNA polymerase and alkaline phosphatase, and is required for cell division and differentiation. All are associated with the development of immune cells. See Katona and Katona-Apte, "The Interaction between Nutrition and Infection," 1584; H. H. Sandstead and R. A. Rinaldi, "Impairment of Deoxyribonucleic Acid Synthesis by Dietary Zinc Deficiency in the Rat," *Journal of Cellular Physiology* 73 (1969): 81–83; Shetty, *Nutrition Immunity Infection*, 101–3.

108 Zinc deficiency has been shown to be associated with decreased number of immune cells, reduced function of neutrophils and natural killer cells, and compromised cytotoxic activity and antibody production. See Shetty, *Nutrition Immunity Infection*, 104–6; P. Bonaventura, "Zinc and Its Role in Immunity and Inflammation," *Autoimmunity Reviews* 14, no. 4 (April 2015): 277–85; A. H. Shankar, "Zinc and Immune Function: The Biological Basis of Altered Resistance to Infection," *American Journal of Clinical Nutrition* 68, no. 2 suppl. (August 1998): 447S–463S; H. Haase and L. Rink, "Functional Significance of Zinc-Related Signaling Pathways in Immune Cells," *Annual Review of Nutrition* 29 (2009): 133–52; P. J. Fraker et al., "The Dynamic Link between the Integrity of the Immune System and Zinc Status," *Journal of Nutrition* 130, 5S suppl. (May 2000): 1399S–406S; A. R. Sherman, "Zinc, Copper, and Iron Nutriture and Immunity," *Journal of Nutrition* 122, no. 3 suppl. (March 1992): 604–9.

109 S. C. Liberato et al., "Zinc Supplementation in Young Children: A Review of the Literature Focusing on Diarrhoea Prevention and Treatment," *Clinical Nutrition* 34, no. 2 (2015): 181–88; A. S. Prasad, "Zinc Deficiency in Sickle Cell Disease," *Progress in Clinical and Biological Research* 165 (1984): 49–58. Zinc supplementation has also been found to improve the cell-mediated immune response in children using the multitest cell-mediated immune skin test. See S. Sazawal et al., "Effects of Zinc Supplementation on Cell-Mediated Immunity and Lymphocyte Subsets in Preschool Children," *Indian Paediatrics* 34 (1997): 589–97.

110 Shetty, *Nutrition Immunity Infection*, 101–3; R. Bahl et al., "Plasma Zinc as a Predictor of Diarrhoeal and Respiratory Morbidity in Children in an Urban

Slum Setting," *American Journal of Clinical Nutrition* 68 (suppl. 2) (1998): 414S–7S; Bhaskaram, "Micronutrient Malnutrition, Infection, and Immunity," S43; R. Bahl et al., "Increased Diarrhoeal and Respiratory Morbidity in Association with Zinc Deficiency—A Preliminary Report," *Acta Paediatrica* 85 (1996): 148–50.

111   Katona and Katona-Apte, "The Interaction between Nutrition and Infection," 1584.

112   Indeed, during the pre-antibiotic era, vitamin A was used in the treatment of many infectious diseases. Milk, butter and cheese consumption was recommended to reduce childhood infection, due to their incorporation of the vitamin. See N. Scrimshaw et al., *Interactions of Nutrition and Infection* (Geneva, Switzerland: World Health Organization, Monograph series no. 37, 1968), 64; C. E. Bloch, "Blindness and Other Diseases in Children Arising in Consequence of Deficient Nutrition (Lack of Fat Soluble a Factor)," *Journal of Dairy Science* 7, no. 1 (1924):1–9. Vitamin A was thus labeled as an anti-infective vitamin in 1928. Subsequently, its deficiency has been linked with increased morbidity and mortality from infectious disease. See Bhaskaram, "Micronutrient Malnutrition, Infection, and Immunity," S40–S42.

113   Shetty, *Nutrition Immunity Infection*, 78.

114   The reason for mucus reduction is twofold. Vitamin A is required for correct cell differentiation of the epithelial cells, and lack of vitamin A causes the mucus-secreting cells to be replaced by keratin-producing cells. Vitamin A is required directly for the synthesis of the mucopolysaccharides, glycoproteins and glycosaminoglycans that constitute the mucus. See Shetty, *Nutrition Immunity Infection*, 78.

115   R. K. Chandra, "Increased Bacterial Binding to Respiratory Epithelial Cells in Vitamin A Deficiency," *British Medical Journal* 297 (1988): 834–35.

116   Bhaskaram, "Micronutrient Malnutrition, Infection, and Immunity," S40; P. Chambon, "A Decade of Molecular Biology of Retinoic Acid Receptors," *FASEB Journal* 10, no. 9 (1996): 940–54.

117   Retinoic acid is required for differentiation of activated B lymphocytes to antibody-producing cells, leading to increased secretion of immunoglobulins (proteins involved in the recognition of pathogen-derived molecules). See Shetty, *Nutrition Immunity Infection*, 31–32.

118   Ibid., 31 and 74–76.

119   Katona and Katona-Apte, "The Interaction between Nutrition and Infection," 1583–84; Shetty, *Nutrition Immunity Infection*, 79–82; "Joint WHO/UNICEF Statement on Use of Vitamin A for Measles," *Weekly Epidemiological Record* 62 (1987):133–34; A. H. Shankar et al. *Vitamin A Supplementation As Nutrient-Based Intervention To Reduce Malaria Related Morbidity*. Report of the XVIII International Vitamin A Consultative Group Meeting. Cairo, Egypt, September 22–26, 1997. ILSI, 1998.

120   Shetty, *Nutrition Immunity Infection*, 75.

121   Tang Guangwen, "Bioconversion of Dietary Provitamin A Carotenoids to Vitamin A in Humans," *American Journal of Clinical Nutrition* 91, no. 5 (2010): 1468S–1473S.

122   In vitro studies have shown that proliferation of lymphocytes; activation of B lymphocytes and synthesis of antibodies by B lymphocytes; phagocytosis by neutrophils; and cytokine secretion are all influenced by glutamine concentration. See Shetty, *Nutrition Immunity Infection*, 29. The role of glutamine in the immune system is reviewed in P. C. Calder and P. Yaqoob, "Glutamine and the Immune System," *Amino Acids* 17, no. 3 (1999): 227–41.

123   Prakash Shetty, *Nutrition Immunity Infection* (Wallingford, Oxfordshire, UK: CABI, 2010), 29.

124 Cited in Potter, *Commoners, Tribute, and Chiefs*, 195. On this situation, see also Michael Leroy Oberg, *Dominion and Civility: English Imperialism and Native America, 1585–1685* (Ithaca, NY: Cornell University Press, 2003), 184.

125 Helen C. Rowntree, *Pocahontas's People: The Powhatan Indians of Virginia through Four Centuries* (Norman: University of Oklahoma Press, 1990), 92–94, 117–24 and 128; Potter, *Commoners, Tribute, and Chiefs*, 195; James H. Merrell, "Cultural Continuity among the Piscataway Indians of Colonial Maryland," *William and Mary Quarterly* 36 no. 4 (Oct., 1979): 548–70.

126 Perdue, *Cherokee Women*, 63–70; Christina Synder, "The South," in *The Oxford Handbook of American Indian History*, 322; Greg O'Brien, "The Conqueror Meets the Unconquered: Negotiating Cultural Boundaries on the Post-Revolutionary Southern Frontier," *Journal of Southern History* 67, no. 1 (2001): 39–72; Andrew K. Frank, *Creeks and Southerners: Biculturalism on the Early American Frontier* (Lincoln: University of Nebraska Press, 2005). Traditional "subsistence activities became hazardous as raiders lurked near the corn fields, hoping to capture women and children, the very individuals whom the English most valued as slaves." Male hunters, moreover, "were also not safe in their hunting territories and often abandoned the hunt to stay at home to protect their loved ones." See Kelton, *Epidemics and Enslavement*, 159.

127 A. N. Mudryj et al., "Nutritional and Health Benefits of Pulses," *Applied Physiology, Nutrition, and Metabolism* 39, no. 11 (November 2014): 197–204; V. Messina, "Nutritional and Health Benefits of Dried Beans," *American Journal of Clinical Nutrition* 100, suppl. 1 (July 2014): 437S–42S.

128 For an overview of the association between antioxidants and immunity/diseases, see M. A. Puertollano, "Dietary Antioxidants: Immunity and Host Defense," *Current Topics in Medicinal Chemistry* 11, no. 14 (2011): 1752–66; M. Wojcik et al., "A Review of Natural and Synthetic Antioxidants Important For Health and Longevity," *Current Medicinal Chemistry* 17, no. 28 (2010): 3262–88. On the vital status of vitamin C (often from plant sources) and immunity/long-term health, see S. Chambial et al., "Vitamin C in Disease Prevention and Cure: An Overview," *Indian Journal of Clinical Biochemistry* 28, no. 4 (October 2013): 314–28; A. Sorice et al., "Ascorbic Acid: Its Role in Immune System and Chronic Inflammation Diseases," *Mini-Reviews in Medicinal Chemistry* 14, no. 5 (May 2014): 444–52. For more on vitamin A and immunity, see C. C. Brown and R. J. Noelle, "Seeing through the Dark: New Insights into the Immune Regulatory Functions of Vitamin A," *European Journal of Immunology* 45, no. 5 (May 2015): 1287–95.

129 Puertollano, "Dietary Antioxidants: Immunity and Host Defense," 1752; Ruiz-Núñez et al., "Lifestyle and Nutritional Imbalances Associated with Western Diseases," 1193. For more on their roles in immune function, and their occurrence in fruit and vegetables, see K. A. Steinmetz and J. D. Potter, "Vegetables, Fruit, and Cancer Prevention: A Review," *Journal of the American Dietetic Association* 96, no. 10 (October 1996): 1027–39; Y. F. Chu et al., "Antioxidant and Antiproliferative Activities of Common Vegetables," *Journal of Agricultural and Food Chemistry* no. 50, no. 23 (November 2002): 6910–16; M. A. Van Duyn, "Overview of the Health Benefits of Fruit and Vegetable Consumption for the Dietetics Professional: Selected Literature," *Journal of the American Dietetic Association* 100, no. 12 (December 2000): 1511–21. For more on how a diet high in antioxidants has been shown to reduce oxidative stress and to lower inflammation levels, see Ruiz-Núñez et al., "Lifestyle and Nutritional Imbalances Associated with Western Diseases: Causes and Consequences of Chronic Systemic

Low-grade Inflammation in an Evolutionary Context," *Journal of Nutritional Biochemistry* 24, no. 7 (2013): 1193; G. Egger and J. Dixon, "Non-nutrient Causes of Low-grade, Systemic Inflammation: Support for a 'Canary in the Mineshaft' View of Obesity in Chronic Disease," *Obesity Reviews* 12, no. 5 (2010): 339–45; Jason K. Hou et al., "Dietary Intake and Risk of Developing Inflammatory Bowel Disease: A Systematic Review of the Literature," *American Journal of Gastroenterology* 106, no. 4 (2011): 563–73. On their abundance in fresh fruits, leafy plants and vegetables, see also Fred Ottoboni and Alice. Ottoboni, *The Modern Nutritional Diseases: Heart Disease, Stroke, Type-2 Diabetes, Obesity, Cancer: And How to Prevent Them* (Sparks, NV: Vincente Books, 2002). 119.

130   Puertollano, "Dietary Antioxidants: Immunity and Host Defense," 1755.

131   Dean P. Jones, "Redefining Oxidative Stress," *Antioxidants & Redox Signaling* 8, no. 9–10 (2006): 1865; A. A. Hala Abou-Zeina et al., "Effects of Dietary Antioxidants Supplementation on Cellular Immune Response and Evaluation of Their Antimicrobial Activity against Some Enteric Pathogens in Goats," *Global Veterinaria* 11, no. 2 (2013): 145; Puertollano, "Dietary Antioxidants: Immunity and Host Defense," 1752. Oxidizing molecules can cause peroxidation of lipids in the cell membrane, which decreases the fluidity of the cell membrane and adversely affects the function of immune cells. See Manuel A. De Pablo and Gerardo Alvarez De Cienfuegos, "Modulatory Effects of Dietary Lipids on Immune System Functions," *Immunology and Cell Biology* 78, no. 1 (2000): 31–39.

132   E. J. Anderson et al., "H_2O_2 Emission and Cellular Redox State Link Excess Fat Intake to Insulin Resistance in Both Rodents and Humans," *Journal of Clinical Investigation* 119, no. 3 (2009): 574–75. Ruiz-Núñez, "Lifestyle and Nutritional Imbalances Associated with Western Diseases," 1193.

133   Puertollano, "Dietary Antioxidants: Immunity and Host Defense," 1754–55.

134   Bhaskaram, "Micronutrient Malnutrition, Infection, and Immunity," S44; Melinda A. Beck et al., "Dietary Oxidative Stress and the Potentiation of Viral Infection," *Annual Review of Nutrition* 18, no. 1 (1998): 93–116.

135   Puertollano, "Dietary Antioxidants: Immunity and Host Defense," 1755–58.

136   Ibid.; B. Frei et al., "Ascorbate Is an Outstanding Antioxidant in Human Blood Plasma," *Proceedings of the National Academy of Sciences of the United States of America* 86, no. 16: 6377–81; R. Anderson and P. T. Lukey, "A Biological Role for Ascorbate in the Selective Neutralization of Extracellular Phagocyte-Derived Oxidants," *Annals of the New York Academy of Sciences* 498 (1987): 229–47.

137   M. M. Grant et al., "Dose-Dependent Modulation of the T Cell Proteome by Ascorbic Acid," *British Journal of Nutrition* 97 (2007): 19. "Neutrophils, when stimulated, take up molecular oxygen (O2) and generate reactive free radicals and singlet oxygen, which, along with other reactive molecules, can kill bacterial pathogens. This process, called the *oxidative burst* because it can be observed in vitro as a rapid consumption of O2, also involves the enzymatic generation of bactericidal halogenated molecules via myeloperoxidase. These killing processes are usually localized in intracellular vacuoles containing the phagocytized bacteria." See Gerald F. Combs Jr., *The Vitamins* 4th ed. (Amsterdam: Elsevier, 2012): 247.

138   H. Hemilä, "Vitamin C Intake and Susceptibility to the Common Cold," *British Journal of Nutrition* 77, no. 1 (January 1997): 59. Updated in *Cochrane Database of Systematic Reviews* January 31, 2013, (1): CD000980.

139   Combs Jr., *The Vitamins*, 248–50; J. A. Simon et al., "Relation of Serum Ascorbic Acid to Helicobacter Pylori Serology in US Adults: The Third National Health and

Nutrition Examination Survey," *Journal of the American College of Nutrition* 22, no. 4 (2003): 283–89.

140   Puertollano, "Dietary Antioxidants: Immunity and Host Defense," 1758; E. S. Wintergerst, "Immune-Enhancing Role of Vitamin C and Zinc and Effect on Clinical Conditions," *Annals of Nutrition and Metabolism* 50, no. 2 (2006): 85–94; B. Leibovitz and B. V. Siegel, "Ascorbic Acid and the Immune Response," *Advances in Experimental Medicine and Biology* 135 (1981): 1–25; S. J. Rayment et al., "Vitamin C Supplementation in Normal Subjects Reduces Constitutive ICAM-1 Expression," *Biochemical and Biophysical Research Communications* 308, no. 2 (2003): 339–45.

141   Puertollano, "Dietary Antioxidants: Immunity and Host Defense," 1758–59.

142   Ibid.; S. N. Meydani, "Vitamin E and Immune Response in the Aged: Molecular Mechanisms and Clinical Implications," *Immunological Reviews* 205 (2005): 269–84. In particular, the Th1 cytokine mediated response is increased in association with vitamin E.

143   Ibid., 1758; J. M. Graat et al., "Effect of Daily Vitamin E and Multivitamin-Mineral Supplementation on Acute Respiratory Tract Infections in Elderly Persons: A Randomized Controlled Trial," *JAMA* 288, no. 6 (2002): 715–21; S. N. Meydani et al., "Vitamin E and Respiratory Tract Infections in Elderly Nursing Home Residents: A Randomized Controlled Trial," *JAMA* 292, no. 7 (2004): 828–36.

144   A. A. Hala et al., "Effects of Dietary Antioxidants Supplementation, 146; S. A. Elliot, "Selenium: A Major Antioxidant Player," *Proceedings of Four-State Dairy Nutrition and Management Conference*, Dubuque, IA. http://www.dairyweb.ca/Resources/4SDNMC2006/Elliot.pdf

145   Puertollano, "Dietary Antioxidants: Immunity and Host Defense," 1759; Lidia Kiremidjian-Schumacher et al., "Supplementation with Selenium and Human Immune Cell Functions. II. Effect on Cytotoxic Lymphocytes and Natural Killer Cells," *Biological Trace Element Research* 41, no. 1–2 (1994): 115–27; M. K. Baum, "Selenium and Interleukins in Persons Infected with Human Immunodeficiency Virus Type 1," *Journal of Infectious Diseases* 182, no. S1 (2000): S69–73.

146   Puertollano, "Dietary Antioxidants: Immunity and Host Defense," 1760; Shu Yu Yu et al., "Protective Role of Selenium against Hepatitis B Virus and Primary Liver Cancer in Qidong," *Biological Trace Element Research* 56, no. 1 (1997): 117–24; M. Yu et al., "Plasma Selenium Levels and Risk of Hepatocellular Carcinoma among Men with Chronic Hepatitis Virus Infection," *American Journal of Epidemiology* 150, no. 4 (1999): 367–74. In patients suffering from HIV, low plasma selenium has been associated with a tenfold increased risk of death. See Puertollano, "Dietary Antioxidants: Immunity and Host Defense," 1760; Marianna K. Baum, "High Risk of HIV-Related Mortality Is Associated with Selenium Deficiency," *Journal of Acquired Immune Deficiency Syndromes and Human Retrovirology* 15, no. 5 (1997): 370–74.

147   One mechanism by which zinc exerts antioxidant effects is the regulation of expression of metallothionein-like proteins with antioxidant activity. See A. A. Hala et al., "Effects of Dietary Antioxidants Supplementation," 149; Ananda S. Prasad, "Zinc: Role in Immunity, Oxidative Stress and Chronic Inflammation," *Current Opinion in Clinical Nutrition and Metabolic Care* 12, no. 6 (2009): 646–52; A. H. Shankar and A. S. Prasad, "Zinc and Immune Function: The Biological Basis of Altered Resistance to Infection," *American Journal of Clinical Nutrition* 68 (1998) (suppl.): 447S–463S. The antioxidant activity of zinc is crucial for the activity of superoxide

dismutase enzymes and for T cell proliferation, maturation and differentiation. See Puertollano, "Dietary Antioxidants: Immunity and Host Defense," 1760.

148 Puertollano, "Dietary Antioxidants: Immunity and Host Defense," 1759.

149 Ibid.; M. S. Santos et al., "Natural Killer Cell Activity In Elderly Men Is Enhanced by Beta-Carotene Supplementation," *American Journal of Clinical Nutrition* 64, no. 5 (1996): 772–77. Studies in patients with HIV suggest that low serum concentrations of Beta-carotene and vitamin A decrease CD4+ lymphocyte counts and increase mortality, and that dietary supplementation with beta-carotene reduces the risk of AIDS development and death. See Ajani Nimmagadda et al., "The Significance of Vitamin A and Carotenoid Status in Persons Infected by the Human Immunodeficiency Virus Type 1 Infection," *Clinical Infectious Diseases* 26 (1998): 711–18; A. M. Tang et al., "Effects of Micronutrient Intake on Survival in Human Immunodeficiency Virus Type 1 Infection,: *American Journal of Epidemiology* 143, no. 12 (1996): 1244–56.

150 Puertollano, "Dietary Antioxidants: Immunity and Host Defense," 1759; S. S. Percival, "Neutropenia Caused by Copper Deficiency: Possible Mechanisms of Action," *Nutrition Reviews* 53 (1995): 59–66.

151 C. Castillo-Durán et al., "Controlled Trial of Copper Supplementation during the Recovery from Marasmus," *American Journal of Clinical Nutrition* 37, no. 6 (1983): 898–903.

152 M. Mutlu, "Magnesium, Zinc and Copper Status in Osteoporotic, Osteopenic and Normal Post-Menopausal Women," *Journal of International Medical Research* 35 (5 (September–October 2007): 692–95: M. J. Laires et al., "Role of Cellular Magnesium in Health and Human Disease," *Frontiers in Bioscience* 9 (January 2004): 262–76.

153 Laires et al., "Role of Cellular Magnesium in Health and Human Disease"; R. K. Rude and M. E. Shils, "Magnesium," in *Modern Nutrition in Health and Disease*, ed. M. E. Shills et al. (New York: Lippincott Williams & Wilkins, 2006), 223–47; C. Masterjohn, "Nutritional Adjuncts to the Fat-Soluble Vitamins," *Wise Traditions* (winter 2012). https://www.westonaprice.org/health-topics/abcs-of-nutrition/nutritional-adjuncts-to-the-fat-soluble-vitamins/.

154 Laires et al., "Role of Cellular Magnesium in Health and Human Disease," 262–76.

155 See also H. McCoy and M. A. Kenney, "Magnesium and Immune Function: Recent Findings," *Magnesium Research* 5, no. 4 (December 1992): 281–93; H. McCoy, "Interactions between Magnesium and Vitamin D: Possible Implications in the Immune System," *Magnesium Research* 9, no. 3 (October 1996): 185–203; Carl L. Keen et al., "The Plausibility of Micronutrient Deficiencies Being a Significant Contributing Factor to the Occurrence of Pregnancy Complications," *Journal of Nutrition* 133, no. 5 (May 2003): 1597S–1605S.

156 M. Mutlu, "Magnesium, Zinc and Copper Status in Osteoporotic, Osteopenic and Normal Post-Menopausal Women," *Journal of International Medical Research* 35, no. 5 (September–October 2007): 692–905; Laires et al., "Role of Cellular Magnesium in Health and Human Disease," 262–76.

157 R. M. Neer, "The Evolutionary Significance of Vitamin D, Skin Pigment, and Ultraviolet Light," *American Journal of Physical Anthropology* 43, no. 3 (November 1975): 409–16.

158 Patricia K. Galloway, *Choctaw Genesis: 1500–1700* (Lincoln: University of Nebraska Press, 1995), 183–99.

159 Kelton, *Epidemics and Enslavement*, 156.

160 For a summary of the expansion of white American settlers and the eventual decline of Native American population numbers in the half century after the Seven Years War and the American Revolution, see Claudio Saunt, "The Age of Imperial Expansion, 1763–1821," in *The Oxford Handbook of American Indian History*, 83; Ubelaker, "North American Indian Population Size," 173; Colin G. Galloway, *The Scratch of a Pen: 1763 and the Transformation of the North America* (New York: Oxford University Press, 2006); Colin G. Galloway, *The American Revolution in Indian Country: Crisis and Diversity in Native American Communities* (New York: Cambridge University Press, 1995); Alan Taylor, *The Divided Ground: Indians, Settlers, and the Northern Borderland of the American Revolution* (New York: Alfred A. Knopf, 2006), 66–70.

161 Cited in Matthew Dennis, "Cultures of Nature: To CA. 1810," in *A Companion to American Environmental History*, ed. Douglas Cazaux Sackman (Oxford: Blackwell Press, 2014), 225.

162 M. Simmons, "History of Pueblo-Spanish Relations to 1821," in *Handbook of North American Indians*, vol. 9, *Southwest*, ed. A. Ortiz (Washington, DC: Smithsonian Institution Scholarly Press, 1979), 178–93.

163 Ann L. W. Stodder and Debra L. Martin, "Health and Disease in the Southwest before and after Spanish Contact," in *Disease and Demography in the Americas*, 178–93.

164 According to Ethridge, these settlement patterns were "specifically adapted to the dry, desert environments" and their disruption by "forced year-round occupancy strained local resources." See Ethridge, "European Invasions and Early Settlement, 1500–1680," 52; Colin Galloway, *One Vast Winter Count: The Native American West before Lewis and Clark* (Lincoln: University of Nebraska Press, 2003), 165–96; Richard C. Chapman, "Sixteenth-Century Indigenous Settlement Dynamics in the Upper Middle Rio Grande Valley," in *Native and Spanish New Worlds: Sixteenth Century Entradas in the American Southwest and Southeast*, ed. Clay Mathers, Jeffrey M. Mitchem and Charles M. Haecker (Tucson: University of Arizona Press, 2013), 155–70.

165 Some communities even reluctantly replaced maize with wheat, because "it was more frost-resistant than maize." As Adams and Fish have summarized, "Wheat was adopted early in the postcontact period as a winter crop by indigenous peoples of southern Arizona and northern Sonara, and it equaled or exceeded the importance of maize in many locals [...] [so that] By the early decades of the 20th century, the Akimel O'odham no longer maintained the full complement of colored maize varieties." See Karen R. Adams and Suzanne K. Fish, "Subsistence through Time in the Greater Southwest," in *The Subsistence Economies of Indigenous North American Societies: A Handbook*, ed. Bruce D. Smith (Washington, DC: Smithsonian Institution Scholarly Press, 2011), 166.

166 M. Schoeninger, "Reconstructing Prehistoric Human Diet," in *The Chemistry of Prehistoric Human Bone*, ed. T. D. Price (New York: Cambridge University Press, 1989); K. A. Spielmann, "Colonists, Hunters, and Famers: Plains Pueblo Interaction in the Seventeenth Century," in *Columbian Consequences*, ed. D. Thomas (Washington, DC: Smithsonian Institution Scholarly Press, 1989), 1: 101–14.

167 According to Spielmann, "nutritional health [in the Southwest] decreased dramatically in the seventeenth century." See K. A. Spielmann, "Colonists, Hunters, and Famers," 110.

168 Ibid., 101–14; Ann L. W. Stodder and Debra L. Martin, "Health and Disease in the Southwest before and after Spanish Contact," 61.

169   According to Adams and Fish, hunting and gathering remained important alongside agriculture before sustained contact during the seventeenth century, when "farming gained significance and hunting-gathering declined in importance, except for pueblos whose agricultural lands became restricted, such as Taos." See Karen R. Adams and Suzanne K. Fish, "Subsistence through Time in the Greater Southwest," in *The Subsistence Economies of Indigenous North American Societies: A Handbook*, 161.

170   John Kantner, *Ancient Puebloan Southwest* (Cambridge: Cambridge University Press, 2004), 241.

171   See K. A. Spielmann, "Colonists, Hunters, and Famers," 110.

172   K. Kang et al., 'Effect of L-arginine on Immune Function: A Meta-analysis," *Asia Pacific Journal of Clinical Nutrition* 23, no. 3 (2014): 351–59. Turkey remains were found to rise substantially after around AD 1100 in several Puebloan regions and were found to reach 17 percent of the total fauna at Pueblo Alto in Chaco Canyon. Scholars have suggested this phenomenon responded specifically to nutrient deficiencies in maize, coupled with the inability to source wild game, due to overhunting among populations that had expanded unsustainably because of the grain. See B. E. Beacham and S. R. Durand, "Eggshell and the Archaeological Record: New Insights into Turkey Husbandry in the American Southwest," *Journal of Archaeological Science* 34 (2007): 1610–21; T. C. Windes, "Eggshell and the Archaeological Record: New Insights into Turkey Husbandry in the American Southwest," *Journal of Archaeological Science* 34, no. 10 (October 2007): 1610–21; Thomas C. Windes, "The Use of Turkeys at Pueblo Alto Based on the Eggshell and Faunal Remains," in *Investigations at the Pueblo Alto Complex, Chaco Canyon, New Mexico, 1975–1979*, vol. 3, part 2, *Artifactual and Biological Analyses*, ed. Frances Joan Mathien and Thomas C. Windes (E. Publications in Archaeology 18F, Chaco Canyon Studies. National Park Service, US Department of the Interior, Sante Fe, NM, 1997); K. A. Spielmann and E. Angstadt-Leto, "Hunting, Gathering and Health in the Prehistoric Southwest," in *Evolving Complexity and Environmental Risk in the Prehistoric Southwest*, ed. J. Tainter and B. B. Tainter. *Santa Fe Institute Studies in Complexity*, vol. 24 (Boston: Addison-Wesley, 199), 79–106; P. L. Walker, "The Causes of Porotic Hyperostosis and Cribra Orbitalia: A Reappraisal of the Iron-Deficiency-Anemia Hypothesis," *American Journal of Physical Anthropology* 139, no. 2 (2009): 109–25; John Kantner, *Ancient Puebloan Southwest* (Cambridge: Cambridge University Press, 2004), 241.

173   The recognition of pathogenic molecules is contingent on the MHC-peptide complex in antigen presenting cells. For a discussion of this process, see Chapter 1 of this study and Shetty, *Nutrition Immunity Infection*, 28–29.

174   Kang et al., "Effect of L-arginine on Immune Function," 351–69.

175   Shetty, *Nutrition Immunity Infection*, 29.

176   A. C. Millman et al., "Natural Killer Cells, Glutathione, Cytokines, and Innate Immunity against Mycobacterium Tuberculosis," *Journal of Interferon and Cytokine Research* 28, no. 3 (2008): 153–56.

177   P. Li et al., "Amino Acids and Immune Function," *British Journal of Nutrition* 98, no. 2 (August 2007): 237–52; A. Jackson et al., "Comparison of Urinary Excretion of 5-L-Oxoproline (L-Pyroglutamate) during Normal Pregnancy in Women in England and Jamaica," *British Journal of Nutrition* 77, no. 2 (February 1997) 183–96; E. Meléndez-Hevia, "A Weak Link in Metabolism: The Metabolic Capacity for Glycine Biosynthesis Does Not Satisfy the Need for Collagen Synthesis," *Journal of Bioscience* 34, no. 6 (December 2009): 853–72. For a discussion of the abundance of

folate in liver, see C. Masterjohn, "Beyond Good and Evil: Synergy and Context with Dietary Nutrients," *Wise Traditions*, fall 2012. https://www.westonaprice.org/health-topics/abcs-of-nutrition/beyond-good-and-evil/. On the importance of folate, found in liver (as well as many plant sources), see below.

178 Adams and Fish, "Subsistence through Time in the Greater Southwest," in *The Subsistence Economies of Indigenous North American Societies: A Handbook*, 169.

179 As Duval has pointed out, the knock-on effect of European market forces led many Osage people to stop "farming altogether, ending or at least altering women's longstanding complementary contribution to the feeding their people as well as their ownership of farmland." These phenomena were likely problematic in reducing nutrient diversity, particularly antioxidants and folate, which are necessary for sound immunity and fertility. See Kathleen Duval, "Living in a Reordered World, 1680–1763," in *The Oxford Handbook of American Indian History*, 67; Galloway, *One Vast Winter Count*, 273.

180 Louis S. Warren, "The Nature of Conquest: Indians, Americans, and Environmental History," 297.

181 Gary Clayton Anderson, *The Indian Southwest, 1580–1830: Ethnogenesis and Reinvention* (Norman: University of Oklahoma Press, 1999), 61.

182 One study highlights the importance of folate in oocyte maturation: subjects receiving IVF treatment who also received folate were found to have more mature eggs than those who did not receive folate. See C. O'Neill, "Endogenous Folic Acid Is Essential for Normal Development of Preimplantation Embryos," *Human Reproduction* 13, no. 5 (May 1998): 1312–16; W. Szymański, "Effect of Homocysteine Concentration in Follicular Fluid On a Degree of Oocyte Maturity," *Ginekologia Polska* 74, no. 10 (October 2003): 1392–96.

183 C. Castillo-Lancellotti, "Impact of Folic Acid Fortification of Flour on Neural Tube Defects: A Systematic Review," *Public Health Nutrition* 16, no. 5 (May 2013): 901–11; L. George L. et al., "Plasma Folate Levels and Risk of Spontaneous Abortion," *JAMA* 288, no. 15 (October 2002): 1867–73; A. M. Molloy et al., "Effects of Folate and Vitamin B12 Deficiencies during Pregnancy on Fetal, Infant, and Child Development," *Food Nutrition Bulletin* 29, no. 2 suppl. June 2008): S101–11; discussion S112–15; T. O. Scholl and W. G. Johnson, "Folic Acid: Influence on the Outcome of Pregnancy," *American Journal of Clinical Nutrition* 71, no. 5 suppl. (May 2000): 1295S–303S.

184 W. Y. Wong et al., "Effects of Folic Acid and Zinc Sulfate on Male Factor Subfertility: A Double-Blind, Randomized, Placebo-Controlled Trial," *Fertility and Sterility* 77, no. 3 (March 2002): 491–98; G. Bentivoglio et al., "Folinic Acid in the Treatment of Human Male Infertility," *Fertility and Sterility* 60, no. 4 (October 1993): 698–701; S. S. Young, "The Association of Folate, Zinc and Antioxidant Intake with Sperm Aneuploidy in Healthy Non-Smoking Men," *Human Reproduction* 23, no. 5 (May 2008): 1014–22.

185 X. Wu, "Association between the MTHFR C677T Polymorphism and Recurrent Pregnancy Loss: A Meta-Analysis," *Genetic Testing and Molecular Biomarkers* 16, no. 7 (July 2012): 806–11; M. Rodríguez-Guillén, "Maternal MTHFR Polymorphisms and Risk of Spontaneous Abortion," *Salud Pública de Mexico* 51, no. 1 (January–February 2009): 19–25.

186 A properly working MTHFR enzyme normally transfers 5,10-methylenetetrahydrofolate into an activated form, 5-MTHF (5-methyl tetrahydrofolate). Such a process is crucial for DNA methylation, nucleic acid

biosynthesis, neurotransmitter synthesis and the creation of signaling molecules that are central to the development of embryos in the first trimester of pregnancy. Folate plays a vital role in remethylation of homocysteine to methionine, which is essential for DNA-synthesis, DNA-repair, and DNA-imprinting processes. See H. D. Morgan et al., "Epigenetic Reprogramming in Mammals," *Human Molecular Genetics* 14, spec. no. 1 (April 2005): R47–58.

187   Scrimshaw et al., "Interactions of Nutrition and Infection," *Monograph Series World Health Organization* 57 (1968): 3–329; G. J. Armelagos, A. H. Goodman and K. H. Jacobs, "The Origins of Agriculture: Population Growth during a Period of Declining Health," *Population and Environment* 13, no. 1 (Fall 1991): 9–22.

188   Theodore Binnema, *Common and Contested Ground: A Human and Environmental History of the Northwestern Plains* (Toronto: University of Toronto Press, 2004), 75–78.

189   Pekka Hämäläinen, "The Rise and Fall of Plains Indian Horse Cultures," *Journal of American History* 90, no. 3 (2003): 833–62; James F. Brooks, *Captives and Cousins: Slavery, Kinship, and Community in the Southwest Borderlands* (Chapel Hill: University of North Carolina Press, 2002).

190   Jones, *Rationalizing Epidemics*, 173–74.

191   Dean R. Snow, "The First Americans and the Differentiation of Hunter Gatherer Cultures," in *The Cambridge History of the Native Peoples of the Americas:* vol. 1, *North America*: part 1, ed. Bruce G. Trigger and Wilcomb E. Washburn (Cambridge: Cambridge University Press, 1996), 193. The historical development of pemmican, a dense mixture of meat and fat eaten by Plains Native Americans from the eighteenth century onward, suggests that indigenous communities endeavored to maintain their attachment to animal fats even after they lost access to these newly hunted meats. On the nutrient profile of pemmican, see R. G. Sinclair and G. M Brown et al., "The Tolerance of Eskimos for Pemmican and for Starvation," *Revue Canadienne De Biologie* 7, no. 1 (1948): 197.

192   Ann L. W. Stodder and Debra L. Martin, "Health and Disease in the Southwest before and after Spanish Contact," 60; M. Simmons, "History of Pueblo-Spanish Relations to 1821," 178–93; Pekka Hämäläinen, "The Rise and Fall of Plains Indian Horse Cultures," 833–62; Galloway, *One Vast Winter Count*, 267–312.

193   See Brooks, *Captives and Cousins*, 1–116; Ned Blackhawk, *Violence over the Land: Indians and Empires in the Early American West* (Cambridge, MA: Harvard University Press, 2006), 16–54; Jeffrey Ostler, "The Plains," in *The Oxford Handbook of American Indian History*, 239.

194   Kathleen Duval, *The Native Ground: Indians and Colonists in the Heart of the Continent* (Philadelphia: University of Pennsylvania Press, 2007), 103–27.

195   Claudio Saunt, "The Age of Imperial Expansion, 1763–1821," 83; Galloway, *The Scratch of a Pen*; Galloway, *The American Revolution in Indian Country;* Taylor, *The Divided Ground*, 66–70.

196   Ostler, "The Plains," 238–39.

197   Pekka Hämäläinen, "The Politics of Grass: European Expansion, Ecological Change, and Indigenous Power in the Southwest Borderlands," *William and Mary Quarterly* 67, no. 2 (2010): 173–208.

198   Pekka Hämäläinen, *The Comanche Empire* (New Haven, CT: Yale University Press, 2008), 179; Claudio Saunt, "The Age of Imperial Expansion, 1763–1821," 82.

199   On the initial height gains among Plains communities in close proximity to animals, which subsequently diminished relative to other populations, see R. H. Steckel,

"Stature and Living Standards in the United States," in *American Economic Growth and Standards of Living before the Civil War*, ed. Robert E. Gallman and John J. Wallis (Chicago: University of Chicago Press, 1992), 265–308; Richard H. Steckel and Joseph M. Prince, "Tallest in the World: Native Americans of the Great Plains in the Nineteenth Century," *American Economic Review* 91, no. 1 (2001): 287–94; R. Steckel, "Inequality amidst Nutritional Abundance: Native Americans on the Great Plains," *Journal of Economic History* 70, no. 2 (2010): 265–86.

200 Andrew C. Isenberg, *The Destruction of the Bison: An Environmental History, 1750–1920* (Cambridge: Cambridge University Press, 2000), 131–34.

201 See this narrative in Elizabeth A. Fenn, *Encounters at the Heart of the World: A History of the Mandan People* (New York: Hill and Wang, 2014).

202 Jeffrey Ostler, "The Plains," 238–39.

203 "Euro-American encroachments on key resource sites could disrupt Native subsistence across wide areas." See Gregory E. Smoak, "The Great Basin," in *The Oxford Handbook of American Indian History*, 381.

204 Ibid., 382.

205 Ibid., 383–84

206 William H. McNeill, *Plagues and Peoples* (Garden City, NY: Anchor Books, 1976), chapters 3–5; Alfred W. Crosby, "Virgin Soil Epidemics as a Factor in the Aboriginal Depopulation in America," *William and Mary Quarterly*, 3rd ser., 33 (1976): 289–99; Neil Salisbury, *Manitou and Providence: Indians, Europeans, and the Making of New England, 1500–1643* (New York: Oxford University Press, 1982).

207 Salisbury, *Manitou and Providence*, 57.

208 Calvin Martin, *Keepers of the Game: Indian-Animal Relationships and the Fur Trade* (Berkeley: University of California Press, 1978); Shepard Krech III, *The Ecological Indian: Myth and History* (New York: W. W. Norton, 1999), 173–209.

209 As Salisbury notes, by the beginning of the seventeenth century communities such as the Micmac came to lead "a precarious existence every winter, relying on the French and other outside sources of food for survival." See Salisbury, *Manitou and Providence*, 57; Calvin Martin, "The Four Lives of a Micmac Copper Pot," *Ethnohistory* 22 (1975): 113–16.

210 Salisbury, *Manitou and Providence*, 76; Dean R. Snow, "Abenaki Fur Trade in the Sixteenth Century," *Western Canadian Journal of Anthropology* 6 (1976): 3 and 117–18.

211 Alfred W. Crosby, "Virgin Soil Epidemics as a Factor in the Aboriginal Depopulation in America," *William and Mary Quarterly*, 3d ser., 33 (1976), 289–99; Salisbury, *Manitou and Providence*, 102–3.

212 See Ethridge and Such-Hall eds., *Mapping the Mississippian Shatter Zone*, 30–33; Daniel Richter, *The Ordeal of the Longhouse: The Peoples of the Iroquois League in the Era of European Colonization* (Chapel Hill: University of North Carolina Press, 1992), 32–49 and 51–62.

213 Kathleen Duval, "Living in a Reordered World, 1680–1763," 70–73.

214 Timothy J. Shannon, "Iroquoia," in *The Oxford Handbook of American Indian History*, 204.

215 Sir George Peckham, cited in Peter C. Mancall, ed., *Envisioning America: English Plans for the Colonization of North America, 1580–1640* (Boston: Bedford Books, 1995), 64.

216 For men like William Bradford, as Dennis has pointed out, "wilderness surrounded and dominated the pilgrims' Canaan, which lacked a vantage point for any latter-day Moses to see into their future land of milk and honey." As Puritan leader William Bradford noted, nobody in his party could yet, in the third decade of the seventeenth

century, "as it were, go up to the top of Pigsah, to view from this wilderness a more goodly country to feed their hopes [...] [T]he whole country, full of woods & thickets, represented a wild & savage hue. If they looked behind them, there was a might ocean which they had passed, and was now as a main bar & gulf to separate them from all the civil parts of the world." See Matthew Dennis, "Cultures of Nature: To CA. 1810," in *A Companion to American Environmental History*, 223.

217   Thornton, "Health, Disease, and Demography," 70; Cronon, *Changes in the Land*, 142–46; Anderson, "King Philip's Herds," 606.

218   Anderson, *Creatures of Empire*, 188; Sherburne F. Cook, "The Significance of Disease in the Extinction of the New England Indians," *Human Biology*, 45 (1973): 485–508; Robert R. Gradie, "New England Indians and the Colonizing Pigs," in *Papers of the Fifteenth Algonquian Conference*, ed. William Cowan (Ottawa: Carleton University Press, 1984), 159–62; Daniel Gookin, *Historical Collections of the Indians in New England* (1674; reprinted in New York, 1972), 33.

219   Anderson, *Creatures of Empire*, 188.

220   Anderson, "King Philip's Herds," 622–23.

221   Armelagos et al., "The Origins of Agriculture: Population Growth during a Period of Declining Health," 9–22. See also C. M. Cassidy, "Nutrition and Health In Agriculturalists and Hunter-Gatherers: A Case Study of Two Prehistoric Populations," in *Nutritional Anthropology: Contemporary Approaches to Diet & Culture*, ed. N. W. Jerome (Pleasantville, NY: Redgrave Publishing Company 1980), 117–45.

222   S. Polgar, "Evolution and the Ills of Mankind," in *Horizons of Anthropology*, ed. S. Tax (Chicago: Aldine Publishing Company, 1964), 200–11.

223   Thornton, "Health, Disease, and Demography," 70.

224   Ibid.; Louis S. Warren "The Nature of Conquest: Indians, Americans, and Environmental History," in *Companion to American Indian History*, 287–306.

225   Crosby, *Ecological Imperialism*, 289; Cronon, *Changes in the Land*, 142–46; Anderson, "King Philip's Herds," 606.

226   Miantonomi, Narragansett sachem, to the Montauk Indians of eastern Long Island, Summer 1642, cited in Salisbury, *Manitou and Providence*, 13,

227   C. A. Daley, "A Review of Fatty Acid Profiles and Antioxidant Content in Grass-Fed and Grain-Fed Beef," *Nutrition Journal* 9 (March 2010):10; P. French, "Fatty Acid Composition, Including Conjugated Linoleic Acid, of Intramuscular Fat from Steers Offered Grazed Grass, Grass Silage, Or Concentrate-Based Diets,: *Journal of Animal Science* 78, no. 11 (November 2000): 2849–55; E. N. Ponnampalam, "Effect of Feeding Systems on Omega-3 Fatty Acids, Conjugated Linoleic Acid and Trans Fatty Acids in Australian Beef Cuts: Potential Impact on Human Health," *Asia Pacific Journal of Clinical Nutrition* 15, no. 1 (2006): 21–29; S. K. Duckett, "Effects of Winter Stocker Growth Rate and Finishing System On: III. Tissue Proximate, Fatty Acid, Vitamin, and Cholesterol Content," *Journal of Animal Science* 87, no. 9 (September 2009): 2961–70.

228   For relatively recent research on the importance of fat for the bioavailability of vitamins such as A, K, C and D (some from mouse studies), see N. W. Solomons and J. Bulus, "Plant Sources of Provitamin A and Human Nutriture," *Nutrition Review* 51 (July 1993): 1992–94; R. Bouillon et al, "Polyunsaturated Fatty Acids Decrease the Apparent Affinity of Vitamin D Metabolites for Human Vitamin D-Binding Protein," *Journal of Steroid Biochemistry and Molecular Biology* 42 (1992): 855–61; H. H. W. Thijssen and M. J. Drittij-Reijnders, "Vitamin K Distribution in

Rat Tissues: Dietary Phylloquinone Is a Source of Tissue Menquinone-4," *British Journal of Nutrition* 72 (1994): 415–25; J. E. Ronden et al., "Tissue Distribution of K-Vitamins under Different Nutritional Regimens in the Rat," *Biochimica et Biophysica Acta* 1379 (1998): 16–22; H. H. W. Thijssen and M. J. Drittij-Reijnders, "Vitamin K Status in Human Tissues: Tissue-Specific Accumulation of Phylloquinone and Menaquionone-4," *British Journal of Nutrition* 75 (1996): 121–27; B. L. M. G. Gijsbers et al., "Effect of Food Composition on Vitamin K Absorption in Human Volunteers," *British Journal of Nutrition* 76 (1996): 223–29; L. J. Schurgers and C. Vermeer, "Determination of Phylloquinone and Menaquinones in Food," *Haemostasis* 30 (2000): 298–307; A. K. Garber, "Comparison of Phylloquinone Bioavailability from Food Sources or a Supplement in Human Subjects," *Journal of Nutrition* 129 (1999): 1201–203; N. C. Binkley et al., "A High Phylloquinone Intake Is Required to Achieve Maximal Osteocalcin Gamma-Carboxylation," *American Journal of Clinical Nutrition* 76 (2002): 1055–60.

229   Shetty, *Nutrition Immunity Infection*, 27.

230   On plant micronutrient bioavailability in association with fats from separate sources, see M. Brown et al., "Carotenoid Bioavailability Is Higher from Salads Ingested with Full-Fat Than with Fat-Reduced Salad Dressings as Measured with Electrochemical Detection 1,2,3," *American Journal of Clinical Nutrition* 80, no. 2 (August 2004): 396–403; K. H. Van Het Hof et al., "Dietary Factors That Affect the Bioavailability of Carotenoids," *Journal of Nutrition* 130, no. 3 (March 2000): 503–6; N. Kono and H. Arai, "Intracellular Transport of Fat-Soluble Vitamins A and E," *Traffic* 16, no. 1 (January 2015): 19–34; N. W. Solomons and J. Bulus, "Plant Sources of Provitamin A and Human Nutriture," *Nutrition Review* 51 (July 1993): 1992–94; R. Bouillon et al., "Polyunsaturated Fatty Acids Decrease the Apparent Affinity of Vitamin D Metabolites for Human Vitamin D-Binding Protein," *Journal of Steroid Biochemistry and Molecular Biology* 42 (1992): 855–61; 16; Thijssen, "Vitamin K Status in Human Tissues: Tissue-Specific Accumulation of Phylloquinone and Menaquionone-4," 121–27; Gijsbers et al., "Effect of Food Composition on Vitamin K Absorption in Human Volunteers," 223–29; L. J. Schurgers and C. Vermeer, "Determination of Phylloquinone and Menaquinones in Food," *Haemostasis* 30 (2000): 298–307; A. K. Garber et al., "Comparison of Phylloquinone Bioavailability from Food Sources or a Supplement in Human Subjects," *Journal of Nutrition* 129 (1999): 1201–203. For evidence that "consuming beta-carotene with beef tallow rather than sunflower oil increases the amount we absorb from 11 to 17 percent," see X. Hu, "Intestinal Absorption of Beta-Carotene Ingested with a Meal Rich in Sunflower Oil Or Beef Tallow: Postprandial Appearance in Triacylglycerol-Rich Lipoproteins in Women," *American Journal of Clinical Nutrition* 71, no. 5 (May 2000): 1170–80.

231   Anderson, "King Philip's Herds," 615–17.

232   Salisbury, *Manitou and Providence*, 126.

233   Dean R. Snow, "The First Americans and the Differentiation of Hunter Gatherer Cultures" in *The Cambridge History of the Native Peoples of the Americas*, vol. 1, *North America*: part 1, 194; Anderson, *Creatures of Empire*, 79; Salisbury, *Manitou and Providence*, 176–77.

234   Chickataubut and Sagamore John were called to an English court for attacking livestock near Massachusetts Bay, in what Salisbury has described as an "ironic comment on the rationalizations of the English that they were stable horticulturalists while the Indians primarily roamed and hunted oblivious to notions of territoriality."

In the court documents, the two men were keen to point out their land management techniques, and the gendered cultivation of plant foods in their community, which complemented animals that were hunted outside those settlements. See Salisbury, *Manitou and Providence*, 187. On the expansion of English settlement and the disruption of Native American lands following the 1680s, see, for example, Daniel R. Mandell, *King Philip's War: Colonial Expansion, Native Resistance, and the End of Indian Sovereignty* (Baltimore, MD: Johns Hopkins University Press, 2010), 80–83; Jean O'Brien, *Dispossession by Degrees: Indian Land and Identity in Natick, Massachusetts, 1650–1790* (New York: Cambridge University Press, 1997), 65–91; Kathleen Duval, "Living in a Reordered World, 1680–1763," 70; Anderson, "King Philip's Herds," 601–24.

235   On the scholarly debate regarding the Iroquois diminution of Delaware gender norms, see Amy C. Schutt, *Peoples of the River Valleys: The Odyssey of the Delaware Indians* (Philadelphia: University of Pennsylvania Press, 2007), 90–93; William J. Bauer Jr., "The Atlantic Northeast," in *The Oxford Handbook of American Indian History*, 347.

236   Richard White, *The Middle Ground: Indians, Empires, and Republics in the Great Lakes Region, 1650–1815* (Cambridge: Cambridge University Press, 1991); Ethridge, "European Invasions and Early Settlement, 1500–1680," in *The Oxford Handbook of American Indian History*, 52.

237   Bauer Jr., "The Atlantic Northeast," 350–53.

238   Karim M. Tiro, "A 'Civil' War? Rethinking Iroquois Participation in the American Revolution," *Explorations in Early American Culture* 4 (2000): 148. On Iroquois nutritional strategies in the context of the war, see also Rachel B. Herrmann, "No useless mouth": Iroquoian Food Diplomacy in the American Revolution," *Diplomatic History* 41, no. 1 (2016): 20–49.

239   Bauer Jr., "The Atlantic Northeast," 350–53.

240   On Iroquois losses by the 1840s, see Laurence M. Hauptman, *Conspiracy of Interests: Iroquois Dispossession and the Rise of New York State* (Syracuse, NY: Syracuse University Press, 1999).

241   See Drew R. McCoy, *The Elusive Republic: Political Economy in Jeffersonian America* (Chapel Hill: University of North Carolina Press, 1980), 203–4; Robert M. Owens, "Jeffersonian Benevolence on the Ground: The Indian Land Cession Treaties of William Henry Harrison," *Journal of the Early Republic* 22, no. 3 (2002): 419–20; Claudio Saunt, *A New Order of Things: Property, Power, and the Transformation of the Creek Indians, 1733–1816* (Cambridge and New York: Cambridge University Press, 1999), 271–72.

242   Synder, "The South," 326.

243   Michael D. Green, *The Politics of Indian Removal: Creek Government and Society in Crisis* (Lincoln: University of Nebraska Press, 1982); Theda Perdue and Michael D. Green, *The Cherokee Nation and the Trail of Tears* (New York: Penguin, 2007); Mary E. Young, *Redskins, Ruffleshirts, and Rednecks: Indian Allotments in Alabama and Mississippi, 1830–1860* (Norman: University of Oklahoma Press, 1961).

244   The Mandan population, for example, reduced from 9,000 in the 1750s to 150 in 1838. See Ostler, "The Plains," 241.

245   Clark Spencer Larsen, "Biological Changes in Human Populations with Agriculture," *Annual Review of Anthropology* 24, no. 1 (1995): 188; Kelton, *Epidemics and Enslavement*, 13; Goodman and Armelagos, "Disease and Death Dr. Dickson's Mounds," 15–16; Jane E. Buikstra et al, "Diet, Demography, and the Development of Horticulture,"

in *Emergent Horticultural Economies of the Eastern Woodlands*, ed. William F. Keegan (Southern Illinois University at Carbondale Center for Archaeological Investigations, Occasional Paper 7), 87–107; Bruce D. Smith, "Origins of Agriculture in Eastern North America," *Science* 246 (1989): 1566–71.

246 Anderson, "King Philip's Herds," 615–17; Thomas Hatley, "Cherokee Women Farmers Hold Their Ground," in *Appalachian Frontiers: Society and Development in the Preindustrial Era*, ed. Robert D. Mitchell (Lexington: University Press of Kentucky, 1991), 44.

4. Metabolic Health and Immunity in Native America, 1750–1950

1 Jaspinder Kaur, "A Comprehensive Review on Metabolic Syndrome," *Cardiology Research and Practice* (2014): 1–21; J. Jakelić et al., "Nonspecific Immunity in Diabetes: Hyperglycemia Decreases Phagocytic Activity of Leukocytes in Diabetic Patients," *Medical Archives* 49, no. 1–2 (1995): 9–12; Rebecca Ilyas et al., "High Glucose Disrupts Oligosaccharide Recognition Function via Competitive Inhibition: A Potential Mechanism for Immune Dysregulation in Diabetes Mellitus," *Immunobiology* 216, no. 1–2 (2011): 126–31.

2 Pedro Carrera-Bastos et al., "The Western Diet and Lifestyle and Diseases of Civilization," *Research Reports in Clinical Cardiology* 2 (2011): 15–35; Begoña Ruiz-Núñez et al., "Lifestyle and Nutritional Imbalances Associated with Western Diseases: Causes and Consequences of Chronic Systemic Low-grade Inflammation in an Evolutionary Context," *Journal of Nutritional Biochemistry* 24, no. 7 (2013): 1183–201; Rosário Monteiro and Isabel Azevedo, "Chronic Inflammation in Obesity and the Metabolic Syndrome," *Mediators of Inflammation* (2010): 1–10; Dana T. Graves and Rayyan A. Kayal, "Diabetic Complications and Dysregulated Innate Immunity," *Frontiers in Bioscience* 13 (2008): 1227–39.

3 Prakash Shetty, *Nutrition Immunity Infection* (Wallingford, Oxfordshire, UK: CABI, 2010), 23.

4 Michael P. Muehlenbein, *Human Evolutionary Biology* (Cambridge: Cambridge University Press, 2010), 466; Ben C. Sheldon and Simon Verhulst, "Ecological Immunology: Costly Parasite Defences and Trade-offs in Evolutionary Ecology," *Trends in Ecology & Evolution* 11, no. 8 (1996): 317–21.

5 T. W. McDade et al., "Prenatal Undernutrition and Postnatal Growth Are Associated with Adolescent Thymic Function," *Journal of Nutrition* 131, no. 4 (2001): 1225–31; Sheldon and Verhulst, "Ecological Immunology," 317–21.

6 That such a state can be defined as a syndrome began to be noted in the 1920s, when the Swedish physician Eskil Kylin described the strong "association of high blood pressure (hypertension), high blood glucose (hyperglycemia), and gout." Obesity, insulin resistance and high blood triglycerides are said to be part of the syndrome, which was formally described as "metabolic syndrome" in 2005. Kaur, "A Comprehensive Review on Metabolic Syndrome," 1–21; Shetty, *Nutrition Immunity Infection*, 166; Ruiz-Núñez et al., "Lifestyle and Nutritional Imbalances Associated with Western Diseases," 1183.

7 Kaur, "A Comprehensive Review on Metabolic Syndrome," 1; Monteiro and Azevedo, "Chronic Inflammation in Obesity and the Metabolic Syndrome," 1–10; Ana Azevedo et al., "The Metabolic Syndrome," in *Oxidative Stress, Inflammation and Angiogenesis in the Metabolic Syndrome*, 1–19.

8   "IDF Worldwide Definition of the Metabolic Syndrome," International Diabetes Federation. Accessed November 30, 2016, http://www.idf.org/metabolic-syndrome. See also Ruiz-Núñez et al., "Lifestyle and Nutritional Imbalances Associated with Western Diseases," 1189; Dariush Mozaffarian, "Trans Fatty Acids—Effects on Systemic Inflammation and Endothelial Function," *Atherosclerosis Supplements* 7, no. 2 (2006): 29–32; D. Mozaffarian et al., "Health Effects of Trans-Fatty Acids: Experimental and Observational Evidence," *European Journal of Clinical Nutrition* 63 (suppl. 2) (2009): 5–21; Katherine Esposito and Dario Giugliano, "Mediterranean Diet and the Metabolic Syndrome: The End of the Beginning," *Metabolic Syndrome and Related Disorders* 8, no. 3 (2010): 197–200; D. Giugliano et al., "The Effects of Diet on Inflammation: Emphasis on the Metabolic Syndrome," *Journal of the American College of Cardiology* 48, no. 4 (2006): 677–85; Dariush Mozaffarian and Eric B. Rimm, "Fish Intake, Contaminants, and Human Health," *JAMA* 296, no. 15 (2006): 1885–99.

9   Peter Katona and Judit Katona-Apte, "The Interaction between Nutrition and Infection," *Clinical Infectious Diseases* 46, no. 10 (2008): 1582–88.

10 Andrew L. Kau et al., "Human Nutrition, the Gut Microbiome and the Immune System," *Nature* 474, no. 7351 (2011): 329–30.

11 Kau et al., "Human Nutrition, the Gut Microbiome and the Immune System," 329.

12 Ibid.; Angus W. Thomson et al., "Immunoregulatory Functions of MTOR Inhibition," *Nature Reviews Immunology* 9, no. 5 (2009): 324–37; Takahisa Nakamura et al., "Double-Stranded RNA-Dependent Protein Kinase Links Pathogen Sensing with Stress and Metabolic Homeostasis," *Cell* 140, no. 3 (2010): 338–48; Brigitta Stockinger, "Beyond Toxicity: Aryl Hydrocarbon Receptor-mediated Functions in the Immune System," *Journal of Biology* 8, no. 7 (2009): 61.

13 Fleur Ponton et al., "Integrating Nutrition and Immunology: A New Frontier. *Journal of Insect Physiology* 59, no. 2 (2013): 131; Janelle S. Ayres and David S. Schneider, "Tolerance of Infections," *Annual Review of Immunology* 30, no. 1 (2012): 271–94. On Leptin's important metabolic role in immunity, see Claudio Procaccini et al., "Leptin as Immune Mediator: Interaction between Neuroendocrine and Immune System," *Developmental & Comparative Immunology* 66 (2017): 120–29; Antonio La Cava and Giuseppe Matarese, "The Weight of Leptin in Immunity," *Nature Reviews Immunology* 4, no. 5 (2004): 371–79; G. M. Lord et al., "Leptin Modulates the T-cell Immune Response and Reverses Starvation-Induced Immunosuppression," *Nature* 394 (1998): 897–901; X. Guo et al., "Leptin Signaling in Intestinal Epithelium Mediates Resistance to Enteric Infection by Entamoeba Histolytica," *Mucosal Immunology* 4, no. 3 (2010): 294–303. The mTOR metabolic pathway senses energy status, oxygen levels, and even the effects of emotional stress, and regulates cellular metabolism accordingly. Numerous studies have shown mTOR signaling affects aspects of the innate and adaptive immune responses, including T cell formation and activity, dendritic cell formation, and memory T-cell formation. See Carla Garza-Lombó et al., "Mammalian Target of Rapamycin: Its Role in Early Neural Development and in Adult and Aged Brain Function," *Frontiers in Cellular Neuroscience* 10 (2016): 157; Kau et al., "Human Nutrition, the Gut Microbiome and the Immune System," 329; Thomson et al., "Immunoregulatory Functions of MTOR Inhibition," 324–37; Anna Mondino and Daniel L. Mueller, "MTOR at the Crossroads of T Cell Proliferation and Tolerance," *Seminars in Immunology* 19, no. 3 (2007): 162–72; H. Hackstein, "Rapamycin Inhibits IL-4–induced Dendritic Cell Maturation in Vitro and Dendritic Cell Mobilization and Function in Vivo," *Blood* 101, no. 11 (2003): 4457–63; Jianxun Song et al., "The

Kinases Aurora B and MTOR Regulate the G1–S Cell Cycle Progression of T Lymphocytes," *Nature Immunology* 8, no. 1 (2006): 64–73. doi:10.1038/ni1413; H. R. Turnquist et al., "Rapamycin-Conditioned Dendritic Cells Are Poor Stimulators of Allogeneic CD4 T Cells, But Enrich for Antigen-Specific Foxp3 T Regulatory Cells and Promote Organ Transplant Tolerance," *Journal of Immunology* 178, no. 11 (2007): 7018–31; S. L. Weinstein et al., "Phosphatidylinositol 3-kinase and mTOR Mediate Lipopolysaccharide-Stimulated Nitric Oxide Production in Macrophages via Interferon-Beta," *Journal of Leukocyte Biology* 67 (2000): 405–14; Koichi Araki et al., "The Role of MTOR in Memory CD8 T-cell Differentiation," *Immunological Reviews* 235, no. 1 (2010): 234–43; Nutrient-sensing signaling pathways such as the mTOR pathway have been shown to directly influence T cell behavior. See Kai Yang et al., "T Cell Exit from Quiescence and Differentiation into Th2 Cells Depend on Raptor-mTORC1-Mediated Metabolic Reprogramming," *Immunity* 39, no. 6 (2013): 1043–56.

14   On dendritic cell differentiation and T cell differentiation in association with tryptophan, see B. Platzer et al., "Aryl Hydrocarbon Receptor Activation Inhibits In Vitro Differentiation of Human Monocytes and Langerhans Dendritic Cells," *Journal of Immunology* 183, no. 1 (2009): 66–74; Francisco J. Quintana et al., "Control of Treg and TH17 Cell Differentiation by the Aryl Hydrocarbon Receptor," *Nature* 453, no. 7191 (2008): 65–71; Marc Veldhoen et al., "The Aryl Hydrocarbon Receptor Links TH17-Cell-Mediated Autoimmunity to Environmental Toxins," *Nature* 453, no. 7191 (2008): 106–9.

15   Fred Ottoboni and M. Alice Ottoboni, *The Modern Nutritional Diseases: And How to Prevent Them* (Sparks, NV: Vincente Books, 2002): 218–19. A recent meta-analysis concluded that the risk of diabetes is increased with consumption of foods with a high glycemic index. Intervention studies suggest that low glycemic index foods improve insulin levels in diabetic patients. See Carrera-Bastos et al., "The Western Diet and Lifestyle and Diseases of Civilization," 24; Alan Barclay, "CD1-1 Glycemic Index, Glycemic Load and Diabetes Risk: A Meta-analysis," *Diabetes Research and Clinical Practice* 79 (2008): 627–37. Type 2 diabetes (or non-insulin-dependent diabetes) involves "diminished reduction of the circulating glucose concentration by insulin," also described as insulin resistance. Insulin is a hormone secreted by the pancreas in response to an increase in blood glucose levels following the consumption of glucose-containing foods. Insulin secretion causes increased glucose uptake by several organs and tissues in the body, so that the dangerous state of hyperglycaemia is avoided. The insulin resistance that occurs in Type 2 diabetes therefore affects the ability of insulin to perform this role. Chronic inflammation from excess blood glucose and insulin insensitivity is strongly linked with metabolic syndrome. According to a recent overview, "it has become clear that chronic systemic low grade inflammation is at the basis of many, if not all, typically Western diseases centered on the metabolic syndrome." See Ruiz-Núñez et al., "Lifestyle and Nutritional Imbalances Associated with Western Diseases," 1186; Gerald M. Reaven, "The Insulin Resistance Syndrome: Definition and Dietary Approaches to Treatment," *Annual Review of Nutrition* 25, no. 1 (2005): 391–406; Lindgärde et al., "Traditional versus Agricultural Lifestyle among Shuar Women of the Ecuadorian Amazon: Effects on Leptin Levels," *Metabolism* 53, no. 10 (2004): 1355–58; Paul Z. Zimmet et al., "The Global Epidemiology of Non-Insulin-Dependent Diabetes Mellitus and the Metabolic Syndrome," *Journal of Diabetes and Its Complications* 11, no. 2 (1997): 60–68.

16   Isabelle Wolowczuk et al., "Feeding Our Immune System: Impact on Metabolism. *Clinical and Developmental Immunology* 2008 (2008): 1–19; Casey J. Fox et al., "Fuel Feeds Function: Energy Metabolism and the T-Cell Response," *Nature Reviews Immunology* 5, no. 11 (2005): 844–52.

17   Gisela Wilcox, "Insulin and Insulin Resistance," *Clinical Biochemist Reviews* 26, no.2 (2005): 19–39; Graves and Kayal, "Diabetic Complications and Dysregulated Innate Immunity," 1227–39; Ruiz-Núñez et al., "Lifestyle and Nutritional Imbalances Associated with Western Diseases," 1186. On these metabolic abnormalities increasing the risk of conditions such as type 2 diabetes, cardiovascular disease, and even some cancers, see Azevedo et al., "The Metabolic Syndrome," 2; I. D. Caterson et al., "Prevention Conference VII: Obesity, a Worldwide Epidemic Related to Heart Disease and Stroke: Group III: Worldwide Comorbidities of Obesity," *Circulation* 110, no. 18 (2004); Robert H. Eckel et al., "The Metabolic Syndrome," *The Lancet* 365, no. 9468 (2005): 1415–28; Andrea Galassi et al., "Metabolic Syndrome and Risk of Cardiovascular Disease: A Meta-Analysis," *American Journal of Medicine* 119, no. 10 (2006): 812–19.

18   Ilyas et al., "High Glucose Disrupts Oligosaccharide Recognition Function," 126– 31; T. C. Alba-Loureiro et al., "Diabetes Causes Marked Changes in Function and Metabolism of Rat Neutrophils," *Journal of Endocrinology* 188, no. 2 (February 2006): 295–303; Y. Takeda et al., "Immunological Disorders of Diabetes Mellitus in Experimental Rat Models," *Nihon Eiseigaku* 69, no. 3 (2014):166–76; J. Jakelić et al., "Nonspecific Immunity in Diabetes," *Medical Arhives* 49, no. 1–2 (1995): 9– 12. Experiments in Drosophila suggest that insulin signaling has a profound role in immunity. See Ponton et al., "Integrating Nutrition and Immunology," 130–37. Mutations in the chico receptor (a homologue of the mammalian insulin receptor) result in superior pathogen resistance. See Sergiy Libert et al., "Realized Immune Response Is Enhanced in Long-lived Puc and Chico Mutants But Is Unaffected by Dietary Restriction," *Molecular Immunology* 45, no. 3 (2008): 810–17; Pankaj Kapahi et al., "With TOR, Less Is More: A Key Role for the Conserved Nutrient-Sensing TOR Pathway in Aging," *Cell Metabolism* 11, no. 6 (2010): 453–65. The Forkhead Transcription Factor (FOXO), an evolutionarily conserved protein in the insulin pathway, has also been implicated in the immune response. FOXO can induce expression of antimicrobial peptides, molecules involved in the immune response that are highly conserved between species, in Drosophila and in cultured human cells. See Nissim Hay Nissim, "Interplay between FOXO, TOR, and Akt," *Biochimica Et Biophysica Acta (BBA)—Molecular Cell Research* 1813, no. 11 (2011): 1965–70; Thomas Becker et al., "FOXO-dependent Regulation of Innate Immune Homeostasis," *Nature* 463, no. 7279 (2010): 369–73; Phillipe Bulet et al., "Anti-microbial Peptides: From Invertebrates to Vertebrates," *Immunological Reviews* 198, no. 1 (2004): 169–84.

19   Monteiro and Azevedo, "Chronic Inflammation in Obesity and the Metabolic Syndrome," 3.

20   The relevant cytokines here include TNFα, IL-6, and IL-18. See Monteiro and Azevedo, "Chronic Inflammation in Obesity and the Metabolic Syndrome," 3; M. Qatanani and M. A. Lazar, "Mechanisms of Obesity-Associated Insulin Resistance: Many Choices on the Menu," *Genes & Development* 21, no. 12 (2007): 1443–55; T. Skurk et al., "The Proatherogenic Cytokine Interleukin-18 Is Secreted by Human Adipocytes," *European Journal of Endocrinology* 152, no. 6 (2005): 863–68.

21 Monteiro and Azevedo, "Chronic Inflammation in Obesity and the Metabolic Syndrome Monteiro," 4; Y. E. Okamoto et al., "Adiponectin Inhibits the Production of CXC Receptor 3 Chemokine Ligands in Macrophages and Reduces T-Lymphocyte Recruitment in Atherogenesis," *Circulation Research* 102, no. 2 (2008): 218–25; Satoshi Nishimura et al., "CD8 Effector T Cells Contribute to Macrophage Recruitment and Adipose Tissue Inflammation in Obesity," *Nature Medicine* 15, no. 8 (2009): 914–20; V. Z. Rocha et al., "Interferon-γ , a Th1 Cytokine, Regulates Fat Inflammation: A Role for Adaptive Immunity in Obesity," *Circulation Research* 103, no. 5 (2008): 467–76.

22 Monteiro and Azevedo, "Chronic Inflammation in Obesity and the Metabolic Syndrome," 4; Okamoto et al., "Adiponectin Inhibits the Production of CXC Receptor 3 Chemokine Ligands," 218–25; Nishimura et al., "CD8 Effector T Cells Contribute to Macrophage Recruitment," 914–20; Rocha et al., "Interferon-γ , a Th1 Cytokine, Regulates Fat Inflammation," 467–76.

23 Monteiro and Azevedo, "Chronic Inflammation in Obesity and the Metabolic Syndrome," 3; Qatanani and Lazar, "Mechanisms of Obesity-Associated Insulin Resistance," 1443–55.

24 Monteiro and Azevedo, "Chronic Inflammation in Obesity and the Metabolic Syndrome," 2–3; Martin Laclaustra et al., "Metabolic Syndrome Pathophysiology: The Role of Adipose Tissue," *Nutrition, Metabolism and Cardiovascular Diseases* 17, no. 2 (2007): 125–39. doi:10.1016/j.numecd.2006.10.005; K. G. Parhofer and P. H. Barett, "Thematic Review Series: Patient-Oriented Research; What We Have Learned about VLDL and LDL Metabolism from Human Kinetics Studies," *Journal of Lipid Research* 47, no. 8 (2006): 1620–30. doi:10.1194/jlr.r600013-jlr200.

25 Monteiro and Azevedo, "Chronic Inflammation in Obesity and the Metabolic Syndrome," 3; J. K. Sethi et al., "Thematic Review Series: Adipocyte Biology. Adipose Tissue Function and Plasticity Orchestrate Nutritional Adaptation," *Journal of Lipid Research* 48, no. 6 (2007): 1253–62.

26 Ian Spreadbury, "Comparison with Ancestral Diets Suggests Dense Acellular Carbohydrates Promote an Inflammatory Microbiota, and May Be the Primary Dietary Cause of Leptin Resistance and Obesity," *Diabetes, Metabolic Syndrome and Obesity: Targets and Therapy* (2012): 175–82; Jared Diamond, "The Double Puzzle of Diabetes," *Nature* 423, no. 6940 (2003): 599–602.

27 L. J. Baier and R. L. Hanson, "Genetic Studies of the Etiology of Type 2 Diabetes in Pima Indians: Hunting for Pieces to a Complicated Puzzle," *Diabetes* 53, no. 5 (2004): 1181; R. L. Hanson and W. C. Knowler, "Type 2 Diabetes and Maturity-Onset Diabetes of the Young," in *Analysis of Multifactoral Disease*, ed. T. Bishop and P. Sham (Oxford: BIOS Science Publishers, 2000), 131–47.

28 A study of inheritance patterns in two Mexican American families with partly indigenous heritage suggested that one particular gene, of unknown identity, exerted a strong influence on the development of early onset type 2 diabetes in these individuals. See M. P. Stern et al., "Evidence for a Major Gene for Type II Diabetes and Linkage Analyses with Selected Candidate Genes in Mexican-Americans," *Diabetes* 45, no. 5 (1996): 563–68. For genetic variation in diabetes etiology in Native American and Caucasian families, see also Baier and Hanson, "Genetic Studies of the Etiology of Type 2 Diabetes in Pima Indians," 1181; J. T. Cook et al., "Segregation Analysis of NIDDM in Caucasian Families," *Diabetologia* 37, no. 12 (1994): 1231–40; R. L. Hanson et al., "A Genome-Wide Association Study in American Indians Implicates DNER as a Susceptibility Locus for Type 2 Diabetes," *Diabetes* 63, no. 1

(2014): 369–76. A genome-wide association study has identified polymorphisms in the DNER locus that are associated with increased risk of diabetes in Pima Indians. W. C. Knowler et al., "Diabetes Incidence and Prevalence in Pima Indians: A 19-fold Greater Incidence Than in Rochester, Minnesota," *American Journal of Epidemiology* 108 (1978): 497–505; Devon A. Mihesuah, *Recovering Our Ancestors' Gardens: Indigenous Recipes and Guide to Diet and Fitness* (Lincoln: University of Nebraska Press, 2005), 3 and 16; L. Ma et al., "PCLO Variants Are Nominally Associated with Early-Onset Type 2 Diabetes and Insulin Resistance in Pima Indians," *Diabetes* 57, no. 11 (2008): 3156–60.

29   See C. N. Hales and D. J. Barker, "The Thrifty Phenotype Hypothesis," *British Medical Bulletin* 60 (2001): 5–20. The original proposition for the Thrifty Gene Hypothesis can be found in J. V. Neel, "Diabetes Mellitus: A 'Thrifty' Genotype Rendered Detrimental by "Progress"? *The American Journal of Human Genetics* 14 (1962): 353–62. For an even more nuanced account of the hypothesis that incorporates potential metabolic differences among the ancestors of modern human populations, see D. Sellayah et al., "On the Evolutionary Origins of Obesity: A New Hypothesis," *Endocrinology* 155, no. 5 (2014), 1573–88. It has been suggested that the feast/famine cycle may have selected for thrifty genes only in agricultural societies. See A. M. Prentice, "Early Influences on Human Energy Regulation: Thrifty Genotypes and Thrifty Phenotypes," *Physiology & Behavior* 86, no. 5 (2005): 640–45. The TGH provides several testable predictions. One such prediction, if the postagricultural model is assumed, is that genetic loci associated with obesity and diabetes should show characteristic signs of recent positive selection. However, a study by Southam et al. testing 13 obesity- and 17 type-2-diabetes-associated genetic variants (comprising a comprehensive list of the most well-established obesity- and diabetes-associated loci at the time of publication) found little evidence for recent positive selection. See L. Southam et al., "Is the Thrifty Genotype Hypothesis Supported by Evidence Based on Confirmed Type 2 Diabetes- and Obesity-Susceptibility Variants?" *Diabetologia* 52, no. 9 (2009): 1846–51. For a strong critique of the hypothesis, see J. R. Speakman, "Thrifty Genes for Obesity, an Attractive But Flawed Idea, and an Alternative Perspective: The 'Drifty Gene' Hypothesis," *International Journal of Obesity* 32, no. 11 (2008): 1611–17.

30   Taubes, *Good Calories, Bad Calorie: Fats, Carbs, and the Controversial Science of Diet and Health* (New York: Anchor, 2007) 238; Peggy Halpern, *Obesity and American Indians/Alaska Natives Prepared for US Department of Health and Human Services Office of the Assistant Secretary* (April 2007) . https://aspe.hhs.gov/pdf-report/obesity-and-american-indiansalaska-natives

31   K. West, "Diabetes in American Indians and Other Native Populations of the New World," *Diabetes* 23 (1974): 841–55.

32   Spreadbury, "Comparison with Ancestral Diets," 181; Lindgärde et al., "Traditional versus Agricultural Lifestyle among Shuar Women," 1355–58; Zimmet et al., "The Global Epidemiology of Non-insulin-dependent Diabetes Mellitus," 60–68; Diamond, "The Double Puzzle of Diabetes," 599–602.

33   J. C. Brand et al., "Plasma Glucose and Insulin Responses to Traditional Pima Indian Meals," *American Journal of Clinical Nutrition* 51, no. 3 (March 1990): 416–20; D. E. Williams et al., "The Effect of Indian or Anglo Dietary Preference on the Incidence of Diabetes in Pima Indians," *Diabetes Care* 24, no. 5 (May 2001): 811–16.

34   R. Cowen, "Seeds of Protection: Ancestral Menus May Hold a Message for Diabetes-Prone Descendants," *Science News* 137 (1990): 350–51.

35   T. F. Burns Kraft et al., "Phytochemical Composition and Metabolic Performance-Enhancing Activity of Dietary Berries Traditionally Used by Native North Americans," *Journal of Agricultural and Food Chemistry* 56, no. 3 (February 2008): 654–60.

36   For the disruption of season patterns of consumption in the Southeast, where year-round maize consumption increased at the expense of hunted animals and other plants, see Paul Kelton, *Epidemics and Enslavement: Biological Catastrophe in the Native Southeast, 1492–1715* (Lincoln: University of Nebraska Press, 2007), 13.

37   Virginia P. Miller, "Aboriginal Micmac Population: A Review of the Evidence," *Ethnohistory* 23 (1976): 12. See the discussion of Miller's assessment in Catherine C. Carlson et al., "Impact of Disease on the Precontact and Early Historic Populations of New England and the Maritimes," in *Disease and Demography in the Americas*, ed. John W. Verano and Douglas H. Ubelaker (Washington, DC: Smithsonian Institution Scholarly Press, 1992), 142.

38   Father Pierre Biard, cited in Carlson et al., "Impact of Disease on the Precontact and Early Historic Populations," 142.

39   Cited in ibid., 148.

40   Virginia DeJohn Anderson, "King Philip's Herds: Indians, Colonists, and the Problem of Livestock in Early New England," *William and Mary Quarterly* 3rd series, 51, no. 4 (October 1994): 606; R. White, *The Roots of Dependency: Subsistence, Environment, and Social Change among the Choctaws, Pawnees, and Navajos* (Lincoln: University of Nebraska Press, 1983).

41   Howard R. Lamar and Sam Truett, "The Greater Southwest and California from the beginning of European Settlement to the 1880s," in *The Cambridge History of the Native Peoples of the Americas*, vol. 1, *North America*: part 2, ed. Bruce G. Trigger and Wilcomb E. Washburn (Cambridge: Cambridge University Press, 1996), 62–63.

42   Ibid.

43   Weston A. Price, *Nutrition and Physical Degeneration*. 6th ed., 14th printing (La Mesa, CA: Price-Pottenger Nutrition Foundation, 2000): 260.

44   On greater historical carbohydrate consumption at lower global latitudes, see Alexander Ströhle and Andreas Hahn, "Diets of Modern Hunter-Gatherers Vary Substantially in Their Carbohydrate Content Depending on Ecoenvironments: Results from an Ethnographic Analysis," *Nutrition Research* 31, no. 6 (2011): 429–35.

45   W. E. Connor et al., "The Plasma Lipds, Lipoproteins, and Diet of the Tarahumara Indians of Mexico," *American Journal of Clinical Nutrition* 31 (1978): 1131; D. L. Christensen et al., "Physical Activity, Cardio-Respiratory Fitness, And Metabolic Traits In Rural Mexican Tarahumara," *American Journal of Human Biology* 24, no. 4 (July–August 2012): 558–61. Problematically, many studies of Tarahumara cardiovascular health have focused on low HDL levels, which other recent studies have found to be ineffective as a health marker (in comparison to small dense LDL particles). The Tarahumara were a subject of Christopher McDougall's bestselling book, *Born to Run: A Hidden Tribe, Superathletes, and the Greatest Race the World Has Never Seen* (New York: Knopf, 2009).

46   H. R. et al., "Cardiovascular Damage Resulting from Chronic Excessive Endurance Exercise," *Missouri Medicine* 109, no. 4 (July–August 2012): 312–21; J. H. O'Keefe et al., "Potential Adverse Cardiovascular Effects from Excessive Endurance Exercise," *Mayo Clinic Proceedings* 87, no.6 (2012):587–95.

47   Melissa A. Walker et al., "Powering the Immune System: Mitochondria in Immune Function and Deficiency," *Journal of Immunology Research* 2014 (2014): 1; R. Rossignol

et al., "Threshold Effect and Tissue Specificity: Implication for Mitochondrial Cytopathies," *Journal of Biological Chemistry* 274, no. 47 (1999): 33426–32.

48 Michael D. Buck et al., "T Cell Metabolism Drives Immunity," *Journal of Cell Biology* 210, no. 4 (2015): 1352; G. J. Van Der Windt et al., "Mitochondrial Respiratory Capacity Is a Critical Regulator of CD8 T Cell Memory Development," *Immunity* 36, no. 1 (2012): 68–78.

49 T. N. Seyfried et al., "Cancer as a Metabolic Disease: Implications for Novel Therapeutics," *Carcinogenesis* 35, no. 3 (2013): 516; O. Warburg, "On the Origin of Cancer Cells," *Science* 123, no. 3191 (1956): 309–14; Peter L. Pedersen, "Warburg, Me and Hexokinase 2: Multiple Discoveries of Key Molecular Events Underlying One of Cancers' Most Common Phenotypes, the 'Warburg Effect,' i.e., Elevated Glycolysis in the Presence of Oxygen," *Journal of Bioenergetics and Biomembranes* 39, no. 3 (2007): 211–22; O. Warburg, "On Respiratory Impairment in Cancer Cells," *Science* 124, no. 3215 (1956): 269–70. Mitochondria are required for the energy-producing process known as oxidative phosphorylation, which relies on the electron transport chain in the mitochondrial membrane. See Bernhard Kadenbach, "Introduction to Mitochondrial Oxidative Phosphorylation," *Advances in Experimental Medicine and Biology Mitochondrial Oxidative Phosphorylation* 748 (2012): 1–11. The process is required for the burning of fatty acids and the complete oxidation of glucose. See Seyfried et al., "Cancer as a Metabolic Disease," 517–19.

50 A deficiency in the metabolic efficiency of cells can be exhibited through a decreased ability to perform oxidative phosphorylation. See Seyfried et al., "Cancer as a Metabolic Disease," 517; Paloma Acebo et al., "Cancer Abolishes the Tissue Type-Specific Differences in the Phenotype of Energetic Metabolism," *Translational Oncology* 2, no. 3 (2009): 138–45; J. M. Cuezva et al., "The Bioenergetic Signature of Cancer: A Marker of Tumor Progression," *Cancer Research* 62 (2002): 6674–81; Seyfried et al., "Cancer as a Metabolic Disease," 521–22; Thomas N. Seyfried et al., "Is the Restricted Ketogenic Diet a Viable Alternative to the Standard of Care for Managing Malignant Brain Cancer?" *Epilepsy Research* 100, no. 3 (2012): 310–26; Thomas Seyfried, *Cancer as a Metabolic Disease: On the Origin, Management, and Prevention of Cancer* (New York: Wiley, 2012) 291–354 and 516–77; Gabriele D. Maurer et al., "Differential Utilization of Ketone Bodies by Neurons and Glioma Cell Lines: A Rationale for Ketogenic Diet as Experimental Glioma Therapy," *BMC Cancer* 11, no. 1 (2011): 315; Robert Skinner et al., "Ketone Bodies Inhibit the Viability of Human Neuroblastoma Cells," *Journal of Pediatric Surgery* 44, no. 1 (2009): 212–16; Pedersen, "Warburg, Me and Hexokinase 2," 211–22; O. Warburg, *The Metabolism of Tumours* (New York: Richard R. Smith, 1931). Research supports the hypothesis that the health of mitochondria is one of the primary determinants of the aberrant metabolism of cancer cells: several studies show mitochondrial abnormalities in tumor cells. See Seyfried et al., "Cancer as a Metabolic Disease," 517–18. Transplantation of mitochondria from one cell to another has been shown to convert a cancerous cell to a healthy cell and vice versa, thereby illustrating the ability of mitochondria to determine the metabolic health of a cell. See Seyfried et al., "Cancer as a Metabolic Disease," 516–18; Benny Abraham Kaipparettu et al., "Crosstalk from Non-Cancerous Mitochondria Can Inhibit Tumor Properties of Metastatic Cells by Suppressing Oncogenic Pathways," *PLoS ONE* 8, no. 5 (2013): e61747; R. L. Elliott et al., "Mitochondria Organelle Transplantation: Introduction of Normal Epithelial Mitochondria into Human Cancer Cells Inhibits Proliferation and

Increases Drug Sensitivity," *Breast Cancer Research and Treatment* 136, no. 2 (2012): 347–54; Peter L. Pedersen, "Tumor Mitochondria and the Bioenergetics of Cancer Cells," *Membrane Anomalies of Tumor Cells Progress in Tumor Research* 22 (1978): 190–274; Gabriel Arismendi-Morillo, "Electron Microscopy Morphology of the Mitochondrial Network in Gliomas and Their Vascular Microenvironment," *Biochimica Et Biophysica Acta (BBA)—Bioenergetics* 1807, no. 6 (2011): 602–8; Gabriel Arismendi-Morillo, "Electron Microscopy Morphology of the Mitochondrial Network in Human Cancer," *International Journal of Biochemistry & Cell Biology* 41, no. 10 (2009): 2062–68; G. J. Arismendi-Morillo and A. V. Castellano-Ramirez, "Ultrastructural Mitochondrial Pathology in Human Astrocytic Tumors: Potentials Implications Protherapeutics Strategies," *Journal of Electron Microscopy* 57, no. 1 (2008): 33–39; Simone Fulda et al., "Targeting Mitochondria for Cancer Therapy," *Nature Reviews Drug Discovery* 9, no. 6 (2010): 447–64; Y. Shapovalov et al., "Mitochondrial Dysfunction in Cancer Cells Due to Aberrant Mitochondrial Replication," *Journal of Biological Chemistry* 286, no. 25 (2011): 22331–38. Mitochondrial dysfunction, likely from excess glucose metabolism, is also strongly implicated in Parkinson's disease, which involves disruptions to normal cellular metabolism. See Nicole Exner et al., "Mitochondrial Dysfunction in Parkinson's Disease: Molecular Mechanisms and Pathophysiological Consequences," *EMBO Journal* 31, no. 14 (2012): 3038–62; C. Perier and M. Vila, "Mitochondrial Biology and Parkinson's Disease," *Cold Spring Harbor Perspectives in Medicine* 2, no. 2 (2012); R. F. Peppard et al., "Cerebral Glucose Metabolism in Parkinson's Disease with and without Dementia," *Archives of Neurology* 49, no. 12 (1992): 1262–68.

51   On the role of Reactive Oxygen Species such as superoxide and hydroxyl, see Mostafa I. Waly et al., "Low Nourishment of Vitamin C Induces Glutathione Depletion and Oxidative Stress in Healthy Young Adults," *Preventive Nutrition and Food Science* 20, no. 3 (2015): 198–203; Joan Montero et al., "Cholesterol and Peroxidized Cardiolipin in Mitochondrial Membrane Properties, Permeabilization and Cell Death," *Biochimica Et Biophysica Acta (BBA)——Bioenergetics* 1797, no. 6–7 (2010): 1217–24.

52   Dean P. Jones, "Redefining Oxidative Stress," *Antioxidants & Redox Signaling* 8, no. 9–10 (2006): 1865–879.

53   In order to emphasize the role that oxidative stress plays in signaling, Jones recently suggested that oxidative stress should be defined as "a disruption of redox signalling and control." See Jones, "Redefining Oxidative Stress," 1865–79.

54   Monteiro and Azevedo, "Chronic Inflammation in Obesity and the Metabolic Syndrome," 4; Qatanani and Lazar, "Mechanisms of Obesity Associated Insulin Resistance," 1443–55. ROS have been shown to cause secretion of cytokines via activation of the MAP protein kinase pathway. See Graves and Kayal, "Diabetic Complications and Dysregulated Innate Immunity," 1227–39.

55   A. Tsatsoulis et al., "Insulin Resistance: An Adaptive Mechanism Becomes Maladaptive in the Current Environment—An Evolutionary Perspective," *Metabolism* 62 (2013): 622–33. For new research on the link between vitamin D and insulin sensitivity (higher vitamin D mitigating or reducing the insulin-producing effects of carbohydrates, declining vitamin D from the sun increasing insulin insensitivity and producing negative health outcomes, including cardiovascular disease), see A. Zitterman, "Vitamin D and Disease Prevention with Special Reference to Cardiovascular Disease," *Progress in Biophysics & Molecular Biology* 92, no.1 (September 2006): 39–48; C. V. Harinarayan, "Vitamin D and Diabetes Mellitus," *Hormones*

(Athens). 13, no. 2 (April–June 2014): 163–81; J. A. Alvarez and A. Ashraf. "Role of Vitamin D in Insulin Secretion and Insulin Sensitivity for Glucose Homeostasis," *International Journal of Endocrinology* 2010, Article ID 351385, 18 pages; Priyanka Prasad, "Interplay of Vitamin D and Metabolic Syndrome: A Review," *Diabetes & Metabolic Syndrome: Clinical Research & Reviews* (March 2015): 105–12; C-C. Sung et al., "Role of Vitamin D in Insulin Resistance," *Journal of Biomedicine and Biotechnology* (2012): 634195; B. Maestro et al., "Identification of a Vitamin D Response Element in the Human Insulin Receptor Gene Promoter," *Journal of Steroid Biochemistry and Molecular Biology* 84, no. 2–3 (2003): 223–30; U. Zeitz et al., "Impaired Insulin Secretory Capacity In Mice Lacking A Functional Vitamin D Receptor," *FASEB Journal* 17, no. 3 (2003): 509–11; A. W. Norman et al., "Vitamin D Deficiency Inhibits Pancreatic Secretion of Insulin," *Science* 209 (1980):823–825; M. F. Holick, "Diabetes and the Vitamin D Connection," *Current Diabetes Reports* 8 (2008): 393–398; C. Mattila et al., "Serum 25-Hydroxy Vitamin D Concentration and Subsequent Risk of Type 2 Diabetes," *Diabetes Care* 30 (2007): 2569–70; Jatupol Kositsawat et al., "Association of A1C Levels with Vitamin D Status in U.S. Adults Data from the National Health and Nutrition Examination Survey," *Diabetes Care.* 33, no. 6 (June 2010): 1236–38.

56   I. Sekirov et al., "Gut Microbiota in Health and Disease," *Physiological Reviews* 90 (2010): 859–904.

57   Giada De Palma et al., "The Microbiota-Gut-Brain Axis in Gastrointestinal Disorders: Stressed Bugs, Stressed Brain or Both?" *Journal of Physiology* 592, no. 14 (2014): 2990; J. K. Nicholson et al., "Host-Gut Microbiota Metabolic Interactions," *Science* 336, no. 6086 (2012): 1262–267; Felix Sommer and Fredrik Bäckhed, "The Gut Microbiota—Masters of Host Development and Physiology," *Nature Reviews Microbiology* 11, no. 4 (2013): 227–38.

58   Matthew J. Bull and Nigel T. Plummer, "Part 1: The Human Gut Microbiome in Health and Disease," *Integrative Medicine* 13, no. 6 (2014): 18.

59   Catherine A. Lozupone et al., "Diversity, Stability and Resilience of the Human Gut Microbiota," *Nature* 489, no. 7415 (2012): 220–30. doi:10.1038/nature11550; P. B. Eckburg, "Diversity of the Human Intestinal Microbial Flora," *Science* 308, no. 5728 (2005): 1635–38.

60   See the account of these first encounters in M. Kat Anderson, *Tending the Wild: Native American Knowledge and the Management of California's Natural Resources* (Berkeley and Los Angeles: University of California Press, 2005), 64–67; William J. Bauer, Jr., "California," in *The Oxford Handbook of American Indian History*, 281.

61   Sebastian Rodriguez Cermeno (November 1595), cited in Anderson, *Tending the Wild*, 67.

62   Sherburne F. Cook, "Historical Demography," in *Handbook of North American Indians*, vol. 8, *California* (Washington, DC: Smithsonian Institution Scholarly Press, 1978), 91.

63   Philip L. Walker and John R. Johnson, "Effects of Contact on the Chumash Indians," in *Disease and Demography in the Americas*. ed. John W. Verano and Douglas H. Ubelaker (Washington, DC: Smithsonian Institution Scholarly Press, 1992), 131–32. See also David Hornbeck, *California Patterns: A Geographical and Historical Atlas* (Palo Alto, CA: Mayfield Publishing, 1983), 46; Sherburne F. Cook and Cesare Marino, "Roman Catholic Missions in California and the Southwest," in *Handbook of North American Indians*, vol. 4, *History of Indian-White Relations* (Washington, DC: Smithsonian Institution Scholarly Press, 1988), 474; Robert L. Hoover, "Spanish-Native Interactions and Acculturation in Alta California Missions," in *Archaeological and Historical Perspectives*

on the Spanish Borderlands West, ed. David H. Thomas (Washington, DC: Smithsonian Institution Scholarly Press, 1989), 401.

64 Anderson, *Tending the Wild,* 74.

65 Steven W. Hackel, "From Ahogado to Zorrillo: External Causes of Mortality in the California Missions," *History of the Family* 17, no. 1 (2012): 77–104; Ubelaker, "Population Size, Contact to Nadir," 699.

66 Alan K. Brown, *The Aboriginal Population of the Santa Barbara Channel* (Berkeley: University of California Press, 1967), 76.

67 Cited in Maynard Geiger and Clement Meighan, *As the Padres Saw Them* (Santa Barbara, CA: Santa Barbara Mission Archive Library, 1976), 86. See also the discussion in Kent G. Lightfoot, *Indians, Missionaries, and Merchants: The Legacy of Colonial Encounters on the California Frontiers* (Berkeley: University of California Press, 2005), 101; Glenn J. Farris, "Depriving God and the King of the Means of Charity: Early Nineteenth-Century Missionaries' Views of Cattle Ranchers near Mission La Purisima, California," in *Indigenous Landscapes and Spanish Missions: New Perspectives from Archaeology and Ethnohistory,* ed. Lee M. Panich and Tsim Schneider (Tucson: University of Arizona Press, 2014), 151; Walker and Johnson, "Effects of Contact on the Chumash Indians," 132.

68 Bauer Jr., "California," 283.

69 Lisabeth Haas, *Pablo Tac, Indigenous Scholar: Writing on Luiseño Language and Colonial History, c.1840* (Berkeley: University of California Press, 2011), 151, 163–83; James A. Sandos, *Converting California: Indians and Franciscans in the Missions* (New Haven, CT: Yale University Press, 2004), 141–53; Quincy D. Newell, *Constructing Lives at Mission San Francisco: Native Californians and Hispanic Colonists, 1776–1821* (Albuquerque: University of New Mexico Press, 2009); Steven W. Hackel, *Children of Coyote, Missionaries of Saint Francis: Indian-Spanish Relations in Colonial California, 1769–1850* (Chapel Hill: University of North Carolina Press, 2005), 76–78; Dianne Kirkby, "Colonial Policy and Native Depopulation in California and New South Wales, 1770–1840," *Ethnohistory* 31, no. 1 (1984): 1–16

70 Lightfoot, *Indians, Missionaries and Merchants,* 56.

71 Jan Timbrook et al., "Vegetation Burning by the Chumash," *Journal of California and Great Basin Anthropology* 4, no. 2 (1982): 163–86.

72 William R. Hildebrandt and Kimberly Carpenter, "Native Hunting Adaptations in California: Changing Patterns of Resource Use from the Early Holocene to European Contact," in *The Subsistence Economies of Indigenous North American Societies: A Handbook,* ed. Bruce D. Smith (Washington, DC: Smithsonian Institution Scholarly Press, 2011), 132.

73 Lightfoot, *Indians, Missionaries and Merchants,* 59; Bauer Jr., "California," 284–85.

74 Bauer Jr., "California," 286.

75 Albert L. Hurtado, *Indian Survival on the California Frontier* (New Haven, CT: Yale University Press, 1988), 205–7; William J. Bauer Jr., *We Were All Like Migrant Workers Here: Work, Community and Memory on California's Round Valley Reservation, 1850–1941* (Chapel Hill: University of North Carolina Press, 2009), 60.

76 Anderson, *Tending the Wild,* 76.

77 Louis S. Warren, "The Nature of Conquest: Indians, Americans, and Environmental History," ," in *A Companion to American Indian History* ed. Philip J. Deloria and Neal Salisbury (Malden, MA: Wiley-Blackwell, 2002), 297.

78 Hackel, *Children of Coyote, Missionaries of Saint Francis,* 76–78.

79 Philip L. Walker et al., "The Effect of European Contact on the Health of California Indians," in *Columbian Consequences,* vol. 2, *Archaeological and Historical Perspectives on the Spanish Borderlands West,* ed. David H. Thomas (Washington, DC: Smithsonian

Institution Scholarly Press, 1989), 354; Lytt I. Gardner, "Deprivation Dwarfism," *Scientific American* 227 (1) (1972): 76–82; Walker and Johnson, "Effects of Contact on the Chumash Indians," 132.

80   Brendan C. Lindsay, *Murder State: California's Native American Genocide, 1846–1873* (Lincoln: University of Nebraska Press, 2012); Benjamin Madley, "California's Yuki Indians: Defining Genocide in Native American History," *Western Historical Quarterly* 39, no. 3 (2008): 303–32.

81   David Rich Lewis, *Neither Wolf Nor Dog: American Indians, Environment, and Agrarian Change* (New York: Oxford University Press, 1994), 84–118; Bauer Jr., "California," 290.

82   Brian Fagan, *Before California: An Archaeologist Looks at Our Earliest Inhabitants* (Walnut Creek, CA: Alta Mira, 2003), 125–214.

83   As Fritz has shown, up to AD 1000 and after the consolidation of maize agriculture, nuts "were critical sources of fats, proteins, and carbohydrates from early Holocene into historic times"—including hickory nuts, walnuts, acorns, hazelnuts, chestnuts, and chinquapins. Wherever oak and hickory forests grew—in California, the Great Basin, the Midwest, the Great Lakes, and the Northeast and Atlantic coastal regions—they constituted a "staple storable plant." See Gayle J. Fritz, "Levels of Native Biodiversity in Eastern North America," in *Biodiversity and Native America*, ed. Paul E. Minnis and Wayne J. Elisens (Norman: University of Oklahoma Press, 2000), 233.

84   We now know that a good source of resistant starch can be found in acorn powder See M. Tadayoni et al., "Isolation of Bioactive Polysaccharide from Acorn and Evaluation of Its Functional Properties," *International Journal of Biological Macromolecules* 72 (January 2015): 179–84.

85   Andrew B. Shreiner et al., "The Gut Microbiome in Health and in Disease," *Current Opinion in Gastroenterology* 31, no. 1 (2015): 69–75; Erica D. Sonnenburg and Justin L. Sonnenburg, "Starving Our Microbial Self: The Deleterious Consequences of a Diet Deficient in Microbiota-Accessible Carbohydrates," *Cell Metabolism* 20, no. 5 (2014): 780; Harry J. Flint et al., "Microbial Degradation of Complex Carbohydrates in the Gut," *Gut Microbes* 3, no. 4 (2012): 289–306; Nicole M. Koropatkin et al., "How Glycan Metabolism Shapes the Human Gut Microbiota," *Nature Reviews Microbiology* 10 (2012): 323–35.

86   Sonnenburg and Sonnenburg, "Starving Our Microbial Self," 780; Koropatkin et al., "How Glycan Metabolism Shapes the Human Gut Microbiota," 323–35.

87   Sekirov et al., "Gut Microbiota in Health and Disease," 859–904.

88   Harry J. Flint et al., "Polysaccharide Utilization by Gut Bacteria: Potential for New Insights from Genomic Analysis," *Nature Reviews Microbiology* 6, no. 2 (2008): 121.

89   Audrey Rivière, "Bifidobacteria and Butyrate-Producing Colon Bacteria: Importance and Strategies for Their Stimulation in the Human Gut," *Frontiers in Microbiology* 7 (2016): 1.

90   D. L. Topping and P. M. Clifton, "Short-Chain Fatty Acids and Human Colonic Function: Roles of Resistant Starch and Nonstarch Polysaccharides," *Physiological Reviews* 81, no. 3 (July 2001): 1031–64; K. M. Behall et al., "Consumption of Both Resistant Starch and Beta-Glucan Improves Postprandial Plasma Glucose and Insulin in Women," *Diabetes Care* 29, no. 5 (May 2006): 976–81; K. L. Johnston et al., "Resistant Starch Improves Insulin Sensitivity In Metabolic Syndrome. *Diabetic Medicine* 27, no. 4 (April 2010): 391–97; O. J. Park et al., "Resistant Starch Supplementation Influences Blood Lipid Concentrations and Glucose Control in Overweight Subjects. *Journal of Nutritional Science and Vitaminology* 50, no. 2 (April 2004): 93–99.

91   Narinder Kaur and Anil K. Gupta, "Applications of Inulin and Oligofructose in Health and Nutrition," *Journal of Biosciences* 27, no. 7 (2002): 704; Rivière et al., "Bifidobacteria and Butyrate-Producing Colon Bacteria," 8; X. Wang and G.r. Gibson, "Effects of the in Vitro Fermentation of Oligofructose and Inulin by Bacteria Growing in the Human Large Intestine," *Journal of Applied Bacteriology* 75, no. 4 (1993): 373–80; Glen R. Gibson et al., "Selective Stimulation of Bifidobacteria in the Human Colon by Oligofructose and Inulin," *Gastroenterology* 108, no. 4 (1995): 975–82; M. B. Roberfroid et al., "Colonic Microflora: Nutrition and Health," *Nutrition Reviews* 53 (1995): 127–30; J. H. Cummings et al., "Prebiotic Digestion and Fermentation," *American Journal of Clinical Nutrition* 73 (suppl) (2001): 415–20; H. Hidaka et al., "Effects of Fructooligosaccharides on Intestinal Flora and Human Health," *Bifidobacteria and Microflora* 5 (1986): 37–50; R. K. Buddington et al., "Dietary Supplementation of Neosugar Alters the Faecal Flora and Decreases Activities of Some Reductive Enzymes in Human Subjects," *American Journal of Clinical Nutrition* 63 (1996): 709–16; B. Kleessen et al., "Effects of Insulin and Lactose on Faecal Microflora, Microbial Activity and Bowel Habit in Elderly Constipated Persons," *American Journal of Clinical Nutrition* 65 (1997): 1397–1402. Bifidobacteria have been shown to have a number of beneficial effects on the immune system. See Rivière et al., "Bifidobacteria and Butyrate-Producing Colon Bacteria," 1–3; R. Miller-Catchpole, "Bifidobacteria in Clinical Microbiology and Medicine," in *Biochemistry and Physiology of Bifidobacteria*, ed. Anatoly Bezkorovainy and Robin Miller-Catchpole (Boca Raton, FL: CRC Press, 1989): 177–200; Gibson et al., "Selective Stimulation of Bifidobacteria in the Human Colon by Oligofructose and Inulin," 975–82; S. C. Leahy et al., "Getting Better with Bifidobacteria," *Journal of Applied Microbiology* 98, no. 6 (2005): 1303–15; Lara Gorissen, "Production of Conjugated Linoleic Acid and Conjugated Linolenic Acid Isomers by Bifidobacterium Species," *Applied Microbiology and Biotechnology* 87, no. 6 (2010): 2257–66; M. Rossi and A. Amaretti, "Probiotic Properties of Bifidobacteria," in *Bifidobacteria, Genomics and Molecular Aspects*, ed. B. Mayo and D. van Sinderen (Norwich: Caister Academic Press, 2011): 97–123; Mérilie Gagnon et al., "Bioaccessible Antioxidants in Milk Fermented by Bifidobacterium Longum subsp.longum Strains," *BioMed Research International* 2015 (2015): 1–12; Diana Di Gioia et al., "Bifidobacteria: Their Impact on Gut Microbiota Composition and Their Applications as Probiotics in Infants," *Applied Microbiology and Biotechnology* 98, no. 2 (2013): 563–77; Remo Frei et al., "Prebiotics, Probiotics, Synbiotics, and the Immune System," *Current Opinion in Gastroenterology* 31, no. 2 (2015): 153–58.

92   Sonnenburg and Sonnenburg, "Starving Our Microbial Self," 783; J. L. Sonnenburg et al., "Glycan Foraging in Vivo by an Intestine-Adapted Bacterial Symbiont," *Science* 307, no. 5717 (2005): 1955–59.

93   Sonnenburg and Sonnenburg, "Starving Our Microbial Self," 783.

94   Christoph A. Thaiss et al., "The Interplay between the Innate Immune System and the Microbiota," *Current Opinion in Immunology* 26 (2014): 41–48. Experiments in mice with altered immune receptor signaling illustrate such a phenomenon. They show alterations in the composition of their microbiota, which predisposes them to inflammatory disease, indicative of aberrant immune function. See Seth Rakoff-Nahoum et al., "Recognition of Commensal Microflora by Toll-Like Receptors Is Required for Intestinal Homeostasis," *Cell* 118, no. 2 (2004): 229–41. Germ-free (gnotobiotic) mice, which lack a gut microbiome community entirely, often show abnormalities in immune function. See Kau et al., "Human Nutrition, the Gut Microbiome and the Immune System," 327–36.

95   The Nod-like receptor signaling is thought to play an attendant role in maintaining the
     intestinal microbiotal community. The Nod1 receptor pathway is activated in intes-
     tinal cells by peptidoglycans in the cell walls of some bacterial species, and induces
     changes in the intestinal lymphoid tissues necessary for maintenance of the microbiotal
     community. See Djahida Bouskra et al., "Lymphoid Tissue Genesis Induced by
     Commensals through NOD1 Regulates Intestinal Homeostasis," *Nature* 456, no. 7221
     (2008): 507–10. Similarly, the Nod2 signaling pathway has been shown to regulate the
     microbiotal composition: experiments in mice lacking the Nod2 receptor were found
     to have perturbations in their microbiota. See T. Petnicki-Ocwieja et al., "Nod2 Is
     Required for the Regulation of Commensal Microbiota in the Intestine," *Proceedings of
     the National Academy of Sciences* 106, no. 37 (2009): 15813–18. The microbiota, in turn,
     regulate Nod-like receptor signaling. Expression of the receptor has been found to
     depend on the presence of the microbiotal community. See Petnicki-Ocwieja et al.,
     "Nod2 Is Required for the Regulation of Commensal Microbiota in the Intestine,"
     15813–18. This feedback loop may keep the microbiotal populations in a symbi-
     otic balance, preventing overcolonization and resulting dysbiosis. Signaling through
     the NLR pathway has been shown to prevent infection by *Salmonella Typhimurium*,
     suggesting a role in preventing invasion by pathogenic species. See Thaiss et al., "The
     Interplay between the Innate Immune System and the Microbiota," 44; Petr Broz
     et al., "Redundant Roles for Inflammasome Receptors NLRP3 and NLRC4 in Host
     Defense against Salmonella," *Journal of Experimental Medicine* 207, no. 8 (2010): 1745–
     55. Research suggests that signaling through the NLR pathway affects microbiotal
     composition in ways that encourage the development of inflammatory bowel dis-
     ease and colorectal cancer. See Thaiss et al., "The Interplay between the Innate
     Immune System and the Microbiota," 41–42. Signaling through the NLR pathways
     is also thought to affect microbiotal composition in ways that may encourage the
     development of metabolic syndrome. See Thaiss et al., "The Interplay between
     the Innate Immune System and the Microbiota," 42–44; Jorge Henao-Mejia et al.,
     "Inflammasome-Mediated Dysbiosis Regulates Progression of NAFLD and Obesity,"
     Nature, 482 (2012): 179–85.
96   Thaiss et al., "The Interplay between the Innate Immune System and the Microbiota,
     41. Toll-like receptors (TLR) are pattern recognition receptors that are present in T
     cells. See Adeeb H. Rahman et al., "The Contribution of Direct TLR Signaling to T
     Cell Responses," *Immunologic Research* 45, no. 1 (2009): 25. TLRs have been suggested
     to be involved in the recognition of the microbiota. See Thaiss et al., "The Interplay
     between the Innate Immune System and the Microbiota," 41–42; Rakoff-Nahoum
     et al., "Recognition of Commensal Microflora by Toll-Like Receptors," 229–41;
     R. Medzhitov et al., "A Human Homologue of the Drosophila Toll Protein Signals
     Activation of Adaptive Immunity," *Nature* 388 (1997): 394–97; A. Poltorak, "Defective
     LPS Signaling in C3H/HeJ and C57BL/10ScCr Mice: Mutations in Tlr4 Gene,"
     Science 282, no. 5396 (1998): 2085–88. Signaling through toll-like receptors has been
     shown to affect the specific species present in the microbiota: TLR2 activation on
     CD4+ T cells is required for colonization by *Bacteroides fragilis*——signaling through
     this pathway restricts the response of T helper cells so that *Bacteroides fragilis* is tolerated
     by the immune system. See Thaiss et al., "The Interplay between the Innate Immune
     System and the Microbiota," 41–42; J. L. Round et al., "The Toll-Like Receptor
     2 Pathway Establishes Colonization by a Commensal of the Human Microbiota,"
     Science 332, no. 6032 (2011): 974–77.

97 Stephanie C. Ganal et al., "Priming of Natural Killer Cells by Nonmucosal Mononuclear Phagocytes Requires Instructive Signals from Commensal Microbiota," *Immunity* 37, no. 1 (2012): 171–86. In the lamina propria of the intestine, they activate an innate immune response to pathogenic but not commensal bacteria. See Thaiss et al., "The Interplay between the Innate Immune System and the Microbiota," 45–46. In mice, specific types of mononuclear phagocytes have been shown to be required for the clearance of pathogens invading the intestinal lumen, and during dysbiosis the movement of phagocytes is affected, and an immune response is activated against commensal bacteria. See Thaiss, "The Interplay between the Innate Immune System and the Microbiota," 43–44; Gretchen E. Diehl et al., "Microbiota Restricts Trafficking of Bacteria to Mesenteric Lymph Nodes by CX3CR1hi Cells," *Nature* 494, no. 7435 (2013): 116–20. Such mechanisms are hypothesized to affect the development of inflammatory conditions such as inflammatory bowel disease, and also to compromise the working immune system. See Kau et al., "Human Nutrition, the Gut Microbiome and the Immune System," 327–36; De Palma et al., "The Microbiota-Gut-Brain Axis in Gastrointestinal Disorders," 2989–97; Diehl et al., "Microbiota Restricts Trafficking of Bacteria," 116–20.

98 Thaiss et al., "The Interplay between the Innate Immune System and the Microbiota," 41–48. Gnotobiotic mice have been used in many studies to examine effects of the microbiome on immune function. Perturbations in immune function are found in these mice, indicating that the microbiome has a vital role in immune function. Studies of gnotobiotic mice have also shown that the function and development of several types of immune cells depends on the microbiota. For example, the function of specific classes of innate lymphoid immune cells (ILCs) has been shown to be dependent on intestinal microbes. See Kau et al., "Human Nutrition, the Gut Microbiome and the Immune System," 327–36; Thaiss et al., "The Interplay between the Innate Immune System and the Microbiota," 45–46; Naoko Satoh-Takayama et al., "Microbial Flora Drives Interleukin 22 Production in Intestinal NKp46 Cells That Provide Innate Mucosal Immune Defense," *Immunity* 29, no. 6 (2008): 958–70; Stephanie L. Sanos et al., "RORγt and Commensal Microflora Are Required for the Differentiation of Mucosal Interleukin 22–producing NKp46 Cells," *Nature Immunology* 10, no. 1 (2008): 83–91; S. Sawa et al., "Lineage Relationship Analysis of ROR t Innate Lymphoid Cells," *Science* 330, no. 6004 (2010): 665–69; Shinichiro Sawa et al., "RORγt Innate Lymphoid Cells Regulate Intestinal Homeostasis by Integrating Negative Signals from the Symbiotic Microbiota," *Nature Immunology* 12, no. 4 (2011): 320–26. Conversely, studies have shown that ILCs regulate microbiotal populations and aid the host response against pathogens. See Thaiss et al., "The Interplay between the Innate Immune System and the Microbiota," 45–46; Matthias Lochner et al., "Microbiota-induced Tertiary Lymphoid Tissues Aggravate Inflammatory Disease in the Absence of RORγt and LTi Cells," *Journal of Experimental Medicine* 208, no. 1 (2010): 125–34; G. F. Sonnenberg et al., "Innate Lymphoid Cells Promote Anatomical Containment of Lymphoid-Resident Commensal Bacteria," *Science* 336, no. 6086 (2012): 1321–25; Christoph S. Klose et al., "A T-bet Gradient Controls the Fate and Function of CCR6–RORγt Innate Lymphoid Cells," *Nature* 494, no. 7436 (2013): 261–65. Studies on gnotobiotic mice, and mice with a restricted number of species in their microbiota, suggest a role of the microbiota in regulating T cells: the levels of invariant natural killer T (iNKT) cells is reduced in these mice. See Thaiss et al., "The Interplay between the Innate Immune

System and the Microbiota," 45–46; B. Wei et al., "Commensal Microbiota and CD8+ T cells Shape the Formation of Invariant NKT Cells," *Journal of Immunology* 184 (2010): 1218–26. Levels of iNKT cells are increased in the colonic lamina propia and lungs of adult germ-free mice, which are susceptible to ulcerative colitis and asthma, which provides some support to the suggestion that these cells play a role in allergies and asthma. See Thaiss et al., "The Interplay between the Innate Immune System and the Microbiota," 45; Patrick J. Brennan et al., "Invariant Natural Killer T Cells: An Innate Activation Scheme Linked to Diverse Effector Functions," *Nature Reviews Immunology* 13, no. 2 (2013): 101–17; Dingding An et al., "Early Life Exposure to Microbiota Has Persistent Effects on Colonic Lamina Propria INKT Cells and Colitis," *Inflammatory Bowel Diseases* 17 (2011): S70; T. D. Olszak et al., "Microbial Exposure during Early Life Has Persistent Effects on Natural Killer T Cell Function," *Science* 336, no. 6080 (2012): 489–93.

99   Ponton et al., "Integrating Nutrition and Immunology," 131.

100   Thaiss et al., "The Interplay between the Innate Immune System and the Microbiota," 45; Olszak and colleagues also showed that expression of a ligand (signaling molecule) for a receptor expressed in NKT cells, CXCL16, was dependent on the microbiota: germ-free mice had reduced methylation and expression of the gene encoding this receptor. See Olszak et al., "Microbial Exposure during Early Life Has Persistent Effects," 489–93.

101   Kau et al., "Human Nutrition, the Gut Microbiome and the Immune System," 329; Jennifer J. Bird et al., "Helper T Cell Differentiation Is Controlled by the Cell Cycle," *Immunity* 9, no. 2 (1998): 229–37; Luying Peng et al., "Effects of Butyrate on Intestinal Barrier Function in a Caco-2 Cell Monolayer Model of Intestinal Barrier," *Pediatric Research* 61, no. 1 (2007): 37–41. Experiments have suggested that the SCFAs and proprionate may exert anti-inflammatory effects by binding to the G-protein-coupled receptor GPR43, which may result in changes in gene expression in immune cells including neutrophils and eosinophils. See A. J. Brown et al., "The Orphan G Protein-coupled Receptors GPR41 and GPR43 Are Activated by Propionate and Other Short Chain Carboxylic Acids," *Journal of Biological Chemistry* 278, no. 13 (2002): 11312–19; E. Le Poul et al., "Functional Characterization of Human Receptors for Short Chain Fatty Acids and Their Role in Polymorphonuclear Cell Activation," *Journal of Biological Chemistry* 278, no. 28 (2003): 25481–89; Kendle M. Maslowski et al., "Regulation of Inflammatory Responses by Gut Microbiota and Chemoattractant Receptor GPR43," *Nature* 461, no. 7268 (2009): 1282–86.

102   Kau et al., "Human Nutrition, the Gut Microbiome and the Immune System," 330.

103   Ibid.

104   B. S. Reddy et al., "Effect of Intestinal Microflora on Iron and Zinc Metabolism, and on Activities of Metalloenzymes in Rats," *Journal of Nutrition* 102 (1972): 101–7.

105   T. Werner et al., "Depletion of Luminal Iron Alters the Gut Microbiota and Prevents Crohn's Disease-like Ileitis," *Gut* 60, no. 3 (2010): 325–33.

106   Some recent studies have suggested that corrinoids (molecules related to vitamin B12) may affect the health of the host. It has been hypothesized that folate and cobalamin produced in the gut by bacteria could "affect host DNA methylation patterns," and that acetate produced by microbes in the gut could modify chromatin structure and gene transcription. Some of these modifications may occur in immune cells or result in changes to immune cell function. See Kau et al., "Human Nutrition, the Gut Microbiome and the Immune System," 330; R. H. Allen and S. P. Stabler,

"Identification and Quantitation of Cobalamin and Cobalamin Analogues in Human Feces," *American Journal of Clinical Nutrition* 87 (2008): 1324–35; Andrew L. Goodman et al., "Identifying Genetic Determinants Needed to Establish a Human Gut Symbiont in Its Habitat," *Cell Host & Microbe* 6, no. 3 (2009): 279–89; P. J. Anderson et al., "One Pathway Can Incorporate Either Adenine or Dimethylbenzimidazole as an -Axial Ligand of B12 Cofactors in Salmonella Enterica," *Journal of Bacteriology* 190, no. 4 (2008): 1160–71.

107   Katona and Katona-Apte, "The Interaction between Nutrition and Infection," 1583–84. Enteric infection specifically has been linked to vitamin A deficiency. See A. Sommer, "Increased Risk of Xerophthalmia Following Diarrhea and Respiratory Disease," *American Journal of Clinical Nutrition* 45 (1987): 977–80. In germ-free mice, vitamin A deficiency has been shown to result in loss of $T_H 17$ cells in the small intestine. A reduction in segmented filamentous bacteria (SFB) was also found in the gut biome of the vitamin A deficient mice. See H.-R. Cha et al., "Downregulation of Th17 Cells in the Small Intestine by Disruption of Gut Flora in the Absence of Retinoic Acid," *Journal of Immunology* 184, no. 12 (2010): 6799–806; Given that SFB is known to affect the behavior of $T_H 17$ cells, the authors hypothesized that the effect of vitamin A on immune cell function was a result of the reduction in SFB. See I. Ivanov et al., "Induction of Intestinal Th17 Cells by Segmented Filamentous Bacteria," *Cell* 139, no. 3 (2009): 485–98; Valérie Gaboriau-Routhiau et al., "The Key Role of Segmented Filamentous Bacteria in the Coordinated Maturation of Gut Helper T Cell Responses," *Immunity* 31, no. 4 (2009): 677–89; Cha et al., "Downregulation of Th17 Cells in the Small Intestine by Disruption of Gut Flora," 6799–806.

108   H. V. Kuhnlein and N. J. Turner, "Traditional Plant Foods of Canadian Indigenous Peoples: Nutrition, Botany, and Use," *Food and Nutrition in History and Anthropology*, ed. S. Katz, vol. 8 (Philadelphia: Gordon and Breach Science Publishers, 1991); Fiona Hamersley Chambers and Nancy J. Turner, "Plant Use by Northwest Coast and Plateau Indigenous Peoples," in *The Subsistence Economies of Indigenous North American Societies: A Handbook*, ed. Bruce D. Smith (Washington, DC: Smithsonian Institution Scholarly Press, 2011), 68–69; Charles B. Heiser Jr., *The Sunflower* (Norman: University of Oklahoma Press, 1976), Jefferson Chapman et al., "Archaeological Evidence for Precolumbian Introduction of Portulaca oleracea and Mollugo verticililata into Eastern North America," *Economic Botany* 28 (1974): 411–12.

109   Robert Boyd, *The Coming of the Spirit of Pestilence: Introduced Infectious Diseases and Population Decline among Northwest Coast Indians, 1774–1874* (Vancouver: University of British Columbia Press; Seattle: University of Washington Press, 1999), 21–45 and 84–85; Andrew H. Fisher, "The Pacific Northwest," in *The Oxford Handbook of American Indian History*, 258; Lynda V. Mapes, *Breaking Ground: The Lower Elwha Klallam Tribe and the Unearthing of Tse-whit-zen Village* (Seattle: University of Washington Press, 2009), 45.

110   See the discussion of these links in Chambers and Turner, "Plant Use by Northwest Coast and Plateau Indigenous Peoples," 67; B. Hayden, ed., *Complex Cultures of the British Columbia Plateau: Traditional Stl'atl'imx Resource Use* (Vancouver: University of British Columbia Press); T. Lantz and N. J. Turner, "Traditional Phenological Knowledge (TPK) of Aboriginal Peoples in British Columbia," *Journal of Ethnobiology* 23, no. 2: 263–86.

111   Chambers and Turner, "Plant Use by Northwest Coast and Plateau Indigenous Peoples," 71.

112   Inulin is found in over 3,000 vegetables, including chicory roots, Jerusalem arti-
      choke, dahlia tubers, yacon, asparagus, leek and onion corms. On inulin as a form
      of RS, see Kaur and Gupta, "Applications of Inulin and Oligofructose in Health and
      Nutrition," 704. Some strains of butyrate-producing bacteria such as *F. prausnitzii*
      can ferment non-digestible carbohydrates such as inulin-type fructans. See Audrey
      Rivière et al., "Bifidobacteria and Butyrate-Producing Colon Bacteria: Importance
      and Strategies for Their Stimulation in the Human Gut," *Frontiers in Microbiology* 7
      (2016): 8; S. Wichienchot et al., "Extraction and Analysis of Prebiotics from Selected
      Plants from Southern Thailand," *Journal of Science and Technology* 33 (2011): 517–23;
      Francis R. J. Bornet, "Fructo-Oligosaccharides and Other Fructans: Chemistry,
      Structure and Nutritional Effects," in *Advanced Dietary Fibre Technology*, ed. Barry
      V. McCleary and Leon Prosky (Oxford: Wiley Blackwell, 2001), 480–93; M. B.
      Roberfroid, "Inulin-Type Fructans: Functional Food Ingredients," *Journal of Nutrition*
      137, no. 11 (2007): 2493S–2502S.
113   Experiments by Oku and colleagues in which oligofructose was given to rats as 10%
      of the diet for 30 days showed a reduction in postprandial glycemia by 17% and a
      reduction in postprandial insulinemia by 26%, and feeding of synthetic fructan for
      three months resulted in a lower glycemic response to saccharose and maltose. See
      Kaur and Gupta, "Applications of Inulin and Oligofructose," 707; T. Oku et al.,
      "Non-digestibility of a New Sweetener, 'Neosugars' in the Rat," *Journal of Nutrition*
      114 (1984): 1574–81.
114   Diabetic subjects showed a decrease in fasting blood glucose after 14 days of daily
      ingestion of 8g of synthetic fructan. See Kaur and Gupta, "Applications of Inulin and
      Oligofructose," 707; Kamejiro Yamashita et al., "Effects of Fructo-oligosaccharides
      on Blood Glucose and Serum Lipids in Diabetic Subjects," *Nutrition Research* 4, no. 6
      (1984): 961–66.
115   J. J. Rumessen et al., "Fructans of Jerusalem Artichokes: Intestinal Transport,
      Absorption, Fermentation and Influence," *American Journal of Clinical Nutrition* 52
      (1990): 675–781.
116   K. G. Jackson et al., "The Effect of the Daily Intake of Inulin on Fasting Lipid,
      Insulin and Glucose Concentrations in Middle-aged Men and Women," *Journal of
      Manipulative and Physiological Therapeutics* 23, no. 5 (2000): 375.
117   Inclusion of inulin in a high-saturated fat diet in rats was shown to reduce triglyceride
      levels in the blood and liver. Experiments on the effects of inulin and oligfructose on
      lipid metabolism in humans have not shown consistent results, though some suggest
      beneficial effects such as lowering of triglyceride levels and lowering of LDL levels.
      For example, a study by Williams and Jackson found that inulin or oligofructose sup-
      plementation resulted in reductions in triacylglycerol and a decrease in LDL in some
      individuals. Experiments in rats suggest that this effect is a result of decreased expres-
      sion of genes involved in lipogenesis; a similar mechanism may occur in humans. See
      N. Kaur et al., "Hypotriglyceridaemic Effect of *Cichorium intybus* Roots In Ethanol
      Injected And Saturated Fat-Fed Rats," *Medical Science Research* 16 (1988): 91–92; S. C.
      Williams, "Effects of Inulin on Lipid Parameters in Humans," *Journal of Nutrition* 129
      (1999): 1471S–1473S; Muhammad Shoaib et al., "Inulin: Properties, Health Benefits
      and Food Applications," *Carbohydrate Polymers* 147 (2016): 447; C. M. Williams et al.,
      "Inulin and Oligofructose: Effects on Lipid Metabolism from Human Studies,"
      British Journal of Nutrition 87, no. S2 (2002): S261–S264; Roberfroid, "Inulin-Type
      Fructans: Functional Food Ingredients," 2493S–502S.

118 E. S. Hunn, "On the Relative Contribution of Men and Women to Subsistence among Hunter-Gatherers of the Columbia Plateau: A Comparison with Ethnographic Atlas Summaries," *Journal of Ethnobiology* 1 (1981): 124–34; Nancy J. Turner, "'Passing on the News': Women's Work, Traditional Knowledge and Plant Resource Management in Indigenous Societies of N.W. N. America," in *Women and Plants: Case Studies on Gender Relations in Local Plant Genetic Resource Management*, ed. P. Howard (London: Zed Books, 2003), 133–49.

119 Sonnenburg and Sonnenburg, "Starving Our Microbial Self," 781; Alan W. Walker et al., "Dominant and Diet-responsive Groups of Bacteria within the Human Colonic Microbiota," *ISME Journal* 5, no. 2 (2010): 220–30. One study compared the gut microbiota of children in a rural village in Burkina Faso with the microbiota of children in Italy, and found differences in the composition of the microbiota as well as a fourfold increase in the amount of SCFAs butyrate and propionate produced by the microbiota in the children from Burkina Faso. Similarly, a greater diversity of bacteria was found in the Hadza hunter-gatherers in Tanzania. See C. De Filippo et al., "Impact of Diet in Shaping Gut Microbiota Revealed by a Comparative Study in Children from Europe and Rural Africa," *Proceedings of the National Academy of Sciences* 107, no. 33 (2010): 14691–96; Stephanie L. Schnorr et al., "Gut Microbiome of the Hadza Hunter-Gatherers," *Nature Communications* 5 (2014): 3654. doi:10.1038/ncomms4654.

120 Spreadbury, "Comparison with Ancestral Diets," 181.

121 Ibid., 179; H. Ghanim et al., "Increase in Plasma Endotoxin Concentrations and the Expression of Toll-Like Receptors and Suppressor of Cytokine Signaling-3 in Mononuclear Cells after a High-Fat, High-Carbohydrate Meal: Implications for Insulin Resistance," *Diabetes Care* 32, no. 12 (2009): 2281–87; Mariann I. Lassenius et al., "Bacterial Endotoxin Activity in Human Serum Is Associated With Dyslipidemia, Insulin Resistance, Obesity, and Chronic Inflammation," *Diabetes Care* 34, no. 8 (2011): 1809–15.

122 Huss-Ashmore et al., "Nutritional Inference from Paleopathology," 396.

123 J. D. Soderholm and M. H. Perdu, "Stress and Gastrointestinal Tract. II. Stress And Intestinal Barrier Function," *American Journal of Physiology-Gastrointestinal and Liver Physiology* 280 (2001): G7–G13; S. M. Collins, "Stress and the Gastrointestinal Tract IV: Modulation of Intestinal Inflammation by Stress: Basic Mechanisms and Clinical Relevance," *American Journal of Physiology-Gastrointestinal and Liver Physiology* 280 (2001): G315–G318; P. C. Konturek et al., "Stress and the Gut: Pathophysiology, Clinical Consequences, Diagnostic Approach And Treatment Options," *Journal of Physiology and Pharmacology* 62 (2011): 591–99; De Palma et al., "The Microbiota-Gut-Brain Axis in Gastrointestinal, Disorders," 2989–97.

124 Mark Lyte et al., "Stress at the Intestinal Surface: Catecholamines and Mucosa–Bacteria Interactions," *Cell and Tissue Research* 343, no. 1 (2010): 23–32.

125 De Palma et al., "The Microbiota-Gut-Brain Axis in Gastrointestinal Disorders," 2991.

126 Alper Evrensel and Mehmet Emin Ceylan, "The Gut-Brain Axis: The Missing Link in Depression," *Clinical Psychopharmacology and Neuroscience* 13, no. 3 (2015): 241; M. A. C. Stephens and G. Wand, "Stress and the HPA Axis Role of Glucocorticoids in Alcohol Dependence," *Alcohol Research: Current Reviews* 34, no. 4 (2012):468; Ronald Glaser, "Stress Damages Immune System and Health," *Discovery Medicine* (July 2009): 165–69; Rachel D. Moloney et al., "Stress and the Microbiota-Gut-Brain

Axis in Visceral Pain: Relevance to Irritable Bowel Syndrome," *CNS Neuroscience & Therapeutics* 22, no. 2 (2015): 103.

127 De Palma et al., "The Microbiota-Gut-Brain Axis in Gastrointestinal Disorders," 2991; Stephen M. Collins and Premsyl Bercik, "The Relationship Between Intestinal Microbiota and the Central Nervous System in Normal Gastrointestinal Function and Disease," *Gastroenterology* 136, no. 6 (2009): 2003–14.

128 De Palma et al., "The Microbiota-Gut-Brain Axis in Gastrointestinal Disorders," 2989–997. Experiments in mice have suggested that stress affects the microbiota. For example, Lyte and colleagues found that mice subject to social stress, when a male mouse was placed into the cage, experienced changes in their gut microbota. See Michael T. Bailey et al., "Exposure to a Social Stressor Alters the Structure of the Intestinal Microbiota: Implications for Stressor-induced Immunomodulation," *Brain, Behavior, and Immunity* 25, no. 3 (2011): 397–407.

129 Giada De Palma et al., "Su1990 The Role of Microbiota in the Maternal Separation Model of Depression," *Gastroenterology* 142, no. 5 (2012): S554.

130 L. Desbonnet et al., "Effects of the Probiotic Bifidobacterium Infantis in the Maternal Separation Model of Depression," *Neuroscience* 170, no. 4 (2010): 1179–88.

131 De Palma et al., "The Microbiota-Gut-Brain Axis in Gastrointestinal Disorders," 2993; Mark Lyte, "Probiotics Function Mechanistically as Delivery Vehicles for Neuroactive Compounds: Microbial Endocrinology in the Design and Use of Probiotics," *BioEssays* 33, no. 8 (2011): 574–81.

132 Evrensel and Ceylan, "The Gut-Brain Axis: The Missing Link in Depression," 240; Lyte, "Probiotics Function Mechanistically as Delivery Vehicles," 574–81.

133 Kau et al., "Human Nutrition, the Gut Microbiome and the Immune System," 329; Maslowski et al., "Regulation of Inflammatory Responses by Gut Microbiota," 1282–86.

134 Robert Dantzer et al., "From Inflammation to Sickness and Depression: When the Immune System Subjugates the Brain," *Nature Reviews Neuroscience* 9, no. 1 (2008): 46–56.

135 Rosita Kahaani Worl, "Alaska," in *The Oxford Handbook of American Indian History*, 301.

136 Robert A. McKennan, *The Upper Tanana Indians* (New Haven, CT: Yale University Press, 1959).

137 Annaliese Jacobs, "Empire at the Floe Edge: Western Empires and Indigenous Peoples in the Bering Sea and Arctic Ocean, c. 1820–1900," in *The Routledge History of Western Empires*, ed. Robert Aldrich and Kirsten McKenzie (New York: Routledge, 2014), 139.

138 Claudio Saunt, "The Age of Imperial Expansion, 1763–1821," in *The Oxford Handbook of American Indian History*, 80.

139 For early salmon consumption several thousand years ago, see Matthew Betts, "Zooarcheology and the Reconstruction of Ancient Human-Animal Relationships in the Arctic," in *The Oxford Handbook of the Arctic*, ed. T. Max Friesen et al. (Oxford: Oxford University Press, 2016), 84. For the gradual disruption of indigenous salmon consumption in southern Alaska, see David F. Arnold, *The Fishermen's Frontier: People and Salmon in Southeast Alaska* (Seattle: University of Washington Press, 2008), 40–65.

140 Saunt, "The Age of Imperial Expansion, 1763–1821," 80; Donald W. Clark, "Kodiak Island: The Later Cultures," *Arctic Anthropology* 35, no. 1 (1998): 172–86;

Jon Erlandson et al., "Spatial and Temporal Patterns of Alutiiq Paleodemography," *Arctic Anthropology* 29, no. 2 (1992): 42–62.

141 J. C. Joordens et al., "A Fish Is Not a Fish: Patterns in Fatty Acid Composition of Aquatic Food May Have Had Implications for Hominin Evolution," *Journal of Human Evolution* (2014): 107–16; E. Dewailly et al., "Cardiovascular Disease Risk Factors and N-3 Fatty Acid Status in the Adult Population of James Bay Cree," *American Journal of Clinical Nutrition* 76, no. 1 (2002): 85–92; Y. E. Zhou et al., "Decreased Activity of Desaturase 5 in Association with Obesity and Insulin Resistance Aggravates Declining Long-Chain N-3 Fatty Acid Status in Cree Undergoing Dietary Transition," *British Journal of Nutrition* 102, no. 6 (2009): 888–94; A. I. Adler et al., "Lower Prevalence of Impaired Glucose Tolerance and Diabetes Associated with Daily Seal Oil Or Salmon Consumption among Alaska Natives," *Diabetes Care* 17, no. 12 (December 1994): 498–501; Y. Yan, "Omega-3 Fatty Acids Prevent Inflammation and Metabolic Disorder through Inhibition of NLRP3 Inflammasome Activation," *Immunity* 38, no. 6 (June 2013): 1154–63.

142 Following contact in regions such as Florida and the Southwest, evidence of increasing skeletal lesions such as cribra orbitalia may suggest vitamin B12 deficiency alongside declining DHA. See Henrik Tauber, "13c Evidence for Dietary Habits of Prehistoric Man in Denmark," *Nature* 292 (1981): 332–33; Margaret J. Schoeninger et al., "Stable Nitrogen Isotope Ratios of Bone Collagen Reflect Marine and Terrestrial Components of Prehistoric Human Diet," *Nature* 220 (1983): 1381–83; P. L. Walker et al., "The Causes of Porotic Hyperostosis and Cribra Orbitalia: A Reappraisal of the Iron-Deficiency-Anemia Hypothesis," *American Journal of Physical Anthropology* 139, no. 2 (2009): 115.

143 See the discussion in Reply to W.B. Grant, "Re: Vitamin D Deficiency among Northern Native Peoples," *Peter Frost International Journal of Circumpolar Health* 71, no. 1 (2012): 18001.

144 Vitamin D is obtained in the diet from fatty fish and fish liver oil, and is produced in the skin on exposure to sunlight. See Cynthia Aranow, "Vitamin D and the Immune System," *Journal of Investigative Medicine* 59, no. 6 (2011): 881.

145 Previtamin D3 undergoes thermal isomerization into vitamin D3 (the conversion of molecules with the same number of atoms but different arrangements). The vitamin is then converted to 25-hydroxyvitamin D3 in the liver and into the biologically active form $1,25(OH)_2D3$ in the kidneys. See Aranow, "Vitamin D and the Immune System," 881–82.

146 S. V. Ramagopalan et al., "A ChIP-seq Defined Genome-wide Map of Vitamin D Receptor Binding: Associations with Disease and Evolution," *Genome Research* 20, no. 10 (2010): 1352–360.

147 Leng Khoo et al., "Translating the Role of Vitamin D 3 in Infectious Diseases," *Critical Reviews in Microbiology* 38, no. 2 (2012): 122; D. Provvedini et al., "1,25-dihydroxyvitamin D3 Receptors in Human Leukocytes," *Science* 221, no. 4616 (1983): 1181–83; Ashok K. Bhalla et al., "Specific High-Affinity Receptors for 1,25-Dihydroxyvitamin D3In Human Peripheral Blood Mononuclear Cells: Presence in Monocytes and Induction in T Lymphocytes Following Activation," *Journal of Clinical Endocrinology & Metabolism* 57, no. 6 (1983): 1308–10.

148 The VDR is now known to regulate the expression of many genes involved in immune function. See Malcom D. Kearns and Vin Tangpricha, "The Role of Vitamin D in Tuberculosis," *Journal of Clinical & Translational Endocrinology* 1, no. 4 (2014): 167–69;

Jacques M. Lemire, "Immunomodulatory Role of 1,25-dihydroxyvitamin D3," *Journal of Cellular Biochemistry* 49, no. 1 (1992): 26–31; Leng Khoo et al., "Translating the Role of Vitamin D 3 in Infectious Diseases," 122. Moreover, during an immune response, expression of the VDR has shown to be upregulated (more receptors are produced so that the cell can amplify its response to the signaling pathway). See P. T. Liu, "Toll-Like Receptor Triggering of a Vitamin D-Mediated Human Antimicrobial Response," *Science* 311, no. 5768 (2006): 1770–73.

149 Kearns and Tangpricha, "The Role of Vitamin D in Tuberculosis," 167–69; A. R. Martineau et al., "IFN- gamma- and TNF-Independent Vitamin D-Inducible Human Suppression of Mycobacteria: The Role of Cathelicidin LL-37," *Journal of Immunology* 178, no. 11 (2007): 7190–98; T.-T. Wang et al., "Cutting Edge: 1,25-Dihydroxyvitamin D3 Is a Direct Inducer of Antimicrobial Peptide Gene Expression," *Journal of Immunology* 173, no. 10 (2004): 2909–12. Indeed, immunity-dependent B cells and T cells are able to synthesize $1,25(OH)_2D3$, offering further evidence of the important role that vitamin D plays in the immune response. See Aranow, "Vitamin D and the Immune System," 882.

150 Leng Khoo et al., "Translating the Role of Vitamin D 3 in Infectious Diseases," 122–35.

151 Aranow, "Vitamin D and the Immune System," 883–84; Leng Khoo et al., "Translating the Role of Vitamin D 3 in Infectious Diseases," 123; L. E. Jeffery et al., "1,25-Dihydroxyvitamin D3 and IL-2 Combine to Inhibit T Cell Production of Inflammatory Cytokines and Promote Development of Regulatory T Cells Expressing CTLA-4 and FoxP3," *Journal of Immunology* 183, no. 9 (2009): 5458–67. Expression of the VDR has been found to be increased in the presence of the pathogen-derived molecules lipopolysaccharide (LPS), which in turn increases production of bacteriacidal proteins such as cathelocidin. See Aranow, "Vitamin D and the Immune System," 881–86; Richard L. Gallo et al., "Biology and Clinical Relevance of Naturally Occurring Antimicrobial Peptides," *Journal of Allergy and Clinical Immunology* 110, no. 6 (2002): 823–31; Liu, "Toll-Like Receptor Triggering," 1770–73; Wang et al., "Cutting Edge: 1,25-Dihydroxyvitamin D3 Is a Direct Inducer," 2909–12.

152 On the potential importance of dietary Vitamin D in immunity, see A. R. Martineau et al., "A Single Dose of Vitamin D Enhances Immunity to Mycobacteria," *American Journal of Respiratory and Critical Care Medicine* 176, no. 2 (July 2007): 208–13; S. L. Yang, "Vitamin D Deficiency Suppresses Cell-Mediated Immunity in Vivo," *Archives of Biochemistry and Biophysics* 303, no. 1 (May 1993): 98–106; N. Talat et al., "Vitamin D Deficiency and Tuberculosis Progression," *Emerging Infectious Diseases* 16, no. 5 (May 2010): 853–55; M. Urashima et al., "Randomized Trial of Vitamin D Supplementation to Prevent Seasonal Influenza A in Schoolchildren," *American Journal of Clinical Nutrition* 91, no. 5 (May 2010): 1255–60; P. Frost, "Vitamin D Deficiency among Northern Native Peoples: A Real Or Apparent Problem?" *International Journal of Circumpolar Health* 71 (2012): 18001. Many observational studies have reported a correlation between vitamin D levels and immunity to infectious diseases such as respiratory tract infections, and a seasonal effect of increased infections due to lower vitamin D levels in the winter has been recognized for respiratory tract infections. See Cynthia Aranaow, "Vitamin D and the Immune System," 882; James Sabetta et al., "Serum 25-Hydroxyvitamin D and the Incidence of Acute Viral Respiratory Tract Infections in Healthy Adults," *PLoS ONE* 5, no. 6 (2010); J. J. Cannell

et al., "Epidemic Influenza and Vitamin D," *Epidemiology and Infection* 134, no. 06 (2006): 1129–40; M. Rodríguez et al., "High Frequency of Vitamin D Deficiency in Ambulatory HIV-Positive Patients," *AIDS Research and Human Retroviruses* 25, no. 1 (2009): 9–14. Some trials have found a decrease in infection rates following vitamin D supplementation. A recent study noted a reduction in cases of influenza in schoolchildren following vitamin D supplementation, for example. See Aranow, "Vitamin D and the Immune System," 883; Urashima et al., "Randomized Trial of Vitamin D Supplementation," 1255–60.

153   G. A. Rook, "The Role of Vitamin D in Tuberculosis," *American Review of Respiratory Disease* 138, no. 4 (1988): 768–70.

154   Nilay Sutaria et al., "Vitamin D Status, Receptor Gene Polymorphisms, and Supplementation on Tuberculosis: A Systematic Review of Case-control Studies and Randomized Controlled Trials," *Journal of Clinical & Translational Endocrinology* 1, no. 4 (2014): 151–60. Mortality from tuberculosis increases during the winter, when serum levels of vitamin D are much lower. Though such an association may be confounded by other factors, such as greater proximity of individuals in enclosed spaces, the role of vitamin D should not be discounted. See A. S. Douglas et al., "Seasonality of Tuberculosis: The Reverse of Other Respiratory Diseases in the UK," *Thorax* 51, no. 9 (1996): 944–46. The disease is spread by the inhalation of respiratory secretions from infected individuals. Some bacteria may escape destruction by immune cells in the respiratory system and cross the membranes of cells in the respiratory tract. Once inside a cell, the bacteria replicate, kill the host cell, and invade other tissues. Further immune responses limit the spread of the bacteria, but at the cost of tissue necrosis. See R. K. Chandra, "Nutrition, Immunity and Infection: From Basic Knowledge of Dietary Manipulation of Immune Responses to Practical Application of Ameliorating Suffering and Improving Survival," *Proceedings of the National Academy of Sciences* 93, no. 25 (1996): 14304. Interestingly, in Europe and the United States from the mid-nineteenth century, fish liver oil was used a primary treatment of tuberculosis. See C. J. B. Williams, "Cod-Liver Oil in Phthisis," *London Journal of Medicine* 1 (1849): 1–18. Sun exposure was also described as effective treatment, with summer facilities built in locations such as the Swiss Alps. See Katona and Katona-Apte, "The Interaction between Nutrition and Infection," 1584.

155   Iain Mathieson et al., "Genome-Wide Patterns of Selection in 230 Ancient Eurasians," *Nature* 528, no. 7583 (2015): 499–503; Iñigo Olalde et al., "Derived Immune and Ancestral Pigmentation Alleles in a 7,000-year-old Mesolithic European," *Nature* 507, no. 7491 (2014): 225–28.

156   Peter Heinbecker, "Studies on the Metabolism of Eskimos," *Journal of Biological Chemistry* 80, no. 2 (1928): 464–65.

157   G. S. Mouratoff et al., "Diabetes Mellitus in Eskimos," *Journal of the American Medical Association* 199 (1967): 961–66; E. M. Scott and I. V. Griffith, "Diabetes Mellitus in Eskimos," *Metabolism* 6 (1957): 320–25.

158   Martín de Santa Olalla L. et al., "N-3 Fatty Acids In Glucose Metabolism And Insulin Sensitivity," *Nutricion Hospitalaria* 24, no. 2 (March–April 2009): 113–27; P. Flachs et al., "The Effect of n-3 Fatty Acids on Glucose Homeostasis and Insulin Sensitivity," 63 (suppl. 1) (2014): S93–118; S. M. Eraky et al., "Modulating Effects of Omega-3 Fatty Acids and Pioglitazone Combination on Insulin Resistance through Toll-Like Receptor 4 in Type 2 Diabetes Mellitus," *Prostaglandins, Leukotrienes & Essential Fatty Acids* 16 (June 2017): 30239-3.

159 Adler et al., "Lower Prevalence of Impaired Glucose Tolerance and Diabetes," 1498–1501; Sven O. E. Ebbesson et al., "Omega-3 Fatty Acids Improve Glucose Tolerance and Components of the Metabolic Syndrome in Alaskan Eskimos: The Alaska Siberia Project," *International Journal of Circumpolar Health* 64, no. 4 (2005): 396–408.

160 Ebbesson et al., "Omega-3 Fatty Acids Improve Glucose Tolerance," 396–408.

161 See B. Maestro et al., "Transcriptional Activation of the Human Insulin Receptor Gene by 1,25-dihydroxyvitamin D_3," *Cell Biochemistry and Function* 20 (2002): 227–32; Alvarez and Ashraf, "Role of Vitamin D in Insulin Secretion," 351–85; Guri Grimnes et al., "Vitamin D, Insulin Secretion, Sensitivity, and Lipids," *Diabetes* 60, no. 11 (November 2011): 2748–57; C. Cade and A. W. Norman, "Vitamin D3 Improves Impaired Glucose Tolerance and Insulin Secretion in the Vitamin D-Deficient Rat in Vivo," *Endocrinology* 119, no. 1 (July 1986): 84–90.

162 Heinbecker, "Studies on the Metabolism of Eskimos," 462–63.

163 For a description of the metabolic state of ketosis, see Richard L. Veech et al., "Ketone Bodies, Potential Therapeutic Uses," *IUBMB Life (International Union of Biochemistry and Molecular Biology: Life)* 51, no. 4 (2001): 241–47. For research suggesting that the metabolism of ketones decreases inflammation, see T. N. Seyfried, "Ketone Strong: Emerging Evidence for a Therapeutic Role of Ketone Bodies in Neurological and Neurodegenerative Diseases," *Journal of Lipid Research* 55, no. 9 (2014): 1815. Maciej Gasior et al., "Neuroprotective and Disease-Modifying Effects of the Ketogenic Diet," *Behavioural Pharmacology* 17, no. 5–6 (2006): 438; Tim E. Cullingford, "The Ketogenic Diet: Fatty Acids, Fatty Acid-activated Receptors and Neurological Disorders," *Prostaglandins, Leukotrienes and Essential Fatty Acids* 70, no. 3 (2004): 253–64.

164 When glucose is limited, ketone bodies are produced in the liver as a result of β-oxidation of fatty acids from adipose tissue, and from specific amino acids. See V. D. Longo and M. P. Mattson, "Fasting: Molecular Mechanisms and Clinical Applications," *Cell Metabolism* no. 19 (2014): 182. The concentration of ketone bodies in the blood increases as the concentration of free fatty acids increases. See R. L. Veech, "Ketone Ester Effects on Metabolism and Transcription," *Journal of Lipid Research* 55, no. 10 (2014): 2004–6; H. A. Krebs, "The Regulation of the Release of Ketone Bodies by the Liver," *Advances in Enzyme Regulation* 4 (1966): 339–53. The ketones cannot be used by the liver, which lacks the enzyme succinyl CoA:3-ketoacid CoA transferase, and so they flow out of the liver and into the brain and other organs. See Anssi H. Manninen, "Metabolic Effects of the Very-Low-Carbohydrate Diets: Misunderstood 'Villains' of Human Metabolism," *Journal of the International Society of Sports Nutrition* 1, no. 2 (2004): 8. The ketones are metabolized by these organs in the process of ketolysis: the conversion of ketone bodies into acetoacetyl-CoA and then acetyl-CoA. See Longo and Mattson, "Fasting: Molecular Mechanisms and Clinical Applications," 182.

165 Seyfried et al., "Cancer as a Metabolic Disease," 516; Thomas N. Seyfried et al., "Metabolic Management of Brain Cancer," *Biochimica Et Biophysica Acta (BBA)— Bioenergetics* 1807, no. 6 (2011): 577.

166 Longo and Mattson, "Fasting: Molecular Mechanisms and Clinical Applications," 182.

167 Manninen, "Metabolic Effects of the Very-Low-Carbohydrate Diets," 8; J. D. Fernstrom and M. H. Fernstrom, "Nutrition and the Brain," in *Nutrition & Metabolism*, ed. M. J. Gibney, I. A Macdonald and H. M. Roche (Oxford, UK: Blackwell Science, 2003), 145–67.

168   Veech et al., "Ketone Bodies, Potential Therapeutic Uses," 241–47; Antonio Paoli,
      "Ketogenic Diet for Obesity: Friend or Foe?" *International Journal of Environmental Research
      and Public Health* 11, no. 2 (2014): 2092–107; Longo and Mattson, "Fasting: Molecular
      Mechanisms and Clinical Applications," 181; George F. Cahill, "Fuel Metabolism
      in Starvation," *Annual Review of Nutrition* 26, no. 1 (2006): 1–22. Evidence for the
      role of ketosis in life extension comes from the experiments involving calorie restric-
      tion: calorie restriction extends the lifespan of many organisms (including *E. coli*,
      S.cerveviae and *C.elegans*); this life extension in *E.coli* is reversed by the addition of many
      nutrients, but not by the addition of acetate (a ketone-body-like carbon source). See
      Longo and Mattson, "Fasting: Molecular Mechanisms and Clinical Applications,"
      181–82; Stavros Gonidakis et al., "Genome-wide Screen Identifies Escherichia Coli
      TCA-Cycle-Related Mutants with Extended Chronological Lifespan Dependent on
      Acetate Metabolism and the Hypoxia-inducible Transcription Factor ArcA," *Aging
      Cell* 9, no. 5 (2010): 868–81; Valter D. Longo et al., "Human Bcl-2 Reverses Survival
      Defects in Yeast Lacking Superoxide Dismutase and Delays Death of Wild-Type
      Yeast," *Journal of Cell Biology* 137, no. 7 (1997): 1581–88; Tammi L. Kaeberlein et al.,
      "Lifespan Extension in Caenorhabditis Elegans by Complete Removal of Food."
      Aging Cell 5, no. 6 (2006): 487–94. Gonidakis et al., "Genome-wide Screen Identifies
      Escherichia Coli TCA-cycle-related Mutants," 868–81.
169   Longo and Mattson, "Fasting: Molecular Mechanisms and Clinical Applications,"
      181.
170   C. Tóth and Z. Clemens, "Halted Progression of Soft Palate Cancer in a Patient
      Treated with the Paleolithic Ketogenic Diet Alone: A 20-Months Follow-up,"
      American Journal of Medical Case Reports 4, no. 8 (2016): 288–92; Cordain, Loren,
      The Paleo Diet: Lose Weight and Get Healthy by Eating the Food You Were Designed to Eat.
      New York: J. Wiley, 2002.
171   J. M. Freeman and E. H. Kossoff. "Ketosis and the Ketogenic Diet: Advances In
      Treating Epilepsy and Other Disorders," *Advances in Pediatrics* 57 (2010): 315–29; J. G.
      Mantis et al., "Management of Multifactorial Idiopathic Epilepsy in EL Mice with
      Caloric Restriction and the Ketogenic Diet: Role of Glucose and Ketone Bodies,"
      Nutrition & Metabolism 1 (2004): 11; Seyfried et al., "Metabolic Management of Brain
      Cancer," 577–94; Seyfried et al., "Cancer as a Metabolic Disease," 515–27.
172   Tóth and Clemens, "Halted Progression of Soft Palate Cancer," 288–92; Seyfried
      et al., "Metabolic Management of Brain Cancer, 583; Giulio Zuccoli et al.,
      "Metabolic Management of Glioblastoma Multiforme Using Standard Therapy
      Together with a Restricted Ketogenic Diet: Case Report," *Nutrition & Metabolism*
      7, no. 1 (2010): 33; L. C. Nebeling et al., "Effects of a Ketogenic Diet on Tumor
      Metabolism and Nutritional Status in Pediatric Oncology Patients: Two Case
      Reports," *Journal of the American College of Nutrition* 14, no. 2 (1995): 202–08. In 1956,
      Warburg drew attention to the importance of metabolism in disease, suggesting that
      cancer results from abnormal cellular metabolism in which tumor cells exhibit an
      increased reliance on glucose as an energy source. See Tóth and Clemens, "Halted
      Progression of Soft Palate Cancer," 288; Warburg, "On the Origin of Cancer Cells,"
      309–14. Recently, for example, a patient with a soft palate tumor was treated exclu-
      sively with a ketogenic paleolithic diet (a diet based primarily on non-lean animal
      meat including organ meats, with plant content less than 30%). This treatment
      halted growth of the tumor during the 20-month period of the study. Another trial
      using the ketogenic diet to treat brain cancers in two children resulted in decreased

uptake of glucose in tumors in both patients, and halted disease progression over 12 months for one patient. See Tóth and Clemens, "Halted Progression of Soft Palate Cancer," 288–92; L. C. Nebeling et al., "Effects of a Ketogenic Diet on Tumor Metabolism," 202–8. Experiments in animals have shown that dietary restriction slows the growth of brain tumours. See Seyfried et al., "Metabolic Management of Brain Cancer," 581–84; T. N. Seyfried et al., "Role of Glucose and Ketone Bodies in the Metabolic Control of Experimental Brain Cancer," *British Journal of Cancer* 89, no. 7 (2003): 1375–82; Laura M. Shelton et al., "Calorie Restriction as an Anti-invasive Therapy for Malignant Brain Cancer in the VM Mouse," *ASN Neuro* 2, no. 3 (2010): 171–77.

173 Experiments have shown that oxidative stress is reduced in the metabolic state of ketosis. See T. N. Seyfried, "Ketone Strong: Emerging Evidence," 1815; Richard L. Veech, "The Therapeutic Implications of Ketone Bodies: The Effects of Ketone Bodies in Pathological Conditions: Ketosis, Ketogenic Diet, Redox States, Insulin Resistance, and Mitochondrial Metabolism," *Prostaglandins, Leukotrienes and Essential Fatty Acids* 70, no. 3 (2004): 309–19. The supplementation of ketone body esters (which are converted into ketones) has been shown to lower blood glucose level and insulin levels in rats, supporting the notion that ketones provide a direct metabolic benefit distinct from lowering glucose, likely through the reduction in oxidative stress. See Kieran Clarke et al., "Kinetics, Safety and Tolerability of (R)-3-hydroxybutyl (R)-3-hydroxybutyrate in Healthy Adult Subjects," *Regulatory Toxicology and Pharmacology* 63, no. 3 (2012): 401–8; R. Veech and M. A. Mehlman, "Liver Metabolite Content, Redox and Phosphorylation States in Rats Fed Diets Containing 1,3-Butanediol and Ethanol," *Energy Metabolism and the Regulation of Metabolic Processes in Mitochondria* (1972): 171–83. Ketone bodies have been shown to reduce production cellular concentration of ROS via several mechanisms. The production of ROS is likely reduced via decreased levels of coenzyme Q semiquinone (a component of the electron transport chain in mitochondria) in the presence of ketone bodies. See Gasior et al., "Neuroprotective and Disease-Modifying Effects of the Ketogenic Diet," 436; Veech, "Ketone Bodies, Potential Therapeutic Uses," 241–47. Increased activity of gluta-thione peroxidize, an enzyme with antioxidant activity required to neutralize ROS, is likely to reduce levels of ROS. See Gasior et al., "Neuroprotective and Disease-Modifying Effects of the Ketogenic Diet," 437; D. R. Ziegler et al., "Ketogenic Diet Increases Glutathione Peroxidase Activity in Rat Hippocampus," *Neurochemical Research* 28 (2003): 1793–97. Ketones are also likely to reduce ROS levels by indu-cing increased expression of uncoupling proteins in mitochondria, which dissipates the membrane potential of the mitochondrial membrane, thereby lowering ROS formation. See Gasior et al., "Neuroprotective and Disease-Modifying Effects of the Ketogenic Diet," 437; Patrick G. Sullivan et al., "The Ketogenic Diet Increases Mitochondrial Uncoupling Protein Levels and Activity," *Annals of Neurology* 55, no. 4 (2004): 576–80. Studies in rats have shown that the ketogenic diet simulates mito-chondrial biogenesis as well as increased expression of mitochondrial enzymes. See Gasior et al., "Neuroprotective and Disease-Modifying Effects of the Ketogenic Diet," 436; Kristopher J. Bough et al., "Mitochondrial Biogenesis in the Anticonvulsant Mechanism of the Ketogenic Diet," *Annals of Neurology* 60, no. 2 (2006): 223–35. The resulting increase in the phosphocreatine:creatine ratio suggests an increase in cel-lular energy generation as a result of a greater number of mitochondria. See Gasior et al., "Neuroprotective and Disease-Modifying Effects of the Ketogenic Diet," 436.

It is also thought that β-hydroxybutyrate may be a more efficient fuel than oxygen for the brain than glucose (it releases more ATP per molecule), which would again be expected to reduce metabolic stress. See Gasior, "Neuroprotective and Disease-modifying Effects of the Ketogenic Diet," 436; Veech et al., "Ketone Bodies, Potential Therapeutic Uses," 241–47. Consumption of a ketogenic diet has been suggested to reduce inflammation. A link between the ketogenic diet and inflammation is currently "highly tentative," though some experiments suggest that ketosis decreases inflammation. See Gasior et al., "Neuroprotective and Disease-modifying Effects of the Ketogenic Diet," 438. Rats that have undergone intermittent fasting have increased expression of interferon-γ, which conferred protection against cell death. See Gasior et al., "Neuroprotective and Disease-modifying Effects of the Ketogenic Diet," 438; Jaewon Lee et al., "Interferon-γ Is Up-regulated in the Hippocampus in Response to Intermittent Fasting and Protects Hippocampal Neurons against Excitotoxicity," *Journal of Neuroscience Research* 83, no. 8 (2006): 1552–57. It has also been suggested that the high concentrations of fatty acids in the ketogenic diet may activate anti-inflammatory mechanisms. For example, the fatty acids activate the peroxisome proliferator-activated receptor α, which may inhibit inflammation. See Gasior et al., "Neuroprotective and Disease-Modifying Effects of the Ketogenic Diet," 438; Cullingford, "The Ketogenic Diet: Fatty Acids, Fatty Acid-Activated Receptors and Neurological Disorders," 253–64.

174 B. A. Gower and A. M. Goss, "A Lower-Carbohydrate, Higher-Fat Diet Reduces Abdominal and Intermuscular Fat and Increases Insulin Sensitivity in Adults at Risk of Type 2 Diabetes," *Journal of Nutrition* 145, no. 1 (2014): 177S–83S; Hussein M. Dashti et al., "Long Term Effects of Ketogenic Diet in Obese Subjects with High Cholesterol Level," *Molecular and Cellular Biochemistry* 286, nos. 1–2 (2006): 1–9; Megan R. Ruth et al., "Consuming a Hypocaloric High Fat Low Carbohydrate Diet for 12 weeks Lowers C-reactive Protein, and Raises Serum Adiponectin and High Density Lipoprotein-Cholesterol in Obese Subjects," *Metabolism* 62, no. 12 (2013): 1779–87; J. O. Holloszy and E. F. Coyle, "Adaptations of Skeletal Muscle to Endurance Exercise and Their Metabolic Consequences," *Journal of Applied Physiology: Respiratory, Environmental and Exercise Physiology* 56, no.4 (1984): 831–38; A. L. Carey et al., "Effects of Fat Adaptation and Carbohydrate Restoration on Prolonged Endurance Exercise," *Journal of Applied Physiology* 91, no. 1 (1985): 115–22; Wee Kian Yeo et al., "Fat Adaptation in Well-Trained Athletes: Effects on Cell Metabolism," *Applied Physiology, Nutrition, and Metabolism* 36, no. 1 (2011): 12–22; Pete J. Cox et al., "Nutritional Ketosis Alters Fuel Preference and Thereby Endurance Performance in Athletes," *Cell Metabolism* 24, no. 2 (2016): 256–68.

175 S. D Phinney, "Ketogenic Diets and Physical Performance," *Nutrition & Metabolism* 1 (2004): 2. E. V. Lambert et al., "High-Fat Diet versus Habitual Diet Prior go Carbohydrate Loading: Effects of Exercise Metabolism and Cycling Performance," *International Journal of Sport Nutrition and Exercise Metabolism* 11 no. 2 (2001): 209–25; D. S. Rowlands and W. G. Hopkins, "Effects of High-Fat and High-Carbohydrate Diets on Metabolism and Performance in Cycling," *Metabolism* 51, no.6 (June 2002): 678–90; Carey et al., "Effects of Fat Adaptation and Carbohydrate Restoration," 115–22; Yeo et al., "Fat Adaptation In Well-Trained Athletes," 12–22; D. Cameron-Smith, "A Short-Term, High-Fat Diet Up-Regulates Lipid Metabolism and Gene Expression in Human Skeletal Muscle." *American Journal of Clinical Nutrition* 77, no. 2 (Feb

2003): 313–18; Holloszy and Coyle, "Adaptations of Skeletal Muscle to Endurance Exercise," 831–38; J. A. Romijn et al., "Strenuous Endurance Training Increases Lipolysis and Triglyceride-Fatty Acid Cycling at Rest," *Journal of Applied Physiology* 75, no. 1 (July 1993): 108–13.

176   Heinbecker, "Studies on the Metabolism of Eskimos," 461–75; A. C. Corcoran and M. Rabinowitch, "A Study of the Blood Lipoids and Blood Protein in Canadian Eastern Arctic Eskimos," *Biochemical Journal* 31, no. 3 (1937): 343–48. Some studies have questioned the notion of a sole reliance on fat and ketosis. See, for example, Kang-Jey Ho et al., "Alaskan Arctic Eskima: Responses to a Customary High Fat Diet," *American Journal of Clinical Nutrition.* 25, no. 8 (1972): 737–45, which states that "Carbohydrate accounted for only 15% to 20% of their calories, largely in the form of glycogen." See also R. G. Sinclair et al., "The Tolerance of Eskimos for Pemmican and for Starvation," *Revue Canadienne De Biologie* 7, no. 1 (1948): 197.

177   Heinbecker, "Studies on the Metabolism of Eskimos," 462–63.

178   Ibid., 461–75.

179   Ho et al., "Alaskan Arctic Eskima," 737–45.

180   Heinbecker, "Studies on the Metabolism of Eskimos," 461–62; Philip A. Shaffer, "Antiketogenesis: III. Calculation of the Ketogenic Balance From the Respiratory Quotients," *Journal of Biological Chemistry* 49, no. 1 (1921): xlvii and 449.

181   Corcoran and Rabinowitch, "A Study of the Blood Lipoids and Blood Protein in Canadian Eastern Arctic Eskimos," 343–48.

182   Patil et al., "Cardiovascular Damage Resulting from Chronic Excessive Endurance Exercise," 312–21; O'Keefe et al., "Potential Adverse Cardiovascular Effects From Excessive Endurance Exercise," 587–95; Hayden W. Hyatt et al., "A Ketogenic Diet in Rodents Elicits Improved Mitochondrial Adaptations in Response to Resistance Exercise Training Compared to an Isocaloric Western Diet," *Frontiers in Physiology* 7 (2016): 533.

183   D. W. Foster, "Studies in the Ketosis of Fasting," *Journal of Clinical Investigation* 46, no. 8 (August 1967): 1283–96; M. Lv et al., "Roles of Caloric Restriction, Ketogenic Diet and Intermittent Fasting during Initiation, Progression and Metastasis of Cancer in Animal Models: A Systematic Review and Meta-Analysis," *PLoS ONE* 9, no. 12 (2014): e115147.

184   George C. Frison, *Survival by Hunting: Prehistoric Human Predators and Animal Prey* (Berkeley: University of California Press, 2004): 18, 99, 116, 127 and 171; George C. Frison, *Prehistoric Hunters of the High Plains* (St. Louis: Academic Press, 1991).

185   E. H. Kossoff, "More Fat and Fewer Seizures: Dietary Therapies for Epilepsy," *The Lancet Neurology* 3, no. 7 (July 2004): 415–20; B. Cheng et al., "Ketogenic Diet Protects Dopaminergic Neurons against 6-OHDA Neurotoxicity via Up-Regulating Glutathione in a Rat Model of Parkinson's Disease," *Brain Research* 1286 (August 2009): 25–31; S. T. Henderson et al., "Study of the Ketogenic Agent AC–1202 in Mild to Moderate Alzheimer's Disease: A Randomized, Double-Blind, Placebo-Controlled, Multicenter Trial," *Nutrition & Metabolism* 10, no. 6 (August 2009): 31; L. C. Costantini et al., "Hypometabolism as a Therapeutic Target in Alzheimer's Disease," *BMC Neuroscience 9* (Suppl 2) (December 2008): S16; A. Zhao et al., "A Ketogenic Diet as a Potential Novel Therapeutic Intervention in Amyotrophic Lateral Sclerosis," *BMC Neuroscience* 3, no. 7 (April 2006): 29; K. W. Barañano and A. L. Hartman, "The Ketogenic Diet: Uses in Epilepsy and Other Neurologic Illnesses," *Current Treatment Options in Neurology* 10, no. 6 (November 2008): 410–19; N. S. Al-Zaid

et al., "Low Carbohydrate Ketogenic Diet Enhances Cardiac Tolerance to Global Ischaemia," *Acta Cardiologica* 62, no. 4 (August 2007): 381–89.

186   The production of ketone bodies during starvation may help stimulate the process of autophagy: in vitro experiments with human cells showed that autophagy is stimulated by physiological concentrations of the ketone bodies β-hydroxybutyrate and acetoacetate. See Patrick F. Finn and J. Fred Dice, "Ketone Bodies Stimulate Chaperone-Mediated Autophagy," *Journal of Biological Chemistry* 280, no. 27 (2005): 25864–70.

187   Payal Mehta et al., "Noncanonical Autophagy: One Small Step for LC3, One Giant Leap for Immunity," *Current Opinion in Immunology* 26 (2014): 69; David C. Rubinsztein et al., "Autophagy Modulation as a Potential Therapeutic Target for Diverse Diseases," *Nature Reviews Drug Discovery* 11, no. 9 (2012): 709–30.

188   Yuting Ma et al., "Autophagy and Cellular Immune Responses," *Immunity* 39, no. 2 (August 2013): 211–12; D. R. Green et al., "Mitochondria and the Autophagy-Inflammation-Cell Death Axis in Organismal Aging," *Science* 333, no. 6046 (2011): 1109–12.

189   Mehta et al., "Noncanonical Autophagy," 69–70; Rubinsztein et al., "Autophagy Modulation," 709–30. The autophagy mechanism involves formation of a double-membraned vesicle (compartment) around the debris (the "autophagosome") and fusion of this vesicle with lysosomes (organelles specialized in the degradation of cellular debris). See Mehta et al., "Noncanonical Autophagy," 69–70.

190   Rubinsztein et al., "Autophagy Modulation," 709–30. Signaling pathways such as the AMP-activated protein kinase (AMPK) pathway and mammalian target of rapamycin (mTOR) pathways upregulate autophagy when nutrients are limited. See Ma et al., "Autophagy and Cellular Immune Responses," 212.

191   Beth Levine et al., "Autophagy in Immunity and Inflammation," *Nature* 469, no. 7330 (2011): 323. Autophagy has been found to play an essential role in maintaining survival in conditions of short-term starvation in many eukaryotic organisms, including yeasts, nematode worms and some mammals; conservation of the process among different organisms indicates the physiological importance of the process. See Uma M. Sachdeva and Craig B. Thompson, "Diurnal Rhythms of Autophagy: Implications for Cell Biology and Human Disease," *Autophagy* 4, no. 5 (2008): 582; Mehrdad Alirezaei et al., "Short-Term Fasting Induces Profound Neuronal Autophagy," *Autophagy* 6, no. 6 (2010): 702. Autophagy plays a role in survival of the neonate in some mammalian species immediately after birth, when the placental supply of nutrients ceases; in mice, autophagy reaches peak levels three to six hours after birth, before returning to normal levels. See Sachdeva and Thompson, "Diurnal Rhythms of Autophagy," 582; Akiko Kuma et al., "The Role of Autophagy during the Early Neonatal Starvation Period," *Nature* 432, no. 7020 (2004): 1032–036; Masaaki Komatsu et al., "Impairment of Starvation-Induced and Constitutive Autophagy in Atg7 -deficient Mice," *Journal of Cell Biology* 169, no. 3 (2005): 425–34. Mice with mutations in the autophagy gene Atg5 die sooner than wild-type mice on starvation after birth, suggesting that the role of autophagy is provision of metabolic substrates to allow cell survival. See Sachdeva and Thompson, "Diurnal Rhythms of Autophagy," 582; Kuma et al., "The Role of Autophagy during the Early Neonatal Starvation Period," 1032–036. Michael Lazarou, "Keeping the Immune System in Check: A Role for Mitophagy," *Immunology and Cell Biology* 93, no. 1 (2014): 6; Ma et al., "Autophagy and Cellular Immune Responses," 214–15; Kiichi Nakahira et al.,

"Autophagy Proteins Regulate Innate Immune Responses by Inhibiting the Release of Mitochondrial DNA Mediated by the NALP3 Inflammasome," *Nature Immunology* 12, no. 3 (2010): 222–30; M. C. Tal et al., "Absence of Autophagy Results in Reactive Oxygen Species-Dependent Amplification of RLR Signaling," *Proceedings of the National Academy of Sciences* 106, no. 8 (2009): 2770–75; Rongbin Zhou et al., "A Role for Mitochondria in NLRP3 Inflammasome Activation," *Nature* 469, no. 7329 (2011): 221–25.

192   Longo and Mattson, "Fasting: Molecular Mechanisms and Clinical Applications," 182 and 186–87; Laura Castello et al., "Alternate-Day Fasting Protects the Rat Heart against Age-Induced Inflammation and Fibrosis by Inhibiting Oxidative Damage and NF-kB Activation," *Free Radical Biology and Medicine* 48, no. 1 (2010): 47–54; Veech et al., "Ketone Bodies, Potential Therapeutic Uses," 241–47. Fasting has been used to improve health in patients suffering from chronic diseases and to delay aging. See T. N. Seyfried, "Ketone Strong: Emerging Evidence," 1815–17; Longo and Mattson, "Fasting: Molecular Mechanisms and Clinical Applications," 181–92; R. Weindruch et al., "The Retardation of Aging in Mice by Dietary Restriction: Longevity, Cancer, Immunity and Lifetime Energy Intake," *Journal of Nutrition* no. 116 (1986): 641–54. Fasting can result in improvements in markers of metabolic syndrome. See Longo and Mattson, "Fasting: Molecular Mechanisms and Clinical Applications," 187; Castello et al., "Alternate-Day Fasting Protects the Rat Heart against Age-induced Inflammation and Fibrosis," 47–54; R. Wan et al., "Intermittent Fasting and Dietary Supplementation with 2-deoxy-D-glucose Improve Functional and Metabolic Cardiovascular Risk Factors in Rats," *FASEB Journal* 17: (2003) 1133–34. Alternate-day fasting experiments in humans and animals show reduced rates of diabetes, lower fasting insulin and glucose concentrations, lower incidence of cancer and other improvements in markers of metabolic health. See K. A. Varady and M. K. Hellerstein, "Alternate-Day Fasting and Chronic Disease Prevention: A Review of Human and Animal Trials," *American Journal of Clinical Nutrition* 86 (2007): 7–13. Experiments in mice showed that time-restricted feeding (feeding restricted to eight hours a day) protected against obesity, hyperinsulinemia, inflammation and other metabolic perturbations associated with metabolic syndrome. (This was not due to calorie reduction: the mice consumed the same number of calories as control mice with constant access to food). See Megumi Hatori et al., "Time-Restricted Feeding without Reducing Caloric Intake Prevents Metabolic Diseases in Mice Fed a High-Fat Diet," *Cell Metabolism* 15, no. 6 (2012): 848–60. Fasting is even associated with improvements in cognitive performance: experiments in mice and rats have shown that intermittent fasting can decrease age-related cognitive decline. See Longo and Mattson, "Fasting: Molecular Mechanisms and Clinical Applications," 183; Rumani Singh et al., "Late-Onset Intermittent Fasting Dietary Restriction as a Potential Intervention to Retard Age-Associated Brain Function Impairments in Male Rats," *Age* 34, no. 4 (2011): 917–33; A. Fontan-Lozano et al., "Caloric Restriction Increases Learning Consolidation and Facilitates Synaptic Plasticity through Mechanisms Dependent on NR2B Subunits of the NMDA Receptor," *Journal of Neuroscience* 27, no. 38 (2007): 10185–95. Experiments in mice have shown the upregulation of autophagy (described below) in neurons during 24-hour fasts. See Alirezaei et al., "Short-Term Fasting Induces Profound Neuronal Autophagy," 702–10. Some studies have also suggested that intermittent fasting can cause changes in the composition of the gut microbiota that may improve health. See

Longo and Mattson, "Fasting: Molecular Mechanisms and Clinical Applications," 187; Valentina Tremaroli and Fredrik Bäckhed, "Functional Interactions between the Gut Microbiota and Host Metabolism," *Nature* 489, no. 7415 (2012): 242–49.

193   Levine et al., "Autophagy in Immunity and Inflammation," 323–35; Green et al., "Mitochondria and the Autophagy-Inflammation-Cell Death Axis in Organismal Aging," 1109–12. Owing to the effect of autophagy on immune function, it has been suggested that it reduces oxidative stress and chronic inflammation, and vice versa. Autophagy has been shown to influence the secretion of immune modulators such as cytokines, thereby limiting the inflammatory response. It limits the secretion of proinflammatory cytokines such as IL-1β. The mechanism is thought to involve production of ROS by mitochondria, which activates the NLR family, pyrin domain-containing 3 (NLRP3) inflammosome signaling pathway, which in turn stimulates IL-1β secretion. See Michael Lazarou, "Keeping the Immune System in Check: A Role for Mitophagy," *Immunology and Cell Biology* 93, no. 1 (2014): 6. Autophagy has been shown to stimulate the removal of damaged mitochondria, which in turn decreases inflammation through decreased NLR signaling. See Ma et al., "Autophagy and Cellular Immune Responses," 214; Nakahira et al., "Autophagy Proteins Regulate Innate Immune Responses," 222–30; Tal et al., "Absence of Autophagy Results in Reactive Oxygen Species-Dependent Amplification of RLR Signaling," 2770–75. In support of this mechanism, defective clearance of mitochondria has been shown to result in accumulation of ROS. See Lazarou, "Keeping the Immune System in Check," 6; Zhou et al., "A Role for Mitochondria in NLRP3 Inflammasome Activation," 221–25; Nakahira et al., "Autophagy Proteins Regulate Innate Immune Responses," 222–30.

194   In mice, mutation in the Atg5, a protein involved in autophagy, in macrophages and neutrophils, increases susceptibility to infection with the pathogens L. monocytogenes and T. gondii. See Levine et al., "Autophagy in Immunity and Inflammation," 328; Zijiang Zhao et al., "Autophagosome-Independent Essential Function for the Autophagy Protein Atg5 in Cellular Immunity to Intracellular Pathogens," *Cell Host & Microbe* 4, no. 5 (2008): 458–69. The processes xenophagy and virophagy describe the autophagic destruction of bacteria and viruses respectively. See Ma et al., "Autophagy and Cellular Immune Responses," 213–14. One mechanism of pathogen destruction involves the fusion of vesicles containing antimicrobial peptides with phagosomes (organelles specialized in destruction of extracellular material) containing bacteria, which results in destruction of the pathogen. See Ma et al., "Autophagy and Cellular Immune Responses," 213; Marisa Ponpuak et al., "Delivery of Cytosolic Components by Autophagic Adaptor Protein P62 Endows Autophagosomes with Unique Antimicrobial Properties," *Immunity* 32, no. 3 (2010): 329–41. Several recent studies have supported the hypothesis that autophagy plays an important role in disease resistance to mycobacteria in humans. For example, variants of the protein IRGM, which has been shown to be involved in clearance of mycobacteria in vitro, have been found to increase susceptibility to tuberculosis. Mutations in a protein NOD2, which is involved in autophagy, have been found to be associated with susceptibility to Mycobacterium leprae. See Levine, "Autophagy in Immunity and Inflammation," 328; Vojo Deretic and Beth Levine, "Autophagy, Immunity, and Microbial Adaptations," *Cell Host & Microbe* 5, no. 6 (2009): 527–49; Christopher D. Intemann et al., "Autophagy Gene Variant IRGM −261T Contributes to Protection from Tuberculosis Caused by Mycobacterium Tuberculosis But Not by M. Africanum Strains," *PLOS Pathogens* 5, no. 9 (2009): e1000577; Fu-Ren Zhang

et al., "Genomewide Association Study of Leprosy," *New England Journal of Medicine* 361, no. 27 (2009): 2609–18.

195 Recently, the discovery of a novel autophagy pathway (LC3-associated phagocytosis; LAP) has suggested further roles of autophagy in immunity. This pathway involves the formation of a single-membraned vesicle, containing the protein LC3, around the pathogen. See Ma et al., "Autophagy and Cellular Immune Responses," 214; Mehta et al., "Noncanonical Autophagy," 69–75. LAP has been shown to be involved in the destruction of the bacterium Burkholderia psuedomallie as well as the presentation of fungal antigens by macrophages. See Ma et al., "Autophagy and Cellular Immune Responses," 214; Lan Gong et al., "The Burkholderia Pseudomallei Type III Secretion System and BopA Are Required for Evasion of LC3-Associated Phagocytosis," *PLoS ONE* 6, no. 3 (2011): e17852; Jun Ma et al., "Dectin-1-Triggered Recruitment of Light Chain 3 Protein to Phagosomes Facilitates Major Histocompatibility Complex Class II Presentation of Fungal-Derived Antigens," *Journal of Biological Chemistry* 287, no. 41 (2012): 34149–56; J. Martinez et al., "Microtubule-Associated Protein 1 Light Chain 3 Alpha (LC3)-Associated Phagocytosis Is Required for the Efficient Clearance of Dead Cells," *PNAS* 108, no. 42 (2011): 17396–401. This pathway has recently been suggested to modulate the immune response in additional ways, including antigen presentation, dead cell clearance and cytokine secretion. See Mehta et al., "Noncanonical Autophagy," 69–75. As well as its involvement in pathogen destruction, the autophagy pathway has been shown to play a vital role in regulating the numbers of B and T cells, which are vital for immunological function. See Levine et al., "Autophagy in Immunity and Inflammation," 329; Herbert W. Virgin and Beth Levine, "Autophagy Genes in Immunity," *Nature Immunology* 10, no. 5 (2009): 461–70; F. Liu et al., "FIP200 Is Required for the Cell-Autonomous Maintenance of Fetal Hematopoietic Stem Cells," *Blood* 116, no. 23 (2010): 4806–14. Autophagy serves as a determinant of the viability of T cells. It is thought that T cell maturation, which involves withdrawal of growth factors, may depend on autophagy, via a mechanism that involves "mitophagy," the autophagy of mitochondria. Recent research also suggests that antigen presentation by T cells and dendritic cells is facilitated by autophagy. See Heather H. Pua et al., "Critical Role for the Autophagy Gene Atg5 in T Cell Survival and Proliferation," *Journal of Experimental Medicine* 204, no. 1 (2006): 25–31; C. Li et al., "Autophagy Is Induced in CD4 T Cells and Important for the Growth Factor-Withdrawal Cell Death," *Journal of Immunology* 177, no. 8 (2006): 5163–68; Luc English et al., "Autophagy Enhances the Presentation of Endogenous Viral Antigens on MHC Class I Molecules during HSV-1 Infection," *Nature Immunology* 10, no. 5 (2009): 480–87; Magarian J. Blander and Ruslan Medzhitov, "Toll-Dependent Selection of Microbial Antigens for Presentation by Dendritic Cells," *Nature* 440, no. 7085 (2006): 808–12.

196 These inflammatory diseases include Crohn's disease (which involves inflammation of the small intestine), systemic lupus erythematosus (SLE), obesity and diabetes, and cystic fibrosis. Recent genome-wide association studies identified three genes that confer susceptibility to Crohn's disease which are also involved in autophagy: IRGM, NOD2 and ATG16L1. See Levine et al., "Autophagy in Immunity and Inflammation," 330–31; Jeffrey C. Barrett et al., "Genome-Wide Association Defines More than 30 Distinct Susceptibility Loci for Crohn's Disease," *Nature Genetics* 40, no. 8 (2008): 955–62. The disrupted behavior of dendritic cells could trigger the aberrant intestinal inflammation characteristic of Crohn's disease. Similarly, mutations in ATG16L1 have been found to result in defective antigen presentation in dendritic cells, and so

aberrant inflammation could be triggered in the same way. Studies have suggested that one mutation in ATG16L1 results in reduced clearance of pathogens, as a result of disrupted autophagy. Studies on mice with this ATG16L1 mutation show increased proinflammatory cytokine production by macrophages and other abnormalities associated with Crohn's disease, further supporting the hypothesis that disruptions in the autophagy pathway can trigger the aberrant inflammation in Crohn's disease. An interaction between autophagy and the microbiome has also been suggested to contribute to Crohn's disease: in mice raised in a pathogen-free facility (so that they lack a microbiome), a virus trigger caused abnormalities associated with Crohn's disease in mice with a mutation in the Atg16l1 protein required for autophagy, but not in wild-type mice. This suggests that the intestinal microbes affect the process of autophagy, thereby influencing the inflammatory response. See Levine et al., "Autophagy in Immunity and Inflammation," 335; Pierre Lapaquette et al., "Crohn's Disease-Associated Adherent-Invasive E.coli Are Selectively Favoured by Impaired Autophagy to Replicate Intracellularly," *Cellular Microbiology* 12, no. 1 (2010): 99–113; Petric Kuballa et al., "Impaired Autophagy of an Intracellular Pathogen Induced by a Crohn's Disease Associated ATG16L1 Variant," *PLoS ONE* 3, no. 10 (2008): e3391; Ken Cadwell et al., "A Key Role for Autophagy and the Autophagy Gene Atg16l1 in Mouse and Human Intestinal Paneth Cells," *Nature* 456, no. 7219 (2008): 259–63; Tatsuya Saitoh et al., "Loss of the Autophagy Protein Atg16L1 Enhances Endotoxin-induced IL-1β Production," *Nature* 456, no. 7219 (2008): 264–68. Ken Cadwell and Herbert W. Virgin, "Virus-Plus-Susceptibility Gene Interaction Determines Crohn's Disease Gene Atg16L1 Phenotypes in Intestine," *Cell* 141, no. 7 (2010): 1135–45. Mice deficient in a protein involved in autophagy, p62, develop insulin resistance and obesity. In part this mechanism may involve the negative regulation of inflammation caused by activation of a signaling pathway activated by fatty acids. Additionally, autophagy may protect against metabolic diseases through the limitation of ER stress associated with metabolic syndrome. See Levine et al., "Autophagy in Immunity and Inflammation," 333; Angelina Rodriguez et al., "Mature-Onset Obesity and Insulin Resistance in Mice Deficient in the Signaling Adapter P62," *Cell Metabolism* 3, no. 3 (2006): 211–22. ER stress is thought to be closely linked to oxidative stress, and involves an accumulation of damaged proteins in the ER membrane, which leads to metabolic inefficiency. Consistent with this hypothesis, suppression of expression of a gene required for autophagy, Atg7, in the liver cells of mice results in an increase in ER stress and insulin resistance. Mice deficient in another protein involved in autophagy, p62, also develop insulin resistance as well as obesity. Experiments in mice showed that time-restricted feeding (feeding restricted to eight hours a day) protected against obesity, hyperinsulinemia, inflammation and other metabolic perturbations associated with metabolic syndrome. (Mice consumed the same number of calories as control mice with constant access to food). See Randal J. Kaufman, "Endoplasmic Reticulum Stress and Oxidative Stress: A Vicious Cycle or a Double-Edged Sword?" *Antioxidants & Redox Signaling* 9, no. 12 (2007): 2277; Rodriguez et al., "Mature-Onset Obesity and Insulin Resistance," 211–22; Ling Yang et al., "Defective Hepatic Autophagy in Obesity Promotes ER Stress and Causes Insulin Resistance," *Cell Metabolism* 11, no. 6 (2010): 467–78; Hatori et al., "Time-Restricted Feeding without Reducing Caloric Intake," 848–60. Autophagy is known to maintain cellular metabolism in short-term starvation, but the role in long-term starvation is not currently known. Recent studies in mice using a fluorescent molecular marker that allows visualization of autophagosomes (cellular organelles involved in autophagy) show that autophagosome density increases after 24 hours, but returns to normal levels after 48 hours. This suggests that the process of autophagy may be important for the maintenance of cellular homeostasis in short-term starvation, but does not have a prominent role in long-term starvation, though more research is needed. See Sachdeva and Thompson, "Diurnal Rhythms of Autophagy," 582; N. Mizushima, "In Vivo Analysis of Autophagy in Response to Nutrient Starvation Using Transgenic Mice Expressing a Fluorescent Autophagosome Marker," *Molecular Biology of the Cell* 15, no. 3 (2003): 1101–11.

197   Saunt, "The Age of Imperial Expansion, 1763–1821," 80; Hubert Howe Bancroft, *History of Alaska, 1730–1886* (San Francisco: A. L. Bancroft, 1886), 124–25; Margaret Lantis, *Ethnohistory in Southwestern Alaska and the Southern Yukon: Method and Content, Studies in Anthropology 7* (Lexington: University Press of Kentucky, 1970), 283; Dorothy Knee Jones, *A Century of Servitude: Pribilof Aleuts under U.S. Rule* (Washington, DC: University Press of America, 1980), 4–6; Boyd, *The Coming of the Spirit of Pestilence*, 204.

198   Worl, "Alaska," 304–10; George Betts, "The Coming of the First White Man," in *Haa Shuka, Our Ancestor Tlingit Oral Narratives*, ed. Nora Marks Daunhauer and Richard Dauenhauer (Seattle: University of Washington Press, and Juneau: Alaska Heritage Foundation, 1987), 309.

199   James R. Gibson, "European Dependence upon American Natives: The Case of Russian America," *Ethnohistory* 25, no. 4 (1978): 359–85. On the fragility of smaller autonomous communities with niche ecological and food cultures, see Margaret Lantis, "Aleut," in *Handbook of North American Indians*, vol. 5, *Arctic*, ed. David Damas and William C. Sturtevant (Washington, DC: Smithsonian Institution Scholarly Press, 1984), 163 and 176–77; Donald W. Clark, "Pacific Eskimo: Historical Ethnography," in ibid., 185–87.

200   Edward H. Hosley, "Intercultural Relations and Cultural Change in the Alaska Plateau," in *Handbook of North American Indians*, vol. 6, *Subarctic*, ed. June Helm (Washington, DC: Smithsonian Institution Scholarly Press, 1981), 547; Worl, "Alaska," 304–7.

201   I am grateful to one of the anonymous reviewers of this book for pointing out this association. See Ernest S. Burch Jr., *The Cultural and Natural Heritage of Northwest Alaska*, vol. 5, *The Iñupiaq Nations of Northwest Alaska.* (Kotzebue: NANA Museum of the Arctic and Anchorage: US National Park Service, Alaska Region, 1994); Ernest S. Burch Jr., *The Iñupiaq Eskimo Nations of Northwest Alaska* (Fairbanks: University of Alaska Press, 1998)

202   R. S. Kuipers et al., "Estimated Macronutrient and Fatty Acid Intakes from an East African Paleolithic Diet," *British Journal of Nutrition* 104, no. 11 (2010): 1666–87. Analysis of modern hunter-gatherer diets suggests that ancient hunter-gatherer diets also incorporated carbohydrates to some degree. See Spreadbury, "Comparison with Ancestral Diets," 176; A. Strohle et al., "Latitude, Local Ecology, and Hunter-Gatherer Dietary Acid Load: Implications From Evolutionary Ecology," *American Journal of Clinical Nutrition* 92, no. 4 (2010): 940–45; Strohle and Hahn, "Diets of Modern Hunter-Gatherers Vary Substantially," 429–35.

203   Levine et al., "Autophagy in Immunity and Inflammation," 323–35.

204   Gasior et al., "Neuroprotective and Disease-Modifying Effects of the Ketogenic Diet," 438.

205   Kau et al., "Human Nutrition, the Gut Microbiome and the Immune System," 327–36.

Epilogue. Decolonizing the Diet: Food Sovereignty and Biodiversity

1   On the potential to define Type I and II diabetes as autoimmune conditions, see Eiji Kawasaki, "Type 1 Diabetes and Autoimmunity," *Clinical Pediatric Endocrinology* 23, no. 4 (October 2014): 99–105; M. A. Syed et al., "Is Type 2 Diabetes a Chronic Inflammatory/Autoimmune Disease?" *Diabetes, Nutrition & Metabolism* 15, no. 2 (April 2002): 68–83.

2   In addition to the studies discussed in Chapters 1 and 4, see Surapon Tangvarasittichai, "Oxidative Stress, Insulin Resistance, Dyslipidemia And Type 2 Diabetes Mellitus," *World Journal of Diabetes* 6, no. 3 (April 2015): 456–80. An earlier generation of studies focused on obesity, the end result of high-sugar diets, without highlighting the specific metabolic cause, and thus assumed that anything that causes obesity, including high-calorie diets from fat, might cause type 2 diabetes.

3   Karethy (Kay) Edwards and Beverly Patchell, "State of the Science: A Cultural View of Native Americans and Diabetes Prevention," *Journal of Cultural Diversity* 16, no. 1 (Spring 2009): 32–35 (citing work in M. Bass and L. Wakefield, "Nutrient Intake and Food Patterns of Indians on Standing Rock Reservation," *Journal of the American Dietetic Association* 64, no. 1 (1974): 3.

4   T. L. Cleave and G. D. Campbell, *Diabetes, Coronary Thrombosis and Saccharine Disease* (Bristol: Wright Publishers, 1969), 25 and 110–14; A. M. Cohen et al., "Genetics and Diet as Factors in Development of Diabetes Mellitus," *Metabolism* 21 (1972): 235–40; P. Wise et al., "Hyperglycaemia in the Urbanized Aboriginal," *Medical Journal of Australia* 2 (1970) 1001–6; K. West, "Diabetes in American Indians and other Native Populations of the New World," *Diabetes* 23 (1974): 841–55.

5   Devon A. Mihesuah, "Diabetes in Indian Territory: Revisiting Kelly M. West's Theory of 1940," *American Indian Culture and Research Journal* 40, no. 4 (2016): 1–21.

6   Edwards and Patchell, "State of the Science," 32–35.

7   J. T. Rand, *Kiowa Humanity and the Invasion of the State* (Lincoln: University of Nebraska Press, 2008): 71–93; K. P. Schweinfurth, *Prayer on Top of the Earth: The Spiritual Universe of the Plains Apaches* (Boulder: University of Colorado Press, 2002); D. Wiedman, "Native American Embodiment of the Chronicities of Modernity: Reservation Food, Diabetes, and the Metabolic Syndrome among the Kiowa, Comanche, and Apache," *Medical Anthropology Quarterly* 26 (2012): 599–600.

8   Troy D. Smith, "Indian Territory and Oklahoma," in *The Oxford Handbook of American Indian History*, 375.

9   See also Richard Irving Dodge, *The Plains of the Great West and Their Inhabitants, Being a Description of the Plains, Game, Indians, &C., of the Great North American Desert* (New York, 1877) for more potential dietary and ecological evidence.

10   Wiedman, "Native American Embodiment of the Chronicities of Modernity," 599–600; Mariana K. Ferreira and Gretchen Lang, *Indigenous Peoples and Diabetes: Community Empowerment and Wellness* (Durham, NC: Carolina Academic Press, 2006), 462; M. BraveHeart, "Gender Differences in the Historical Trauma Response among the Lakota," *Journal of Health and Social Policy* 10, no. 4 (1999): 1–21. For a general outline of the sedentary thesis for increased blood sugar levels, see M. T. Hamilton et al., "Role of Low Energy Expenditure and Sitting in Obesity, Metabolic Syndrome, Type 2 Diabetes, and Cardiovascular Disease," *Diabetes* 56 (2007): 2655–67.

11   Having worked with Pima Indians during the 1950s, Frank Hesse, physician at the Public Health Service Indian Hospital on the Gila Reservation, noted that the diet

among those on reservations consisted of "mainly beans, tortillas, chili peppers and coffee, while oatmeal and eggs are occasionally eaten for breakfast. Meat and vegetables are eaten only once or twice a week. [...] a large amount of soft drinks of all types are consumed between meals." Cited in Gary Taubes, *Good Calories, Bad Calories* (New York: Anchor Press, 2007), 238. See also the following report and literature review: Peggy Halpern, *Obesity and American Indians/Alaska Natives Prepared for US Department of Health and Human Services Office of the Assistant Secretary*, April 2007.

12   Gretchen Goetz, "Nutrition a Pressing Concern for American Indians," *Food Safety News*, March 5, 2012. http://www.foodsafetynews.com/2012/03/nutrition-a-pressing-concern-for-american-indians/#.WefeuzBrxPZ.

13   Edwards and Patchell, "State of the Science," 32–35.

14   W. C. Knowler et al., "Diabetes Incidence and Prevalence in Pima Indians: A 19-Fold Greater Incidence Than in Rochester, Minnesota" *American Journal of Epidemiology* 108 (1978): 497–505; Devon Mihesuah, *Recovering Our Ancestors' Gardens: Indigenous Recipes and Guide to Diet and Fitness* (Lincoln: University of Nebraska Press, 2005), 3 and 16.

15   David S. Jones, "Population, Health, and Public Welfare," in *The Oxford Handbook of American Indian History*, 425–26; Christopher J. L. Murray et al., "Eight Americas: Investigating Mortality Disparities across Races, Counties, and Race-Counties in the United States," *PLoS Medicine* 3, no. 12 (2006): 2.

16   M. A. Hill, "The Diabetes Epidemic in Indian Country," *Winds of Change* 12, no. 3 (Summer 1997): 26–31.

17   For an account of the failure to identify sudden sugar proliferation among communities that became obese and suffered from type 2 diabetes, see Gary Taubes, *The Case against Sugar* (New York: Knopf, 2016), 216–20. See also "Systematic Review and Meta-Analysis of Dietary Carbohydrate Restriction in Patients with Type 2 Diabetes: Comparative Study of the Effects of a 1-Year Dietary Intervention of a Law-Carbohydrate Diet Versus a Low-Fat Diet on Weight and Glycemic Control in Type 2 Diabetes," *BMJ Open Diabetes Research and Care* 2017, no. 5: e000354.

18   Taubes, *The Case against Sugar*, 216–20.

19   Russell Thornton, *American Indian Holocaust and Survival: A Population History since 1492* (Norman: University of Oklahoma Press, 1990): 169–72; Mihesuah, *Recovering Our Ancestors' Gardens*, 3 and 16.

20   United States Department of Agriculture: Food and Nutrition Service: Food Distribution Program on Indian Reservations. https://www.fns.usda.gov/fdpir/food-distribution-program-indian-reservations-fdpir.

21   Pedro Carrera-Bastos et al., "The Western Diet and Lifestyle and Diseases of Civilization," *Research Reports in Clinical Cardiology* 2 (March 2011): 15–35.

22   On the notion of "diseases of civilization," see Mark Nathan Cohen, *Health and the Rise of Civilization* (New Haven, CT: Yale University Press, 1989); Jennie R. Joe and Robert S. Young, eds. *Diabetes as a Disease of Civilization: The Impact of Culture Change on in Indigenous Peoples* (Berlin: De Gruyter, 1994).

23   See Taubes, *Good Calories, Bad Calories*, 9–60; G.M. Oppenheimer and I. D. Benrubi, "McGovern's Senate Select Committee on Nutrition and Human Needs versus the Meat Industry on the Diet-Heart Question (1976–1977)." *American Journal of Public Health* 104, no. 1 (January 2014): 59–69; Z. Harcombe et al., "Food for Thought: Have We Been Giving the Wrong Dietary Advice?" *Food and Nutrition Sciences* 4, no. 3 (2013): 240–44.

24   R. Chowdhury et al., "Association of Dietary, Circulating, and Supplement Fatty Acids with Coronary Risk: A Systematic Review and Meta-Analysis," *Annals of*

Internal Medicine 160 (2014): 398–406; Mahshid Dehghan et al., "Associations of Fats and Carbohydrate Intake with Cardiovascular Disease and Mortality in 18 Countries from Five Continents (PURE): A Prospective Cohort Study," *The Lancet* 390, no. 10107 (November 2017): 2050–62; S.A. Kelly et al., "Whole Grain Cereals for Cardiovascular Disease," *Cochrane Review* 24, no. 8 (August 2017): CD005051; Steven Hamley, "The Effect of Replacing Saturated Fat with Mostly N-6 Polyunsaturated Fat on Coronary Heart Disease: A Meta-Analysis of Randomised Controlled Trials," *Nutrition Journal* 16. No. 3 (May 2017): 30; A. Malhotra et al., "Saturated Fat Does Not Clog the Arteries: Coronary Heart Disease Is a Chronic Inflammatory Condition, the Risk of Which Can Be Effectively Reduced From Healthy Lifestyle Interventions," *British Journal of Sports Medicine* 51, no. 15 (August 2017): 1111–12; Z. Harcombe, "Dietary Fat Guidelines Have No Evidence Base: Where Next for Public Health Nutritional Advice?" *British Journal of Sports Medicine* 51, no. 10 (2017): 769–74; Z. Harcombe et al., "Evidence from Prospective Cohort Studies Does Not Support Current Dietary Fat Guidelines: A Systematic Review and Meta-Analysis," *British Journal of Sports Medicine* 51 (December 2017): 1743–49; Pavel Grasgruber et al., "Food Consumption and the Actual Statistics of Cardiovascular Diseases: An Epidemiological Comparison of 42 European Countries," *Food & Nutrition Research*, 60 (2016): 31694; D. Unwin et al., "It Is the Glycaemic Response to, Not the Carbohydrate Content of Food That Matters in Diabetes and Obesity: The Glycaemic Index Revisited," *Journal of Insulin Resistance* 1, no. 1 (August 2016): 9; Z. Harcombe et al., "Evidence from Randomised Controlled Trials Does Not Support Current Dietary Fat Guidelines: A Systematic Review and Meta-Analysis," *BMJ Open Heart* 3 (2016): e000409; Z. Harcombe et al., "Evidence From Prospective Cohort Studies Did Not Support the Introduction of Dietary Fat Guidelines in 1977 and 1983: A Systematic Review," *British Journal of Sports Medicine* 51, no. 24 (2017): 1737–42; J. J. DiNicolantonio et al., "Problems with the 2015 Dietary Guidelines for Americans: An Alternative," *Missouri Medicine* 113, no. 2 (March–April 2016): 93–97; Jaike Praagman et al., "The Association between Dietary Saturated Fatty Acids and Ischemic Heart Disease Depends on the Type and Source of Fatty Acid in the European Prospective Investigation into Cancer and Nutrition–Netherlands Cohort," *American Journal of Clinical Nutrition* 103, no. 2 (February 2016): 356–65; Nina Teicholz, "The Scientific Report Guiding the US Dietary Guidelines: Is It Scientific?" *The BMJ* 351 (Sep. 2015): h4962; Nina Teicholz, *The Big Fat Surprise: Why Butter, Meat and Cheese Belong in a Healthy Diet* (New York: Simon & Schuster, 2014); Taubes, *Good Calories, Bad Calories*, 9–60.

25 D. S. Ludwig, "Lowering the Bar on the Low-Fat Diet," *JAMA* 316, no. 20 (2016): 2087–88.

26 See, for example, Arndt Manzel et al. "Role of "Western diet" in inflammatory auto-immune diseases," *Current Allergy and Asthma Reports* 14, no. 1 (2014): 404; William Parker and Jeff Ollerton, "Evolutionary biology and anthropology suggest biome reconstitution as a necessary approach toward dealing with immune disorders," *Evolution, Medicine, and Public Health* 1 (2013): 89–103

27 I. Levine, "Cancer among the American Indians and Its Bearing upon the Ethnological Distribution of the Disease," *Journal of Cancer Research and Clinical Oncology* 9 (1910): 422–35; A. J. Orenstein, "Freedom of Negro Races from Cancer," *British Medical Journal* 2 (1923): 342; Prentice G. "Cancer among Negroes," *British Medical Journal* 2 (1923): 1181; G. M. Brown et al., "The Occurrence of Cancer in

an Eskimo," *Cancer* 5 (1952): 142–43; S. B. Eaton et al., "Stone Agers in the Fast Lane: Chronic Degenerative Diseases in Evolutionary Perspective," *American Journal of Medicine* 84 (1988): 739–49. doi: 10.1016/0002-9343(88)90113-1. Carrera-Bastos et al., "The Western Diet and Lifestyle and Diseases of Civilization," *Research Reports in Clinical Cardiology* 2 (2011): 15–35; L. Cordain et al, "Macronutrient Estimations in Hunter-Gatherer Diets," *American Journal of Clinical Nutrition* 72 (2000): 1589–92. G J. Armelagos et al. "Evolutionary, Historical and Political Economic Perspectives on Health and Disease," *Social Science & Medicine* 61, no. 4 (2005): 755–65; Armelagos et al., "Epidemiological and Nutrition Transition in Developing Countries: Impact on Human Health and Development," *Proceedings of the Nutrition Society* 67, no. 1 (February 2008): 82–90.

28   Richard Teague and Matt Barnes, "Grazing management that regenerates ecosystem function and grazingland livelihoods," *African Journal of Range & Forage Science* 34, no. 2 (2017):77-86; David R. Montgomery, "Healthy Soil is the Real Key to Feeding the World," *The Conversation*, April 3, 2017 https://theconversation.com/healthy-soil-is-the-real-key-to-feeding-the-world-75364 .

29   Donald Worster, "Climate and History: Lessons from the Great Plains," in *Earth, Air, Fire, Water*, ed. Jill Ker Conway, Kenneth Kenistton and Leo Marx (Amherst: University of Massachusetts Press, 1999), 51–77.

30   Kate Kelland, "Special Report: Cancer Agency Left In The Dark Over Glyphosate Evidence," Reuters, June 4, 2017. https://www.reuters.com/article/us-glyphosate-cancer-data-specialreport/special-report-cancer-agency-left-in-the-dark-over-glyphosate-evidence-idUSKBN1951VZ?utm_campaign=Storylift+-+ZG32-_OE&utm_source=Storylift&utm_medium=ZG32-_OE&utm_content=A.

31   See American Society of Agronomy, "Is Biodiversity The Future of Farming?" *ScienceDaily*, February 19, 2007. www.sciencedaily.com/releases/2007/02/0702181 35635.htm. See also, on Salatin, http://www.theatlantic.com/health/archive/2011/07/inside-polyface-farm-mecca-of-sustainable-agriculture/242493/.

32   Donald Worster, "The Living Earth: History, Darwinian Evolution, and the Grasslands," in *A Companion to American Environmental History*, ed. Douglas CazauxSackman (Oxford: Blackwell Press, 2014), 64; Jason Moore, "'The Modern World-System' as Environmental History? Ecology and the Rise of Capitalism," *Theory and Society* 32 (2003): 307–77.

33   Smith, "Indian Territory and Oklahoma," in *The Oxford Handbook of American Indian History*, 375.

34   The National Indian Youth Council described protests against state laws that constrained fishing rights as "fish ins." See Trova Heffernan, *Where the Salmon Run: The Life and Legacy of Billy Frank Jr.* (Seattle: University of Washington Press, 2012), 5–9; Wilkinson, *Messages from Frank's Landing*, 38; Fay G. Cohen, *Treaties on Trial: The Continuing Controversy of over Northwest Indian Fishing Rights* (Seattle: University of Washington Press, 1986), 67–70.

35   William J. Bauer Jr., "The Atlantic Northeast," in *The Oxford Handbook of American Indian History*, 355–56.

36   Dan Kraker, "Changing the Protection of Wild Rice Waters: What You Need to Know," MPR News, October 27, 2015. https://www.mprnews.org/story/2015/10/27/wild-rice-water-standard; Josephine Marcotty, "Research, Legal Wrangling Reap Wild Rice Protections," *Star Tribune*, March 12, 2014. http://www.startribune.com/feb-26-wild-rice-protections-costly/247183881/

37   Jill Doerfler and Erik Redix, "The Great Lakes," in *The Oxford Handbook of American Indian History*, 192

38   Shakopee Mdewakanton Sioux Community, *Omakatob Wowapi Four Year Report (2008–2011)*, Shakopeedakota.org, 38–71. http://www.shakopeedakota.org/pdf/4yrRptii.pdf; Jill Doerfler and Erik Redix, "The Great Lakes," in *The Oxford Handbook of American Indian History*, 192; Joseph P. Kalt and Joseph William Singer, *Myths and Realities of Tribal Sovereignty: The Law and Economics of Indian Self-Rule* (Cambridge, MA: Harvard Project on American Indian Economic Development, 2004), 1.

39   Catherine S. Fowler, "'We Live by Them': Native Knowledge of Biodiversity in the Great Basin of Western North America," in *Biodiversity and Native America*, ed. Paul E. Minnis and Wayne J. Elisens (Norman: University of Oklahoma Press, 2000), 123–24.

40   Sandra L. Peacock and Nancy J. Turner, "'Just Like a Garden': Traditional Resource Management and Biodiversity Conservation on the Interior Plateau of British Columbia," in *Biodiversity and Native America*, ed. Paul E. Minnis and Wayne J. Elisens (Norman: University of Oklahoma Press, 2000), 164–65 and 167.

41   Robert Boyd, ed., *Indians, Fire and the Land in the Pacific Northwest* (Corvallis: Oregon State University Press, 1999).

42   Fiona Hamersley Chambers and Nancy J. Turner, "Plant Use by Northwest Coast and Plateau Indigenous Peoples," in *The Subsistence Economies of Indigenous North American Societies: A Handbook*, ed. Bruce D. Smith (Washington, DC: Smithsonian Institution Scholarly Press, 2011), 77–78.

43   Kim Severson, "Squash, Rice and Roadkill: Feeding the Fighters of Standing Rock," *New York Times*, November 16, 2016. https://www.nytimes.com/2016/11/17/us/squash-rice-and-roadkill-feeding-the-fighters-of-standing-rock.html?_r=2&utm_source=SFFB.

44   Alysa Landry, "What Is a Food Desert? Do You Live in One? 23.5 Million in This Country Do," Indian Country Media Network, April 28, 2015. https://indiancountrymedianetwork.com/culture/health-wellness/what-is-a-food-desert-do-you-live-in-one-235-million-in-this-country-do/.

45   On the DDP, see http://www.foundmichigan.org/wp/2012/05/03/decolonizing-diet-project/. For Mihesua's work, see Mihesuah, *Recovering Our Ancestors' Gardens*. The "Native Paleo" project at the Native Wellness Institute in California has adopted and advocated similar practices. See http://www.nativewellness.com/native-paleo.html. On the CDC NDWP Traditional Foods Program grantee partner programs, see D. Satterfield et al., "Health Promotion and Diabetes Prevention in American Indian and Alaska Native Communities–Traditional Foods Project, 2008–2014," *Morbidity and Mortality Weekly Report* suppl. 65, no. 1 (February 2016): 4–10. doi: 10.15585/mmwr.su6501a3, and also a list of the umbrella programs at https://www.cdc.gov/diabetes/ndwp/traditional-foods/traditional-foods-program/index.html.

46   On the preponderance of associated conditions of metabolic syndrome among Native American communities since the 1960s, see for example, Wiedman, "Native American Embodiment of the Chronicities of Modernity," 595–612; Thornton, *American Indian Holocaust and Survival*, 169–72; Mihesuah, *Recovering Our Ancestors' Gardens*, 3 and 16. On the Cherokee and Muskogee efforts, see Rayna Green, "Mother Corn and Dixie Pig: Native Food in the Native South," *Southern Cultures* 14, no. 4 (Winter 2008): 116. For Nabham's statements, see Gary Paul Nabhan, "Native American Management and Conservation of Biodiversity in the Sonoran Desert Bioregion: An Ethnoecological Perspective," in *Biodiversity and Native America*, 41.

INDEX

CPSIA information can be obtained
at www.ICGtesting.com
Printed in the USA
BVHW071830310820
587711BV00001B/70

9 781785 271588